JAMES
PAIN
ARCHITECT

Written by David Lee
Edited by Debbie Jacobs

A Limerick Civic Trust Publication in association with FÁS

Limerick Civic Trust wish to acknowledge and thank all the assistance received during the course of research and production.

In Particular, we wish to recognise the financial support we received from FÁS.

Limerick Civic Trust
Bishops' Palace
Church Street
Limerick
Ireland

Tel: +353 61 313399   Fax: +353 61 315513

Design & Layout: John Paul Dowling
Published by: Limerick Civic Trust © 2005
Printed by: Limerick Leader
ISBN: 0-9531224-7-6

This Publication is part of a FÁS Training Project funded by the local community, the Employment Levy and European Union Structural Funds.

All errors of fact and detail in this publication have been deliberately inserted to remind both reader and author that only God is Perfect !

Acknowledgments

We wish to acknowledge the help and support of the following people and organisations without whose assistance this publication would not have been possible:

Denis M. Leonard, Director, Limerick Civic Trust; Angela Alexander; Geoffrey Ashton, North Munster Masonic and Community Centre; Lorraine Barrett, Eleanore Morrissey, Office of Public Works, Cahir Castle; Gerald Bourke; Laoise Bourke, Anita Carey, John Greville, Gillian Griffin, Mr. King, Michael Wenkel, Adare Manor; Tony Brazil, Ethel O'Driscoll, Limerick Travel; Sarah Cullinan, FÁS; Kieran Devery; Tom Donovan; The Earl and Countess of Dunraven; Desmond FitzGerald, Knight of Glin; Seamus Flynn; Rev. Jane Galbraith, St. Michael's Church; Shay Gardiner, Mark Nolan, Gary Redmond, Thomas O'Toole, Dromoland Castle; Mossy Geary; Patricia Hassette, Swiss Cottage; Rebecca Hayes, Grand Lodge of Freemasons; Jackie Hayes, Limerick Archives; Terence Higgins, St. Mary's Cathedral; Irish Georgian Society; Susie Gwyn Jones, Edward Somerville, Eloisa Souza Coelho, Jackie Stubbs, Lough Cutra Castle; Dan Lawless; Arnold Leahy Architects; Simon Lincoln, Architectural Archives, Dublin; John Logan, University of Limerick; Declan McLoughlin, Limerick Film Archive; James McMahon; Trevor Morrow; Matthew Potter; Yan Ryan; Sean Spellissy; Joe Walsh.

A special thank you to the staff of Limerick Civic Trust; Peggy Barry; Margaret Franklin, Limerick County Library; David Gaynor; Ferga Grant; Elis Kennedy; Mike McGuire, Fiona Ismail, Limerick City Library; Lucia Martinez; Mary O'Riodan; Larry Walsh, Brian Hodkinson, Tom Keogh, Limerick City Museum

The Staffs of:
Limerick City Library;
Limerick County Library;
Limerick School of Art and Design;
Mary Immaculate College Library;
National Library, Dublin;
Representative Church Body Library, Dublin.

David Lee has been project leader of the History and Folklore Research Project at Limerick Civic Trust since 1994. Publications he has edited and contributed to include *Georgian Limerick* Vol. I & II, *Remembering Limerick*, and *Made in Limerick* Vol. I.

Debbie Jacobs has been assistant project leader of the History and Folklore Research Project at Limerick Civic Trust for over five years. She has contributed to and edited *Made in Limerick* Vol. I and is currently working on Vol. II due to be published later this year.

Foreword

It is generally recognised that Limerick is experiencing the greatest level of development since Edward Sexton Pery and his contemporaries built the Georgian town, known as Newtown Pery, on lands which he owned beyond the confines of the walled Medieval City. In the 1760s Limerick was proclaimed to be an open city and the dismantling of the city walls, around the Englishtown and Irishtown, began.

Some fifty years later the Pain brothers, James and George Richard, moved to Limerick and established themselves as the foremost architects of their time in Munster. They were leading exponents of the Gothic style and were specialists in castellated country houses, bridges and churches. They also built schools, courthouses and prisons. Examples of their work are to be seen throughout Ireland. George moved to Cork in the 1820s and James lived in Limerick until he died in 1877 aged 97.

The importance of these architect brothers, particularly from a Limerick perspective, cannot be underestimated in any way. As the current developments throughout Limerick continue at an unprecedented scale, examples of Pains' architecture abound throughout the City as some of our most prominent buildings.

This book, *James Pain, Architect*, concentrates mostly on the Limerick area and yet at the same time informs the reader to a lesser degree about their buildings in other parts of Ireland. It is the first published study on the legacy of the Pain brothers. The book is designed to appeal to the wider audience and not just for the architect or lovers of architecture. The story behind the building is often far more interesting than the finished article. Thomond Bridge falling into the river and Pain's philosophy about Limerick Prison would be classic examples in this regard.

James Pain, Architect is a valuable addition to our already impressive list of publications. It's a new departure for us being a specialist topic.
I congratulate Dave Lee and Debbie Jacobs, from our FÁS sponsored History Project, and the designer of the book, John Paul Dowling, on the excellence of this work. This is a book, which will appeal to a wide range of readership throughout Ireland. We in Limerick Civic Trust are very proud of this publication *James Pain, Architect* and are confident that it will get the nationwide acclaim it deserves.

Pat Daly
Chairman
Limerick Civic Trust.

Introduction

This study deals with the architectural practice of Munster architect James Pain (*c.*1780-1877) who lived in Limerick during the period from *c.*1811 until his death. This is the first book to be devoted to the work of James Pain and includes a considerable amount of information not previously known. As such, it is a major contribution to architectural studies.

Working in conjunction with his younger brother George Richard who died in Cork in 1838, James Pain is mainly known for his country house commissions and his work as a church architect for the Munster area. However, either individually or in partnership with George Richard, he carried out work in many other fields as well. He made a major contribution to prison architecture in Ireland, as well as constructing bridges and roads. In addition to this, he designed schools, courthouses and bridewells, and banks. A major part of his practice involved making additions and renovations to country houses, most of this work being unrecorded.

Before James Pain came to Ireland he was a pupil of John Nash, the famous London Regency architect, and as such learnt that the success of an architect lies in his versatility and an ability to please his patrons. James and his brother George Richard, also a pupil of Nash, were capable of working in various styles including Gothic Revival, Tudor-Revival and Classical. No job was too big or too small. This gained James a great reputation amongst his patrons. His attention to detail and professionalism ensured that he was in steady employment until only a few years before his death aged 97.

With the ability to design anything from ice houses and mausoleums to great Gothic mansions, a great deal of his work can still be seen throughout Munster. A legacy that forms part of the rich and diverse cultural and architectural history of this country.

David Lee
Debbie Jacobs

Contents

Currency:

Before the introduction of decimalisation in 1971 the currency used in Britain and Ireland was based on the Sterling system of the Pound (£), Shilling (s) and Pence (d) with Ireland's currency linked in value to the British pound sterling. In this system there were 12 pennies in a shilling and 20 shillings in a pound - hence there were 240 pennies in a pound. Each penny was subdivided, with both a half-penny coin and a quarter-penny coin (known as a Farthing) in circulation. The farthing was withdrawn from circulation in 1961. A Guinea was a sum of 21 shillings and although the guinea coin had long been out of circulation a number of items, such as professional fees and auctioned *objets d' art,* were valued in guineas.

Between 1971 and 2002 the chief monetary unit in the Republic of Ireland was the Punt (£Ir), there being 100 pence in a Punt (*Irish*: Pound). In 1979 the Irish Punt entered the European Monetary Union, unlinking its value to Sterling. Although the southern Irish economy adopted the Euro in January 2002, Britain and Northern Ireland remained outside the Euro zone (1 Euro = 100 cents).

Measurements
Linear Measure

1 inch = 25.4 millimetres exactly

1 foot (12 inches) = 0.3048 metre exactly

1 yard (3 feet) = 0.9144 metre exactly

1 statute mile (1,760 yards) = 1.609 kilometres

ARRIVAL IN IRELAND

Introduction

In Britain and Ireland during the nineteenth century wealthy landed families, church authorities and public institutions, seeking to communicate a sense of social status, historical continuity and ancestral rights commissioned architects to design buildings in a style known as 'Gothic' - this being a revival of a style of architecture characteristic of the High Middle Ages in Northern Europe during the twelfth to fifteenth centuries.

The two leading exponents of this Gothic style in Munster in the early nineteenth century were Limerick and Cork based architects James and George Richard Pain. Born in England, the two brothers served their professional apprenticeship under Regency architect John Nash, the favoured architect of the Prince Regent. They first came to Ireland during the second decade of the century, James about 1811/12 to supervise the building of Lough Cutra Castle near Gort in Co. Galway, a castellated house designed by Nash for Colonel Charles Vereker.[1] Subsequently James, along with his brother George Richard who arrived in Ireland about 1815, went on to establish an extensive fashionable architectural practice of their own - one of their particular specialities being castellated country houses. They were also involved in the building of numerous parish churches for the Church of Ireland in the Gothic style.

David Gaynor

Lough Cutra Castle, Co. Galway designed by John Nash 1811. James Pain was the executing architect.

Although the exact date of James's coming to Ireland is not known it is fairly certain that he established himself in Limerick upon his arrival, for a news item in the *Limerick Chronicle* of 15 December 1877, reporting the architect's death in the city, stated that 'it is now upwards of 70 years since he settled in Limerick'. A vague enough statement, in truth, but it does establish that James was living in Limerick c1811/12, if not before. By about 1820 George Richard had moved to Cork where he married and had a number of children. He died there in December 1838.

As former pupils of the eminent Nash their acceptance by Society was assured. They assiduously cultivated and enjoyed the patronage of the aristocracy and among their major commissions can be counted Dromoland Castle in Co. Clare for Sir Edward O'Brien; Mitchelstown Castle in Co. Cork for George King, Earl of Kingston and Adare Manor, Co. Limerick for Windham Henry, Earl of Dunraven. Their period of prominence was the 1820s and '30s and although much of their country house practice was in Picturesque Gothic or Tudor-Gothic, they were equally capable of carrying out commissions in Classical for public and private buildings and, in the case of G. R. Pain, for the Catholic Church.

Gothic Revival and Classicism

Architecture in eighteenth and nineteenth century Britain and Ireland was strongly influenced by the past, especially by the Classical architecture of Ancient Greece and Rome and the Gothic style of the medieval period, the latter characterised by pointed windows and arches, window tracery, pinnacles, spires and battlements. Gothic is also known as 'Pointed' architecture since the pointed arch is such a key element. Buildings that sought inspiration from the High Middle Ages are generally termed 'Gothic Revival'. Within this very broad category architectural historians employ other definitions. 'Gothick' refers to mainly eighteenth century architecture that is vaguely based on medieval Gothic and tends towards a taste for the exotic. 'Neo-Gothic', on the other hand, describes a scholarly nineteenth century movement that faithfully adhered to the archaeological correctness of the original.

The expression 'Historicism' is applied to architectural styles that are strongly influenced by the past. Besides Gothic Revival, another form of Historicism very popular in the eighteenth century, and the first forty years of the nineteenth, was 'Classicism' based on the art and architecture of Greece and Rome. 'Classicism' is itself an overarching label covering a number of fashionable stylistic movements, each of which emphasised particular aspects of Classical archaeology - the main stylistic sub-divisions in Britain and Ireland being 'Palladianism' (early eighteenth century), 'Neoclassicism' (late eighteenth and early nineteenth centuries) and 'Greek Revival' (introduced in

Limerick Savings Bank (1840) on Glentworth Street in Greek Revival architectural style. William H. Owen, architect.

the 1750s, but mainly popular during the period of the Napoleonic Wars up until the 1830s). To confuse matters slightly, the term 'Neoclassicism' is sometimes loosely used as a synonym for Classicism, but the context should give an indication as to the sense.

The Greeks and the 'Goths' were not the only source of inspiration for nineteenth century architects and other historical periods were utilised for nostalgic retro-architecture. There were revivals in Norman, Tudor, Elizabethan and Jacobean architecture as well as a fad for Egyptian. Hybrid styles such as Tudor-Gothic and Jacobethan also enjoyed periods of popularity. In Ireland, as part of the nineteenth and early twentieth Celtic Revivalist movement, a style known as Hiberno-Romanesque was resurrected, modelled on Irish ecclesiastical architecture of the tenth to twelfth centuries. Hence the popularity of the Celtic Cross for church monuments and grave markers.

This reliance on the past for exemplary models was broken in the twentieth century with the Modern Movement that sought to completely break the connection with history and produce a totally new and non-traditional form of architecture emphasising the need to construct functional, minimalist buildings to serve the needs, and utilise the technology, of twentieth century industrialised society. Post-Modernism was itself a late twentieth century reaction against Modernism. Although it did not attempt to faithfully copy the past, as did the Historicist movements, Post-Modernism incorporated motifs and elements associated with earlier historical styles and architectural traditions, sometimes in an eclectic manner.

Significant Contribution

Besides being involved in country house and ecclesiastical architecture the Pain brothers also built schools, courthouses and prisons and were involved in a number of civil engineering projects including the design of Limerick City's Athlunkard and Thomond Bridges over the Shannon River and Baal's Bridge over the Abbey River. A tally of their buildings in Limerick includes Villiers Alms Houses on King's Island and the austere County Gaol on Mulgrave Street. The brothers, in particular George Richard, also made a significant contribution to the built heritage of Cork City, being credited for such notable structures as the Cork City and County Courthouse (completed 1835) built in the grand Classical manner, and Blackrock Castle (1828-29), a delightful Gothic construction on the banks of the River Lee.

A further point of interest is that James Pain was a shareholder in the Pery Square Tontine Company that was responsible for financing the construction of six fashionable terraced houses in Pery Square, unquestionably the finest terrace to be built in the city's Georgian quarter. He served the Company as supervising architect for the project.

As well as being architects the brothers also ran a substantial business as builders and contractors, including acting as contractors on a number of their own designs. So adaptable were they that their work ranged from building majestic Gothic mansions and Classical churches to constructing roads. Successful businessmen as well as accomplished architects, the brothers gained an early reputation for being professionally competent, reliable and honest. Able to complete commissions on time, and generally within budget, their services were very much in demand.

Following the death of his brother in 1838 James Pain entered into a fallow period creatively and he appears not to have produced any major original work or to have been given any large-scale commissions comparable to the works he was involved with during the high tide of his career in the 1820s and '30s. Nevertheless he continued working until a few years before his death in 1877, aged 97.[2]

John Nash – Architect of Eminence

One of the principal architects of the Regency period was John Nash (1752-1835), best remembered for such achievements as the exotic Royal Pavilion at Brighton (remodelled 1815-22) and the layout of London's West End (1811 onwards). Nash was also influential in the rise of the Picturesque movement and the development of an interest in Gothic Revival among England's elite, building his own castellated mansion, East Cowes Castle (1798 onwards; demolished 1950) on the Isle of Wight and carrying out Gothic commissions for patrons in Britain who wanted a touch of the romantic in their lives.

John Nash (1752-1835) leading Regency architect.

Brighton Pavilion remodelled 1815-22 by John Nash. Externally decorated in a style borrowed from Mogul India incorporating features such as minarets, onion domes and pierced latticing.

Nor was he overlooked by the landed wealth of Ireland. In the early years of the nineteenth century the name of Nash is associated with the design of four Irish castellated houses: Shanbally Castle in Co. Tipperary (completed 1819; demolished 1960); Kilwaughter, Co. Antrim (1807; dismantled 1951); Killymoon Castle, Cookstown, Co. Tyrone (built 1801-3) and Lough Cutra in Co. Galway (work commencing 1811/12; enlarged 1856),[4] the latter designed for Colonel Charles Vereker who later became 2nd Lord Gort. Despite the amount of work that Nash carried out in Gothic, and the number of lucrative castellated commissions he acquired, it seems that 'Feudal' may not have been his style of first choice, for he was reputed to have once said 'I hate this Gothic style, one window costs more trouble to design than two houses.'[5] However, despite this alleged remark, Nash was one of the foremost architects of Picturesque practising in Britain at this time, for he had a remarkable eye for pictorial composition - his design for Luscombe Castle (1799) in Devon amply illustrating this quality.

Regardless of personal preferences, architects must learn to please their patrons and Nash was equally flexible in serving both the dictates of fashion as well as catering for more traditional tastes. As proof, Nash's other commissions included a number of neoclassical style houses, the outstanding Irish example being Rockingham House in Co. Roscommon[6] (built 1809-10;

Luscombe Castle, Devon (1799) designed by John Nash, amply illustrates his talent for pictorial composition.

destroyed by fire 1957). His design work in this country also included, very possibly, the Swiss Cottage near Cahir in Co. Tipperary, a superb example of *cottage orné* designed for Richard and Emily Butler, Lord and Lady Caher, and restored in the mid-1980s with the assistance of the Irish Georgian Society (Sybil Connolly, the fashion designer, reinterpreting the interiors).

With the commencement of his work in 1811 for the Prince Regent, later George IV (1820-30), in laying out London's West End it proved impossible for Nash to exercise any personal control over his Irish projects. He therefore recommended to Colonel Vereker that James Pain, one of his assistants, oversee the building of Lough Cutra as resident architect in Ireland, an indication of the trust that Nash had in the professionalism and integrity of James Pain, then about 32 years old. A surviving architectural drawing by John Nash of the front elevation of the house is signed and dated October 1811[7] and it is generally accepted that construction work began about 1811,[8] or perhaps in the building season of 1812, work not having been completed until at least 1817.[9] If so, James came to Ireland in 1811 or 1812. We certainly know that he had become professionally established in Ireland by 1813 for he submitted drawings to Sir Edward O'Brien for the proposed rebuilding of Dromoland House, Co. Clare - drawings signed and dated 'James Pain/ July 31 1813'.[10]

Apprenticed to Eminence

James and his brother George Richard were born into a family of builders and architects, James *c*1780 at Isleworth in Middlesex and George *c*1793 in London. It can be justly said that they were well and truly bred to the profession, for their grandfather, William Pain (*c*1730 - *c*1790),[11] who described himself as 'an architect and joiner' and 'architect and carpenter', was the author of at least twelve practical architectural treatises and pattern books published during the second half of the eighteenth century with titles such as *The Practical House Carpenter* (1788 – 2nd edition) and *The Builder's Pocket Treasure; or Palladio Delineated and Explained* (1763).[12] They were to prove popular and were republished several times during the late eighteenth and early nineteenth centuries. In at least one of these publications he was assisted by his son James, a builder and surveyor by profession who, in turn, was father to at least five male children including the James and George of this study, and at least one daughter. James Pain's Will, drawn up in 1863 (See Appendix IV), mentions four brothers: George Richard, Henry, John and Benjamin, and a sister, Sarah (Sally). Colvin lists just four brothers in all: James, George Richard, Henry and a Thomas who is not mentioned in James's Will.[13]

How effectively the two brothers assimilated Gothic while working with Nash, while at the same time gaining an easy familiarity with Classical, can be seen in their subsequent work in Ireland. Exactly when James became a pupil with

Cumberland Terrace, Regents Park, London (1826) by John Nash in the grand neoclassical style.

Nash is not known, but he was aged about 16 in 1796 when Nash returned to London to re-establish his practice in the capital (16 was the usual age for a pupil to be taken on by an architectural firm). Nash had left London in 1783 after being declared a bankrupt, his first attempt to establish himself in the capital city as an architect and builder ending in failure. He went to live in Carmarthen, Wales. Gaining a reputation as an architect of the Picturesque, his return to London in 1796 signalled the commencement of a glittering and triumphal career until his eventual fall from grace in 1828-30 when he was suspected of profiteering and sharp practice at the public expense. His career came to an abrupt end when his royal patron George IV died in 1830. John Nash himself dying five years later.[14] It can be assumed that James signed his articles of apprenticeship about 1796, his future prospects benefiting greatly from being associated at the start of his career with the rise to fame of one of England's most renowned architects. Besides James and George Richard, another brother, Henry, also served as a pupil of Nash.[15]

Their father, James Pain is not to be confused with the celebrated James Paine, spelt with an 'e' (1717-89), the well-known English architect involved in a large number of country house commissions in England, including Chatsworth, Kedleston Hall and Alnwick Castle, as well as major public projects such as Middlesex Bridge, Surrey (1771-7) and Middlesex Hospital (1755-78). His only son, also James Paine (1745-1829), vacillated between architecture, water-colours and sculpture but was completely overshadowed by the achievements of his father. A portrait of father and son was painted by Joshua Reynolds in 1764.[16]

George Richard Pain - Accomplished Artist

George arrived in Ireland several years later than James, for he was only 18 in 1811 and still serving his time. The date of his arrival is vague. It does seem, however, that George was still in England in 1814 as he exhibited at the Royal Academy that year and gave a London address: 1 Diana Place, New Road, London.[17] The Royal Society of Arts archives for 1812 records his address as 'Dixon's Place, New Road, London', then as 'Diana Place' in 1813.[18] George Richard regularly exhibited architectural designs at the Royal Academy between 1810 and 1814 and was awarded the Gold Medal of the Royal Society of Arts in 1812 for 'an original design of a Gothick church' and the Silver Medal in 1813 for 'a design for a gothic palace'. His view of Henry VIII's Chapel at Westminster was shown at the Academy in 1813.[19] According to the *National Dictionary of National Biography* George 'exhibited at the Royal Academy designs in the Gothic style in 1810-14 while living at '1 Diana Place, Fitzroy Square.'[20]

The available information seems to suggest that George Richard had not moved to Ireland earlier than 1814. He was certainly resident here by the spring of 1816, at the very latest, as reference is made in a local newspaper to the 'Messrs. Pain' who had been awarded, in March of that year, a joint contract with Limerick builders Nicholas and William Hannon to build the new County Limerick Gaol.[21] Another early 'sighting' of G. R. Pain is in the Limerick Corporation minutes for 29 January 1817 on the occasion of his conferral with the Freedom of the City, being described as 'Geo. Richard Payne [sic], Architect, City Limerick.'[22] His undoubted skill with architect's pen and artist's brush stood the brothers' architectural partnership in good stead over the following years for, according to an article in a 1911 edition of *The Builder*, it was accepted tradition that 'James was the better at planning, and more the man of affairs, whereas George was the draughtsman and designed the elevations.' Information for the article being provided by James's nephew, Benjamin.[23] Elsewhere, George is described as 'an accomplished draughtsman.'[24] George's skill as a water-colouristist is indicated by two paintings he exhibited at the Royal Hibernian Academy in 1832, his *Destruction of the Castle of Otranto* depicts the collapse of Horace Walpole's massive Gothic fortress, while *Caius Marcius at the Ruins of Carthage* portrays a Classical architectural theme on an epic scale.[25]

Both brothers lived in Ireland for the remainder of their lives, George dying in Cork in December 1838 at the early age of 45,[26] while his elder brother died in Limerick in December 1877, aged 97,[27] being laid to rest in the Vereker family vault in the grounds of St. Mary's Cathedral.[28] Although not born in Ireland, the Pain brothers can both be regarded primarily as Irish architects. This is not only due to their outstanding and prolific contribution to Ireland's built heritage and their length of residence, but also because their architecture is so very much an integral part of the historical fabric and social history of this country. Their achievement deserves wider recognition beyond the narrow circle of architectural historians.

George Richard Pain's water-colour *Caius Marcius at the Ruins of Carthage* (*c*.1831) portrays a Classical architectural theme on an epic scale.

Endnotes

1 *The Dictionary of Architecture* s.v. 'Pain, James and George Richard', Architectural Publications Society. This source of information on the Pain brothers, compiled in 1877, states that Nash 'having designed Loughcooter castle for Lord Gort, recommended the brothers as builders. They consequently went to Ireland . . .' However, it is unlikely that George Richard accompanied his elder brother to commence work on Lough Cutra (known at the time as Loughcooter) because in 1814 G. R. Pain gives a London address, '1. Diana Place, New Road' when he exhibits at the Royal Academy, see *Dictionary of National Biography* s.v. 'Pain, James'.

2 'The Late James Pain', obituary by W. F. (probably architect William Fogerty) published in the *Limerick Chronicle*, 22 December 1877; *The Builder*, 29 December 1877 and *The Irish Builder*, 1 January 1878.

3 For biographical details of John Nash and listing of his works: Colvin, H. *A Biographical Dictionary of British Architects 1600-1840*, s.v. 'Nash, John', 3rd edition, Yale University Press, New Haven & London, 1995, pp. 687-94.

4 Colvin loc. cit.; Davis, T. 'John Nash in Ireland', *Bulletin of the Irish Georgian Society* Vol. VIII, No. 2, April-June 1965.

5 Quoted in Clark, K. *The Gothic Revival: An Essay in the History of Taste*, John Murray, London, 1962.

6 Davis *op. cit.*

7 Guinness, D. & Ryan, W. *Irish Houses and Castles*, Thames & Hudson Ltd., London, 1971, p. 176.

8 Bence-Jones, M. *A Guide to Irish Country Houses*, Constable, London, 1982, 2nd revised edition, 1999, p.192.

9 *Limerick Gazette*, 21 October 1817.

10 Richardson, Douglas Scott *Gothic Revival Architecture in Ireland*, 2 Vols., Garland Publishing Inc., New York and London, 1983, Vol. I, p. 132.

11 *Dictionary of National Biography* s.v. 'Pain, James', Vol. XV, Oxford University Press, 1917.

12 Colvin *op. cit.* s.v. 'Pain, William', p. 721.

13 ibid. p. 721.

14 ibid. s.v. 'Nash, John'.

15 ibid. s.v. 'Pain, William'.

16 ibid. s.v. 'Paine, James (1717-1789)', pp. 721-6; s.v. 'Paine, James (1745-1829) ', pp. 726-7.

17 *Dictionary of National Biography*, s.v. 'Pain, James'. George Richard's address is given as '1 Diana Place, Fitzroy Square'.

18 Graves, Algernon *The Royal Academy of Arts: A Complete Dictionary of Contributors and Their Work from its Foundation in 1769 to 1904*, 9 Vols, The Royal Academy, London, 1905-6, Vol. VI., p. 41.

19 *ibid.*

20 *Dictionary of National Biography* s.v. 'Pain, James'.

21 *Limerick Gazette*, 5 April 1816.

22 *Limerick Corporation Minute Book*, 29 January 1817, Limerick Archives.

23 Anon. 'Some Forgotten Books and a Family of Architects', *The Builder*, 23 June 1911, p. 772.

24 *The Dictionary of Architecture* s.v. 'Pain (James and George Richard)', Architectural Publications Society – entry compiled in 1877.

25 Crookshank, A. & Knight of Glin *The Watercolours of Ireland*, Barrie and Jenkins, London, 1994, p. 107.

26 *Limerick Chronicle*, 29 December 1838.

27 *Limerick Chronicle*, 15 December 1877.

28 Civil Death Record and Church Burial Record of James Pain, Limerick Archives; *A Historic and Descriptive Sketch of St. Mary's Cathedral*, Printed by M'Kerns & Sons, Limerick, 1881, 1st edition, p. 20.

CHAPTER TWO

ESTABLISHING AN ARCHITECTURAL PRACTICE

James's first employer in Ireland was the very same dashing Colonel Charles Vereker who had distinguished himself at the Battle of Collooney in Co. Sligo when, during the 1798 Rebellion, he led the Limerick City Militia into battle against General Humbert's French expeditionary force on 5 September.[1] Vereker, as the sitting MP for Limerick City, was a powerful figure in local politics in conjunction with his power-broking uncle, John Prendergast Smyth. Members of the Smyth/Vereker family exercised dominant control over the 'Corrupt Corporation', a conservative, mainly Protestant Ascendancy clique that controlled the city's parliamentary seat by dubious methods. Many of the city's leading merchants, traders and artisans were excluded from exercising the franchise and the electoral roll was stacked in favour of the 'Clique of Corruption' by giving the vote to politically reliable supporters who lived outside the constituency. Charles Vereker, later 2nd Viscount Gort, was to become a lifetime friend of the Englishman James Pain as well as being a useful social contact.

David Gaynor

Lough Cutra Castle, Co. Galway pleasantly sited beside the lough.

Rib vaulting inside Lough Cutra Castle.

Lough Cutra Castle

Rising grandly over a lake in south Co. Galway, John Nash's design for Vereker's Lough Cutra Castle[2] was quite simple in plan and fairly modest in scale, consisting of just one round and two octagonal towers linked by low, two-storey battlemented ranges. In plan the layout of the house is exceedingly straightforward, basically consisting of two parallel ranges back to back with connecting doors, with the hall in the middle of the front range and the drawing room in the centre of the rear. It was similar to Nash's own East Cowes Castle on the Isle of Wight, since demolished, that Vereker had visited and admired.[3] Though not remarkable for its size, Lough Cutra is neat in proportion and comfortable within. The exterior exudes robustness and boldness of feature so that all the elements of a well-designed castellated country house are represented in the overall composition: a sense of it being a superior, comfortable mansion for a gentleman of substance; a sense of commanding power and strength; a sense of historical continuity; a sense of Gothic romance; a sense of the dramatic; a sense of the Picturesque. All expressed and combined in Nash's design.[4]

Very romantically sited, Lough Cutra relies for its picturesque charm on its lakeside setting. Set on a rise beside the lough, the mansion, which stands on a terrace to resolve the problem of a sloping site, has no need to rely on a mountain of masonry piled high, stone upon stone, to achieve elevation and express social status. Vereker had been born to command, a natural leader of men who, as a youth, had served as an adventurous midshipman at the age of

14 on a ship o' war and had distinguished himself in action in the Mediterranean; a warrior who led his regiment into battle against the French; a city political boss who disdained the whinging and whining of reformers and liberals and who served as a Member of the Westminster Parliament, the political hub at the centre of Britain's growing economic and maritime power.[5] Such a practical man of affairs had no need of vulgar, extravagant architectural displays to puff himself up, extravagant displays that ruined less sensible men. If any man had fully earned the privilege of being the proprietor of a Gothic mansion it was Colonel Charles Vereker. He had certainly 'put in the hours' serving and protecting England's interests against designing foreign foes and traitorous Irish rebels.

North Munster Masonic Centre, King's Island, Limerick with St. Munchin's Church in the background.

014

Freemasonry

Not long after arriving in Ireland James joined the Freemasons as an Entered Apprentice, being initiated into the Ancient Union Lodge No. 13, Limerick, on 3 August 1813 according to a membership scroll of Lodge 13 in possession of the Limerick Freemasons - the surname being spelt 'Paine'. This date is confirmed by the archives of the Grand Lodge of Freemasons Ireland, but he was not marked on the main membership register at Grand Lodge in Dublin, for whatever reason, until 21 March 1814.[6] Presented with its Warrant in November 1732, No 13 is one of the oldest Masonic Lodges in Ireland and it still functions, or 'works', to this day. Lodge 13 presently meets in a purpose-built

David Gaynor

Masonic Centre constructed to very high standards by a FÁS Local Training Initiative Scheme. Located beside the Bishops' Palace on Castle Street, King's Island, and officially known as the North Munster Masonic Centre, it was built under the supervision of Noel McCarthy and completed in 2005. This substantially sized, two-storey building is faced with random rubble limestone making it sympathetic to the architecture of the area. It features Gothic style windows and doors and has a semicircular 'bastion' housing the staircase. The Masonic Centre, which houses a museum and a community hall on the ground floor and private lodge rooms on the upper, is adjacent to the churchyard of St. Munchin's (1827), a former Anglican parish church designed by the James Pain.

Gothic ogee door as seen in the North Munster Masonic Centre.
It is believed that this door came originally from St. Munchin's Church.

James was to be in well-connected company as some of the most prominent men in the city and county were, or were to become, Masons in the same Lodge, including Henry Watson, proprietor of *The Limerick Chronicle*; James Spaight, prominent merchant; Michael Furnell, High Sheriff of Co. Limerick, as were various members of the influential Barrington, Maunsell and Vereker families, along with many other leading citizens. Traditionally Lodge members were 'Private and professional gentlemen, Merchants and other respectable persons.'[7] There were many Lodges to be found throughout Ireland composed of persons of a similar degree, indeed, some were of the very first rank in society. The various British army regiments stationed in the country also had their own military lodges, so a Mason travelling the country would soon find fellow brothers of the Craft to aid him if in need of assistance.

Freemasonry in Ireland is popularly associated with Protestantism due in part to the traditional hostility of the Catholic Church. But in the early nineteenth century there were a number of prominent Catholics involved in Irish lodges including Daniel O'Connell whose profession was that of barrister. He became a member of Lodge 189, Dublin, in 1799, becoming Worshipful Master in 1801. A Lodge 189 minute book mentions Daniel O'Connell as joining Lodge 13, Limerick in 1800, but there is no reference in the Lodge 13 minute books held in the archives of Grand Lodge of him being one of their members. He was also founding member of Lodge 886, Tralee, in 1800. When the Irish Hierarchy strictly enforced the 1738 Papal Bull condemning Freemasonry, O'Connell had to repudiate the institution at the time of Catholic Emancipation in 1829.

Provincial Grand Architect

On 13 December 1824 James was marked on the main membership register at Grand Lodge as a member of Lodge 95, Cork. There are no minute books extant for this lodge, so the actual date of the architect joining No. 95 is not known.[8] There was nothing to preclude a mason from being a member of more than one lodge; he could join two, three, four, five or more if he so choose. It was perfectly natural for James to join a Cork lodge since he spent time in the city on professional business.

When the aged architect died in 1877 the *Limerick Chronicle* described the deceased as 'an old and much esteemed member of the Masonic body'[9] and records for Lodge 13 show that he was quite often in attendance at meetings.[10] Although a long-standing member for over sixty years James was only Worshipful Master of the Lodge once. This was for the six month period of June-December 1844, James taking up the position on 24 June.[11] Up until 1875 the Worshipful Master and other Lodge officers were elected twice yearly, in June and December; thereafter the position was held for a year.[12]

In 1844 James held the position 'Provincial Grand Superintendent of Works' in the North Munster Provincial Grand Lodge and he is also recorded in the same document as being a member of No. 13, Royal Arch Chapter.[13] About 1864 James served as Provincial Grand Senior Deacon of the Province of Munster.[14] At some stage during his progress through the various orders and degrees associated with the Masonic fraternity James Pain was conferred with the title 'Provincial Grand Architect'.[15] Whether or not his Masonic contacts proved beneficial to his professional career we know not, but in the pursuit of making friends and influencing people we can safely assume that membership of the Freemasons proved no disadvantage in the social milieu in which James moved. There is no record of George Richard Pain having been a member of the Freemasons in Ireland.[16]

New City Gaol

As well as being given responsibility by John Nash for overseeing the Lough Cutra project, it is very likely that James was entrusted with other of Nash's uncompleted Irish commissions as executing architect and builder. In an obituary of James that appeared shortly after his death, and signed 'W. F.' (probably William Fogerty, a Limerick architect who would have known James personally), it is stated that he was sent to Ireland by Nash 'to superintend some important works.'[17] James, and later his brother George Richard, were the obvious choice as overseers of Nash's commissions in Ireland, their familiarity with the great man's work making them the ideal candidates for the task. Some evidence for this is to be found amidst Maurice Lenihan's voluminous footnotes in his *Limerick; Its History and Antiquities* (1866). Lenihan states that the plans for the new Limerick City Gaol, which the City Grand Jury had decided at the Spring Assizes of 1811 should be built at a cost of £6,123 4 shillings (s) 6 pence (d), were 'perfected by Mr. Nash, Architect, and the place selected was the Dean's Close, near the Cathedral of St. Mary's in Bow Lane.' Lenihan further notes that on 13 March 1814 an engine to supply water to the new Gaol was 'put up . . . by Mr. Paine [*sic*], architect, the builder of the city gaol'; the prison having being completed in the latter part of November 1813.[18]

Presumably Nash drew up the plans for the new City prison when he was in the Limerick/Clare area working on the design of Lough Cutra for Colonel Charles Vereker who, at the time, was Foreman of the Limerick City Grand Jury. So, the hand of genius of John Nash, the man who created the oriental exoticism of Brighton's Royal Pavilion, once touched Limerick.

Grand Juries

Grand juries were to be a source of employment for James Pain over the coming years and some explanation of their various functions is necessary. Nowadays the term 'Grand Jury' is commonly associated with the United States legal system in which it is a jury selected to examine the validity of an accusation prior to a trial. This function is directly derived from the seventeenth century English judicial system whereby a grand jury, comprised of prominent local landlords selected by the sheriff, was concerned with the administration of justice. As time progressed grand juries in England, Wales and Ireland acquired other functions, becoming an important body of local government for a city or county as well as maintaining their legal function. By the early nineteenth century grand juries were responsible for the provision of roads and bridges and the construction and maintenance of prisons, courthouses, bridewells, 'lunatic' asylums, dispensaries and county hospitals. Local taxes known as the 'county cess' were levied to finance this work.

Traditionally meeting in a room in the city or county courthouse, grand juries met twice yearly at the Spring and Summer Assizes for the purpose of passing 'presentments'. Presentments were printed lists of works and payments that had been approved of by the grand jury and were published under the title, for example, *Presentments Made on the County of Limerick, at Summer Assizes, 1822*.[19] Various reports were also published in the presentments, including the 'Gaol Report' drawn up by the Board of Superintendence responsible for the maintenance of the local prison, courthouses and bridewells.

Assizes were court sittings that were held twice a year in each county in the spring and summer to hear civil and criminal cases. Assize judges also had to approve the grand jury presentments, often a mere formality.

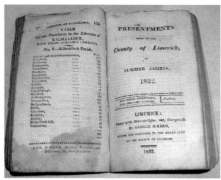

Presentments for Limerick County Grand Jury, Summer Assizes, 1822. On left page, final page of Presentments for Spring Assizes, 1822.

Spiky Gothic

The assertion that James Pain was sent to Ireland by Nash 'to superintend some important works'[20] does suggest that projects on a par with Lough Cutra were placed into his portfolio by Nash. One project that may qualify, and would have been within James's travelling radius, was Shanbally Castle in Co. Tipperary. Designed by Nash for 1st Viscount Lismore,[21] this substantial castellated mansion was conceived about 1812[22] and completed in 1819.[23]

It is possible that it was during this period that James also supervised the construction of St. Paul's (Church of Ireland) in Cahir, Co. Tipperary,[24] built for £2,307 13s 4d, the money a loan from the Board of First Fruits.[25] In Lewis's *Topographical Dictionary of Ireland* (1837) St. Paul's is described as being 're-built in 1817 . . . it is a spacious structure of stone, in the later English style, with an embattled tower surmounted by a finely proportioned spire, the whole after a design by John Nash of London.'[26] Sir John Summerson, author of two studies of John Nash,[27] expressed the opinion in 1982, in correspondence with Cahir historian Joe Walsh, that,

> 'I think we may certainly take it that Cahir parish church is by Nash, Lewis's Top. Dict. [Topographical Dictionary] is a reliable authority

St. Paul's Church (1817), Cahir, Co. Tipperary designed by John Nash. It was built as a garrison church, it has a very militaristic exterior but a very warm interior.

and the vaulting . . . is of a type which Nash used, e.g. at Ravensworth and Longner. The chancel looks to me like a Victorian addition.'[28]

But when exactly the church was designed, we have no knowledge. The examples cited by Sir John are Ravensworth Castle, Co. Durham and Longner Hall.

While St. Paul's has been described as Nash's 'best Gothic Revival church', [29] it is not to everybody's taste with its overly feudal, militarist look and its squat, heavy appearance. Every available piece of wall on the building is battlemented; bartizans 'decorate' the exterior corners of the transepts; the cross shaped windows of the corner towers flanking the east facing doorway recall the loopholes of fortifications and the whole structure is over endowed with a blistering array of spires and pinnacles. The term 'Spiky Gothic' is particularly apposite as regards St. Paul's.

Internally three galleries were installed under a fine plasterwork ceiling and they are unusual in that they can only be entered from the outside. This is a similar arrangement to that in Nash's earlier St. Mildred's Church on the Isle of Wight where, in adding the galleries to a small nave, Nash was forced into using external entrances.[30] Associated with the church is the nearby Erasmus Smith School constructed the year after St. Paul's was built with funds provided by the Erasmus Smith Trust.[31] Erasmus Smith (1611-91) was a seventeenth century educational philanthropist who established an endowment fund to build a number of free grammar schools in Ireland. In 1723 the trust also began to grant-aid the building of primary schools wherever a

020

Front elevation of Erasmus Smith School (1818) believed to be designed by John Nash.

landlord so wished. Although by 1811 the trust had only built a total of eight schools, by 1824 the number had dramatically increased to 111, of which 100 were primary schools.[32] The Cahir school, a fine example of early nineteenth century Gothic Revival, is work that Sir John Summerson considered very suggestive of Nash,

> 'The Cahir School looks to me very like a Nash job. We know that he designed the church in 1817 and I presume that the school, 1818, was for the same client. Stylistically it is very like Nash – the pinnacles especially are of a type he used over and over again.'[33]

Swiss Cottage

It has been argued that, during his visit to Ireland in 1810, Nash as well as attending to his designs for two large country houses of respectively Classical and castellated styles, Rockingham House in Co. Roscommon[34] and Lough Cutra Castle, also designed 'Swiss Cottage'. A thatched *cottage orné* (French for 'decorated cottage'), it was built beside the River Suir near Cahir Castle in Co. Tipperary for Richard Butler, 12th Lord Caher, and his wife Lady Emily who, in 1816, were created Earl and Countess Glengall.[35] Although there is no documentary evidence to prove that Nash was the architect, Sir John Summerson expresses the guarded view that Swiss Cottage 'could also be Nash. It is not wholly unlike Royal lodge though the veranda, made up of rough bits of wood is not quite like anything in Nash's known cottage work.'[36]

Two reasons have been advanced for the opinion that it was probably a Nash design: (a) the structure bears a similarity in architectural style and detail with the designs Nash sent to England from Ireland in 1810 for a group of picturesque cottages that were built at Blaise Hamlet at Henbury, Bristol the following year.[37] If Swiss Cottage was built by Irish craftsmen employed by Lord Caher using Nash's drawings as a guide rather than as a set template that may explain the difference in the workmanship concerning Swiss Cottage and Nash's English *cottage orné*. (b) Through Nash's association with Cahir and Co. Tipperary in designing St. Paul's Church and nearby Shanbally Castle he would have been met with Lord Caher whose seat was in Cahir. Lord Caher and Lady Emily were very much in the thick of the London High Society scene at the time and would have met many of those prominent in the Prince Regent's entourage.

Swiss Cottage was built for the private use of Lord and Lady Caher and, as a picturesque and romanticised vision of a rural idyll, it was the perfect place to entertain guests. Various versions as to the origins of the cottage have been circulated, including the colourful story that the 1st Earl of Glengall had it built as a secluded meeting place for himself and his mistresses;[38] a variant version

021

Swiss Cottage (*c*.1812), Cahir, Co. Tipperary.

has it that it was the 2nd Earl who had it built for a mistress.[39] The *Parliamentary Gazetteer* of 1844-6 erroneously says that the cottage was 'erected by the late Countess of Glengall'[40] i.e. Lady Emily who died in the 1830s; her husband died in 1819.

While no definite date has been fixed for its year of construction there is evidence of its existence by 1814, for Waterford born artist Joseph Alpenny drew a pencil sketch of the cottage that year.[41] Alpenny's sketch was discovered while restoration work on Swiss Cottage was taking place during 1985-9 and after the veranda had been restored and re-roofed with cedar shingles, this being thought to have been the original style of the veranda roofing. All previously known illustrations and photographs had shown the veranda so roofed. However, Alpenny's drawing revealed that the veranda was originally thatched. Perhaps the thatch had been replaced by shingles quite early on because it was not able to throw off rain water efficiently. After some debate by the restoration team, it was decided to stay with the cedar shingles. A tentative construction date of 1810/11 has been suggested for the Swiss Cottage coinciding with Nash's visit to Ireland that year and the erection of Blaise Hamlet.[42]

The *cottage orné* was built on that part of Lord Caher's estate in the district of Kilcommon where the annual local races were held and a report written in 1816 on that year's racing event made mention of the,

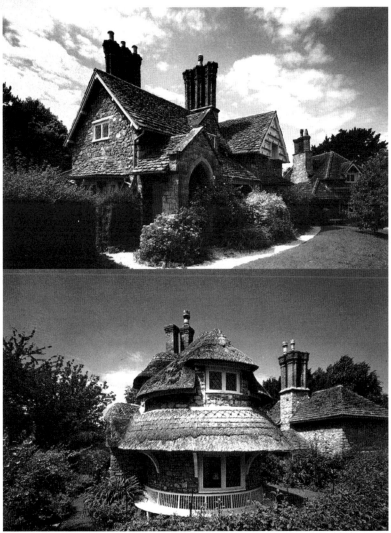

Picturesque cottages at Blaise Hamlet, Henbury, Bristol, England by John Nash.

'. . . scenery over which the bounty of nature has spread her most attractive beauties and upon which the hand of taste has disposed its most bewitching embellishments – the grounds of Kilcommon and the tout ensemble of the Cottage affording a display of rural decoration not easy to be equalled in this country for chasteness of character and richness of fancy.'[43]

In the early part of the nineteenth century the structure was simply known as 'The Cottage'. In 1857 it was called 'Caher Cottage' in a sale catalogue when the estate went onto the market under the Incumbered Estates Act following the bankruptcy of the 2nd Earl of Glengall;[44] whereas a lithograph (1853) of the building by Maurice Collis is captioned 'Cahir Cottage'.[45] It was not until the late nineteenth century that it became more familiar as 'Swiss Cottage' because of its chalet-like appearance.[46] Swiss Cottage predates St. Paul's Church and while James Pain may have supervised the building of this captivating *cottage orné* there is no documentary evidence to prove it and all that can be said for the present is that James's familiarity with Nash's work does make him a possible candidate.

Picturesque Eye

Supposedly emulating the 'Olde' English labourer's cottage of the fifteenth and sixteenth centuries, decorated cottages were usually small, asymmetrical buildings built in a deliberately and highly romanticised rustic style. Positively falling over themselves in proclaiming their rootedness in nature, they expressed the idea that man, nature and the landscape are intimately interconnected. The product of the late eighteenth/early nineteenth century cult of the Picturesque, of which John Nash was a leading figure and in which the Pain brothers were trained, *cottage orné* were invariably roofed with very thick thatch and constructed mainly of wood. Cahir's Swiss Cottage has many of the features associated with the genre: thatch roof of reeds and an elaborate

024

Cahir Castle, Cahir, Co. Tipperary. Lithograph by Maurice Collis, 1853.

rustic veranda supported by tree trunks (the rooted in nature concept); dormer windows and diamond leaded windows (authentic Olde Worlde charm); irregularity of design and an asymmetrical arrangement of forms and details whereby no two views of the structure are the same (suggesting the irregularity of nature). Scenic location was another key element in siting Picturesque architecture and in Swiss Cottage there is simple rustic perfection, set as it on the edge of a wooded bluff beside the River Suir and overlooking a grassy, wooded plain. The whole composition is geared towards evoking an emotional, reflective response in which we are stripped of pretentious details and returned to first principals and our natural self.

In florid word and phrase a contributor to the *Parliamentary Gazetteer of Ireland* goes into raptures about the picturesque beauty of the Glengall demesne within which the cottage is set. The publication speaks of the,

'. . . beauteous course of the limpid and feathery Suir, the ivy-mantled, water-girt, and romantic castle of Cahir . . . the undulated expanse of villa-dotted luxuriance which spreads away in the distance, and the grand perspective of the verdant and wooded declivities of the Galtee mountains, render Cahir unsurpassed for picturesqueness by any town in Munster.'[47]

Nash's corpus of work in Munster alone, ranging from two castellated mansions to a prison, a school, a church and a *cottage orné*, gives some indication of the wide diversity of Nash's architectural abilities and the comprehensive training the Pain brothers received while working with Nash in England, especially in viewing architectural compositions and settings with a 'Picturesque Eye'.

Dromoland House

Besides acting as supervising architect for John Nash, James Pain was naturally ambitious to establish his own reputation as an architect and one of the first signs of him striking out for independence came in the summer of 1813 when he submitted drawings, dated 'July 13 1813',[48] to Sir Edward O'Brien MP whose seat was Dromoland House, an early eighteenth century mansion that stood near Newmarket-on-Fergus in the County of Clare. Sir Edward was actively considering the possibility of replacing his house with a more modern structure and Colonel Vereker may very well have introduced his fellow MP to the eager to please architect, recommending the Englishman highly on the basis of his work at Lough Cutra. Pain's first proposal for Dromoland was not Gothic in design, but was rather conventional and involved retaining part of the old house. It was by no means the only proposal received by Sir Edward during this period, for architect Thomas Hopper also submitted drawings, as did Richard and William Morrison.[49] Hopper (1776-1856) was responsible for the rather plain Greek Revival gate lodge (1812) that still stands at the main entrance to Dromoland.[50]

James Pain's proposed front elevation for Dromoland House, 1813.

James Pain's proposed garden elevation for Dromoland, 1813.

Despite the earnest solicitations of eager architects Sir Edward did not see the need to rush into the project, deciding to proceed cautiously before committing his wealth. Writing to his wife, Lady Charlotte, from London in 1812 he told her of the plans Hopper had given him for Dromoland, but he believed that,

Gate lodge (1812), Dromoland Castle, Co. Clare. Greek Revival architectural style by Thomas Hopper.

'. . . such considerable difficulty will attend the adding and linking the old house to the new that I begin to think it would be almost as well to build a new House entirely & to content ourselves with the one we have till we can do it to suit our Purse & wishes in every respect as we are in no hurry about the matter . . .'[51]

It was not until 1819 that Sir Edward finally made up his mind on the various designs that had been submitted to him over the period 1812-19, including a second Pain submission in asymmetrical castellated style.[52]

Kilnasoolagh Church

James's courting of Sir Edward's favour was not without some gain, for we find in the 16 April 1816 vestry minutes of Kilnasoolagh parish at Newmarket-on-Fergus that the architect had been appointed to rebuild the Anglican church there.[53] This was the church at which the O'Briens of Dromoland worshipped, were wedded and buried[54] and Sir Edward one of the churchwardens.[55] Two years earlier, in 1814, the vestry had come to the conclusion that the church was in so much need of repair that the structure had to be totally rebuilt. Accordingly, a request was made to the Bishop of Killaloe to arrange a £900 loan from the Board of First Fruits to help finance the project.[56]

Considered to be one of Clare's most attractive churches, Pain's Kilnasoolagh is built in the Simple Gothic manner typically associated with early nineteenth century Church of Ireland architecture - basically a rectangular box housing both nave and chancel with a square bell tower at the western end where the entrance porch is situated. The tower, crenellated and three stages in height,[57]

Kilnasoolagh Church, Newmarket-on-Fergus, Co. Clare. In 1816 James Pain was appointed architect to build this church.

is surmounted by a slender octagonal spire. A louvered, round headed opening features on each face of the tower's upper, belfry stage. The present spire is not the original, having been replaced in 1992 by a new spire when the old one was severely damaged by a lightning strike the previous year.[58]

Diagonal staged buttresses (set diagonally at the corner of a building forming an angle of 135° with each wall) are located at the four corners of the main body of the building reaching the full height of the wall, the buttresses being topped by finials. On the north side of the chancel a robing room is attached to the church. The building is five bays in length and a feature of the design is that although there are windows on the south facing elevation there are none on the north. The tracery in the windows is a simple Perpendicular. When built the church could seat 200 in box pews - these were removed in the 1860s.[59] Box pews were a standard feature in seventeenth to nineteenth century churches, consisting of benches enclosed within panelling and provided with a door to exclude drafts. In an attempt to keep the congregation warm in winter a stove was also installed in the aisle sometimes in the centre of the church and sometimes placed near the box pews of the most wealthy members of the congregation who sat at the top of the church. Box pews were available for rent and provided exclusive private seating accommodation for prominent personages and their families. Ordinary bench pews were provided at the rear of the nave, nearer the draughty main doors, for those who could not afford a box pew.

In addition to the church at Kilnasoolagh, built for £1,500, a new glebe house was also provided for the rector at £660. The Board of First Fruits granting £400 as a gift to build the glebe house and £260 as a loan.[60]

Another of James's early Irish church commissions was in 1817 at Drumcliff parish church, Ennis, Co. Clare where the church was in need of renovation after being struck by lightning.[61] Much injured by the strike, the tower was damaged and the bell destroyed. During renovation work the tower was heightened and crowned with battlements and pinnacles.[62] The present parish church, St. Columba's, was erected in 1871.[63]

A late nineteenth century guide to Limerick's St. Mary's Cathedral published four years after his death states that James built a porch onto the west door of the Cathedral in 1816. This information, according to the publication, having being 'ascertained on the authority of a professional gentleman who had personal knowledge of the fact, that it was erected in 1816 . . . by James Paine.'[64]

Surveying Thomond Bridge

James undertook a wide range of work in the Limerick area as he sought to establish his reputation as an architect and builder in his adopted city. In 1814, for instance, he surveyed Limerick's ancient fourteenth century Thomond Bridge, which came under the responsibility of Limerick Corporation, and on 13 September he drew up a plan and elevation of the medieval stone structure and a sketch of its proposed replacement. In his comments on the condition of the aged, fourteen arch structure the architect noted that the 'arches are cracked' and the 'piers undermined.'[65] Pain's drawings show that the arches

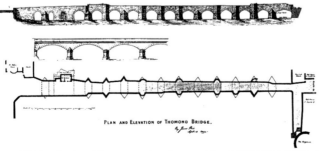

PLAN AND ELEVATION OF THOMOND BRIDGE.

Old Thomond Bridge (top) and its proposed replacement (centre) by James Pain, 1814.

Lithograph by S. Brocas (1826) of the Castle Street end of Thomond Bridge showing the narrowness of the roadway.

were not uniform, eight were flat pointed and the other six semicircular, and were of various spans, ranging from 25 feet (7.62 metres) for the widest arch next to Castle Street to 12 feet and 10 feet (3.01 metres) for the narrowest at the other end of the bridge. In 1814 the roadway between the parapets was only 10 feet 6 inches (3.23 metres) wide at the Castle Street end, gradually widening as one progressed across the bridge; but even at its broadest extent the roadway was only 17 feet (5.18 metres) between the parapets.[66] When the architect drew up his proposal for a replacement bridge he believed that he could design a structure utilising the piers of the old bridge and doubling the span of the original arches.[67]

A visitor to the city in 1810 noted that Thomond Bridge was 'so narrow that Two carriages could with difficulty pass.'[68] There were twelve recesses in the parapet walls, some triangular in plan, others semicircular, to allow pedestrians to step out of the way of traffic. In 1822 the width of the roadway at the Castle Street end was of necessity increased.[69] Despite the poor condition of the antiquated structure another twenty years were to elapse before James and George Richard Pain would eventually be commissioned to build a replacement.

Limerick Corporation

During his early years in Ireland James received work from Limerick Corporation, the Common Council's minutes for 21 April 1815 recording that the Committee of Accounts had authorised a payment to him of £423 17s 5d for sundry repairs and alterations to the Exchange on Nicholas Street where the Corporation had its meeting rooms.[70] He was quite fortunate to receive such a commission, for scrutiny of the accounts for the period 1812-22 reveals that the Corporation very rarely spent money carrying out maintenance of the buildings and infrastructure of those areas of urban Limerick for which it was responsible, viz. Englishtown and Irishtown which were in sore need of repair and attention.

Seven months later, in November 1815, James was in receipt of minor amounts of money from the Corporation for work undertaken on the new Corn Market. The relevant passages stating that 'James Paynne' [*sic*] was to be paid £9 13s 0d for having 'slated the new Corn market and weather slated the Parapet wall' and an additional £8 0s. 8d for 'pointing the Parapet inside and outside in July 1815'. There is no mention of George Pain in that year's Corporation accounts.[71] Four years later, however, in June 1819, £182 1s 2d was paid to 'Messrs. Pain' for further repairs on the Exchange.[72]

In 1815-16 the Commissioners of the County Limerick Gaol undertook an investigation into the state and condition of the prison, a facility located beside the newly built City Gaol. Advice was sought from several expert sources, including an assessment by James Pain of the building's continuing suitability as a prison. His conclusion was in the negative and he urged the construction of an entirely new facility.[73]

Bread and Butter

One of the 'bread and butter' reliables of the architectural and building firm that James was to establish in Limerick was alterations, additions and remodelling work carried out on the private houses of wealthy clients. An early indication of this type of work is possibly Mount Shannon House (near Castleconnell, Co. Limerick) where he may have been associated with the Classical remodelling of the house for John Fitzgibbon, 2nd Earl of Clare. These alterations included the construction of an imposing Ionic portico that served as a porte-cochere for the mansion. Work commenced sometime after 1813 to the specifications of architect Lewis Wyatt and, according to Bence-Jones,

Mount Shannon House near Castleconnell,
Co. Limerick. Photograph shows the
imposing Ionic portico that was added to the
original house. The house was burnt down
in 1920 during the War of Independence.

James Pain worked at Mount
Shannon 'either supervising the
remodelling according to Wyatt's
design, or carrying out subsequent
alterations.'[74] That the architect
did indeed have a professional
relationship with Mount Shannon
during his long career is evidenced
by a gift of books sent by
Fitzgibbon to James Pain on 30
December 1837. In his accompanying letter the Earl of Clare states that he is
sending the books as 'a small proof of my regard and in recollection of this
House which you have done so much to improve.'[75]

Once James had carried out a number of successful renovations and
remodellings in his early years in Limerick his name would soon become
known among the local gentry who often met socially at the assizes, race
meetings etc. In 1813 the County Club was established on George's Street to
cater as an exclusive meeting place for the gentry of the city and county[76] and
it was this social grouping that would provide James Pain with much work
over the coming years. In his early years in Limerick the architect assiduously
cultivated the acquaintance of prominent members of the 'County Set'. The
diary of Sir Vere Hunt of Currah, Co. Limerick records that on 1 March 1816
'Stephen Rice and Mr. Payne [sic] the English architect come here in their way
from Limerick to Mount Trenchard to stay for an hour or two.'[77]

Pain's travelling companion was Stephen Edward Rice, proprietor of Mount
Trenchard, Foynes, Co. Limerick whose daughter Mary Spring Rice was
married to Sir Vere Hunt's son, Aubrey. When his father died in 1818 Sir Aubrey
inherited the estate, changing the family name from Hunt to de Vere about
1832 and renaming the estate Curragh Chase. It was Sir Aubrey's son, also
Aubrey de Vere (1814-1902), who established a reputation as a minor Irish
Victorian poet.[78] Mount Trenchard was to become the seat of Thomas Spring
Rice, 1st Baron Monteagle of Brandon.

The Name of Pain

As is apparent, variant spellings of the surname 'Pain' appear in a number of
contemporary primary sources, including 'Paine' 'Paynne' and 'Payne'. James
was consistent in his use of 'Pain', but even as late as 1877, the year of his
death, his name appears as 'Payne' in a Limerick trade directory.[79] All these
variants are, in a sense, correct, 'Pain' having subsequently become the more
common, standarised spelling of various Middle English (c.1150-1500)
surnames, *Paine, Payne Paynne* and *Pain*, all with a similar origin.

One explanation offered by onomastricians, those who study names, is that the surname can be traced back through the Old French *Paien* to the Latin *Pagamus*, a name derived from the Latin word *pagus*. Originally *pagus* meant a country dweller, as opposed to a town dweller, then it came to denote a

Illustration of the Dominican Church, Limerick consecrated in July 1816. Architect, James Pain.

civilian as opposed to a soldier. During the Christian era *pagus* came to signify a heathen, someone who was not a Christian, not enrolled in the army of Christ. From this, the present meaning of the word 'pagan' is derived. Apparently, although the names *Paine, Payne* etc. had heathenist associations, they were still popular names in the medieval period.[80] A more prosaic explanation is that the surname 'Pain' is derived from the occupation of baker or pantryman, the French word for bread being *pain*.[81] However, it is not uncommon for a surname to have more than one source of meaning.

033

Dominican Church

Despite the possible trace of 'paganism' in the family name, the Pain brothers did quite well in receiving commissions from the Christian authorities in Ireland. Of the two, George Richard carried out the greater number of assignments for the Catholic Church, particularly in the Cork area in the 1820s and '30s, work that is much admired. James's involvement with ecclesiastical architecture, on the other hand, is predominately associated with the Protestant Church of Ireland. However, he did do some work for the Catholic

The Dominican Church was remodelled in the 1860s.

Church during his early years in Limerick, for he was the architect of St. Saviour's Dominican Church on Upper Glentworth Street - the foundation stone being blessed and laid by Bishop Tuohy on Easter Monday 27 March 1815. Fr. James Joseph Carberry, Limerick Dominican and local historian, wrote in 1866 that 'Mr. Wallace, builder', was contracted to build the church while 'the plans were furnished by Payne [sic] Esquire, Architect.'[82]

Although St. Saviour's, consecrated on 6 July 1816,[83] made use of Gothic trappings such as crocketed pinnacles, crenellation and pointed arch fenestration, it lacked the soaring upward thrust one normally associates with ecclesiastical Gothic. Before 1829 Catholic churches in Ireland were not allowed to have a spire or tower and Catholic churches built before that date have the appearance of chapels.[84] Pain's St. Saviour's had a rather subdued, squat appearance on its front elevation, the tracery in the windows being very simple.[85] Nevertheless a visitor to the city in 1817, a Mr. Trotter who penned the near-eponymous *Walks Through Ireland*, commented favourably when he 'saw a new Catholic chapel; just finished in a very handsome Gothic manner, which ornaments the new city very much.' He observed that 'There is considerable harmony between Catholics and Protestants here . . .'[86] When completed in 1816 the chapel stood on Upper Glentworth Street, for Baker Place, which the church now faces, did not exist at the time, nor did Pery Street.[87] With the opening in the 1830s of the Pery Street/Pery Square vista, of which the Dominicans became a focal point, Pain's chapel did not look very prepossessing. To rectify this defect the church was extensively remodelled in the 1860s making a vast improvement in appearance. This work being carried out by William Wallace[88] who added an extra 20 feet (6.1 metres) to the height of the building with the addition of a clerestory. The insertion of a circular rose window in the front elevation of the clerestory, and the replacement of Pain's simple Gothic tracery with the more pleasing elaborate style certainly enhanced the building.

Guard Wall

One of the reasons why James Pain was in constant employment for over sixty years as an architect was his versatility; to keep a wealthy client or public patron happy he was willing to build anything from a family tomb to a monumental mansion, just as happy to build a road as construct a prison. No job was too small or too big for his Limerick office. An example of this versatility is a series of works he is believed to have carried out in the vicinity of Glin Castle and Mount Trenchard along the Shannon estuary.

At the 1815 Summer Assizes the Limerick County Grand Jury allocated £65 to 'Stephen E. Rice [of Mount Trenchard] and Jas. Pain, to repair the guard-wall that separates the north-east part of the new line of mail coach road adjoining the creek of Glin and the newly intended bridge over the river Fergus.'[89] This guard-wall being the estuary wall that flanks the coast road along various stretches of the coastal route from Foynes to Tarbert. It was during this period that a new mail-coach road was being laid down from Limerick to Tralee[90] and James Pain, due to his friendship with influential figures such as Stephen Rice and the Knight of Glin, may have been involved in contractual work on this major civil engineering project. Local gentry were often appointed as supervisors without salary by Grand Juries to oversee construction of new roads that passed by or through their estates and they had some discretion whom to employ. That section of the new road in the vicinity of Foynes and Mount Trenchard came under the supervision of Stephen Rice and was built by the spring of 1812, for a visitor to Mount Trenchard that year records in his diary for Sunday 15 March,

> 'Thomas gives us prayers and we then walk to Stephen Rice's new road. A great and noble work. Henceforth the most interesting feature of the journey from Dublin to Killarney will be this piece of road along the Shannon beginning at the stupendous cliff cut down by Stephen Rice facing Foynes Island . . . '[91]

Since the date of James Pain's arrival in Ireland is a bit vague (c.1811/12) there is no point in speculating whether or not he was involved in the work at Foynes and the blasting down of the cliff just outside the town. Ending in Tarbert, the estuary road is still very scenic.

Glin Castle

Desmond FitzGerald, the present and 29th Knight of Glin and distinguished authority in the field of Irish architecture and the decorative arts, is of the

Glin Castle, Glin, Co. Limerick, an eighteenth century mansion, it was battlemented about 1812 to give the cosmetic appearance of a castle.

strong opinion that James Pain carried out a number of assignments at Glin Castle for John Fraunceis FitzGerald following his attainment of the title as the 25th Knight in 1812.[92] At that time the house was a fairly plain, three-storied Georgian mansion with a double bow on the front. Built in the 1780s, it was known simply as Glin House consisting of the mansion and a long service wing.

Shortly after 1812 the house was given some 'cardboard' Gothic additions in the form of battlements placed on the tops of the walls. The Georgian sash windows on the front and on the six-bay side elevation were replaced by mullioned windows, the detailing on the mullions being identical to that used by John Nash - a feature that suggests that James Pain was involved. The sash windows at the rear of the house were left in place. The service wing was similarly battlemented, given some gimcrack Gothic detailing and further 'tarted up' with several turrets. On the basis of this cosmetic powdering John Fraunceis was able to change the name from Glin House to Glin Castle. As Desmond FitzGerald himself says of his predecessor 'he obviously thought that the holder of such an ancient title should be living in a castle like his medieval ancestors!'[93]

James Pain is also thought to have carried out a number of other improvements and embellishments on the Glin demesne, including erecting a battlemented stable yard and a stone-walled kitchen garden. A hermitage was also constructed in the grounds at this time, the quality of the vaulting indicating that a professional architect was involved rather than a local amateur enthusiast. The Glin hermitage is a simple three-arched pavilion with the inside bare except for a stone slab for a seat. Frugal comfort for any self-respecting hermit and one assumes that this simple shelter was left uninhabited, the position of 'Hermit to the Knight' being unfilled.

Other evidence that an architect of Pain's capabilities was employed by John Fraunceis is the design of the original section of the Steward's Lodge which has distinctive Regency eaves. The architect is also believed to have overseen landscaping to the front of Glin Castle involving raising the level of the ground between the house and the new coast road laid down in 1815. Prior to the building of the highway the land fell naturally to the estuary shore offering an unrestricted picturesque view of the wide expanse of the Shannon and the opposite coast of Clare. To prevent the occupants of Glin Castle having to suffer the inconvenience of having to observe a constant flow of traffic passing along their line of vision it was decided to raise up the soil between the house and the road so as to form a ha-ha to cleverly hide the castle from the view of passers-by.

At the 1815 Spring Assizes held in the County Courthouse in Limerick on 10 March John Fraunceis FitzGerald, a member of the Grand Jury,[94] had been appointed as Supervisor without salary to oversee the construction of a new section of the Glin to Tarbert road, the distance to cover 262 perches 'between the bridge at Glin and the Limekiln on the lands of Ballynamadagh',[95] a distance of just over a mile. It seems reasonable to assume that if James Pain was carrying out landscaping for the Knight of Glin he would have appointed the same architect to build the road and its associated guard-wall. An Irish perch was equal to 21 feet, or 7 yards (6.4 metres); in the British imperial measurement system, a perch is equal to 5 yards (4.6 metres). A perch is also known as a rod or a pole.

It has to be pointed out that there is no documentary evidence to support the contention that James Pain was actually involved in any of the work at Glin - however, the archaeological evidence of the architecture points towards James Pain and Desmond FitzGerald is of the strong belief that he was indeed involved.

In 1815 a very neat looking First Fruits Anglican church with a square tower was built as an eye-catcher on an eminence just outside the village entrance to the demesne and known as the parish church of Kilfergus; it was dedicated to St. Paul.[96] The consecration of the new church was reported in the *Limerick Gazette* and *General Advertizer* of Tuesday, June 20th, 1815 as follows:

> 'On Tursday last, the Lord Bishop of Limerick proceeded from Glin House to the new parish church of Kilfergus, which His Lordship consecrated with the usual ceremonies. After the consecration he publicly baptized the elder son of the Knight of Glen.'

The following year £30 10s 3d is reported to have been allocated to the Knight of Glin and Thomas Madigan at the Spring 1816 County Limerick Grand Jury

Presentments to 'make 31 perches of the new-intended road from Glin to the new Church built near Glin'[97] The main body of the church was a Simple Gothic, rectangular box typical of the period, three bays in length with no vestry room or porch attached. The bays on the northern elevation were equally divided by buttresses topped with pinnacles. There were no windows on the southern elevation. Set several feet above the Gothic windows were rectangular label drip mouldings; there appears to be have been no curved hood mouldings set directly over the windows.[98] The seating arrangement was all box pews. This church is no longer standing, having been replaced in 1868 by one to a Victorian design.[99] Since 1997 the building has served as the Glin Heritage Centre.[100] Simple Gothic was a style of ecclesiastical architecture that James Pain's name would become synonymous with over the coming twenty-five years, in particular after becoming an official architect to the Board of First Fruits *c.*1822.

These early years up to 1816 were to prove the foundation of James Pain's career in Munster and after this period he began to receive major architectural assignments and become recognised as a foremost architect in the province.

Endnotes

1 Lee, David 'The Battle of Collooney, 1798' & Gonzalez, Christine 'Chancer or Hero? General Humbert's Campaign in Ireland, 1798', *Georgian Limerick* Vol. II, Lee, David & Gonzalez, Christine eds., Limerick Civic Trust, Limerick, 2000; *Dictionary of National Biography* s.v. 'Vereker, Charles' Vol. XX, Oxford University Press, 1921-1922.

2 *The Parliamentary Gazetteer of Ireland*, 3 Vols., A. Fullarton, Dublin, London and Edinburgh, 1844-46, s.v. 'Loughcooter', Vol. II, p. 692.

3 Bence-Jones, Mark *A Guide to Irish Country Houses*, 2nd revised edition, Constable, London, 1988 s.v. 'Lough Cutra Castle', p. 192.

4 For further information on Lough Cutra Castle see: Richardson, Douglas Scott *Gothic Revival Architecture in Ireland*, 2 Vols., Garland Publishing Inc., New York and London, 1983, Vol. I. pp. 126-8; Guinness, D. & Ryan, W. *Irish Houses and Castles*, Thames and Hudson Ltd., London, 1971, pp. 176-81; Bence-Jones, Mark *A Guide to Irish Country Houses*, 2nd revised edition, Constable, London, 1988, p.192.

5 For biographical information on Charles Vereker see Lenihan, Maurice *Limerick; Its History and Antiquities* 1866, pp. 225n, 408-15n.

6 Archives of the Grand Lodge of Freemasons, Ireland, Molesworth Street, Dublin. Information from Rebecca Hayes, researcher at Grand Lodge.

7 Haydn, J. A. *Ancient Union Lodge No. 13, Limerick - An Essay on the Bicentenary 1732-1932 of the Lodge No. 13*, Lodge of Research No. 200, Friday 28 April 1933, p.13. Limerick Civic Trust Archive.

8 Archives, Grand Lodge of Freemasons, Ireland (GLFI).

9 *Limerick Chronicle*, 15 December 1877.

10 Archives GLFI.

11 *Limerick Chronicle*, 15 May 1844; Archives GLFI.

12 Haydn *op. cit.* 'Chronological List of Worshipful Masters', pp. 31-2.

13 *List of Officers for the North Munster Provincial Grand Lodge, Limerick, for 24 June-17 December 1844*, printed by George Morgan Goggin, Provincial Grand Librarian, 34 O'Connell Street, Limerick, 1844. Limerick Museum (LM 1996.1494.).

14 *Index of Irish Architects* s.v. 'Pain, James', Irish Architectural Archive, 45 Merrion Square, Dublin.

15 Haydn *op. cit.* p. 14.

16 Archives GLFI.

17 'The Late James Pain, Architect', published in *Limerick Chronicle*, 22 December 1877; *The Builder*, 29 December 1877; *The Irish Builder*, 1 January 1878. The *Index of Irish Architects* s.v. 'Pain James', Irish Architectural Archive says that W. F is 'probably William Fogerty.' Fogerty (1834-78), a Gothic Revivalist, is mainly known for his institutional architecture such as Our Lady's Hospital (1863-8), Ennis; the Methodist College (1865-71), Belfast and the Protestant Orphan Society Hall (1865), Pery Street, Limerick.

18 Lenihan *op. cit.* pp. 428; 428*n*2; 431*n*.

19 The Limerick City Grand Jury Presentments Books for 1791-1887 were destroyed in the fire at the Four Courts in 1922. Copies of the Presentment Books for County Limerick are held in the Local Studies Department, Limerick County Library.

20 'The Late James Pain, Architect', *Limerick Chronicle*, 22 December 1877.

21 *The Parliamentary Gazetteer of Ireland* s.v. 'Shanbally', Vol. III, p. 213.

22 Davis, Terence 'John Nash in Ireland', *Bulletin of the Irish Georgian Society* Vol. VIII, No. 2, April-June 1965, p. 57; Bence-Jones *op. cit.* p. 257.

23 Colvin, Howard *A Biographical Dictionary of British Architects 1600-1840*, 3rd edition, Yale University Press, New Haven and London, 1995, s.v. 'Nash, John', p. 694.

24 Richardson *op. cit.* p. 202.

25 *Parliamentary Gazetteer of Ireland* Vol. 1, p. 293, s.v. 'Cahir, a parish, partly in the barony of East Iffa and Offa'. The contributor to the *Gazetteer* writes that St. Paul's was built 'in 1816.'

26 Lewis, Samuel *A Topographical Dictionary of Ireland*, Two Vols., London, 1837, Vol. I, p. 239; Richardson *op. cit.* pp. 200-2.

27 Summerson, John *The Life and Work of John Nash, Architect*, George Allen and Unwin, London, 1980; *John Nash: Architect to George IV* 1935, 2nd edition 1949.

28 Correspondence from Sir John Summerson to Joe Walsh 29 May 1982.

29 Richardson *op. cit.* p. 200.

30 Mansbridge, Michael *John Nash: A Complete Catalogue* s.v.'179: St Paul's Church', Phaidon, Oxford, 1991.

31 Author's conversation with Cahir historian Joe Walsh.

32 Logan, Dr. John *Book Learning: Schooling and the Promotion of Literacy in Nineteenth Century Ireland*, draft copy, 1994, pp. 39-40, Limerick Civic Trust Archive; Byrne, Joseph *Byrne's Dictionary of Irish Local History* s.v. 'Smith, Erasmus', Mercier Press, Cork, 2004.

33 Correspondence from Sir John Summerson to Joe Walsh 24 October 1987.
34 Colvin *op. cit.* s.v. 'Nash John', p. 693.
35 For discussion of the origins of Swiss Cottage see: O'Reilly, S. *The Swiss Cottage*, Office of Public Works, Criterion Press, Dublin, 1993, pp. 15-7; Girouard, M. 'Swiss Cottage, Cahir', *Country Life*, 22 September 1966; Girouard, M. 'The Swiss Cottage, Cahir, Co. Tipperary', *Country Life*, 26 October 1989.
36 Correspondence from Sir John Summerson to Joe Walsh 29 May 1982.
37 Colvin *op. cit.* s.v. 'Nash, John', p. 693.
38 O'Reilly *op. cit.* p. 17.
39 Lyons, Mary Cecelia *Illustrated Incumbered Estates: Ireland, 1850 - 1905*, Ballinakella Press, Whitegate, County Clare, 1993, p. 71.
40 *The Parliamentary Gazetteer of Ireland* Vol. I, p. 294.
41 O'Reilly *op. cit.* pp. 23-4.
42 Author's conversation with Joe Walsh, Cahir historian who was involved in the restoration. Alpenny's drawing was published in *Cahir Heritage Newsletter* No. 37, Swiss Cottage Edition, 1 September 1989. The original drawing is now in Canada.
43 O'Reilly *op. cit.* p. 17.
44 Lyons *op. cit.* pp. 69-71. *The Parliamentary Gazetteer of Ireland* Vol. I, p. 294 refers to the building as 'a singularly neat cottage'.
45 National Library of Ireland Land Commission Set, Vol. 74 – published in Lyons *op. cit.* p. 73.
46 'The Ld. Cahir's Cottage at Kilcommon', *Cahir Heritage Newsletter* No. 37, Swiss Cottage Edition, 1 September 1989.
47 *Parliamentary Gazetteer of Ireland* Vol. I, s.v. 'Cahir, a market and post town', p. 293.

Queens and Swains: The fashion for *cottage orné* to grace the parklands of country estates was inspired by Queen Marie Antoinette's enthusiasm for an idealised rustic idyll where the Queen and her courtiers could imagine themselves as shepherds and dairymaids and escape, for a while, the tedious duties of royalty. Shakespeare's Henry VI expressing this wistful sentiment to shrug off the burdensome trappings of power:

> 'O God! Methinks it were a happy life,
> To be no better than a homely swain.'
>
> *Henry VI* Part 3, Act II, Scene V. 21-2.

Whatever about the homely life of the English swain (a country youth), the homely life of the Irish swain was a different matter altogether and far from pleasant, as Lady Glengall was only too well aware. In March 1821 she replied to a questionnaire sent by the General Board of Health in Dublin to people of substance throughout the country – landlords, clergymen etc. - enquiring about the living conditions of the poorer classes in their neighbourhoods, particularly as they related to the spread of infectious diseases. The complete text of Lady Glengall's reply to the questionnaire is published, in Luddy, Maria 'The Lives of the Poor in Cahir in 1821', *Tipperary Historical Journal 1991*, Co. Tipperary Historical Society, 1991, pp. 73-9. Originally published in the *First Report of the General Health Board*, Dublin, 1822, her observations about life in the cottages of the underprivileged in Cahir and surrounding district revels that she had no romantic illusions about the charms of Irish rustic idylls,

'Their dwellings are in general wretched hovels, swarming with children, pigs, vermin and fifth, both inside and out . . .' Lady Emily informed the Board of Health. Houses were terribly over-crowded, especially as inhabitants often accommodated other families out of charity, and since 'the usual inhabitants are numerous, they sleep promiscuously, which is of course a dreadful thing.' Up until quite recently [i.e. 1821] dunghills 'were prevalent in the town, nay, they used to pile them up to the top of their houses, and form cesspools of putrid water before their doors.' Through the exertions of Lord and Lady Glengall this nuisance was removed from Cahir, but in the countryside dunghills still flourished 'as usual.'

Lady Emily seems to have had a prejudice against the habits of the local womenfolk, particularly their standards of hygiene, or complete lack of them, for they, 'have not linen next to their skin, whence proceeds the dreadful stench that dirt engenders.' Since these females had not the habits of industry and cleanliness, were totally unemployed except during harvest and potato season, and were 'so ignorant that few know how to do anything, not even to work at their needle' their children were brought up to 'theft and wickedness of all descriptions.'

48 Richardson *op. cit.* Vol. I, pp. 132-4, Figs. 59-61.
49 For discussion on these various proposals see Richardson *op. cit.* pp. 128-39, Figs. 57-68.
50 Colvin *op. cit.* s.v. 'Hopper, Thomas', p. 514.
51 Quoted in O'Brien, Grania R. *These My Friends & Forebears – The O'Briens of Dromoland*, Ballinakella Press, Whitegate, County Clare, 1991, p. 105.
52 Richardson *op. cit.* pp. 140-1.
53 Baily, Edwin R. *Kilnasoolagh Church, Newmarket on Fergus – An Appreciation*, published by Edwin Bailey for Kilnasoolagh Church, Newmarket on Fergus, Co. Clare, 1992, p. 11.
54 O'Brien *op. cit.*
55 Bailey *op. cit.* p. 11.
56 ibid.
57 The correct architectural term for a storey in a tower is 'stage'.
58 Hewson, Adrian *Inspiring Stones: A History of the Church of Ireland Dioceses of Limerick, Ardfert, Aghadoe, Killaloe, Kilfenora, Clonfert, Kilmacduagh & Emly*, Diocesan Council of Limerick, Killaloe and Ardfert, Limerick, 1995, p. 103.
59 Bailey *op. cit.* p. 16.
60 Lewis *op. cit.* s.v. 'Kilnasoolagh'.

61 *Index of Irish Architects* s.v. 'Pain, James', Irish Architectural Archive, Merrion Square, Dublin, citing National Library of Ireland (*Ms 8821*).

62 Lewis *op. cit.* Vol. I p. 601.

63 Hewson *op. cit.* p. 100.

64 *A Historic and Descriptive Sketch of St. Mary's Cathedral*, G. M'Kern & Sons, Limerick, 1881, p. 34.

65 'Note' by Lynch, P. J. to Barry, J. G. 'Old Limerick Bridges', *Journal of the North Munster Archaeological Society*, printed by Guy & Co., Limerick, Vol. I, 1909-1910-1911, p. 13.

66 James Pain's 1814 drawings are reproduced in Barry, J. G. 'Old Limerick Bridges', Journal of the North Munster Archaeological Society Vol. I, 1909-1910-1911, pp. 8-11.

67 Hill, Judith *The Building of Limerick,* The Mercier Press, Cork, 1991, p. 147.

68 Beaufort, Mary *Tour From Upton to Killarney and Limerick in 1810*, MS 4036, Trinity College Dublin, p. 28.

69 Lynch *op. cit.* p. 12n3.

70 MS. *Minutes of Limerick Common Council*, 21 April 1815, Limerick Archives.

71 ibid. 21 November 1815.

72 ibid. 28 June 1819.

73 'Report of the Commissioners of County Limerick Gaol', *Limerick Gazette*, 9 February 1816.

74 Bence-Jones *op. cit.* p. 216.

75 James McMahon file citing The Vereker Papers compiled by Frederick James Wellington Vereker, Limerick Archives. Frederick J. W. Vereker (1866-1946) was the son of Henry Vereker and Sarah (Sally) Pain, niece of James Pain.

76 *County Club, Limerick*, printed for the Committee by Hodges, Figgis, & Co. Ltd., Dublin, 1913, p.5.

77 *The Diary of Sir Vere Hunt. Bart.* Typed transcript of manuscript in De Vere Papers (P 22, Box 1), Limerick Archives.

78 Cronin, Patrick J. *Aubrey de Vere - The Bard of Curragh Chase: A Portrait of his Life and Poetry,* Askeaton Civic Trust, Co. Limerick, 1997, pp. 2-3,7.

79 *Bassett's Directory of the City and County of Limerick . . . 1877-8*, William Bassett, Limerick, pp. 64, 85.

80 *The Oxford Names Companion* s.v. 'Pain', Oxford University Press, Oxford, 2002, pp. 472-3.

81 loc. cit.

82 Carberry, Fr. J. J. *Chronological and Historical Account of Some of the Principal Events Connected with the Dominican Convent Limerick*, privately published 1866. Quoted in Buckley, A. O. P. 'The Present Dominican Church', *Dominicans in Limerick 1227-1977*, Limerick, 1977, p. 25.

83 Lenihan *op. cit.* p. 651.

84 This was one of a number of discriminatory acts against Catholics that were part of the eighteenth century Penal Laws. With the granting of Catholic Emancipation in 1829, this discrimination was finally abolished.

85 A print of the original Dominican Church appeared in Fitzgerald, Rev. P. &

M'Gregor, J. J. *The History, Topography and Antiquities of the County and City of Limerick* 2 Vols., Limerick, 1827, Vol. II, facing page 542.

86 Trotter, J. *Walks Through Ireland in 1812, 1814 and 1817*, (1819), p. 347.

87 *Plan of the City of Limerick 1827*, published in Fitzgerald & M'Gregor *op. cit.* Vol. II, facing page 382.

88 Buckley, A. O.P. *op. cit.* pp. 30-1

89 *Presentments made on the County of Limerick at Summer Assizes, Summer 1815*, p. 15.

90 See, for example *Presentments to the Limerick County Grand Jury, Spring 1811*, p. 19.

91 O'Carroll, Gerald *Robert Day (1746-1841): The Diaries and Addresses to Grand Juries 1793-1829*, Polymath Press, 2005, p. 217.

92 Author's conversation with Knight of Glin on 12 February 2005.

93 Glin, Knight of 'Glin Castle', *The Archaeological Journal* Vol. 153, The Royal Archaeological Institute, 1996, p. 328.

94 *County Limerick Grand Jury Presentments, Spring 1815*, p. 9.

95 ibid. p. 36.

96 Lewis *op. cit.* s.v. 'Glin'.

97 *Presentments to the Limerick County Grand Jury, Spring 1816*, p. 47.

98 Plan and north elevation of Glin Church signed 'James Pain', but not dated, in library of the Representative Church Body (RCB).

99 The date '1868' is inscribed on the exterior ledge of the East window of the church. Consecration took place on 21 July 1868 - Deed of Consecration, Church of Ireland House, Dublin.

100 Moore, Mary M. 'Glin Heritage Centre', *The Glencorby Chronicle*, Vol.I, No. 1, Glin Historical Sciety, 1997, p. 6-8.

CHAPTER THREE
CLIQUE OF CORRUPTION

Freedom of the City

It is in March 1816 that we first begin to hear of George Richard Pain's presence in Ireland when a contract to build a new County Limerick Gaol was awarded to the 'Messrs. Pain.'[1] Both brothers were elected Freemen of Limerick during the following year by Limerick Corporation's Common Council allowing them to vote in Parliamentary elections, the Council minutes revealing that 'James Pain, Esq. Architect, City of Limerick' was granted the franchise by grace on 1 July 1816 while his brother 'Geo. Richard Payne [*sic*], Architect, City Limerick' received the privilege on 29 January 1817 along with 145 other gentlemen.[2] This suggests that the brothers were becoming fully integrated into the life of Limerick as to be trusted by one of the most powerful vested interests in the city.

At that time in Limerick's history only males over the age of 21 formally registered as Freeman of the City were permitted to vote in parliamentary elections and it had been customary since the mid-eighteenth century for the faction in control of the Corporation to grant this privilege predominantly to politically reliable friends and acquaintances, many of them non-residents of the city who were living as far away as Galway, Cork and Dublin.[3]

This ploy was used in order to keep those Limerick voters opposed to the political and financial misdeeds of the Corporation in a permanent electoral minority, the vote being denied to many of the city's long established merchants, artisans and tradesmen who were perceived as being liberal in politics *vis-à-vis* the Corporation. The methods by which the clique maintained their power and distributed patronage among their supporters earned the Council the well-deserved epithet 'Corrupt Corporation' among political opponents. By the early nineteenth century most of Limerick's bourgeoisie and middle-classes lived and carried out their business in the Georgian district of the city which had grown substantially since the area was first developed in the 1760s. Many of its inhabitants, Protestants as well as Catholics and Dissenters, looked askance, to say the least, at the misdeeds of the Ascendancy clique that ran the Corporation and its abuse of public monies and properties. Since 1807 the Georgian Newtown, located in St. Michael's Parish, had run its own local government affairs under a body known as St. Michael's Parish Commissioners. However, the Corporation retained its control over the former medieval quarters of Englishtown and Irishtown as well as the rest of the Borough, a jurisdiction far larger than the present city boundaries. Those opposed to the Corporation were known as the 'Independents' and since the mid-eighteenth century this loose alliance of various interests had fought many a long political and legal tussle with the Corporation whose power, though weakened with the emergence of the St. Michael's Commissioners, remained entrenched until it began to be eroded in the 1820s and '30s.

Colonel Charles Vereker

Levers of Political and Military Power

It is difficult today to imagine the extent of the power and patronage that John Prendergast Smyth, his nephew Colonel Charles Vereker (for whom James Pain superintended the building of Lough Cutra) and their close family relatives exercised in Limerick at that period. But a study of the levers of power held in the hands of both Vereker and his uncle will prove instructive[4] for it gives some idea of an important political and social network in Limerick with which the Pain brothers, especially James, 'the man of affairs', had to maintain friendly relations.

The grip that the Smyth/Vereker/Prendergast clan held over Limerick's parliamentary seat extended back into the mid-eighteenth century. Prior to the Act of Union of 1800 two representatives for Limerick City sat in the Dublin Parliament and one of these seats had been held continuously since 1731 by a member of the Smyth family. In 1785 John Prendergast Smyth inherited the family seat and in the 1790 election both J. P. Smyth and his nephew Charles Vereker were both returned as Members of Parliament for the borough of Limerick.

Following the Act of Union, of which Vereker was a vigorous opponent,[5] Limerick City was allowed to return just one member to the Westminster Parliament and Col. Charles Vereker held this position from 1802 to 1817, winning five elections in a row thanks to the assistance of the ever-obliging non-resident voters. During this period his uncle, J. P. Smyth, was elevated to the titled ranks of society as firstly Baron Kiltarton of Gort in 1810 (at which stage he gave his Lough Cutra property to Charles Vereker) and then 1st Viscount Gort in 1816. When he died the following year Vereker succeeded his uncle as 2nd Viscount Gort on 23 May 1817.[6]

Elevated to the peerage Vereker was obliged to surrender his seat in the House of Commons. Fortunately his son and heir, John Prendergast Vereker, was on hand to fill the breach, winning the prize in the subsequent by-election held in July 1817 in the time-honoured manner,[7] James Pain casting his vote on Tuesday 15 July for Vereker. There is no record of George Richard having voted on this occasion.

Polling in the 1817 election lasted for a total of twenty-one days, the electoral proceedings providing light relief and comic entertainment for those who did not take their politics too seriously.[8] In the days of the open ballot not only did electors have to publicly declare their support for a particular candidate at the Limerick City Courthouse on Bridge Street and their names recorded in the Returning Officers' Books, but the names of all those who polled and who they voted for were published in the local newspapers. A fascinating source of information for historians and a procedure that gave a tremendous advantage to the candidate who held the gift of patronage in a constituency.

The seat remained family property until the celebrated election of 1820 when it was lost to Thomas Spring Rice, the champion of Newtown Pery. On this occasion George Richard Pain voted for Major Vereker on Thursday 23 March 1820[9] and James on Monday 3 April.[10] On the first poll J. P. Vereker won the election by 786 votes to 569, but following an appeal by Rice to Parliament the votes of non-resident Freemen were disallowed and the election result overturned. It was a famous victory for local democracy and a triumphal column in honour of Spring Rice was later erected in the Pery Square park in 1831.

This setback for the Vereker dynasty signalled the beginning of the end for Lord Gort and his crew, but it was not until the introduction of the Reformed Corporations Act of 1840, and the formal abolition of the Corrupt Corporation, that their power structure was finally routed. A new, Reformed Corporation based on a broader, more democratic base incorporating the middle-classes was established to take over the running of the Borough. Even then, the clique controlled by the 2nd Viscount Gort fought a stubborn rearguard action worthy

The entry of the Speaker, Edmond Sexton Pery, into the Irish House of Commons, 1782. Painting by Francis Wheatley

of Charles Vereker's tenacity and undoubted courage. Refusing to acknowledge the authority of the Reformed Corporation and its Mayor, the old body elected its own mayor. For a period there was utter confusion, the city having a dual power situation with two Mayors and two Councils. This opera buffa was finally resolved when the 1840 Act was proclaimed for the city in 1841, but before departing the scene officials of the Corrupt Corporation destroyed its records to hide the evidence of its years of neglect and misrule.

Militias

Political power grows out of the barrel of a gun and the Smyth-Verekers were so placed as to be able to exercise control over locally recruited militia units. During the American War of Independence, which saw the withdrawal of regular army units from garrison duty in Ireland, members of the Smyth family served as Colonels in a number of locally recruited militias to maintain law and order.

When Britain found itself at war with France in 1793 a Militia Act was introduced into Ireland forming battalion-sized units in each county and major city in the country. J. P. Smyth MP was appointed as Colonel Commandant of the Limerick City Regiment of Militia by the Lord Lieutenant, while his nephew Charles Vereker MP was appointed Major. Shortly afterwards, Vereker was promoted to Lieutenant Colonel of the Regiment and in October 1793 a relative, Major Charles Smyth, became Adjutant. The regimental rolls record that several other members of the Vereker/Smyth/Prendergast family network also served in the regiment over the following years, including John Prendergast Vereker, Charles's son and political heir. The regiment in turn being commanded by the 1st, 2nd and 3rd Viscount Gort.[11] With the end of the Napoleonic Wars in 1815 the Limerick City Militia was stood down but the regiment still retained a cadre staff composed of officers, a military band and non-commissioned officers who owed their positions to the patronage of their commanding officer, Charles Vereker.

City Boss

At a local political level the Smyths had exercised a powerful role in Limerick Corporation since the mid-eighteenth century and with the consolidation of the Smyth/Vereker/Prendergast clique the role of 'city boss' was passed from relative to relative along with the inherited transfer of the parliamentary seat. The Corporation's decision-making body, the Common Council, was a self-perpetuating clique whose members, the burgesses, had absolutely no electoral mandate. New members were simply co-opted onto the Council for life by the sitting burgesses who gave the public no prior notice that a co-option was to take place. The office was for life with no bye-law or provision in place to allow for their removal.[12] Decisions relating to the appointment of salaried office holders and the election of mayors were, almost without exception, taken unanimously by the Council. In 1833 of the sixty-three members of the Common Council nineteen were non-residents.[13]

This was the body that had the power to confer the Freedom of the City onto Borough citizens and non-residents alike. A privilege granted wholesale to cronies and the politically reliable, especially when parliamentary elections were due. At one meeting held on 29 January 1817, 146 new Freemen were approved by the Council, including George Richard Pain. An analysis of the list reveals the umbilical link between patronage given and duties owed, for of the 146 names, twenty-nine were non-commissioned officers in the Vereker controlled Limerick City Militia. A further four names on the list were salaried Limerick Corporation appointees, either Serjeants-at-Mace or collectors of Port dues. In addition, some eleven newly appointed Freemen were sons of burgesses, including three sons of the sitting Mayor, John Vereker, brother of Charles. Another twenty-five of the newly appointed Freemen were living in Gort, Co. Galway, many of them tradesmen - carpenters, shoemakers and cabinet-makers - as well as a number of shopkeepers, innkeepers and minor gentry. It is no coincidence that Gort was the nearest town to Col. Vereker's country seat at Lough Cutra, just three miles away, and that the houses in the town were held on lease from Viscount Gort. Samuel Lewis's *Topographical Dictionary* records that in 1837 Gort consisted of 563 houses held in perpetual lease from Lord Gort.[14]

Nepotism was rampant, of course, with plum jobs going to leading members of the 'family' and others within the Golden Circle. To cite one example: the lucrative position of Weigh Master had been given to John Vereker, brother of Charles, on 5 April 1811 when his uncle, John Prendergast Smyth was Corporation boss with the title of Chamberlain.[15] As the person who acted as the treasurer of the Common Council the Chamberlain controlled the purse strings of the Corporation. The duties of Weigh Master, a lifetime appointment, were to weigh the butter and corn presented for sale at the city markets and collect fees for so doing. The job was a sinecure, the actual work being carried out by paid deputies with the Weigh Master keeping the profits of the office after deducting annual expenses amounting to about £250-300. According to the report of a Parliamentary inquiry held in the city in 1833 to investigate the dubious workings of Limerick Corporation, the average yearly income John Vereker received during the period 1827-9 from 'the fees of the butter crane was £1,470'.[16]

Another example of low politics in provincial places also concerns John Vereker who was appointed Mayor of Limerick in June of 1815 with an annual salary of £365; an office he retained for three years until 29 June 1818, on which date the Common Council very kindly increased his salary to £500 a year, backdated to 1815.[17] As well as this flagrant abuse of public monies, the lands owned by the Corporation were also used to feather the nests of the Golden Circle. Lands being leased out for ridiculously small sums of money allowing the leaseholders to extract the maximum profit from their peppercorn investment.

At the time of the Pain brothers' arrival in Ireland Colonel Charles Vereker held the post of Foreman of the City Grand Jury, a body composed, until 1826, almost exclusively of members and supporters of the Common Council and, with a few exceptions, confined to Protestants. Even after some measure of reform was introduced in 1826 the majority of jurors still came from the Common Council.[18] The function of the Grand Jury was to levy a tax on local property owners living within the Borough boundaries and allocate funds for various public institutions and infrastructural projects. Its sphere included the building and maintenance of roads, bridges, city prison, courthouse etc, and the awarding of contracts. Vereker remained Foreman of the City Grand Jury until his elevation to the peerage in 1817 when his son took over the position, naturally.

James Pain had certainly landed on his feet when he came to be acquainted with Colonel Charles Vereker, a man of influence with many valuable social and political connections who could open up doors for an ambitious architect who sought both public commissions and the patronage of those who were the first in consequence in society.

Endnotes

1 *Limerick Gazette*, 5 April 1816.

2 *Minutes of Limerick Common Council* 1/7/1816; 29/1/1817.

3 For a listing of the Freeman of Limerick 1746-1836 giving name, place of residence, occupation and date of admission see 'The Freeman of Limerick', *North Munster Antiquarian Journal*, The Thomond Archaeological Society, Vol. IV, 1944-1945, Appendix I, pp. 103-26.

4 For information on the Smyth-Vereker family see Lenihan, Maurice *Limerick; Its History and Antiquities* (1866), republished by Mercier Press, O'Carroll, Cian ed., Dublin and Cork, 1991. Consult the index.

5 *Dictionary of National Biography* s.v. 'Vereker, Charles', Vol. XX, Oxford University Press, 1917, reprint 1937.

6 loc. cit.

7 A *History of the Proceedings at the Particularly Interesting Elections for a Member to Represent The City of Limerick in Parliament; Containing . . . A List of the Electors, Their Places of Residence, and the Quality in Which They Voted*, printed by William Henry Tyrell, No. 17 College Green, Dublin, 1817, p. 84.

8 ibid. p. 84.

9 *Limerick Gazette*, 28 March 1820. His name is recorded as 'G. R. Paine, Esq.'

10 *Limerick Gazette*, 4 April 1820. His name is recorded as 'J. Paine, Esq.'

11 Lenihan *op. cit.* Appendix G 'The Limerick City Regiment of Militia', pp. 753-5.

12 'Report on the County of the City of Limerick: Section 34 - How Burgesses are Elected', *Reports from Commissioners on Municipal Corporations in Ireland*, British Parliamentary Papers, 1835.

13 ibid. 'Section 83'.

14 Lewis, Samuel *A Topographical Dictionary of Ireland*, Two Vols., London, 1837, Vol. I, p. 666; *Minutes of Limerick Common Council*, 29 January 1817.

15 ibid. 5 April 1811.

16 'Report on the County of the City of Limerick: Sections 102-3', *Reports from Commissioners on Municipal Corporations in Ireland*, British Parliamentary Papers, 1835.

17 *Minutes of Limerick Common Council* 29/6/1818.

18 'Report on the County of the City of Limerick: Section 119', *Reports from Commissioners on Municipal Corporations in Ireland*, British Parliamentary Papers, 1835.

CHAPTER FOUR
BUILDER OF PRISONS

Besides supervising projects designed by John Nash, and obtaining public and private work from various sources, the Pain brothers were eager to establish their own independent fashionable practice in Ireland, for we must remember that by now, 1816, James was 30 and George 23. They were to make a good team, James with his widening circle of influential friends and George with his artistic talent. In addition both had the social cachet of having been pupils of Nash, the Prince Regent's favoured architect. But they would have to wait another three years for their opportunity to be given a major and prestigious country house commission.

Limerick Museum 1987.0458

Limerick City Gaol (an amalgamation of the County and City Gaols) facing onto the River Shannon. Limerick Civic Offices now occupy the site.

051

County Gaol Report

In the meantime, in 1816, James Pain won a public competition to build a new County Gaol[1] on Limerick's New Cork Road (now Mulgrave Street).[2] The process leading to the awarding of the contract began in 1814 when the Gaol Committee of the Limerick County Grand Jury undertook an investigation into the state and condition of the then existing County Gaol in the Englishtown district of Limerick. Facing onto the River Shannon the facility was sited adjacent to the new City Gaol recently built on Dean's Close, once the location of the garden and house of the Dean of St. Mary's Cathedral and now the site of Limerick Civic Offices.[3] Advice was sought from various quarters, including James Pain 'whose architectural abilities have been displayed in the improvements of the City Gaol.'[4]

In his report to the Committee, and in response to supplementary questions put to him, Pain made the observation that the County prison was insecure, there was no chapel for worship and there was only sufficient accommodation for thirty male felons, ten females and ten debtors if a policy of allocating one cell per person was implemented in conformity with current legislation. In response to the Committee's query as to whether the prison could be enlarged to accommodate a population of 100 inmates, with a separate cell for each prisoner, Pain replied 'I think not . . . It would be an inconvenient, unwholesome, and confined prison and not so secure as a place of this description should be - the expense of this would be fully equal to building a new prison.'[5]

The Gaol was overcrowded enough as it was, for in cells measuring 6 feet (1.81 metres) by 8 feet (2.44 metres) 'three human beings are frequently confined; exhibiting instances of suffering unexampled except in the history of Africa slave ships.'[6] That the institution was indeed 'over-subscribed' by inmates is corroborated by information supplied to a Parliamentary Commission on Crime and Punishment that sat in 1818. The data reveals that the greatest number of prisoners held at any one time in the County Gaol during that year was 220, even though its capacity was stated, at the time, to be 130.[7] The latter figure itself being well in excess of Pain's assessment that there was only adequate accommodation for fifty on the basis of one person/one cell. This overcrowding was in contrast with the situation in the new City Gaol, whose construction Pain had supervised when he first came to Limerick, for in that facility the maximum number of inmates held at any one time in 1818 was 107, far below its capacity of 200.[8]

Although the 'old' County prison had only been designed comparatively recently, c.1789 by William Blackburn (1750-90), an English architect who specialised in prison building,[9] the Gaol Committee identified a number of health problems associated with the institution such as poor sanitation and hygiene and, according to Pain's evidence, the water obtained from a well in the prison's forecourt not being fit to drink. The only way to remedy this particular problem was to pump water from the Shannon by an engine. Such a device 'would prevent the intercourse that now exists between the public water-carriers and the prisoners.'[10] Little wonder then that the security system around the County Gaol was a little porous, as evidenced by the escape of eleven prisoners on one occasion in 1813, their example being followed by three other inmates the following year.[11]

Although the County Grand Jury at the 1815 Spring Assizes had sought an advance of £5,000 from the Government to cover the costs 'of repairing and altering the present Gaol,'[12] the Gaol Commissioners in their 1816 report recommended that this money not be wasted on shoring up an institution that was deficient in so many regards. Rather, they were of the very strong opinion 'that the present prison must be altogether abandoned.'[13]

Enough money had been squandered already. Designed about 1789 construction was delayed for several years, Blackburn's plans still being available for inspection in 1791. When Charles Etienne Coquebert de Montbret, French Marine and Commerce attaché to Ireland, visited Limerick that year he recorded that he had seen 'the plan of the new prison by the waterside, two buildings separated by a yard, the one behind for criminals, the first for debtors (county and city separated). Mr. Smyth the architect.'[14] Presumably, Smyth was the executing architect, or the contractor on the project, if it is correct that William Blackburn was indeed the architect. Construction appears to have proceeded exceedingly slowly on what was an architecturally poor structure, the facility still not completed at the turn of the century. When Rev. Foster Archer, Inspector General of the Prisons in Ireland, visited Limerick City in mid-September 1801 he noted that,

> 'A New Gaol is Building for the County, which I examined. The Cells are small and very Badly ventilated. Shewed the Architect a Plan for Remedying this great Defect which He promised to adopt without Delay, also fixed a Site for an Hospital for the Gaol which was Strangely left out of the Plan. Architects Generally know how to Build Private Houses & Churches but I have scarcely met one in Ireland that knew how to Build an Healthy Safe or Convenient Prison.'[15]

Fortunately, the lack of a decent prison architect in the country was to be rectified by the arrival of James Pain.

Contract Awarded

At the 1816 Spring Assizes the Grand Jury announced its decision to allocate £23,000 to building a new prison, the sum to be advanced by the Government and repaid over a period of six years.[16] At a subsequent meeting held in the County Courthouse on Merchants Quay on Saturday 30 March the Gaol Commissioners, after discussing a number of competitive tenders, awarded the contract to the 'Messrs. Pain and Hannons' whose joint proposal of £21,500 was judged the winner, sureties being provided by Colonel Charles Vereker MP and the Limerick merchant company of 'Messrs. Mark, Fisher and Mark.'[17] The Hannons were William and Nicholas Hannon, brothers who were natives of the County and builders and architects by profession. They had built the County Courthouse (commenced 1807, opened 1809, the Doric portico completed 1814) on Merchants Quay.[18] The tenders were structured on a 'plan already approved of' according to a press report;[19] James Pain being credited as the architect by a number of contemporary sources.[20] The site chosen for the facility was located near the Artillery Barracks and opposite the County

Crosbie Row, Limerick. The prison wall facing onto Crosbie Row has been incorporated into the design of the Civic Offices. St. Mary's Cathedral can be seen in the background.

Hospital (1811)[21] (now Limerick Senior College) on the New Cork Road. Construction began in 1817, the project being completed in 1821.[22] When the new Gaol was opened the two Englishtown prisons were both amalgamated into one City Gaol[23] on the site now occupied by Limerick Civic Offices. The buildings associated with this prison have since been demolished; however most of the façade of the prison wall facing onto Crosbie Row, including a pedimented entrance, has been retained and incorporated into the design of the Civic Offices.

It might seem that by taking on a prison commission James, as an architect, was professionally taking a step backwards. But such was not the case, for in the late eighteenth and early nineteenth centuries many of Britain's foremost architects had been involved in prison construction. Leading figures such as John Nash, Robert Adam and James Wyatt had all applied their talents to the task: John Nash having built institutions at Carmarthen (1792), Cardigan (1793) and Hereford (1796); Robert Adam worked on the Edinburgh Bridewell project (1791-4) and James Wyatt the Petworth House of Correction (1785-8).[24] During the course of his career the fashionable English country house architect Thomas Hopper (1776-1856) built two county gaols (Wiltshire and Essex) and two houses of correction over the period 1818-35.[25]

Another weighty, and financially rewarding factor was that the construction of a new prison was a major contract for any builder to be awarded, particularly Limerick County Gaol which took four years to build and involved a considerable amount of masonry and construction work to make the facility secure and inhabitable by a captive population of up to 131 prisoners.[26] At that time it was not unusual for architects to openly compete with other architects

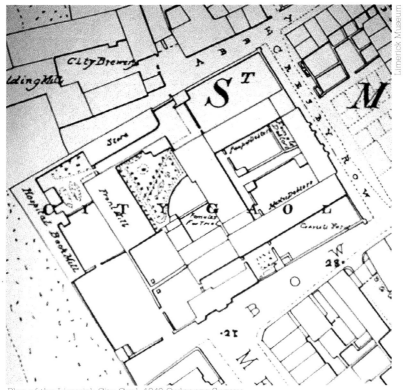

Plan of the Limerick City Gaol, 1840 Ordnance Survey.

and builders to carry out construction work on projects of their own design. In its entry for the Pain brothers, compiled in 1877, *The Dictionary of Architecture* states that 'from the then necessity of the period, they acted as architects and builders; George, an accomplished draughtsman, more especially competing with builders for the execution of his own designs and specifications.'[27]

In his work on the Limerick prison project James was assisted by his younger brother who may have had an input in drawing up the plans and specifications. Their partnership with joint contractors William and Nicholas Hannon continued throughout the construction phase, a number of entries in the Grand Jury Presentments for that period making reference to 'Messrs. Pain and Hannons, contractors for building the county new gaol.'[28] At the 1821 Spring Assizes, for instance, there is an account of a payment of £932 2s to the contractors for the installation of hydraulic machinery in the gaol and 'to make a drain from the prison wall to intersect the sewer from the artillery barracks.'[29]

A quarry behind the construction site supplied stone for the contractors and their masons. Located beside Roxborough Road and Roxborough Avenue [30] (now known colloquially as 'The Jail Boreen'), the quarry was regarded as a source of high quality limestone, containing 'massive limestone beds, capable of yielding large-sized blocks.'[31] The opening up of a new quarry as near as possible to a construction site was a standard practice in Limerick to keep down transportation costs, the city being provided for by a plentiful supply of easily extractable, good quality limestone. At one stage, in 1840, there were as many as twenty-seven active quarries within what is now the city boundary and the suburb of Castletroy supplying not only building stone but also lime and road making material.[32]

Accolades

Evidence for a commencement date in 1817 of the County Gaol is to be found in the files of the local press. In March that year the *Limerick Gazette* carried a notice that tenants in possession of land on the chosen construction site were entitled to compensation at the rate of 20 guineas per acre 'provided they give up immediate and peaceable possession to the contractors.'[33] By early summer work had already started, for in the middle of August the *Gazette* reported that construction was proceeding with great 'rapidity', a substantial section of the outer wall having been built to a height of 30 feet (9.1 metres) and the first range of cells completed. This compared with the situation just two months previously when only the foundation of the outer wall had been laid and little done to the interior.[34] The reporter, obviously impressed with the speed and efficiency with which the task was being carried out, closed with a paean of praise to the brothers Pain:

> 'We can not conclude without paying a small but highly deserved tribute to the gentlemen who have contracted for this building – Messrs. J. and R. [*sic*] Pain. – Their professional characters as architects, is only equalled by their manners as private gentlemen. Their residence amongst us is likely to produce the highest improvements in the erection of our public works if committed to their care. – Their plans evince the most correct taste in ancient and modern architecture, and the execution of some which they have now nearly perfected, are the finest specimens of this ingenious art, combining perfect beauty with durability and will remain as lasting memorials to the professional honour of the architects who have designed them.[35]

Clearly, the two brothers were making a very favourable impression on the people of Limerick. The report does provide evidence that by 1817 the brothers had been working together for some time on a number of projects and that George Richard's contribution was seen by the local press as being the equal of his elder brother. It also suggests that G. R. Pain had a hand in drawing up the plans and specifications for the County Gaol although James Pain is credited with the architectural work by contemporary sources.[36]

James Pain Reported Dead!

Two months later there took place a most,

Melancholy Occurrence

'With the deepest regret we have to state an occurrence which, when known we are convinced, will awaken a [word illegible] feeling in the breast of every reader – On Saturday morning last [18 October 1817] Mr. James Pain, of this city, architect, was surveying some part of the beautiful building now going forward at Loughcooter Castle, County Galway, the intended mansion of Lord Viscount Gort, the scaffolding on which he stood gave way, and he was precipitated from an eminence of four stories high – his side first reached the ground, with the head inclining downwards - the collar bone has been broken, the brain has received a severe concussion, and several bruises on different parts of the body. - A report was current in town on Sunday that he was dead, but we are happy to say, the arrival of Surgeon Franklin who (together with Surgeon Gibson of the City Regt.[37] pofessionally [sic] attended) has not only contradicted that rumour, but has been given sanguine hopes of a speedy recovery. – Lord Gort's anxiety was extreme, his attention polite, friendly and affectionate – it gives evidence of a warm and generous sensibility on the part of one, while, if any were wanting, it affords an additional proof of the respect which Mr. Pain's conduct both as a professional character and private gentleman must ever ensure him. Numerous enquiries continue to be made at this office for his health'.[38]

A heart stopping moment surely for the architect's friends and acquaintances as they read the opening lines. Was James Pain dead? And at such an early age! Tragic, absolutely tragic. (A heart stopping moment also for the researcher who unearthed the report! Was the object of our study prematurely deceased?) As a gentleman we trust that James may have taken the newspaper's little jest in milking the story for all it was worth in good humour.

The report is interesting in a number of regards. It shows the close personal friendship existing between Pain and Charles Vereker and that construction work on Lough Cutra, then known as Loughcooter, was still taking place as late as October 1817. In crashing four stories to the ground the architect must have been working on the upper storey, or the battlements, of one of Lough Cutra's towers.

In October 1817 James Pain fell four stories to the ground when scaffolding gave way on Lough Cutra.

Radiating Principle

The new County Gaol was built on the 'radiating principle', with five cell block wings radiating like spokes from a central, administrative hub.[39] Decagonal in plan, this central tower was 60 feet high (18.29 metres) containing, in successive stories 'the Governor's residence, the committee-room, a chapel and an hospital.'[40] The wings were detached from the tower, each wing being linked by an ornamental cast iron walk bridge to the second floor chapel of the tower.[41]

The prison was rigidly symmetrical and geometric in plan with an outer and inner wall to contain the prisoners. Placed between the cell blocks were self-contained, walled off, exercise yards known as 'airing grounds'. A platform ran around the outside of the second storey of the central tower allowing a sentry to walk around the building and keep an eye on the exercise yards below. Protected from the rain by roofing, this platform was known as the 'arcade'. At ground level the space immediately surrounding the central tower was separated from the exercise yards. The entrance to the institution was suitably bleak, an effect created by the gloomy massing of the unadorned masonry.

The architectural features of the entrance are of the Doric Order, but there is no use of free-standing round columns or pediment. On each side of the main gateway are two substantial, square columns attached to the main wall. These support the horizontal mass of the entablature, which consists of the main horizontal divisions associated with Classical architecture: the architrave, the frieze and the cornice. The frieze is left entirely blank, there being no use of triglyphs to soften the masonry, while underneath the cornice are large, prominent dentils. A badly proportioned engraving in Fitzgerald's and M'Gregor's History of Limerick shows the columns having Ionic capitals, but in their description of the building the authors state that 'The grand entrance is formed of very fine cut stone in the Doric style . . .'

The use of square shafts rather than round for the columns is derived from a feature in Classical architecture known as anta (plural antae) which is a square or rectangular pier or pilaster formed when the side walls of a temple project forward on the front elevation. Antae do not have to conform with the detailing on the base and capitals of the Order used elsewhere in the building. In the case of Limerick prison the three horizontal bands (known as annulets) at the top of the shafts and the plain, undecorated abacus are of the Doric Order. To modern eyes this stripped Classicism is not particularly attractive, but then it is not meant to be. The hard, masculine aspect of the entrance and the bold, projecting angular columns is designedly meant to convey the impression of intimidating robustness and strength.

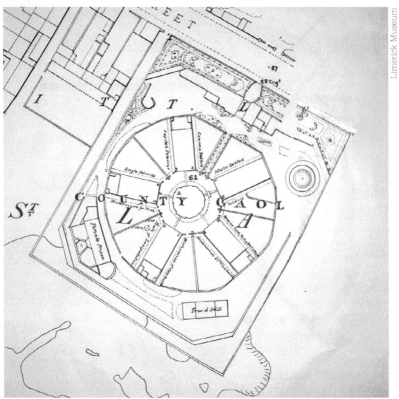

Limerick County Gaol, 1840 Ordnance Survey illustrating the radial design and classification of the prison.

Stripped Classicism was experimented with by late eighteenth and early nineteenth century architects and was again revived in the twentieth century, particularly in Nazi Germany where it was used in public and monumental architecture. One thinks of Hitler's chief architect, Albert Speer, who designed the New Stadium (1935) at Nuremberg with its central, rectangular block of plain masonry standing at the rear of the podium unadorned of any decoration except for ten pilasters and a Grecian doorway. On either side of the central block stands a long open colonnade composed of a row of some thirty-eight square columns supporting a totally unadorned entablature ending in a projecting blank wall. The whole structure in stripped Doric. With its emphasis on phallic, male strength (what else does the Nazi salute symbolise) and aggressive militarism, the Nazi regime had the ideal backdrop for its Party rallies at Nuremberg. Albert Speer recalls how in July 1933 he was summoned to the city to be given the assignment of building the New Stadium and was informed that, 'Preparations were being made there for the first Party Rally of what was now the government party. The victorious spirit of the party was to be expressed even in the architecture of the background.'[42] Just as the Pains' entrance to the Limerick County Gaol symbolises the victory of the social order over criminality and subversion.

As a place both of penitence and thoughtful reflection on a sinful life the prison was built in conformity with contemporary thinking on penal reform. It was intended that each prisoner be housed in a separate cell[43] in contrast with the overcrowded 'old' County Gaol. It was intended to house 131 prisoners at most, accommodation consisting of a small hospital, sleeping cells for 103 prisoners, twenty-two apartments for debtors and five solitary cells reserved for prisoners facing execution or suffering punishment for insubordination.[44] Whereas the old prison was deemed unsatisfactory because there was no proper separation of the various categories of prisoner - young offenders being placed in contact with hardened criminals, and petty offenders having to associate with felons convicted of crimes of the most serious hue - James Pain's new prison on Mulgrave Street provided for the various different categories to be housed apart. The 1840 Ordnance Survey of the prison illustrates the detailed classification of prisoners, with separate areas within the prison being reserved to accommodate categories such as 'Revenue Cases', 'Misdemeanors for Trial' and those under 'Rule of Transportation',[45] the latter category awaiting escort to Cork or Dublin and shipment to the convict colonies of Australia. The area set aside for the accommodation of debtors was divided into two distinct sections - Master Debtors and Pauper Debtors - for even in matters of debt class distinctions were to be maintained.

Penal Reform

To understand the architecture of the new prison it is necessary to have some knowledge of the historical context, for Pain's design was heavily influenced by contemporary thinking in Britain on penal architecture and the social purpose of prisons. His County Gaol was built in the midst of a major early nineteenth century prison building programme then taking place in Britain and Ireland with forty-eight new gaols being erected in England alone during the period 1801-32.[46] This process was driven by a reforming zeal to rationalise and modernise the British penal system and eliminate the abuses and corruption that characterised the penal institutions of the eighteenth century.

One of the bedrock principles behind the reform drive was that prisoners were to be classified according to the nature of their crimes and misdemeanours and that the various categories be housed apart, one from another, and kept strictly separate. There had, of course, been some classification in the eighteenth century, but certainly not sufficient for prison reformers, and from the turn of the century onwards the number of categories increased dramatically. By 1820 the Society for the Improvement for Prison Discipline was recommending twenty categories to prison authorities,[47] but such was the enthusiasm for scientific rationality that individual authorities drew up their own lists, expanding the number of categories further to suit local needs and opinions. In 1826, for instance, it was found that the 460 inmates in Maidstone

County Gaol were housed in thirty-eight wards within four distinct institutions (the Penitentiary, House of Correction, Gaol and Female Prison) and grouped into twenty-nine distinct and separate classifications. Categories that included female vagrants; females under sentence of death; male offenders against the game laws; males found guilty of unnatural crimes. In the Penitentiary the male convicts were subdivided into three groupings; those serving the first third of their sentence; those serving their second third; and those completing the sentence.[48]

The rationale for the separation of the various species of criminal was to prevent prisoners corrupting the virtues and morals of one another. In 1819 architect Thomas Hopper, in his capacity as Surveyor to the County of Essex, stated that the 'division of the prison ought to be so ordered as to prevent the possibility of communication between the different classes of prisoner.'[49] It was felt that unregulated and under-classified prisons allowed such institutions to function as colleges of crime and moral cesspools in which vice and corruption spread like a contagion among prisoners. To prevent these ills it became imperative to separate the vicious and the depraved from the more innocent, the sick from the healthy and to keep those capable of redemption, especially young, impressionable petty offenders, away from the irredeemable recidivist.

A graphic example of the evils of non-classification was offered by Thomas Fowell Buxton, a leading English advocate of prison reform, who, in 1818, cited the case of a youth who had been sent to a London Bridewell for a month for the then crime of selling illegal religious literature. Buxton was concerned that the hitherto uncorrupted youth would be cast during the day among the worst thieves and hardened criminals of the metropolis and spend his nights, 'with those who are infected with a desperate and contagious disorder – taking lessons from the one in blasphemy and dissoluteness, and from the other imbibing the seeds of a disease which you shall carry home to your family.'[50]

Radials and Polygons

The root and branch remodelling of the penal system demanded by the reformers was not achieved overnight and it took a concerted prison building programme lasting many years to replace the old gaols and bridewells with a more orderly system. The new, reformed prisons were consciously designed to facilitate prisoner classification and ensure close supervision of inmates by the prison governor and his staff. Among those who took an interest in the design and layout of gaols two competing opinions vied one with another as to what constituted correct architectural layout; one school arguing for the polygon and the other for the radial plan. Both were highly geometrical and symmetrical in architectural style. As previously stated, the radiating principle was the one chosen for Limerick, its simple layout of central administrative hub and five radiating cellblocks being the height of rationality and regularity.

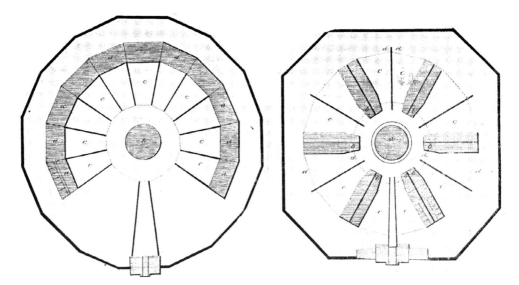

In the early nineteenth century there were two competing designs for prison architecture: on left the polygon plan and on the right, the radial plan.

The impetus for prison reform and the emphasis on radial architecture originally came from John Howard (1726-90) who, while travelling in Europe, was captured by the French during one of her periodic wars with Britain and spent some time in a prison in Brest and then released. His experiences spurred him to make a series of tours of British and Irish prisons in which he investigated the conditions of prisons and prisoners[51] including, in 1788, the Limerick Gaol located in the Thosel on Mary Street which served both the city and the county[52] (this was before any prisons were built beside the river Shannon on Dean's Close). As a result of his investigations he formed the opinion that many of the evils of prison life were due to their plan and that if one were to remedy and rectify these problems the first step to improvement was to change the architecture. Howard published an enormously influential book on the issue, *The State of Prisons* (1777), and his endeavours were rewarded by several Acts of Parliament passed in the late 1770s and early '80s that addressed his concerns and proved the harbinger of penal reform. The legislation covering issues such as the need for new prisons, the separate confinement of prisoners and their being tasked to carry out labour and undergo moral and religious education, minimum cell sizes and regular inspection of institutions.

The following decade William Blackburn (1750-90) was appointed as the official prison architect and, working very closely in association with Howard, he provided plans for a number of prisons and county bridewells during the 1780s until his death in 1790 - sixteen in England plus Limerick County Gaol *c*.1789.[53] It was not to be until after *c*.1800 that radial plans, as envisaged and promoted by Howard and Blackburn, were adopted for the design for county gaols, one of the first being Abingdon Gaol (1805) in Oxfordshire.[54] In terms of radial architecture a tradition had therefore been well established before the

Pains set to work on Limerick Gaol and plans were available from a body known as the Society for the Improvement of Prison Discipline (SIPD) who were keen to promote the new, reformed architecture. For instance, the SIPD presented, c.1820, George Ainslie's 'Design for a County Gaol' to a Parliamentary inquiry dealing with crime and punishment; Ainslie's architectural drawings detailing floor plans and elevations for a radial prison.[55]

The number of wings in radial prisons varied according to the number of prisoners expected to be housed, as illustrated by a sequence of radial plans drawn up by George Thomas Bullar[56] in 1826 for the Society for the Improvement of Prison Discipline. (Bullar was an architect who specialised in the design of prisons.) The smallest of the prisons has two or three wings for those accommodating thirty-to-forty or fifty prisoners. As the number of inmates to be catered for increased, so did the number of wings, the much larger prisons having seven cell blocks for a population of 300. The five-block design was generally considered adequate for a prison population of 200[57] although the ideal number of inmates in the Limerick County Gaol was judged to be 131 of all classes when originally built.[58]

A polygonal prison, on the other hand, typically consisted of a central administrative building surrounded by open exercise yards while on the outer rim of the institution the cell blocks were laid out on the pattern of a regular, geometric polygon. Not perhaps a complete polygon in plan, but a sizeable segment nonetheless. An example of this style of prison architecture in Ireland was Galway County Gaol built in 1811.

The obvious objection to the polygonal gaol was that the layout made it extremely difficult for the governor and his staff to oversee the inmates, divorced as he was from any close, architectural link with the cell blocks and separated from the inmates by the wide expanse of open space created by the exercise yards. Given this factor it is not surprising that the radiating principle proved the most popular with those local authorities and architects charged with the task of planning and building efficiently run prisons with optimum cost in warders' wages. Of the forty-eight new institutions built in England between 1801 and 1832, thirty-eight were built to a concentric plan and of these thirty were radials and only eight polygons.[59] Not only were they very simple to design, the geometry of the radial pattern was best suited to creating a highly segmented prison population that could be easily controlled and kept under constant surveillance by the prison authorities in their central vantage point. It is not surprising then that James Pain and the Limerick County Gaol Commissioners chose the radial against the polygon.

By being built in conformity with the latest thinking in Britain on prison design the Limerick facility was 'state of the art' when built and the most modern prison in Ireland at that time; James Pain being seen as a pioneer in introducing reformed prison architecture into Ireland. It certainly enhanced his reputation as an architect and he achieved some celebrity for the design, commentators speaking very favourably of the institution: 'The county gaol is reputed to be one of the most approved prisons in the kingdom' wrote Henry Inglis in 1834,[60] while four years later Lady Chatterton reported that it was 'a very credible public establishment.'[61] Samuel Lewis, or rather his Limerick correspondent, was of the opinion that its 'internal construction and arrangements are exceedingly well contrived', this being in marked contrast to the City Gaol in Englishtown, it being a 'gloomy quadrangular edifice' that did not 'admit of proper classification.'[62]

A Suitable Model

Such was the reputation of the new Limerick prison in Ireland that James Pain's design proved to be influential, a number of Grand Juries adopting the general layout of Limerick prison for their own county gaols. In 1820 the Jury for King's County decided to replace the old gaol at Philipstown (Daingean) with a more up to date facility. A committee set up to fix upon a site and carry out research for a suitable design visited a number of recently constructed county prisons including Galway (crescent shaped in plan) and Roscommon (a polygon), but it was Limerick's radial plan that impressed the members of the Grand Jury most. It was their considered opinion that Limerick prison was 'possessed of more of the desirable requisites' and had 'fewer defects than any other.'[63] As a result the radial scheme was chosen as the model on which to build the King's County (Offaly) Gaol. To suit local needs some alterations were made, chiefly a reduction in size by about two-fifths to accommodate a prison population of 120 and instead of Limerick's five cell block radial the King's County prison had four radial arms, one at each of the four cardinal points of the central administrative block.[64] This new facility was to be built at Tullamore because it had superseded Philipstown as the principal County town during the eighteenth century. Plans for the Gaol were exhibited at the 1825 Spring Assizes, construction commencing the following year, the prison receiving its first inmates in April 1830.[65] Neighbouring Queen's County (Laois) built its gaol to a similar design at Maryborough (Port Laoise). Completed in 1830, Maryborough also had four radial wings and a central administrative building of three stories (Limerick had four).[66] It seems likely that James Pain, as the leading prison architect in Ireland, would have been asked by the respective Grand Juries to furnish the plans for these two institutions.[67]

Port Laoise was later extended in 1911 and during the Troubles in Northern Ireland was modernised as a high security prison for Republican prisoners. Of Tullamore Gaol, however, nothing remains except for the castellated entrance front on Cormac Street.[68] Battlemented and with false machicolations, the entrance features a Tudor arch gateway flanked by masonry in the form of square turrets. The prison was set on fire during the Civil War, the buildings being demolished in 1937. Since it was first built, Limerick Prison has seen many modifications.

Treadmill

In 1822, at the Summer Assizes, the County Limerick Grand Jury thoughtfully decided to build a mill house and purchase a Cubitt's treadmill[69] for the better exercise of the inmates in the new County Gaol. Since James Pain was retained as prison architect until 1863[70] it is reasonable to assume that he was responsible for drawing up the plans for the mill house and supervising the installation of the treadmill that was to be erected inside the southern angle of the prison wall.[71] The work was completed for just £806 2s 5d,[72] well within the original estimate of £1,000.[73]

Invented and patented in 1818 by English civil engineer William Cubitt, the Cubitt's treadmill proved so attractive to both penal reformers and governors alike that within four years many prisons had installed the new device. A treadmill is basically a long, rotating, horizontal wooden drum (known as a wheel) fitted with rows of steps extending along its length. The wheel is kept in motion by a line of prisoners continuously treading on these boards. Its advantage was that with the minimum amount of supervision it could translate the energy of prisoners into useful labour, the revolving 5 feet (1.52 metres) diameter wheel turning a shaft that set in motion machinery in a mill house. These mills were typically used for grinding corn into flour that was then sold on the open market, or the mill and labour hired out to an outside contractor.[74] Treadmills were also commonly used to operate pumps that raised water into a prison.

In the case of Limerick County Gaol the mill house was used to scutch flax, a plant grown for its textile fibre used in linen-making. Once harvested flax stalks were softened by 'retting' (soaking the stalks in water and then allowing them to dry) then sent to the scutching mill where they were beaten to rid them of their woody fibres. The Limerick prison mill was powered by two treadwheels operated by up to thirty-two prisoners, twelve being sufficient to activate the machinery.[75] Cottage based linen manufacture was a source of considerable employment in the Limerick neighbourhood at this time,[76] the cultivation of flax as a commercial crop in Ireland having been promoted by the activities of the Linen Board since 1711 to encourage the Irish domestic spinning and weaving trades.

In its report to the Grand Jury at the summer 1824 Assizes the Board of Superintendance [sic] of the County Limerick Jails reported that,

'The Tread Mill has been almost constantly at work since last assizes. The Board have every reason to imagine that as an instrument of Prison Discipline, it has produced the best effects. It has not however been, and perhaps never will be made a source of Revenue to the County.'[77]

The profitability or otherwise of treadmills was not the major issue with prison authorities, rather their function was to set prisoners to regular labour that could be measured and controlled by a complicated measuring device. All those set to the wheel would have to rotate the drum a set number of times for a set period. This ensured that there was no malingering on the part of anyone. The typical amount of time spent daily on a treadmill was eight to ten hours in the summer and five to eight hours in the winter with periodic rests. The term 'tread' makes it sound like a non too arduous task akin to walking; whereas in fact the work was far more like being constantly forced to climb all the time, the effort required being quite exhausting. It was certainly no country stroll and women as well as men were set to the wheel. The monotonous drudgery of the task was beneficial, according to the high-minded, to the reform of the idle criminal. But it was mainly used as an instrument by governors and warders for imposing discipline on inmates, the hateful labour being regarded as a punishment.[78] When John Barrow visited Cork County Gaol in 1835 he found that, 'The tread-mill was hard at work, and there were numerous hands, and legs too, employed upon it. They are kept at it, by turns, eight hours out of the twelve, and it seemed fatiguing work.'[79]

Threadmills were typically used for grinding corn into flour or used to operate pumps that raised water into a prison.

Endnotes

1 *Limerick Gazette*, 5 April 1816.

2 Joyce, Gerry *Limerick City Street Names* s.v. 'Mulgrave Street', Limerick Corporation, Limerick, 1995, p. 40. The New Cork Road was later renamed Mulgrave Street in honour of Constantine Phipps, Earl of Mulgrave, Lord Lieutenant of Ireland, who visited the city in 1835 to open the newly completed Wellesley (Sarsfield) Bridge.

3 *A Ground Plan of the Deanery Yard and Adjacent Strand, 25 March 1788*, Limerick Museum (LM 0000.1906); *A Map of the City of Limerick Based on the Civil Survey 1654* drawn up by Claire Lane, 1989, unpublished, Limerick Museum. Dean's Close, also known as the Deanery Yard, was bounded on two of its sides by Crosbie Row and Bow Lane.

4 'Report of the Commissioners of the County Limerick Gaol', *Limerick Gazette*, 9 February 1816.

5 loc. cit.

6 loc. cit.

7 'An Account of all the Gaols, Houses of Correction or Penitentiaries in the United Kingdom', *Crime and Punishment – Prisons 8*, British Parliamentary Papers, 1819, Irish University Press, Shannon, Ireland, 1970, pp. 554-5.

8 ibid.

9 Colvin, Howard *A Biographical Dictionary of British Architects 1600-1840* s.v. 'Blackburn, William', 3rd edition, Yale University Press, New Haven and London, 1995.

10 'Report of the Commissioners of the County Limerick Gaol', *Limerick Gazette*, 9 February 1816.

11 ibid.

12 *Presentments Made on the County of Limerick at Spring Assizes, Spring 1815*, George M'Kern (printer), George Street, Limerick, p. 38.

13 *Limerick Gazette*, 9 February 1816.

14 'A Frenchman's Impressions of Limerick, Town and People, in 1791', Ni Chinneide, Sighle ed. *North Munster Antiquarian Journal*, Thomond Archaeological Society, Vol. V (1946-1949), No. 4, 1948, p. 100; 'Charles Etienne Coquebert de Montbret' *The Grand Tour of Limerick*, Kelly, Cornelius ed., Cailleach Books, Beara, Co. Cork, 2004, p. 61.

15 Archer, Rev. Foster *A Journal Containing a Report on the State of Prisons, County Hospitals, Charter Schools etc. as attained in a Tour thro' the Provinces of Leinster, Munster and Connaught began July 2nd 1801, by Revd. F. Archer, Inspector General of the Prisons in Ireland*, Hardwicke Papers (Additional MSS 35920), British Museum. For Foster's report on the prisons of Limerick see Lynch, Patrick B. 'The Reverend Foster Archer's Visit to Limerick and Clare, 1801', *North Munster Antiquarian Journal*, Vol. XVIII, 1976, pp. 51-2.

16 *Limerick Gazette*, 25 March 1816.

17 *Limerick Gazette*, 5 April 1816; *County Limerick Grand Jury Presentments Spring 1816*, p. 31; Lenihan, Maurice *Limerick: Its History and Antiquities* (1866), pp. 447-8.

18 Lenihan *op. cit.* p. 419-20. *Pigot's 1824 Trade Directory* lists a Nicholas Hannan

(spelt 'Hannon' in the Grand Jury Presentments) as a builder with an address in Taylor Street. Located between Upper Cecil Street and the rear of the Dominican Church, Taylor Street has since been demolished. See Joyce *op. cit.* p. 76.

19 *Limerick Gazette*, 5 April 1816.
20 *Limerick Gazette*, 15 August 1817; Fitzgerald, Rev. P. & M'Gregor, J. J. *The History, Topography and Antiquities of the County and City of Limerick*, 2 Vols., George M'Kern, Limerick, 1827, Vol. II, p. 583, republished by O'Brien Book Publications, Limerick, 1999.
21 Lenihan *op. cit.* p. 415n.
22 *County Limerick Grand Jury Presentments, Summer, 1821*, pp. 41-2.
23 Ordnance Survey, 1840, scale: 5 feet to one statute mile, Limerick City Sheet No. 15.
24 Colvin *op. cit.* s.v. 'Nash, John', p. 689; s.v. 'Adam, Robert', p. 56; s.v 'Wyatt, James', p. 1111; Evans, Robin *The Fabrication of Virtue, English Prison Architecture 1750-1840*, Cambridge University Press, Cambridge, 1982, p. 408.
25 Colvin *op. cit.* s.v. 'Hopper, Thomas', pp. 513-4.
26 'County Limerick Gaol Report', *Limerick County Grand Jury Presentments, Spring Assizes 1848*. The report discusses the chronic overcrowding of the prison at the height of the Famine and makes the comment 'The accommodation originally provided for was 131 prisoners of all classes, the number now in custody is 611 ! - so that legal and healthful accommodation is wanted for 480.'
27 *The Dictionary of Architecture* s.v. 'Pain (James and George Richard)', Architectural Publications Society.
28 *County Limerick Grand Jury Presentments, Summer, 1818*, p. 23; Spring, 1819, p. 27; Spring, 1821, pp. 29-30.
29 ibid. Spring, 1821, pp. 29-30.
30 Ordnance Survey 1840, City of Limerick, Sheet No. 19.
31 Lamplugh, G. W. 'The Geology of the County Around Limerick', *Memoirs of the Geological Survey of Ireland*, Thom & Co., Dublin, 1907, p. 89.
32 Browne, Margaret 'The Limestone Industry of Limerick', *Made in Limerick* Vol. I, Lee, David & Jacobs, Debbie eds., Limerick Civic Trust, Limerick, 2003, pp. 179, 182.
33 *Limerick Gazette*, Friday 7 March 1817.
34 *Limerick Gazette*, Friday 15 August 1817.
35 loc. cit.
36 *Limerick Gazette*, 15 August 1817; Fitzgerald & M'Gregor *op. cit.* Vol. II, p. 583.
37 Limerick City Regiment of Militia; this was Lord Gort's regiment.
38 *Limerick Gazette*, 21 October 1817.
39 Ordnance Survey 1840, City of Limerick, Sheet No. 19.
40 Lewis, Samuel *A Topographical Dictionary of Ireland* (1837), Vol. II, p. 273.
41 *Pigot's Directory* 1824, p. 281.
42 Speer, Albert *Inside the Third Reich*, Book Club Associates/Weidenfeld & Nicolson, London, 1971 edition, pp. 27-8.
43 'Report of the Commissioners of the County Limerick Gaol', *Limerick Gazette*, 9 February 1816.
44 Fitzgerald & M'Gregor *op. cit.* Vol. II, p. 587.
45 Ordnance Survey 1840, City of Limerick, Sheet 19.

46 Evans *op. cit.* p. 283.

47 Evans *op. cit.* p. 265.

48 Evans *op. cit.* pp. 269-70.

49 Quoted in Evans *op. cit.* pp. 265-6.

50 Quoted in Evans *op. cit.* p. 266.

51 *The Cambridge Biographical Encyclopaedia* s.v. 'Howard, John', 2nd edition, Cambridge University Press, 1998.

52 Fitzgerald and M'Gregor *op. cit.* pp. 581-2.

53 Colvin *op. cit.* s.v. 'Blackburn, William'.

54 Cruickshank, Dan *A Guide to the Georgian Buildings of Britain and Ireland*, Weidenfeld and Nicolson, The National Trust, The Irish Georgian Society, 1985, pp. 158-9.

55 'Design for a County Gaol', *Crime and Punishment 8: Reports and Papers relating to the Prisons of the United Kingdom with Minutes of Evidence and Appendices 1818-22*, British Parliamentary Papers, Irish University Press, Shannon, Ireland, 1970.

56 Colvin *op. cit.* s.v 'Bullar, George Thomas'.

57 Evans. op. *cit.* pp. 277-82, Figs. 144-6.

58 'County Limerick Gaol Report', *Limerick County Grand Jury Presentments, Spring Assizes 1848*.

59 Evans *op. cit.* pp. 284-6.

60 Inglis, Henry *A Journey Throughout Ireland During the Spring, Summer and Autumn of 1834*, Two Vols., Whittaker & Co., London, 1834, Vol. I, p. 300.

61 Chatterton, Lady *Rambles in the South of Ireland During the Year 1838*, Two Vols., Saunders and Otley, London, 1839, Vol. II, pp. 231-2.

62 Lewis *op. cit.* Vol. II, p. 273; Fitzgerald & M'Gregor *op. cit.* Vol. II, p. 582. Sections of Samuel Lewis's description of Limerick in his *Topographical Dictionary of Ireland* (1837) are based on Fitzgerald and M'Gregor's 1827 description of the city in their *History, Topography and Antiquities of the County and City of Limerick*, but précised and updated for Lewis's work published ten years later. Lewis, a London publisher, based his celebrated topographical description of Ireland on official sources (census returns, parliamentary reports etc.) and on the contributions of 'nearly all the most intelligent resident gentlemen' in the country. Lewis corresponded with ministers and resident gentlemen who had to vouch for the accuracy of their descriptions before they were published. One assumes that Rev. Patrick Fitzgerald and J. J. M'Gregor were among those recruited by Lewis to provide information on Limerick.

63 'The History of Tullamore Gaol', Offaly Historical and Archaeological Society website.

64 Plan elevation of Tullamore Gaol in Shaffrey, Patrick & Shaffrey, Maura *Buildings of Irish Towns*, The O'Brien Press Ltd., Dublin, 1983, p. 128.

65 'The History of Tullamore Gaol', Offaly Historical and Archaeological Society website.

66 Lewis *op. cit.* p. 346.

67 Architectural historian Dan Cruickshank is of the opinion that Portlaoise was 'probably by James and George Richard Pain.' Cruickshank *op. cit.* p. 159. The Irish

Architectural Archive in its *Index of Irish Architects* s.v. 'Pain, James' attributes Tullamore Gaol to James Pain citing King's County Grand Jury Presentments.

68 Shaffrey *op. cit.* p. 128.

69 *County Limerick Grand Jury Presentments, Summer Assizes, 1822*, p. 16. Local Studies Department, County Limerick Library.

70 James Pain's work for the Limerick County Gaol is recorded in various Presentments of the Limerick County Grand Jury until 1863.

71 Ordnance Survey 1840, City of Limerick, Sheet No. 19.

72 *Limerick County Grand Jury Presentments, Summer, 1824*, p. 20.

73 *Limerick County Grand Jury Presentments, Summer, 1822*, p. 16.

74 Evans *op. cit.* p. 295.

75 Fitzgerald and M'Gregor *op. cit.* Vol. II, p. 584.

76 Fitzgerald and M'Gregor *op. cit.* Vol. II, p. 510. See pp. 510-1.

77 loc. cit.

78 For a discussion on the purposes of the Cubitt's treadmill see Evans *op. cit.* pp. 295-309.

79 Barrow, John *A Tour Around Ireland Through the Sea-Coast Counties, in the Autumn of 1835*, John Murray, London, 1836, p. 326.

CHAPTER FIVE
WICKED MEN & DESIGNING DEMAGOGUES

Local Limerick historians J. J. M'Gregor and Anglican clergyman Rev. Patrick Fitzgerald, writing in 1827, were of the opinion that the County Gaol provided 'a perfect model for all the prisons in Ireland' and were full of praise for the architect:

> 'The grand entrance is formed of very fine cut stone in the Doric style . . . The judgement and taste of Mr. James Pain the Architect, are equally deserving of eulogium for the elegance and connexion of the entire building.'[1]

Beauty lies in the eye of the beholder and perhaps Fitzgerald and M'Gregor's favourable architectural opinion was influenced by the fact that the opening of the prison in 1821 came at a critical time for the authorities. For immediately after its completion a very serious outbreak of agrarian violence broke out in the County and the prison was soon thronged with prisoners arrested in connection with the insurgency.[2]

The unrest, which continued for two years, was occasioned by distress caused to the peasantry by a poor potato harvest and falling grain prices, the crisis leading to a reduction in wages and an increase in unemployment among farm labourers. Spearheaded by oath-bound secret societies known as Rockites who took their name from Captain Rock, their invisible, mythical and non-existent leader, the peasantry sought, by physical force methods,

Limerick County Gaol showing stripped Doric front entrance and in background central administrative block. Two of the radial cell blocks can be seen. The prison has been considerably modified since this photo was taken.

Limerick Museum

reductions in rent and an ending of tithes. Tithes were parish taxes paid to Church of Ireland clergymen for their maintenance and were levied on agricultural produce. Legally binding, tithes were imposed on all producers regardless if one were Protestant, Catholic or Dissenter. The Rev. Patrick Fitzgerald was himself in receipt of £95 a year in tithes from Cahircorney (Cahercorney) parish[3] in East Co. Limerick where he was the incumbent from 1807 to 1857. Cahercorney Church is now in ruins.

The disturbances spread from Co. Limerick to Cork, Kerry and Clare and were characterised by raids for firearms on the homes of farmers and gentry, house burnings, destruction of property, maiming of livestock, shootings, beatings, murders and intimidation. The deployment of para-military police and army units to contain the unrest led to clashes with the security forces, repressive measures and exemplary punishments. Outbreaks of agrarian violence in Munster and other parts of Ireland had become a regular occurrence since the late eighteenth century as the land crisis in rural Ireland became ever more acute, but what was particularly disturbing about the unrest in Co. Limerick for those whose interest lay with the maintenance of the Protestant Ascendancy was evidence of messianic radicalism, the struggle for economic and social justice being viewed by some of the insurgents as an opportunity to destroy Protestantism in Ireland. During the troubles there was much anti-Protestant sectarian feeling and a number of Anglican churches were either burnt down or damaged in 1822.[4]

As the rector for Cahercorney, Rev. Fitzgerald would have been all too aware of the sectarian tensions that came to the fore during the unrest. Although both he and M'Gregor acknowledge the distressed state of the peasantry as a prime cause of the disturbances in their *History, Topography and Antiquities of the County and City of Limerick* (1827), they nevertheless portrayed those involved in leading the insurgency as 'Wicked men' and 'designing demagogues' who took advantage of circumstances 'to infuriate the minds of the people against the government, the gentry and local authorities, whom they were taught to look upon as their cruel oppressors.' Despite 'just retribution' in the form of hangings and transportation, the deluded peasantry continued to engage 'in a conspiracy of the blackest crime, and the most insane folly' until, by Divine Providence, the storm was quelled by that great 'Omnipotent Being, who stills the raging of the seas and the madness of the people' who was pleased, in His Goodness and Mercy, to send 'scarcity, approaching to famine, into the disturbed districts.'[5]

With such views no wonder that the good vicar of Cahercorney and his colleague saw much architectural merit in Pain's prison, now part of the State's apparatus for dealing with crime and social unrest. On 2 August 1822 five men accused of killing a postboy were hung together in front of the new

Limerick County Hospital (now Limerick Senior College) where bodies of executed convicts were sent for dissection.

gaol and their bodies sent across the road to the County Hospital for dissection.[6] The County Hospital (1811) is now Limerick Senior College. Having one's body handed over to local surgeons for anatomical instruction was part of the sentence that could be handed down to condemned convicts of the period. Indeed, in the County Hospital there was a large room in the rear for the reception of the bodies of executed murderers that were, by an Act of Parliament, ordered to be given to the county infirmaries of Ireland for dissection.[7]

Twenty years previously in April 1793 the local authorities were perplexed when the body of a man with his head, hands and legs cut off was found washed up on a strand near Newtown Pery, Limerick's Georgian district. It was first thought that the man had been murdered, but on closer examination it was discovered that the body was that of a criminal recently executed in the city. The body had been given over for dissection and when the corpse had served its purpose the surgeons employed some local men to dispose of the body. Rather than take the trouble of burying the stinking, rotting corpse, they simply dumped it into the river.[8]

Dreadful Murders

Many dreadful murders were committed in the troubles of the early 1820s and one that would have been particularly shocking to James Pain and his neighbours in Newtown Pery was the killing of Mrs. Catherine Torrance, the daughter of prominent Limerick merchant Benjamin Unthank. She was stabbed to death by two men armed with bayonets on Sunday 10 June 1821 while she and her husband were out walking near the village of Adare.[9] The motive for the deadly assault arose from an incident that had taken place three months earlier when Rockites attacked their house at Cunnigar, Co. Limerick. The gang had been beaten off with gunfire, one of the attackers apparently being killed.[10] During the subsequent incident near Adare the husband, John Torrance, received fourteen stab wounds, while his wife was fatally stabbed through the heart. Catherine was buried the following morning in the family vault at St. Munchin's churchyard on King's Island, the city's principal shops and businesses closing their shutters all day as a mark of respect.[11]

Immediately after the murder, citizens were invited to subscribe money to a reward that would be paid to 'whoever shall within twelve months . . . prosecute to conviction' the killers. Such was the public response that by 4 July £1330 had been pledged,[12] James Pain donating £2 5s to the fund.[13] John Torrance survived his wounds, including a stab wound that penetrated his left side, running under the ribs for 6 inches. He was the key prosecution witness against two men arrested on 23 June[14] who were later sentenced to death in December 1821.[15]

Cork House of Correction

Limerick County Gaol was not the only penal commission carried out by the Pain brothers, for in 1818 they designed the House of Correction on Cork City's Western Road. Houses of Correction were distinct institutions within prisons catering for misdemeanants who had committed petty offences and sent to the House for corrective discipline. Typically, inmates were apprentices who had transgressed the terms of their contract,

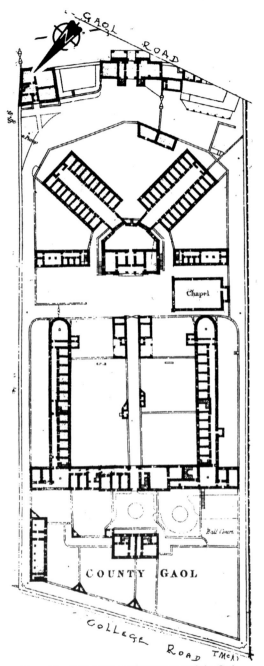

Plan of the Cork House of Correction and the Cork County Gaol. The House of Correction with its central administrative block and radial wings can be seen at the top of the plan. The contrast between the two prison layouts is self-evident.

misbehaving servants, prostitutes, beggars and vagabonds. The Cork House of Correction was purposely built to separate petty offenders from those charged with more serious offences lodged in the County Gaol, which was also known as the 'sheriff's prison.' Each facility had its own governor.[16]

The House of Correction (1818; opened in 1822) was constructed just to the north of the County Gaol (early 1790s) within the same outer boundary wall. Although built on 'improved principles'[17] similar to those used in Limerick the layout differed somewhat from that of Limerick. The Cork prison featuring an impressively large central administrative block with cell blocks radiating from the sides and rear of the building but not from the main, front elevation that faced towards the County Gaol.

The three storey, ashlar, central block, which was *the* significant and dominant element of the entire architectural composition, contained the governor's quarters on the ground floor, a Protestant and a Catholic chapel on the first floor with a hospital on the upper level.[18] The building's architecture was influenced by the Classical Italian Renaissance with its flat roof hidden by stone balustrades, parapets and cornice placed around the roofline of the building:

The windows on the front façade were framed by quoin stonework. An Italian Renaissance motif, quoins were normally used to frame the edges of buildings, but this motif was not used by the Pains on the corners of the administrative block. The building was Classically symmetrical with the ashlar stonework on the ground floor rusticated to suggest a sense of power and solidity, another favoured Renaissance/Palladian technique. The elevation was astylar in style, i.e. a Classical façade having no pilasters or columns. The recesses on the projecting flanks of the main elevation suggest columns extending almost the full height of the structure; these recesses topped by a round-headed, voussoir arch framing a semicircular opening. Within these recesses windows were installed, the ground floor windows having an architrave. Located between the projecting flanks of this southerly facing façade an arcade with elliptical arches, surmounted by a balcony, was placed, conjuring up the feel and image of a sunnier and warmer clime.

In terms of prison architecture the administrative block was a distinguished achievement and a tribute to the skill and proficiency of the brothers Pain. The architecture was of necessity a simple and plain rendition of Italian Renaissance with no fuss, no frills. Nevertheless the manner in which the brothers approached the design is a clear indication that as architects they were cultured and sophisticated, as one would expect from former pupils of Nash.

Shipshape Prison

On either side of the central structure two detached cell blocks were built acting as 'wings' to the main building on the front elevation. Unfortunately this grand effect was later spoilt when a Catholic Chapel was built immediately in front of one of the cell blocks. From the rear of the main building two pairs of cell blocks radiated, one towards the north, the other west. Both of these were attached to the central block. These three storey ranges with their pitched roofs seemed quite narrow, quite reminiscent of the limestone granaries that were once such a prominent feature of Limerick City's commercial architecture. They contained only one row of cells per floor while the standard radical range was designed for two rows of cells on either side of a corridor.

Front elevation of the administrative block of the Cork House of Correction.

Writing in 1846 local Cork historian J. Windele thought it worthy of comment that the cells in the House of Correction 'are fitted up with hammocks' similar to those used on naval ships.[19] This innovation was introduced by Captain Hoare, formerly of the navy, who had been appointed governor of the House. He seems to have believed in good discipline and keeping his prison shipshape and Bristol fashion, for when John Barrow visited the facility in 1835 on behalf of the reading public he found the prison to be kept 'in the most cleanly and neat order; not a speck of dirt to be seen anywhere, and the walls beautifully white throughout, owing to the constant application of the brush.'[20] Those not engaged in whitewashing and cleaning were set to the treadmill that pumped water to the prison.[21]

Grecian Portico

But what impressed Corkonians most was the fact that the design of the House of Correction's entrance portico was 'taken from that of the Temple of Bacchus at Athens' according to local commentators such as J. Windele.[22] A rather ironic mythological association for a penal institution, for Dionysus (Latin name Bacchus) was the Greek God of wine, celebratory drunkenness and ritual ecstasy. Dionysus's female followers, the maenads, went off to the mountains for a girls' night out with their priestesses to engage in rapturous dance and ecstatic rituals resulting, reputedly, according to myth, in live sacrificial animals being seized by the maenads, who had worked themselves up into a state of frenzy, rending the sacrifices asunder with their bare hands.[23] But it is probably unlikely that Captain Hoare, strict disciplinarian that he was, would have allowed such carryings-on and feminist frolics to have taken place in Cork.

The portico is actually inspired by the Temple of Apollo at Delos,[24] the smallest of the Greek Cyclade Islands in the Aegean Sea. This example of Doric architecture was introduced into English architecture by eighteenth century architects James Stuart and Nicholas Revett whose drawings and measurements of Greek temples and monuments in Athens (1751-3) and Asia Minor (1764-6) gave rise to Greek Revival.[25]

The entrance to the House of Correction is composed of a Doric portico in austere Greek Revival style with four round columns supporting a pediment with an unsculptured tympanum. The only decorative feature on the portico is fluting applied a few inches at the very top and bottom of the otherwise unfluted column shafts, and a frieze of triglyphs on the entablature. A frieze of triglyphs was also applied to the corners of the prison walls to very neatly and cleverly round off the Classical effect of the entrance. The drums on the column shafts are quite massive exuding such strength that even Samson, in all his fury, would find great difficulty in toppling them. To impress upon newly arrived inmates that prison life was no pleasure garden the Pain brothers' stark

The Pain brothers' very stern Greek Revival style entrance to the Cork House of Correction.

portico rather resembles the front façade of a melancholy mausoleum. This effect is enhanced by an entrance archway suggesting a corbelled arch (a feature achieved by corbelling from both sides of the archway with horizontal stone blocks) whereby the two topmost courses of the arch are corbelled. Rather than coming to an apex, the arch is bridged by a long lintel. The entire effect gives a primitive look to the entrance, as though it was the portal to some monumental megalithic tomb. The corbelled arch (also known as a false or pseudo-arch) was believed at the time to be a feature of Egyptian architecture. There was some interest among late eighteenth and early nineteenth century architects for Egyptian Revival, the stonework of the gateway and the rustication of the flanking niches being the Pain brothers' nod in that particular direction.

Approached by a bridge, fronted by an esplanade and flanked by high prison walls, the prison entrance was enhanced by its surroundings in a successful attempt to present an imposing, if drear, Grecian aspect to the viewer. Photographs rarely do full justice to the magnitude of the composition and the forceful, visual impact it makes on the naked eye. George Richard Pain designed the approaches in 1823.[26]

The entire prison complex, which later became the Cork Male Prison, was closed in the 1950s and subsequently acquired by University College Cork.[27] The buildings were demolished and all that remains of the Pains' penal work in Cork is the tetrastyle portico that can still be seen in the grounds of UCC facing the Western Road, and a section of the prison wall. The portico still commands admiration among architectural historians.

> 'The transformation of that ubiquitous early nineteenth-century public building embellishment, the Grecian portico, to an awe-inspiring symbol of penal servitude is best illustrated by Cork Male Prison[28] by James and George Pain, which is furnished with the quintessential brooding Delian Doric portico set against a blank wall with sparsely placed, heavily rusticated windows.'[29]

It is by considering the Pain brothers' design for the House of Correction that one comes to fully appreciate the impact that they had on the citizens of Cork. With just one building they immediately became to be recognised as leading architects and from that period onwards the brothers, in particular George, were to be favoured with prestigious assignments in both the City and County of Cork.

Stark Appearance

The stark appearance of the entrances to both the Limerick and Cork prisons cannot be deemed a fault of the architects, for it was considered architecturally correct by prison authorities, architects and penal reformers alike that the outward appearance of prisons be bleak to intimidate the prisoner and reassure the tax-paying public. For as James Elmes (1782-1862), architect, prison builder, as well as prolific writer on artistic and architectural topics,[30] remarked in his *Hints for the Improvement of Prisons* (1817), the express purpose of creating such entrances was to give an appearance 'as gloomy and melancholy as possible.'[31] Simple Doric was well suited to this task and other prison architects also thought the style appropriate. There is extant in the Essex County Records Office a Thomas Hopper drawing (1820) of a prison portico with four plain Doric columns and heavily rusticated walls. Hopper's design is even more severe than the Pains' Cork House of Correction, for his minimalist Doric lacks a pediment.[32]

While early nineteenth century prisons became increasingly standardised in their internal arrangements an architect's individual taste was allowed to manifest itself in the design of the main entrance. As seen with the Pain brothers they made most impact when they worked with Doric, although the

The Gothic style entrance to the Cork City Gaol contrasts with
that of the Greek Revival style of the Cork House of Correction.

entrances to their Limerick and Cork gaols are each distinctly different from one another. Other architects preferred Gothic to create an intimidating effect and to convey the message of sternness and the permanence of Authority. Such was the case with the contemporaneous Cork City Gaol (1818-24) built at Sunday's Well to the design of Kilkenny architect William Robertson (contractor Thomas Deane).[33] Here, a doorway is set within a substantial fortified, battlemented gateway that has imposing depth front to rear as well as boasting a strong front elevation. The doorway is placed between battlemented polygonal towers pierced with arrow loops. While the gatehouse was built in dark brown sandstone, the masonry surrounds of the windows are in white limestone giving the building a striking appearance. The prison walls, though plain, are decorated with battlements on the corners to correspond with the fortified entrance and to create the impression of corner turrets, thereby rounding off the Gothic effect of the gatehouse. The main gateway into the prison is actually placed to the left of the main building and is unfortified. This gate also has limestone surrounds.

The City Gaol, set high up on the ridge at Sunday's Well exactly faces and looks down upon the Pain brothers' portico on the other side of the River Lee, some 2 kilometres away. They face each other in a ritualistic 'Battle of the Styles', each equally valid and impressive according to their own architectural lights. Rivalry in another sense too, for the Pain brothers and Thomas Deane, the builder of the City Gaol, were to become open rivals as architects in Cork over the coming years.

Tullamore prison (1830) also had a castellated entrance, as did Wexford County Gaol (1812). But working with that style did not always bring about the desired effect, the Gothic entrance to the Wexford prison, for instance, does not seem a particularly impressive structure as it lacks depth front to rear, giving it a very flat, stage-set appearance. Compared to the Pains' Grecian it is very weak façade for a prison entrance. Cold, severe Classicism was the most appropriate public expression for early nineteenth century prisons with their emphasis on absolute geometric symmetry in design, structural rationality and strict scientific classification of prisoners. A clinical, utilitarian approach to architecture that would drive ideological Gothic Revivalists such as Augustus Pugin to utter distraction.

Palace of a Prison

It would appear that the County Gaol/House of Correction facility was the better of the two Cork prisons, much of the credit going, one should be in no doubt, to the Pains for the model architectural layout they had provided. According to the *Parliamentary Gazetteer of Ireland* (1844-46), up to the close of 1841 no part of the City Gaol 'was in a state of adaptation to the total separation of prisoners' and that 'various desirable improvements' had been postponed. On the other hand the County Gaol complex was 'one of the most extensive and best conducted establishments in Ireland.'[34]

Despite the best efforts on the part of architects to give a daunting appearance to places of detention, a number of contemporary commentators were quick to point out that the modern reformed prisons were like 'palaces' for the idle. Following his visit to Cork County Gaol in 1842 novelist and travel writer William Thackeray remarked that the prison was 'so neat, spacious and comfortable that we can only pray to see every cottager in the country so cleanly, well lodged, and well fed as the convicts are.' Describing it as 'this palace of a prison' he remarked that the daily diet of a pound of bread and two pints of milk 'would be a luxury' to 'millions of people in this wretched country' and that 'the prison seemed almost a premium for vice.'[35] More an ironic comment, one would have thought, on the social condition of the country rather than a critique of prison pleasures.

Marriage

It was while working in Cork that George Richard presumably met Catherine Benn whom he married. Making their home at 5 St. Patrick's Hill, Cork,[36] the couple had a son, James Richard Pain, born c.1823[37] and a daughter Catherine (Kate). Their father was made a Freeman of Cork City in 1827[38] and by 1832 had moved to Camden Place.[39] Following the death of his first wife, George later married Margaret Atkins who gave birth to a daughter Sarah (Sally). Margaret was aunt to William Atkins who became apprenticed to G. R. Pain in 1832,[40] William Atkins becoming, in turn, a well-known Cork architect who was responsible for, among other commissions, Our Lady's Hospital (1847-52), an asylum at Sunday's Well, Cork.[41] Although James had settled permanently in Limerick, and although they carried out work separately, the two brothers continued to work in close partnership on many projects and assignments. They advertised as a joint practice, for instance Pigot's 1824 Directory for Limerick lists 'Pain James & G. R.' as architects with an office address on the city's Upper George's Street.[42] Together they established a very successful practice in the south of Ireland.

James Pain's Address

For all of his sixty-six odd years in this country James Pain lived in Limerick and since 1824, at least, in a Georgian terraced house on George Street, referred to as George's Street in the early nineteenth century. Pigot's 1824 directory gives James's home and business address as 'upper George's-street' while the 1840 *New Triennial and Commercial Directory* simply states 'George's Street'. It was common in those days for professional people and shopkeepers to live overhead their businesses and offices, usually located on the ground floor. Slater's directories for 1846 and 1856 both offer the information that the architect lived at '33 George Street'. After crossing the junction of Roches Street and George's Street (now O'Connell Street) this house was the second on the left as one headed towards Richmond Place (now The Crescent). The 1840 Ordnance Survey very helpfully numbers all the houses on the street and No. 33 is shown as having an area, now covered over with pavement. No. 32 was the house on the corner, presently (2005) the White Gold Gift Shop.

A slight difficulty in tracing James's address arises due to the fact that his 1863 Will and two subsequent directories all cite '35 George Street' as his address.[43] However, Nos. 33 and 35 are one and the same house, for at some stage during the middle of the nineteenth century the house numbering system in George Street was altered. The corner house, previously 32, becoming 34 and James Pain's residence becoming 35.

A year or so before his death in December 1877 James moved to 17 Glentworth Street,[44] this house since been having demolished to make way for the Glentworth Hotel, now Pery's hotel.

James Pain's house was situated to the right of the White Gold gift shop.

Endnotes

1 Fitzgerald, Rev. P. & M'Gregor, J.J. *The History, Topography and Antiquities of the County and City of Limerick*, 2 Vols., Limerick, 1827, Vol. II, pp. 583-4.

2 Lenihan, Maurice *Limerick; Its History and Antiquities*, 1866, p. 448n1.

3 Lewis, Samuel *A Topographical Dictionary of Ireland*, 2 Vols., London, 1837, Vol. I, s.v. 'Cahircorney'.

4 Curtin, Gerald 'Religious and Social Conflict During the Protestant Crusade in West Limerick 1822-49', *The Old Limerick Journal*, Kemmy, Jim ed., No. 39, Winter 2003; Feeley, Pat 'Whiteboys and Ribbonmen', *The Old Limerick Journal*, Kemmy, Jim ed., No. 4, September 1980.

5 Fitzgerald & M'Gregor *op. cit.* 'Appendix No. VII'. pp. xxxix & xliv.

6 *Limerick Chronicle*, 4 August 1822.

7 Lenihan *op. cit.* p. 415n.

8 *Limerick Chronicle*, 20 April 1793.

9 *Limerick Chronicle*, 13 June 1821.

10 *Limerick Chronicle*, 21 December 1821; Fitzgerald & M'Gregor *op. cit.* Vol. II, p. xl.

11 *Limerick Chronicle*, 13 June 1821.

12 *Limerick Chronicle*, 4 July 1821.

13 *Limerick Chronicle*, 23 June 1821.

14 *Limerick Chronicle*, 23 June 1821.

15 Fitzgerald & M'Gregor *op. cit.* p. xl; *Limerick Chronicle*, 21 December 1821.

16 *Parliamentary Gazetteer of Ireland* 1844-46, Vol. I, p. 524.

17 Windele, J. *Historical and Descriptive Notices of the City of Cork*, Messrs. Bolster, Cork. 1846, p. 25.

18 McNamara, T. F. *Portrait of Cork*, Watermans, Cork, 1981, p. 79.

19 Windele, J. *Historical and Descriptive Notices of the City of Cork and its Vicinity* Longman & Co., London, 1846, p. 25.

20 Barrow, John *A Tour Round Ireland*, John Murray, Albemarle Street, London, 1836, p. 325.

21 Lewis *op. cit.* Vol. I, p. 420.

22 Windele *op. cit.* p. 25.

23 Price, Simon & Kearns, Emily eds. *The Oxford Dictionary of Classical Myth and Religion*, Oxford University Press, 2003 s.v. 'Dionysus'. The renting asunder of live animals by maenads was confined to ancient Greek mythology, poetry and vase paintings and there is no evidence of female devotees engaging in anything other than joyful rituals associated with the cult.

24 Craig, Maurice *The Architecture of Ireland*, Batsford, Ltd., London and Eason & Son, Dublin, 1982, p. 262.

25 Curl, James Stevens *Oxford Dictionary of Architecture* s.v. 'Revett, Nicholas (1720-1804)'; s.v. 'Stuart, James 'Athenian' (1713-88)', Oxford University Press, Oxford, 1999.

26 *Index of Irish Architects* s.v. 'Pain, James', Irish Architectural Archive, Merrion Square, Dublin.

27 Green, J. F. 'James and George Richard Pain', *The Green Book, 1965: The Journal of the Architectural Association of Ireland*, Dublin, 1965.

28 The County Goal/House of Correction facility and the Cork City Goal in Sunday's Well were mutually consolidated in the 1840s - *Parliamentary Gazetteer of Ireland* Vol. I, p. 524. The former becoming the Male Prison and the latter the Female Prison.

29 Cruickshank, Dan *A Guide to the Georgian Buildings of Britain and Ireland*, Weidenfeld and Nicolson, The National Trust, The Irish Georgian Society, 1985, p. 158.

30 Colvin, Howard *A Biographical Dictionary of British Architects 1600-1840* s.v. 'Elmes, James', 3rd edition, Yale University Press, New Haven and London, 1995, pp. 343-4. Elmes's works include the House of Correction (1820) in Waterford and the New Gaol (1819-20) at Bedford, England.

31 Elmes, James *Hints for the Improvement of Prisons*, London, 1817, p. 14.

32 Evans, Robin *The Fabrication of Virtue, English Prison Architecture 1750-1840*, Cambridge University Press, Cambridge, 1982, Fig. 128, p. 253.

33 O'Dwyer, Frederick *The Architecture of Deane and Woodward*, Cork University Press, Cork, 1997, pp. 14, 550n44.

34 *The Parliamentary Gazetteer of Ireland*, Vol. I, p. 524.

35 Thackeray, William Makepeace *The Irish Sketch Book 1842*, J. M. Dent & Co., London, 1903, p. 95

36 *Pigot & Co.'s City of Dublin and Hibernian Provincial Directory*, J. Pigot & Co., London & Manchester, 1824, p. 248.

37 James Richard Pain died aged 28 on 8 February 1852, see *Limerick Chronicle*, 8 February 1852.

38 McNamara, T. F. *Portrait of Cork*, Cork, 1981, p. 155.

39 Royal Hibernian Academy's Index of Exhibitors 1987, III, p. 58.

40 O'Dwyer, Frederick 'A Noble Pile in the Late Tudor Style: Mitchelstown Castle', *Irish Arts Review 2002*, p. 43n31.

41 Williams, Jeremy *Architecture in Ireland 1837-1921*, Irish Academic Press, Dublin, 1994, pp. 66-7.

42 *Pigot's op. cit.* p. 286.

43 Slater's 1870 Directory; Bassett's Directory for 1875-6.

44 Bassett's 1877-8 Directory.

CHAPTER SIX

THE RETURN OF THE GOTHS

The big break for the Pain partnership in establishing themselves as fashionable architects came in 1819 when they were offered their first major, independent country house commission by Sir Edward O'Brien (1773-1837) of Dromoland who had finally made up his mind about the design of his new home to replace his eighteenth century mansion. The gestation period had been rather lengthy, about seven years in fact, involving a number of proposals from various architects before Sir Edward finally accepted a castellated design jointly drawn up in early 1819 by James and George Richard Pain. James's earlier 1813 proposal had been conservative and relatively dull in comparison, the difference illustrating an increase in confidence by James over the intervening six years and the benefits of being in association with his more artistic, imaginative brother.

Before discussing Dromoland Castle and the brothers' other major castellated assignment, Mitchelstown Castle, it would be useful at this stage to consider the historical background to Gothic Revivalist architecture in England and explain why it came to be so popular among the landed elite of Britain and Ireland during the Regency period. As pupils of leading Regency architect John Nash, during their formative years the Englishmen James and G. R. Pain drew upon their native country's rich Gothic Revivalist heritage, a heritage that helped to shape their cultural understanding and architectural skills. Strictly speaking, in political terms, the Regency period covers the years 1811-20 when George, Prince of Wales, was Prince Regent during his father's, George III, ill health. As a description of artistic and architectural style however, the term Regency covers a much broader time frame, generally speaking from the 1790s to the accession, or reign, of William IV (1830-37). As a label, some art historians extend the period into the early Victorian 1840s.

Pleasing Vistas

As an architectural style Gothic Revival grew its wings in Britain during the eighteenth and early nineteenth century and migrated to Ireland where it found favour with the aristocracy. The revival had its roots in changing attitudes towards English landscape design and the employment of garden buildings to enhance and adorn estates. In the early years of the eighteenth century the formal house garden with its rigid geometric lines was still in vogue, as were long radial avenues lined by trees traversing through parklands. However this symmetrical style, imported from the Continent, came to be increasingly seen as an unnatural imposition on Nature that ought to be rejected for a far more freer, more informal interpretation and arrangement of the landscape. 'English Freedom' and informality was to be prized over Continental Absolutism and rigidity; the ideal garden being one that aspired to celebrate the freedom and openness of Nature.[1]

Such thinking led to a revolution in English landscape design that discarded the straight line and the geometric compass, introducing in its stead a landscape of flowing natural forms that resembled a pictorial composition of poetic nature rather than a gardening parade ground. With the remodelling of parklands by landscape designers who considered carefully the correct siting of garden buildings, the perfect placement of artificial lakes, rivers and waterfalls and the calculated planting of trees, this 'naturalist' landscape was as much man-made and contrived as what went before, but it was considerably more pleasing to the eye and terribly more 'real'. If Nature was not as beautiful as She ought to be when viewed by the gentleman of a great house and fortune then an improving landscape designer was drafted in to carry out the necessary cosmetic surgery.

With the emergence, from the 1730s onwards, of this new 'naturalistic' treatment of the country park and garden, in which the undulating line expressed the ideal of natural beauty, estate holders sought to implant into the landscape picturesque buildings of modest size that would add to the pleasing vistas of rolling hills, serpentine waters and clumps of carefully planted trees. An approach to landscape design that sought, in the words of garden historian James Howley,

> '. . . not only to let nature take her true course but also to adorn her with buildings to embellish and thus underline her beauty. The belief was that a natural landscape, no matter how beautiful, could be further enhanced by the addition of a building or structure judiciously placed to represent the presence of civilisation in a balanced and unimposing way. The building could either evoke association through memory or allegory, or simply demonstrate man in harmony with nature.'[2]

To achieve this effect the fashionable landowner in the latter half of the eighteenth century could choose from a variety of styles to create focal points and inject a sense of discernment and aesthetic taste into the garden landscape. But in the early decades of the English landscape movement temples, mausolea and statues in the Roman Classical mode were preferred, as were Palladian bridges spanning rivers. The term 'garden' may be a bit misleading, for the garden park at Stowe in Buckinghamshire was over 400 acres in extent merging into the surrounding estate; while garden buildings, such as the mausoleum at Castle Howard in Yorkshire, could be quite substantial structures. But it was not to everybody's taste or pocket to build on such a large scale, and smaller, more modest structures were popular. Such an example can be seen in the grounds of Dromoland Castle, Co. Clare where a Temple to Mercury was erected at a date prior to 1740.[3]

Temple of Mercury, Dromoland Castle, far left. During World War II Dromoland was taken over as a camp by the Irish Army. To keep themselves occupied they used the Statue of Mercy for target practice. Pictured are bullet holes on the arm and buttocks. The statue, normally found at the top of the temple, is in storage awaiting restoration.

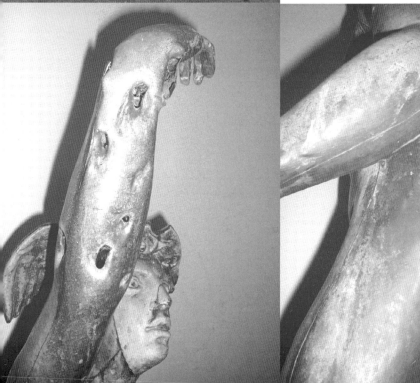

Although Classical remained the dominant force in the landscaped garden in the first half of the eighteenth century, an alternative did emerge in the form of Gothic garden buildings utilising medieval forms and motifs. Foremost among those who incorporated Gothic into their landscaped arrangements were Whig oligarchs who saw positive virtue springing from England's medieval past, men of wealth who saw the English barons of the Middle Ages as the champions of British liberties and founders of Parliamentary rights. For had not the barons, drawing their strength from their estates and fortresses, stood up to King John at Runnymede and extracted, at the point of a sword, Magna Carta (1215), the basis of the English Constitution, from a reluctant and tyrannical king.

Up until the second half of the eighteenth century the Whigs were an influential and powerful grouping of country aristocrats and mercantile interests who supported the supremacy of Parliament, the Protestant Succession and the constitutional monarchy of the House of Hanover. Beneficiaries of the Glorious Revolution of 1688 and the expansion overseas of British mercantile trade - they were opposed to Absolutist Monarchy and a Jacobite restoration, for they wished to dispose of their lands, properties and fortunes as best they saw fit, free of the meddlings of a centralised 'Sun King' state.

Temples to Liberty

Prominent among these Whigs was Richard Temple, Viscount Cobham, who, at his landscaped garden park at Stowe in Buckinghamshire created a series of architectural set pieces in which the use of Classical and Gothick garden buildings expressed, to the initiated, his anti-Absolutist policies and defence of Parliamentary rights. With these buildings, given titles such as the Temple of Ancient Virtue and the Temple of British Worthies, the political message was laid on fairly thickly. Of particular interest is the Gothic Temple (1741) designed by James Gibbs.[4] Although by no means the first Gothic garden building to be erected on an English country estate, it is the one that can stand for the others in its explicit and direct statement of a political idea.

Originally called the 'Temple of Liberty', and built as an intact structure (not as a ruin), it was dedicated to the 'Liberty of our Ancestors'. In Whig historical mythology the term 'Gothic Liberty' referred to the political institutions of Anglo-Saxon England prior to the Norman invasion, in particular the Royal council known as the Witenagemot, a body of nobles and churchmen that advised Anglo-Saxon kings on policy. It also referred to the spirit of resistance to tyranny as exemplified by the ancient Germanic tribes known as Goths. A spirit which though oppressed by the centralisation of Royal power following the Norman invasion of England in 1066 was not crushed and came to manifest itself in Magna Carta and the establishment of an English Parliament during the thirteenth century to restrain the powers of monarchy and

Temple of Liberty, Stowe, Buckinghamshire, England.

maintain the rights of subjects, particularly subjects who happened to be rich and powerful. The legacy of the 'Norman Yoke' persisted, however, and Royalist power was not to be finally curbed until the parliamentary and military struggles waged against the Crown in the seventeenth century finally bore fruit in the overthrow of James II in 1688 and the establishment of the Hanoverian Succession in 1714.[5] Even then, the defenders of this new political dispensation had to be on guard against French supported Jacobite threats of rebellion and invasion, fears that were not finally laid to rest until the defeat of the 1745 Rebellion at the Battle of Culloden (1746).

From an English historical perspective such events as the triumph of Oliver Cromwell over Charles I and the overthrow of James II by William of Orange have traditionally been considered beneficial because they advanced the cause of parliamentary democracy and individual liberty. The Irish, however, have somewhat different views on the merits of these two gentlemen.

Positively Gothic

The term 'Gothic' is interesting in that it is derived from the fact that Roman, and later historians, labelled all the Germanic tribes on the northern borders of the Roman Empire as 'Goths'; 'Gothic' being a synonym for 'barbaric'. During the seventeenth century when Classical Italian Renaissance architecture came into vogue in England led by architects such as Inigo Jones and Christopher

Wren the style represented the triumphs of the Renaissance and Classical learning over medieval ignorance and superstition. Among some circles the cultural bias against medieval architecture was such that it was looked upon as uncouth and it was considered an insult to say that someone or something was 'positively Gothic'. This was following the lead of Renaissance intellectuals and writers such as Giorgio Vasari (1511-74) who believed that the arts had died in the early medieval 'Dark Ages' after being brought to the highest pitch of achievement in Ancient Rome. A civilisation over-run by the Goths who had introduced their accused 'German' architecture into once cultured lands, this architecture later being labelled 'Gothic'.

Nevertheless, in England there was no blanket contempt for the medieval past and seventeenth century Parliamentarians, seeking historical precedents in their struggles against the Crown, argued that the Saxons, as Germanic settlers in England, had inherited the love of liberty and freedom believed to have been an ingrained virtue of the tribal life of the Goths, especially as expressed in their successful resistance to the expansion of the Roman Empire.[6] The term 'Gothic', once used in the negative, was well and truly turned on its head and came to represent positive virtue. Interestingly, the Gothic Temple at Stowe bore the inscription 'I Thank God That I Am Not A Roman' to underline Richard Temple's view of himself as a freedom loving Goth in opposition to Absolutism.

The temple at Stowe, however, is not to be counted as the first structure in Britain to be built in the Gothic mode during the Georgian period for the purpose of making a political point. That distinction goes to the Gothic Temple (1716-17) at Shotover Park in Oxfordshire[7] built by James Tyrell to celebrate the establishment of the House of Hanover on the throne of England in 1714 along with the defeat of the Jacobites and the confounding of all their knavish tricks and devilish deceits. Other Gothic structures were built in the course of the eighteenth century, but nevertheless the Gothic Temple at Stowe is the one that particularly stands out in the history of English architecture, for it formed part, an integral part, of a political manifesto argued out in architectural form.

As the century progressed other features such as mock medieval ruins and Gothick summer houses appeared in country house gardens. This fashion for Gothic a natural part of the development of the English landscape movement expressing the freedom and openness of Nature.

Gothic Romance

The next logical step for the advance of Gothic architecture was to move from the parklands of noble estates to the mansion house itself. During the mid and latter half of the eighteenth century there arose in England the beginnings of a romantic Gothic movement in which gentleman antiquaries at both local and national level established societies to study ancient monuments, preserve authentic ruins and rebuild houses and churches in a pastiche of medieval Gothic with little attention to architectural accuracy. This phase of medieval revivalist architecture is termed 'Gothick' to distinguish it from nineteenth century 'Gothic' which is more true to the original. Nonetheless, the term 'Gothic Revival' is used as an umbrella term to cover all the various phases of mediaeval historicism, from playful Gothick to faithful Victorian reproduction.

To cater for this new Gothick taste, craftsmen and designers such as Batty Langley and Charles Over published pattern books with titles such *as Ancient Architecture, Restored and Improved* (1742) and *Ornamental Architecture in the Gothic, Chinese and Modern Tastes* (1758) illustrated with Gothic and other detailing for builders to reproduce. Henceforth, we find features such as battlements, towers, Gothic pointed arches, tracery windows, drip mouldings, fan-vaulted ceilings, canopied Gothic niches etc. appearing in the dwellings of the rich and fashionable. Much of this Gothicised work was initially carried out on previously built country houses that were being remodelled and adorned, some quite extensively, with fashionable Gothick.

Strawberry Hill, Twickenham, England.

The first country house to be built virtually from the ground up in a medieval manner was Horace Walpole's Strawberry Hill, a small villa at Twickenham near London that Walpole, a Whig MP from 1741 to 1767, extended over a period from 1753 to 1776 into a crenellated mansion with features such as pointed arch windows, battlemented tower and fan-vaulted ceilings. Walpole did not design the interiors and exteriors solely on his own for he was fortunate to have the assistance of two friends who comprised a 'Committee of Taste' with Walpole. Built in the middle of a century when first Palladianism and then neoclassicism were all the rage, Strawberry Hill was to prove a prescient forerunner of country house castellated architecture that was to become so very popular in Britain and Ireland over the following one hundred years. Inspired by the ongoing Strawberry Hill experiment, which was open to visitors, a fashion for building Gothic garden fancies spread and where once small Grecian temples and neoclassical statues had been the preferred element in a picturesque landscape, fashionable people now built Gothic summer houses with small leaded panes, or built Gothic ruins.[8]

Another important mile-stone in the development of the castellated style was Downton Castle (1771-8) in Herefordshire. Built asymmetrically, it was to prove hugely influential on architects such as John Nash and on the succeeding generation of architects, the likes of James and George Richard Pain who designed Dromoland Castle et al. in the same mode. Architectural historian Chris Brooks describes Downton as,

> 'Emphatically asymmetrical in plan, the external massing is strikingly irregular: ranges chopped into different lengths, towers of diverse heights and sorts, a squat off-centre block in the main elevation, odd little turrets and lots of battlements. Dramatically sited high above the River Terme, Downton is designed to be seen obliquely, conceived in terms of how it might look in the eyes of a spectator.'[9]

As the first consciously built Picturesque castle it was to be a worthy 'John the Baptist' to the arrival of the asymmetrical Picturesque movement that became fashionable from the mid-1790s onwards. Prior to that, mainstream castellated architecture in the 1780s and early '90s was predominately symmetrical.

Ireland

In Ireland a number of estate holders also participated in this exciting experimentation and one of the first stirrings of romantic Gothic in this country appeared at Castle Ward in Co. Down. Built c.1762, it is a 'two-faced' mansion in the sense that the front façade is in Classical mode with engaged columns, central pediment and all the other typical trappings of a grand eighteenth century country house, while in complete contrast the rear, garden-facing

Castle Ward, Co. Down, Northern Ireland. Front elevation in Classical mode.

Castle Ward - Gothic inspired garden elevation.

façade is decorated with Gothic detailing such as battlemented parapet, crocketed pinnacles and pointed tracery windows. Castle Ward, however, retains the structural form of a Georgian country mansion.[10]

Gothic garden buildings and eye-catchers were also being built, mainly as ruins, in Ireland on estates and parklands. One such example being the screen wall (1770s) at Heywood, Co Laois which is punctuated with authentic medieval windows taken from a nearby derelict abbey. Nearer home, at Castle Oliver in Co. Limerick we have the example of a sham castle ruin consisting of two ruinous looking towers linked by a curtain wall.[11] Whereas the intact Gothic Temple at Stowe expressed a positive political symbolism, the role of a sham medieval ruin set in a picturesque landscape could play a far more melancholy function, enabling those of a philosophical frame of mind to contemplate the various themes of: Strength overwhelmed by Nature; the Fall of Civilisations and the Mortality of all Man's Endeavours. More significantly, however, the sham Gothic ruin also served the function of associating the estate holder with the hereditary right to own land.

From the 1770s onwards a number of Irish castellated mansions came to be built in a manner known as 'Classical Gothic' whereby the exterior has towers, battlements etc. but the buildings themselves are symmetrical in plan with most of the interior Classically decorated. Many of these castellated houses were not new, but were earlier buildings that were extensively Gothicised on the exterior but still retaining the building's original symmetry.[12] An example being Castle Browne (Clongowes College), Co, Kildare which was originally a three storey house remodelled as a symmetrical Gothic Revival castle in 1788 with round towers at the corners.[13] A feature of Castle Browne, as with many other Irish castellated houses of the period, is the use of Irish stepped battlements. Other Gothicised Irish houses had a more checkered history, as in the case of Ballinlough Castle, Clonmellon in Co. Westmeath, which was an authentic castle converted into a two storey, seven-bay house in the 1730s. It was then given the full Gothic Revival treatment about fifty years later.[14]

Gothic Horror

This taste for Gothic decoration and fascination with ruins also coincided with a literary taste for the sensational, the supernatural and the ghoulishly graveyard-like; a taste that became labelled 'Gothic'. As well as building Strawberry Hill, Horace Walpole is doubly celebrated as the author of *The Castle of Otranto* (1764) which initiated a fashion for the 'Gothic novel', a genre popular in the late eighteenth and early nineteenth centuries and characterised by an atmosphere of mystery and horror located invariably in a pseudo-medieval setting over which reigns a cruel and lascivious tyrant. Walpole's *Castle of Otranto* is full of supernatural and overly melodramatic happenings interspersed with some quite tedious conversations, but the novel is sufficiently short and light enough to provide the modern reader with an easy introduction to the genre. A short description of the novel is not inapposite to this study, as George Richard Pain was to later paint, in 1831, a striking water-colour of the novel's denouement, such was the enduring impact of Walpole's creation on the romantic imagination.

The Castle of Otranto features a capricious Sicilian nobleman, Manfred, Prince of Otranto, given to fits of violent passion who is only brought to his senses after inadvertently stabbing to death his own daughter, Matilda, in a case of mistaken identity, for, in a fit of jealous rage he really intended to kill a highly desirable young lady, Isabella, whom he lusted after, but who fled in terror from his rapacious clutches, and who was to have been his daughter-in-law, that is until his only son and heir, Conrad, had been horribly mangled and crushed to death by a tremendously massive iron helmet that mysteriously fell from the sky and was deliberately dropped onto the poor unsuspecting lad by a revengeful and gigantic ghost called Alfonso who had been foully murdered by the grandfather of the villainous prince . . . the climax of the story comes when the ghost of Alfonso rises high above the castle of Otranto and the walls of the tyrant's fortress come crashing down.[15]

The English Gothic novel was further developed by writers such as Ann Radcliffe who wrote *A Sicilian Romance* (1790), *The Romance of the Forest* (1791) and *The Mysteries of Udolpho* (1794) whose plots typically featured a virginal heroine who, in the course of her adventures, is trapped at midnight in a bewildering labyrinth of dark castle passages, spiral staircases and dungeons while discovering dark secrets during her nocturnal explorations. Gothic novel settings include castles, monasteries and convents situated in a medieval style social order in which feudal aristos and mad monks freely indulge in their favourite pastimes of murder and rape. These dark deeds taking place in foreign lands such as Italy or Sicily where unbridled Latin passions reign and Protestant virtues are absent. The depraved depths to which Gothic lust could drag a man were fully explored in *The Monk* (1796), a novel by Matthew Lewis MP that plumbed the depths of pornographic violence.

The popularity of the Gothic novel, especially among middle-class females, came at a time of rising prosperity in Britain and a wider appreciation of the civilising effects of culture, taste and polite manners on society. However, as Elizabeth Jenkins remarked in her 1938 biography of Jane Austen,

> 'With the impulse natural to the human mind, the period that marked the highest reach of rational elegance in society saw at the same time the reaction towards the fascination with the

mysterious past; and people who liked to live in white-panelled rooms lighted with crystal lustres, who admired china in the delicious apple green and rose colour of Sèvres, who had their carriages painted primrose colour or vermilion, and their waistcoats sprigged with rosebuds, derived an agreeable titillation from reading about ruins infested with bats and screech owls, the nodding horror of forest boughs at nightfall, and the discomforts and perils of life in a haunted Gothic fortress.'[16]

A fascination caricatured in Jane Austen's first mature novel *Northanger Abbey* (written 1798-9, published 1818) in which the young Catherine Morland, her imagination inspired by her reading of Ann Radcliffe's novels, becomes terribly excited when she is invited to stay as a guest of the Tilneys at their country home, Northanger Abbey,

'Her passion for ancient edifices was next in degree to her passion for Henry Tilney . . . Northanger, it's long, damp passages, its narrow cells and ruined chapel, were to be within her daily reach, and she could not entirely subdue the hope of some traditional legends, some awful memorials of an injured and ill-fated nun.'[17] The lure of horror, for Miss Morland, being placed on the same exquisite level as sexual lure.

English Gothic - A Patriotic Style

By the 1790s, therefore, a considerable amount of interest in the romance of the Gothic past had been generated through literature, antiquarian studies and architectural experimentation as to lay the basis for the next phase in the Gothic Revival. Towards the turn of the century Gothic became increasingly acceptable in Britain and Ireland as an architectural style among wealthy estate holders, not only for whimsical buildings of small scale and dilettantish make overs, but also for new country houses of a substantial size incorporating the characteristics of a medieval castle. For, at the time of the French Revolution and Napoleonic Wars, a new accretion of meaning became attached to the Gothic Revivalist style. It came to represent the stability of a constitutional monarchy and aristocratic social order standing firm against the threat of social revolution and violent disinheritance posed by the Jacobin mob and French expansionism.

The identification of Gothic style with a sense of being patriotically English, or British, had, of course, been well established by this time due to the strong historical associations between the medieval past and the foundations of English political liberties. Gothic architecture had come to be regarded as a distinctive British style. To build in Gothic was to express one's nationality and patriotism. In 1796, for example, work commenced on the fantastical Fonthill Abbey in Wiltshire; a Gothic palace built under the instructions of William

Fonthill Abbey, Wiltshire, England. The tower collapsed in 1825.

Beckford who' had inherited a huge fortune largely based on slave sugar plantations in the West Indies, sugar islands over which the British and French fought in the 1790s and where thousands of soldiers died, mainly of disease. Like Walpole, Beckford was a Gothic novelist, publishing *Vathek* in 1786. The central tower at Fonthill was massively and stupendously Gothic, but the architect and masons lacked the skill of their medieval forefathers and the overweening tower collapsed into ruins in 1825.[18]

Separating English Gothic architecture out from the imagined horrors of Continental Gothicism was not that difficult, for English castles kept the enemy out while foreign fortresses and monasteries trapped the virtuous within. Besides, to behave in the depraved manner of The Monk, or the Tyrant of Otranto, was simply just not possible in Albion's fair isle, a belief articulated by Henry Tilney when he gently upbraids Catherine Morland for supposing that his father, General Tilney, the master of Northanger Abbey, had murdered his wife,

'Dear Miss Morland, consider the dreadful nature of the suspicions you have entertained. What have you been judging from? Remembering the country and the age in which we live. Remember that we are English, that we are Christians. Consult your own understanding, your own sense of the probable, your own observation of what is passing around you - Does our education prepare us for such atrocities? Do our laws connive at them? Could they be perpetrated without being known, in a country like this, where social and literary intercourse is on such a footing; where every man is surrounded by a neighbourhood of voluntary spies, and where roads and newspapers lay every thing open? Dear Miss Morland, what ideas have you been admitting?'[19]

There were, of course, many reasons why people were drawn to Gothic, not all of them overtly or consciously political. For there were those who felt that the rigidities of Classicism, with its overly defined rules and 'Orders', imposed too much discipline on artistic style - in the process stifling imagination, individuality and self-expression. The Palladian mansion and the urban Georgian terrace may represent social order, civilisation and regularity for the prospering bourgeoisie, but there is only so much that can be built in that manner before the eye gets weary and the soul revolts and yearns for something more adventurous. That was one of the reasons why Horace Walpole and others turned to Gothic, it was an escape from the humdrum, the conventional and the ordinary and gave flight to imagination and eccentricity. The artistic soul must soar above the Aonian Mount or else fall crashing to the ground and in Gothic adventurous architects and their wealthy patrons found the extraordinary. English Gothic became part of a broader European artistic and intellectual movement that developed from the 1790s onwards that became known as Romanticism; a movement in revolt against Classicism. A movement concerned with feelings, emotions, individualism, the picturesque, the asymmetrical, the awe and grandeur of Nature as a healthy emotive response to the rigidities of Greco-Roman symmetrical form with its emphasis on what constitutes 'correct' aesthetic proportion.

Essentially, two different stylistic approaches to the building of castellated houses had emerged by this stage, the Picturesque inspired by Downton Castle and the symmetrical. Those built in the Picturesque manner, the majority from the 1790s onwards, were asymmetrical in design, the exterior massing being irregular with battlemented and machicolated towers of diverse heights, sizes and shapes (round, square, octagonal) linked by battlemented ranges of various lengths; the ranges being one, two or three stories high. Slender little turrets rose over the entire composition making the exterior massing ever more irregular and asymmetrical, and as one walked around the building the pictorial composition was ever changing, no two

Bodiam Castle (fourteenth century), Sussex, England.

perspectives being identical. The eye of the beholder was foremost in the mind's eye of the designer as on his drawing board he assembled, rearranged, resized and shuffled around the various architectural elements until he achieved the aesthetic, picturesque effect he desired. Key to the success of the overall design was the landscape in which the building was to be set, the more picture painterly the surrounding countryside the better – Nature and Artifice working together in harmony to create a pleasing effect.

John Nash was a master of the Picturesque and he played, in partnership with landscape gardener Humphry Repton, an important role in developing and fine-tuning this style. Their joint work on Luscombe Castle (1799-1804) in Devon amply illustrating their talent for picturesque composition. Nash was to design a number of other castellated country houses in Britain including Ravensworth, (1808), Co. Durham; Caerhays Castle, Cornwall (c.1808) and East Cowes Castle, Isle of Wight, for himself from 1798 onwards.[20] Lough Cutra, Co. Galway was to be modelled on East Cowes. Of course Nash was not the only architect practicing in this field, among the most prominent was James Wyatt.

Besides Picturesque, there was another form of castellated architecture that emphasised the sublime and took a far less subtle approach with its emphasis on massive size, towering height, stern appearance, regularity and symmetry of design to achieve its primary effect of projecting a sense of social power and authority onto the outside world. Both stylistic approaches took inspiration from the many authentic medieval castles to be found throughout Britain, one of the most romantic being the fourteenth century Bodiam Castle in Sussex. Set within a large, pretty moat, its elegance of design casts a spell over the imagination.

Although there was much allusion to medieval splendours on the exteriors of Gothic houses, it was not to be expected that the inhabitants would want to live medieval lives. The romance of living in a stone-cold castle with narrow window openings stuffed with rags to keep out the draughts and nothing on the floor but rushes did not particularly appeal. Hence, Regency luxury within, the best of furnishings and large windows to let in the light, though hood-moulded to provide the authentic touch. In this sense the Picturesque, Regency castle was the ideal compromise between the romance of the past and the needs of the present.

Popularity in Ireland

From 1800 onwards the Picturesque style also began to be popular with Irish estate owners who, in search of the romantic and a sense of identity, engaged the services of a fashionable architect to build a castellated mansion from the ground up. During the first twenty years of the nineteenth century more than forty castles appeared in the country. The first major country house in Ireland to be built in the new style was Charleville Castle in Co. Offaly. Designed in 1801 by architect Francis Johnson for Viscount Charleville, it proved highly influential in popularising Gothic among the Anglo-Irish. Begun just three years after the 1798 Rebellion, Charleville Castle, is heavy in construction and defensive in appearance. With its stepped battlements, narrow entrance gate overhung by a massive corbelled arch and its heavily machicolated octagonal tower, narrow lights and smallish stone mullioned windows, Charleville has the appearance of a fortress, the masonry giving the castle a cold, suspicious air. A high, slender tower stands 125 feet (38.1 metres) above ground level surmounting a round corner turret and one can well imagine a trusty man-at-arms peering over the battlements of the watchtower keeping a wary eye on the restless natives.[21]

Castles and fortified houses of one sort or another had long been associated in Ireland with landed power and social status. Possession of a castle, even a mock one, spelt out ownership of the land going back to Norman times, even though in reality most of the Ascendancy had not come into their property until the Elizabethan, Cromwellian and Williamite conquests. Nevertheless, there were a number of landed Irish families that could genuinely trace their ancestry in Ireland back many generations unto the Middle Ages. The O'Briens of Dromoland, for example, could trace their line back to Irish Chieftan Brian Boru, who died at the Battle of Clontarf at 1016, while the Knights of Glin have been estate holders in Co. Limerick as far back as the thirteenth century.

The comforting, reassuring attraction of the Gothic style was so strong that a number of eighteenth century country houses were given a feudal make-over, a skin-deep Gothicism in which battlements, turrets and Gothic detailing were added on to the existing house to create the pretense of a castle, as in the case

Charleville Castle, Co. Offaly was the first castellated house in Picturesque style built in Ireland.

of Glin House/Castle *c.*1812. These battlemented exteriors have of course absolutely no defensive value, but they are conveying messages about power, status and authority. They go beyond fancy, show and fashion for they are making an explicit political point.

The building of castellated houses in Ireland was also justified by a strongly held belief that Gothic architecture was particularly suited to the rugged, unspoiled and picturesque nature of the Irish countryside. James Brewer in his *The Beauties of Ireland*, published in the mid 1820s, expressed the idea that man-made Gothic and God-given Nature were in complete harmony, one with another,

'This bold and harsh, but splendid species of design is well adapted to the recluse parts of Ireland, where nature reigns in wild and mysterious majesty. The towers, the ramparts, and long irregular lines of military grandeur which characterise the castellated house, assimilate with the lofty mountains and wide-spread lakes of this romantic island.'[22]

John Nash in Ireland

It is at this point in the first decade of the nineteenth century that John Nash steps onto the Irish scene with a series of four Gothic compositions designed over a ten-year period that were generally more gentle in appearance than Charleville Castle. The first being Killymoon, Co. Tyrone, built *c.*1803. Then followed Kilwaughter, Larne, Co. Antrim (built *c.*1807); Col. Vereker's Lough Cutra, Co. Galway (1811 - *c.*1817) and Shanbally Castle, Co. Tipperary (1812-19).[23]

By assisting with the introduction of the fully-fledged Picturesque style into Ireland, a style that had evolved in England over a long number of years, Nash played an important role in the development of country house Gothic in Ireland. Work that continued on through James Pain when Nash handed over his Irish commissions to his favoured pupil as executing architect. When the Pain brothers established their own practice they carried on an architectural tradition able to trace its roots back to Downton Castle, Strawberry Hill and beyond to the garden buildings of Whig grandees.

Shanbally Castle near Cahir in Co. Tipperary, was to be Nash's final and largest Irish castellated house on which, in all probably, James Pain supervised construction over the period 1812-19. However, it was a bit 'overcooked', especially on the garden front which featured a round tower on the left-hand corner, an octagonal tower on the right, and a central feature flanked by two square towers. There was also a Gothic conservatory arcade on this elevation. The entire frontage was altogether too cluttered. In front of the whole stood a symmetrical balustraded terrace from the centre of which two flights of steps, set in a balustraded, symmetrical staircase, led down to the garden. While such a feature is perfectly ideal for buildings in the Classical manner, it was at odds in front of a building posing as medieval.

There were just too many window styles at Shanbally for just the one building - Gothic pointed, Gothic mullioned rectangular, single lancets, as well as several arrangements composed of three long, narrow lights placed close together. The fenestration on one of the round towers saw pointed Gothic windows on the ground floor, rectangular on the first, and narrow lights on the upper. Whereas machicolation and crenellation is an integral part of the castellated country house, in this case, with such a proliferation of window styles, the machicolation was just additional clutter.

Shanbally Castle, Co. Tipperary, John Nash's largest Irish castellated house.

A very wide range of Gothic vaulting styles were employed on the ceilings of the principal rooms of the house. Every conceivable vault seems to have been put in place, the delicate plasterwork and the variety of styles being quite impressive. Fan vaulting was used to great effect overhead the main staircase and in the main hall, while elsewhere could be seen rib vaulting with hanging keystone, rib vaulting with bosses, half vaults used as a cornice and more besides. Shanbally Castle was a veritable treasure house in terms of its Gothic ceilings, so it is highly regrettable that the house is no more.

Shanbally came to a very sad end in the 1950s when the Land Commission, a Government department, acquired the castle and its 1,000-acre estate. By 1957 the decision had been made to level the house to the ground, demolition work beginning in September of that year. With seething anger, architectural historian Randal MacDonnell relates the story of Shanbally's brutal destruction:

'. . . . the Land Commission sold the castle to a Limerick firm who razed it to the ground in order to salvage the materials from the ruins. A Limerick auctioneer sold these at public auction. The philistines who did this were merely symptomatic of the general attitude of the population at the time . . . Finally, in 1960, explosives had to be used to demolish what remained of the castle, so well had it been built. According to one newspaper report, the stone walls were demolished with 'one big bang' by charges of gelignite after demolition experts had bored no fewer than 1400 holes into the walls about 18 inches from the ground.'[24]

The 'philistine' attitude of the Irish populace at that time towards the 'Big House' and Georgian architecture in general was rooted in bitter historical memory and folklore tradition. The very word 'Georgian' conjured up images of exploiting Protestant landlords rack-renting the peasantry, Penal Laws persecuting Catholics, extreme poverty, famine and draconian repression against those who resisted by arms the Imperial power. With the rise of nineteenth century Irish Catholic Nationalism and the foundation of the Free State this once powerful Ascendancy had been reduced to rather sad and pathetic remnants living in ever-crumbling country mansions. In the culturally enclosed, economically challenged, narrow-minded Ireland of the 1950s who among the 'real' Irish would be interested in the preservation and restoration of 'Planter' mansions and bedraggled Georgian terraces.

Happily, such attitudes of neglect towards this country's built heritage have changed quite radically over the past twenty-five years, a sign of Ireland's growing sense of outgoing self-confidence and engagement with Europe and a more mature sense of Irish history. Whatever one's view of that history, Ireland's eighteenth and nineteenth century 'High' architecture was strongly influenced by Europe's Gothic and Classical traditions reaching back centuries and as such is a valuable part of a shared European cultural heritage and identity that should be cherished.

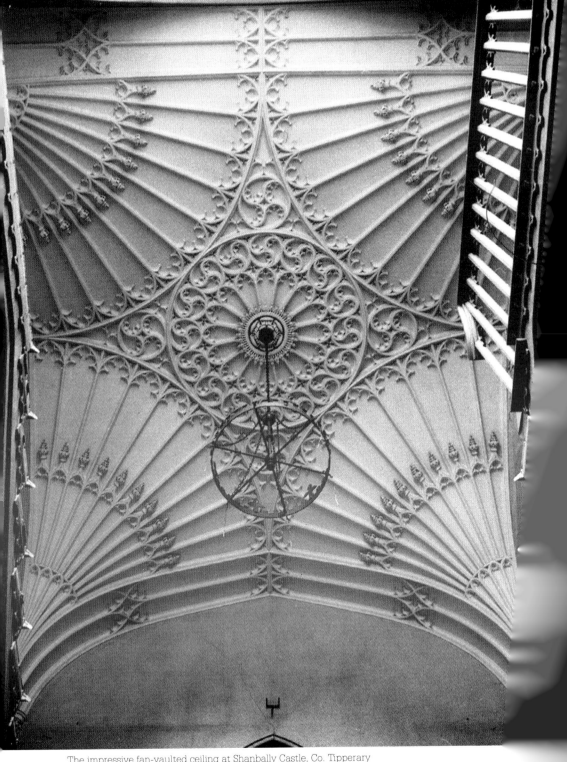

The impressive fan-vaulted ceiling at Shanbally Castle, Co. Tipperary

Endnotes

1 Adams, William Howard *Nature Perfected*, Abbeville Press, New York, 1991, p. 139f.

2 Howley, J. *The Follies and Garden Buildings of Ireland*, Yale University Press, New Haven and London, 1993, p. 4.

3 ibid. p. 141.

4 Brooks, C. *The Gothic Revival*, Phaidon, London, 1999, pp. 54-5.

5 Hill, Christopher 'The Norman Yoke', *Puritanism and Revolution: Studies in Interpretation of the English Revolution of the 17th Century*, Martin Secker & Warburg, 1958.

6 The most spectacular example of Gothic resistance took place in 9 AD when Arminius, a German chieftain, united various Germanic tribes in opposition to Roman expansionism east of the Rhine, utterly annihilating three Roman legions at the Battle of Teutoburger Wald and preventing Germany from being absorbed into the Empire. Arminius, as a supposed blood ancestor of the Saxons, came to be regarded as virtually an English hero. The English admiration for their Germanic roots extended well into the nineteenth century with the English historian Edward Creasy writing in his *Fifteen Decisive Battles of the World* (1852): 'The main stream of our people [the English] was and is Germanic. Our language decisively proves this. Arminius is far more truly one of our national heroes than Caractacus [an Ancient Celtic Briton who fought against the Roman invaders] . . . It may be added that an Englishman is entitled to claim a closer degree of relationship with Arminius than can be claimed by any German on modern Germany.' Creasy, Edward *Fifteen Decisive Battles of the World from Marathon to Waterloo* (1852), republished by Dorset Press, New York, 1987, pp. 116, 129.

7 Brooks *op. cit.* pp. 51-2.

8 ibid. pp. 85-93.

9 Brookes, *op. cit.* p. 163

10 O'Brien, J. & Guinness, D. *Great Irish Houses and Castles*, Weidenfeld & Nicolson Ltd., London, 1993, pp. 142-7.

11 Howley *op. cit.* pp. 109-10; 112-3.

12 For a discussion of Irish Classical Gothic houses see: Rowan, A. J. 'Georgian Castles in Ireland - 1', *Bulletin of the Irish Georgian Society* Vol. VII, No. 1, January-March 1964.

13 Bence-Jones, Mark *A Guide to Irish Country Houses*, Constable, London, revised edition 1988, s.v. 'Castle Browne'.

14 ibid. s.v. 'Ballinlough Castle'.

15 Walpole, Horace *The Castle of Otranto* (1764).

16 Jenkins, Elizabeth *Jane Austen*, Sphere Books, 1973, p. 70. Originally published by Victor Gollancz Ltd., 1938.

17 Austen, Jane *Northanger Abbey*, Chap. 17.

18 Honour, Hugh *Romanticism*, Allen Lane, London, 1979, p. 176; Brooks *op. cit.* pp. 155-7.

19 Austen, Jane *Northanger Abbey* Chap. 24.
20 Covin, H. *A Biographical Dictionary of British Architects 1600*-1840, 3rd edition, Yale University Press, New Haven & London, 1995 s.v. 'Nash, John'.
21 Richardson, Douglas Scott *Gothic Revival Architecture in Ireland*, 2 Vols., Garland Publishing Inc., New York and London, 1983, Vol. I, pp.119-23.
22 Brewer, James *The Beauties of Ireland*, 2 Vols., Sherwood, Jones & Co., London, 1825-6, Vol. I, p. cxxxi.
23 Davis, Terence 'John Nash in Ireland', *Bulletin of the Irish Georgian Society* Vol. VIII, No. 2, April - June 1965; Bence-Jones *op. cit.* s.v. 'Killymoon Castle'; 'Kilwaughter Castle'; 'Lough Cutra Castle'; 'Shanbally Castle'.
24 MacDonnell, Randal *The Lost Houses of Ireland*, Weidenfeld & Nicolson, London, 2002, p. 195.

CHAPTER SEVEN

HIGH GOTHIC PERIOD 1819-1838

Dromoland Castle

Although Burke's *Visitation of Seats* published in 1855 says that Dromoland Castle 'was commenced in 1822', it seems fairly certain that building work began several years earlier in 1820. For, in the spring of that year Sir Edward, writing to Dromoland from London (where he sat as an MP), asks his wife Lady Charlotte to inform 'Mr. Pain', (presumably James Pain as he was the senior partner) that the new house is to be built in 'the very best manner & of the very best materials.' Lady Charlotte was also instructed to tell the architect that with building work about to start he was not to cut down more oak trees on the estate than was necessary. Two years later, in the early summer of 1822, it is evident from Sir Edward's correspondence that building work had been proceeding for some time as, with distress in Clare being caused by a potato failure that year, Sir Edward wrote to his wife saying that since their income from rents had virtually ceased he might have to contemplate halting construction on their new house if finances did not improve. He also writes 'The parts of the House that are finished look very well & executed in the very best manner.'[1]

Water-colour of Dromoland, Co. Clare showing completed western section of Castle standing beside the eighteenth century mansion before the latter was demolished.

The extended period over which Dromoland Castle was built, some nineteen years between 1819 and 1838, makes it difficult to identify precisely the dates of the various construction phases as it was not built in one continuous flow of building activity. Up to the mid-1820s the family lived in the eighteenth century mansion alongside the western section of the new Gothic house as it was being built. The old house was then demolished and, after a delay of several years, work commenced on the eastern section of the Castle about 1832, ending c.1838.[2] When Lady Chatterton visited Dromoland that year she noted that the Castle was 'now nearly finished.'[3]

Throughout, Sir Edward O'Brien insisted that not only was the workmanship and materials to be of the highest quality, he was also determined to be economical in purchasing materials and house furnishings so as to keep the entire project within his financial limits. Cost conscious, he was constantly comparing the prices of furnishings between Limerick and Dublin, London and Manchester, and was quite delighted when he could obtain goods at discount.[4] Sir Edward also took a keen and informed interest in the design of his new home and there was constant dialogue between architects and patron over architectural detailing. In 1820, for example, he wrote instructing the architects that they were to make the 'End window of the Gallery looking on to the yard have a Handsome Gothic Head' as 'it gives an appearance to all the windows of it of Cloisters which I have seen in some Houses . . . so that it would have the appearance of a Chapel.'[5]

The meticulous approach of Sir Edward concerning his new mansion meant that Dromoland Castle was built with tender loving care, with great attention to detail being shown by both the patron and architects alike. It can be judged the most successful of the Pain brother's contribution to country house Gothic - better than their Strancally Castle (c.1830) in Co. Waterford and certainly far superior to Mitchelstown Castle (1823-6) in Co. Cork. Sir Edward died in May 1837 before he saw the finishing touches applied to his grand project, his son Sir Lucius O'Brien (13th Baron Inchiquin b. 1800, d. 1872) succeeding to the inheritance and completing the work.[6]

Dromoland is a most attractive composition in early nineteenth century Picturesque and it owes its attractiveness and enchantment to several features, including the beautiful lakeside setting of the house and the parkland in which it is situated with its woods, pleasant walks and gently rising grassy slopes. Externally Dromoland Castle uses many of the features to be found in asymmetrical castellated architecture. The entire complex of house and service quarters is castellated throughout and the cornices around the principal towers are extensively machicolated, the windows mullioned. But it is how the various architectural features and components are arranged, one with another, that gives Dromoland its pleasing Picturesque qualities. The

Dromoland Castle, Co. Clare, now a hotel.

whole is dominated by an imposing round tower and a strong, military-looking square tower with a number of lesser towers (one a polygon) and turrets to give a varied and eye-engaging medieval skyline to the structure. The castle is friendly and welcoming, with the tall, elegant, slender chimneys rising from the battlements signalling to the weary traveller the prospect of warm cosy fires and comfort within. Lady Chatterton, writing of her visit to Dromoland in 1838, informed her readers that 'Sir Lucius O'Brien lives there in a style of hospitable splendour, which does justice to his good taste and kind heart: the rich are welcome, and the poor taken care of.'[7]

The asymmetrical nature of the castle, the varying heights of the ranges, being one, two or three storeys high, all ensure that the visitor's attention is focused onto the castle and that from whatever angle one chooses to look at Dromoland, each and every perspective is different one from another revealing another facet of the composition, another explanation of what distinguishes excellence in Picturesque Gothic from the mere mediocre and passable. If one had to choose just a few Irish castellated houses to survive while all others were wiped off the face of the earth by some Divine Act of Wrath, then Dromoland Castle has to be included in the list of those to be saved.

It is against this backdrop that the O'Briens might have imagined a tournament being held on their grassy parkland, such as one described by Sir Walter Scott in his celebrated medieval novel *Ivanhoe* published in 1819, the same year Sir Edward made his decision to build Dromoland Castle. Perhaps the fair and lovely Lady Rowena, 'formed in the best proportions of her sex', might appear and preside over the field of Chivalry as 'the Queen of Love and Beauty' to offer the prize to the victor of combats fought lance-to-lance, sword-to-sword, hand-to-hand,

'. . . the knights held their long lances upright, their bright points glancing to the sun, and the streamers with which they were decorated fluttering over the plumage of the helmets . . . The trumpets sounded . . . the spears of the champions were at once lowered . . . the spurs were dashed into the flanks of the horses, and the foremost ranks . . . rushed upon each other in full gallop, and met in the middle of the lists with a shock, the sound of which was heard at a mile's distance.'[8]

Cultural Escapism

Sir Walter Scott's novel *Ivanhoe*, set in late twelve century England at the time of King John and Richard the Lionheart, captured the public imagination and in Scott's wake medievalism became an increasingly important element in British mainstream culture. One of the themes dealt with by the novel is the 'Norman Yoke', the oppression of Saxons by Norman rulers and the loss of Anglo-Saxon liberties. By novel's end this conflict is resolved by a symbolic marriage heralding the reconciliation of the two races and the formation of a new English nation combining the best elements of both. Although at times Scott was critical of the barbarity of the twelfth century, his popular appeal was based on a portrayal of medieval society as an ordered entity that had a clear, ordained hierarchy from castle hall to peasant hearth. A close-knit baronial society of *noblesse oblige* in which the social orders from high to low were harmoniously bound together by a code of mutually understood obligations, duties and sacrifices. Scott further developed the romance of the Middle Ages with subsequent novels emphasising the merits of feudal loyalties and the virtues of chivalry in overcoming threats to the social fabric.

There was a genuine 'spiritual' hunger for such a portrayal, for the High Middle Ages were seen as the Golden Age of English history representing for many artists, writers and conservative members of the educated public an inspiring contrast to the Industrial Revolution then in full flight in Britain. Industrial capitalism had brought dynamic social forces into play that not only undermined the traditional political power and influence of the landed class, but also ushered in the threat of class conflict and social instability. The ruling classes did not have to wait for Karl Marx and Friedrich Engels to thunder in their *Communist Manifesto* of 1848 'A spectre is haunting Europe - the spectre of Communism' before they understood the perils posed by the proletariat. Had not the terrors of the French Revolution provided ample warning enough of the dire consequences attendant upon a ruling elite losing control of society. By contrast, according to a highly romanticised and idealised vision of the Middle Ages, medieval society was believed to have been a harmonious and seamless whole in which masters and craftsmen worked happily together in trade guilds for the common good rather than engaging in strikes, lockouts and bitter disputes. Industrial society was also regarded as the province of cheap and shoddily made factory goods rather than the beautiful, lovingly handcrafted artefacts made by medieval artisans. Accordingly, one aspect of nineteenth century medievalism was an emphasis on handmade goods, crafts and furnishings. The medieval period was also seen as an Age of Faith in which religious unity reigned where the lower orders knew their place and did not go around joining plebian Dissenting and Nonconformist sects that in the early nineteenth century were challenging the authority of the Church of England.

The 1830s and '40s in Britain witnessed a really significant outburst of medievalism in British art and design which brought about an artistic movement known as 'Gothic Revival' (A Victorian church architectural style) to distinguish this phase of neo-Gothic from the preceding phases of Gothick and Romantic Regency Gothic. A key figure associated with this Victorian Gothic Revival was Augustus Pugin (1812-52), an architect who stood forth as the leading theorist and polemicist of this new artistic wave which sought to accurately reproduce the architectural style of the High Middle Ages, especially the ecclesiastical architecture of the thirteenth and fourteenth centuries. In 1835, at the age of 23, Pugin converted to Catholicism and was of the belief that one of the first steps in recreating a harmonious society, in which England would reconvert to Rome, was to build churches in the medieval style; ecclesiastical Gothic being seen as a Trojan Horse for Rome. There was also an Anglican High Church movement that hankered for the power and authority of the pre-Reformation Church, but not in the form of the Catholic Church as advocated by the likes of Pugin.

Of course, all this romantic idealisation of medieval society, with its associated political agenda of lament for the fall of the landed aristocracy and the utopian hope of Pugin & Co. for a return of the old ways was in many ways historically naïve and politically reactionary. Karl Marx writing in 1844 about the sorrow expressed for the replacement of the aristocracy of the land by the aristocracy of money said 'We refuse to join in the sentimental tears which romanticism sheds on this account' (Marx *First Manuscript - Economic and Philosophical Manuscripts*). However, Marx was out of step with current cultural trends, for medievalism became rampant in British society, catching the reactive mood of the period even though the country's wealth was based on industrial capitalism.

Undoubtedly one of the appeals of asymmetrical Gothic for conservatives was that with its greater, lesser and intermediate towers and turrets, its greater and lesser ranges, the architect fixed permanently in stone a hierarchy of architectural features that expressed a vision of an ideal, hierarchical society with everything in its pre-ordained place.

Pomp, Pageantry and Splendour

It was during the first year of construction at Dromoland that the Prince Regent, patron of architect John Nash, succeeded to the Throne as King George IV. To celebrate this happy event a joint military and civic parade of great pomp, pageantry and splendour was held in Limerick on 8 February 1820 in which the trade guilds with their flags and banners, the alderman and burgesses of Limerick Corporation in crimson and black robes, mace bearers and the City Sword Bearer all participated. The military contingent consisted of the 23rd Regiment (Royal Welch Fusileers) with muskets and bayonets fixed, a company of grenadiers, trumpeters, three military bands and a regiment of dashingly handsome hussars, all superbly turned out in their flamboyant Regency uniforms. Also parading that day through the streets of the city were the Worshipful Master, Wardens and Brethren of The Antient Masonic Lodge No. 13 (James Pain's Lodge) 'elegantly attired' and 'wearing robes, Masonic regalia and bearing emblems appropriate to their office and degree.'[9]

It was a glittering affair made even more glorious by the reportage in the *Limerick General Advertiser* of 11 February. Written with gushing overenthusiasm, the account created the image of a city united and loyal behind the British monarchy. It was not merely a large parade, it was 'vast' in size; 'thousands' enthusiastically shouting their homage and hurrahs to the new King, while the artisans of the city were as committed in their attachment to the government of the country as were those of 'rank and fashion'. The editor was to allow no one to rain on this parade.

Goth House

The accession of the new King was to be a factor in the Pain brothers receiving the largest country house commission of their careers. In 1823 they were approached by George King, 3rd Earl of Kingston to build a Gothic pile for him at Mitchelstown in north Co. Cork, a structure that the Earl, known as 'Big George', modestly requested should be the biggest house in all Ireland.[10] This stipulation meant that size predominated over proportion and, as can be seen from surviving photographs (the castle was demolished in the 1920s), Mitchelstown had a certain ponderous architectural quality giving the distinct feeling that, out of pure malice, the building might keel over and crush one under its sheer weight of stone. Part of the problem was that it was built in great haste in the expectation that George IV and his entourage would visit Mitchelstown when he next visited Ireland, the monarch having promised the Earl to do so when he last came to Erin's green shores in 1821.

The contrast between Dromoland and Mitchelstown could not have been more marked, for if Dromoland was in a Picturesque mode, then Mitchelstown was heavy, coercive, and inclined towards the Sublime. Whereas Dromoland was some nineteen years in the making, and built with great care and attention, the great pile of Mitchelstown was thrown up in the space of just three years[11] with little regard for aesthetics. Placed on the top of a windswept hill, its purpose was to impress the multitude. Of all the castellated country house assignments the Pain brothers were involved with during the course of their professional careers, Mitchelstown was the least pleasing to the eye.

A visitor to Mitchelstown in 1828, Furst von Hermann Ludwig Heinrich, Prince of Pückler-Muskau, made the rather apt comment 'We were shown a huge heap of stones . . . but there was one ingredient missing . . . good taste.' A statement with which it would be difficult to disagree. The Prince also observed that the edifice stood 'on the bare turf, without the slightest picturesque break, which castles in the Gothic or kindred styles peculiarly need. The building is much too high for its extent, the style is confused, without variety; the outline heavy, and the effect small though the mass is great.'[12] The Prince was no intellectual light-weight in these matters, for he was a leading landscape designer and theorist who created one of Europe's most spectacular landscape gardens at his estate at Bad Muskau on the Prussian-Polish border.

Mitchelstown Castle, Co. Cork.

The south façade of Mitchelstown, with a vast square tower in the centre, was plain, massive and overbearing. The east front had a tall gate tower, standing seven stories high! Known as the White Tower, it was the main entrance to the castle and boasted a door some 15 feet (4.5 metres) in height standing beneath a 25 feet (7.6 metres) high Tudor arch, the entrance flanked by two slender octagonal towers. Everything about the building was on the grand scale with its 93 feet (28.3 metres) long Gothic vaulted gallery and its suites of guest rooms that could accommodate up to 100 guests at a time. In the middle of the building stood a large courtyard. The entire structure was faced with ashlar limestone.

That the scale of the structure bordered on the grotesque is evidenced by the following description of the King's Bedroom by the Hon. Mrs. Mary Robertson which reads as if it were an extract from Mervyn Peake's *Titus Groan*. Forty-one steps of stairs led to the bedroom which was, 'of such a size that on a misty night it was difficult to see across it . . . The immense canopied four-poster was like a fortress, only gained by assault, crowning, as it did, the summit of a raised platform.'[13]

A contributor to Samuel Lewis's *Topographical Dictionary* (1837) expressed a kinder opinion of the structure, describing the castle as 'noble and sumptuous', the whole pile having the 'character of baronial magnificence.' What particularly impressed the contributor was the 100 feet (30.5 metres) long conservatory with its 'beautiful Ionic pilasters.'[14]

Given the scale of the building project, the manual nature of building work at that time, and the speed with which the castle was erected, the construction site must have been a great hive of activity with a swarm of workers and craftsmen - masons, stonecutters, carpenters, plasterers, painters, bricklayers, plumbers and associated apprentices, carters, labourers and tea boys - all working diligently to achieve Big George's pharaonic vision,

> 'Brick was fired in the demesne brickfield; limestone was cut from local quarries . . . and carted to the building. The best timbers from the Baltic and India were imported through Youghal and Dungarvan and transported by road and boat along the Black water . . . The castle dominated the life and landscape of Mitchelstown for the next hundred years. Standing on a cliff edge with gently sloping woodland and lawns on the southern side, it was a spectacular sight, visible for miles around.'[15]

Improvements

Mitchelstown Castle was said to have cost more than £100,000 to build[16] (Dromoland half that amount), a figure that would translate into many millions of today's money. Despite the huge costs involved this was not to be the end of the 3rd Earl's extravagance. He spent a similar sum on his estate and the town of Mitchelstown, including £3,000 allocated to building a new market house, which included a courtroom overhead.[17] The architects being the ever versatile Pain brothers[18] even though the plaque on the building bears the inscription, 'Built by George, Earl of Kingston. AD 1823.' Other building projects financed by him during this period included the construction of a new Kingston School (1827) in George Street[19] and the building of Brigown Fever Hospital (1823)[20] with its four wards and thirteen beds.

Market House, Mitchelstown, Co. Cork. A typical market house of the period with arcades on the ground floor, now filled in with shop windows.

As proprietor of the town of Mitchelstown 'Big George' did make a number of improvements to the local economy, such as the provision of a number of new access roads into the town including one to Lismore, thereby shortening the distance to this river port and reducing transport costs. He was also responsible for installing a water pump operated by machinery in King's Square. Enclosed in iron railings, this facility was unveiled in 1825.[21]

The patronage of the Earl of Kingston helped to bring about the rebuilding of the church of St. George sited at the southern end of George Street in Mitchelstown. This Anglican house of worship served the parish of Brigown and was originally built as a simple boxlike edifice at the private expense of Caroline, Dowager Countess of Kingston, George's mother, in 1800.[22] Whoever the architect, it was poorly built, for it collapsed in 1802, was rebuilt in 1803 only to collapse once again the following year and resurrected for a second time in 1805.[23] Considered too small to cater for the needs of the congregation, it was significantly remodelled and enlarged by the Pain brothers in 1830 for £1,800, the Earl contributing £500.[24] The brothers' work as architects is acknowledged by the plaque over the entrance to the church, as is the 3rd Earl's donation. With its tall tower and high, slender octagonal spire the church, sited at the higher end of the George Street avenue, can be viewed to best advantage from the King's Square direction and is one of a number of striking vistas to be seen in the town.

The vast Kingstown domain of tens of thousands of acres also incorporated the parish of Marshalstown, which lies to the west of Mitchelstown and Brigown

St. George's Church, Mitchelstown, Co. Cork.

parish, and in 1830 Big George donated £200 towards the cost of building a parish church at Marshalstown[25] to a design by James Pain. The Earl also provided money for a new glebe house.[26] The church is now in ruins.

The Earl also gave the local Catholic community a site in Mitchelstown for their new parish church and a £420 donation towards the building costs. St. Fanahan's, consecrated in 1834[27] and cruciform in plan,[28] was built on a hill overlooking the town and its main square. It is said to be by the Pain brothers[29] since plans to build the church were well advanced in the mid-1820s, the *Limerick Chronicle* reporting on Saturday 29 May 1824, 'The Earl of Kingston has lately appropriated a most eligible site for a new chapel, at Mitchelstown.' This places the Pain brothers well within the time frame, for they were in the midst of their many labours for the Earl and it seems reasonable to suggest that they may have been asked to submit a proposal to the local Catholic authorities.

When first built it had no tower or spire, the entrance front being flanked 'with two octangular [*sic*] towers surmounted by cupolas.' These turrets would have been slender, the intermediate roofline of the gable end presumably battlemented. Since Lewis also states that the front gable was 'embellished with a window of elegant design' and that the church was of the 'later English style of architecture'[30] the window tracery presumably would have been Perpendicular.[31] This central feature occupying a significant area of the gable, being perhaps five lights in width. The doorway would have been Tudor arch. Although no illustration is extant of St. Fanahan's original frontage there were several examples of this type of church built for the Catholic Church elsewhere in Ireland during this period. These also employing a large central window, Tudor doorway and a pair of slender battlemented octagonal turrets terminated with small spires or cupolas, or in other cases just simply battlemented. The use of octagonal corner turrets was actually quite popular in English-speaking countries in the period 1820s - '40s, the architecture based on King's College Chapel (1146-1515), Cambridge in England.[32] An astonishing building, although it has no tower or transcepts, King's College Chapel is an amazing example of Perpendicular Gothic architecture with its spectacular traceried windows and fabulous fan vaulted ceiling.

In 1847 the frontage of St. Fanahan's was remodelled with a square tower installed, surmounted by a slender octagonal spire, and the central bay window and turrets removed; the remaining sections of the gable roofline still retaining their battlements. Given the elevated nature of the site overlooking the town these additions literally raised the architectural profile of the Catholic Church in Mitchelstown and if it could not compete with the vastness of the castle, at least it refused to be intimidated. The church was renamed The Church of the Immaculate Conception in 1855.[33] The tower, with its date stone

'1847', and spire, is now the sole surviving feature of the mid-nineteenth century church, the main body having been removed in controversial circumstances in 1978 and replaced by a modern structure two years later.[34] It is perhaps unlikely that James Pain was involved in the 1847 modification for reasons that will now be made apparent.

Massive Debts

It appears that the architects did not receive full recompense for all their labours at Mitchelstown, for in a will drawn up by James Pain on 11 January 1863 the now elderly architect declares:

> 'There is due and owing to me and secured by the Master in Chancery's returns on the estate of the late George, Earl of Kingston of Mitchelstown Castle the sum of £1,096 - 19 shillings - 3 pence, or thereabouts. If this sum can be obtained . . . .'[35] (Appendix IV - The Will of James Pain).

According to the document, if the sum could be recovered it was to be divided equally between a nephew and two nieces. But I fear the nominated beneficiaries went without for a while longer because the estate remained in chronic debt for many years. It was Big George who had placed the estate's finances into the red by his manic architectural spending spree in the 1820s. He subsequently developed mental illness that manifested itself in April 1830 as acute paranoia; in addition, he suffered two strokes resulting in impaired memory and speech. Packed off to a 'lunatic' asylum in England, he was declared insane and the management of his affairs placed in the hands of the Lord Chancellor that year, the Earl's son being allowed just £6,000 a year to run the great house and estate.[36] It is possible that the debt to the Pains dates from this period and that the architects pulled out of any further involvement with the Kingston estate when the balance of their fees went unpaid.

The 4th Earl, Robert Henry King, the son and heir to Big George who died in 1839, himself became embroiled in serious financial difficulties in the 1840s and much of the estate had to be sold off to pay the creditors. The estate was taken over by the Incumbered Estates Court which by 1856 had sold off 70,800 acres of land;[37] but clearly James Pain received no benefit from this particular sale. It does appear, however, that the debt was finally cleared at a later date, but not until after James's death. In 1876 a major sale of the contents of Mitchelstown Castle and a further sale of lands raised £253,000 to service old debts; the debt to James Pain finally being cleared when 'his will was resworn with the addition of £1,000 in 1879,'[38] a year and a half after the architect's death in December 1877.

The Frenchman's Judgement

From its earliest days, Mitchelstown Castle took on the role of symbolic monument to the overreaching extravagance of the Anglo-Irish Ascendancy and their social decline. When Alexis de Tocqueville (political scientist and author of that great classic in political literature, *Democracy in America*) passed through Mitchelstown on his visit to Ireland in July and August 1835 he saw the Earl's mental and financial problems as representative of a general malaise affecting the Anglo-Irish aristocracy. When, according to de Tocqueville, the Earl of Kingston discovered that he was faced with massive debts of £400,000, without hope of ever being able to repay them, he went mad. 'See the finger of God!' declaims the Frenchman. 'The Irish aristocracy wished to remain separated from the people and remain English. It has striven to imitate the English aristocracy without having its spirit and its resources, and it dies where it has sinned.' Mitchelstown Castle, classic example of architectural monumentalism financed by an unsustainable budget deficit, was but a grandiose fig leaf to cover a social class that had had its day. For de Tocqueville the significance of Big George's debts were that they were owed to the 'Catholic merchants of Cork' who held mortgages on the estate and received all the income. 'The Irish have been dispossessed by force of arms. They return to the estates by industry.'[39]

Writing ten years before the onset of the Great Famine the political philosopher's main conclusion about the role of the Anglo-Irish aristocracy in society was quite damning,

> 'England and Ireland have the same language, the same laws, the same social structure, they are subject to the same government, and there are no [two] countries that present a more different appearance. Both have been for a long time, and are still in many respects, subject to a powerful aristocracy. This aristocracy has produced great wealth in England and frightful poverty in Ireland . . .

> 'The particular misfortune of this country [Ireland] has been to fall into the hands of an upper class who are different from the masses in race, in custom, and in religion and who nevertheless were invested with sovereign power, which they exercise under cover of the all-powerful protection of England. Consequently, therefore, two nations entirely distinct on the same soil. The one rich, civilised, happy; the other poor, half savage and overwhelmed by all the miseries by which God can strike man.'[40]

Prophetic Curse

Before his illness 'Big George', according to local folklore, had a reputation for having a demonic temper. On the larger stage of Irish history George King made an appearance as a less than appealing character, for during the suppression of the 1798 Rebellion he was colonel-commandant of the North Cork Militia, a unit that gained a fearsome reputation as acting with considerable savagery towards suspected rebels. One of the techniques of torture employed by the militiamen was the pouring of molten tar onto a suspect's head - the pain and the agony can only be imagined. At the time George was Viscount Kingsborough (his brother, the 2nd Earl, dying in 1799) and in the spring of 1798 was based in Dublin where, according to one graphic eyewitness account, he took sadistic delight in the torture of prisoners,

> 'As a gentleman of respectability was passing near the old Custom House, in the afternoon of Whit-Sunday, 1798, two spectacles of horror covered with pitch and gore, running as if blind through the streets arrested his attention. They were closely followed out of the old Custom House by Lord Kingsborough, Mr. John Beresford and an officer in uniform. They were pointing and laughing immoderately at these tortured fugitives, one of them John Flemming, a ferry-boatman, and the other Francis Gough, a coachman. They had been unmercifully flogged to extract confession, but, having none to make, melted pitch was poured over their heads . . . Flemming's right ear was cut off, both were sent off without clothes. Lord Kingsborough superintended the flogging, and almost at every lash asked them how they liked it.'[41]

Big George, a latter day Duke of Otranto? Given his Gothic horror character, what better man than the Earl to own an edifice of such scale, magnitude and bad taste.

To be 'fair' to the North Cork Militia, the authorities in Ireland gave the security forces *carte blanche* to carry out State terrorism against the civilian population in order to stamp out the United Irish movement and Kingsborough's Militia were certainly not the only military unit serving in Ireland guilty of brutal acts of repression.

Dramatic Climax

Now here's a curiosity: besides being an architect, George Richard Pain was also an accomplished water-colouristist and in July 1831 he completed a remarkable piece depicting the dramatic climax of Horace Walpole's Gothic novel *The Castle of Otranto* (1764) where 'the buildings echo Pain's Mitchelstown Castle, all is collapsing at a thunderclap, and mighty Alphonso appears in the centre of the ruins.'[42] Indeed, if we compare photographs of Mitchelstown with the painting there is a certain similarity in terms of the heavy Sublime proportions of the two Gothic structures. Was this imaginary destruction on the part of George Richard an expression of his aesthetic

Castle of Otranto (1831). Water-colour by George Richard Pain.

dissatisfaction with his own involvement in devising such an architectural creation as was Mitchelstown? For how could a true artist be pleased with the product? Or was it a case of wishful thinking arising out of the Earl's madness, his violent temper and the debt he owed to the brothers. It would be nice to think that this were true - a dreadful, prophetic curse placed on the House of Kingston by an artist of integrity.

For, if by chance, George Richard Pain was harbouring malicious thoughts towards Mitchelstown then he certainly got his wish, for the pile no longer stands, being burnt and looted in The Civil War of 1922, as if in some Gothic revenge melodrama 'The Great Alphonso' of Catholic Irish Nationalism had stormed and rent asunder the Protestant Ascendancy castle. The house was occupied by the Anti-Treaty IRA in June 1922, looted of its contents and on 12 August 1922 set on fire as the IRA retreated from the advancing Free State forces.[43] A sense of grievance against the Kingston family was certainly present in the district stemming from a shooting incident that had occurred in the main square of Mitchelstown in September 1887 when police opened fire on a rioting crowd at a National League meeting, killing three people. The shooting, known as the 'Mitchelstown Massacre' took place within yards of the market house and courtroom built by the Pain brothers. The incident was connected to an acrimonious and bitter land dispute then taking place between the tenants on the Kingston estate and Anna, Lady Kingston and her husband, William Webber.[44] Lady Kingston died in 1909, but William Webber was still alive in 1922. The burnt-out, derelict, Gothic pile was subsequently demolished in the 1920s, the stones being carted off to build Mount Melleray, a Cistercian abbey at Cappoquin, Co. Waterford. It is said that it took two lorries, two trips a day, six days a week for five years to cart all the stones from Mitchelstown to Mount Melleray.[45] The property was taken over by a farmers' co-operative and there now stands a cheese-processing factory on the site where once stood an aristocrat's castle.

The story of Mitchelstown Castle reads like an allegorical tale full of symbol and meaning about the decline and fall of the Anglo-Irish Ascendancy. It reads as a theatrically over-dramatic epic tale right down to the clichés: 'Whom the Gods wish to Destroy, They first make Mad.'; Protesting peasants gunned down by the agents of an oppressive landlord; Götterdämmerung fire and destruction. The vanquished stones of a Protestant Big House carted off like bonded slaves to build a Catholic Abbey.

Perceptions

Mitchelstown Castle was certainly the most successful of the Pains' designs in terms of its ability to evoke a response, whether it was the visceral hatred of those IRA Volunteers who set the building ablaze, or the admiration of Lady Chatterton who expressed the view that it was a 'noble pile of building, surrounded by fine woods, and commanding extensive views over a broad and fertile plain . . .'[46] Although razed to the ground some eighty years ago the castle still fascinates, due, in part, to the cruel, magisterial personality of its founder, his crashing fall into insanity and the drama and the tragic fate of many of his family members. It is also due to the fact that Mitchelstown was the most expensive private building project ever undertaken in Ireland and its sheer monumentalism is sufficient in itself to invite comment.

If the entrance to the Pain bothers' Limerick County Gaol is an example of nineteenth century stripped Greek Revival, then their Mitchelstown Castle was an outstanding example of partially stripped Gothic Revival. Lacking detailing, this angular mountain of sharp edged masonry appeared severe and uncompromising, projecting a personality of harshness rather than any feeling of harmony with the land and its people. The main body of the castle was very 'male' in appearance, unsoftened due to the absence of 'feminine' round towers.

But one reacts to a building with subjectivity, both conscious and unconscious, a subjectivity informed and ill-informed by personal opinions and experiences, ideologically charged interpretations of history and culturally formed prejudices. Knowing something of the personality of a building's founder and its subsequent history also colours one's emotional response. This is particularly true of Mitchelstown Castle. But one can dislike Mitchelstown simply on the basis that it appears so much at odds with the Picturesque, the building lacking beauty, charm and 'niceness'. Perhaps architectural historian Frederick O'Dwyer has an insight into this negative response when he writes that Mitchelstown 'was a building out of its time, not medieval but a foreshadow of the bold, minimally-ornamented geometric architecture of the early twentieth century . . .'[47] If that was the effect then it was not because the Pain brothers were being deliberately experimental, but simply due to the fact that the massive structure had to be thrown up in the least amount of time. Finesse and detailing were thrown out the window, most of the towers square or rectangular in plan, (although some were octagonal) giving the building a flat 'industrial' appearance.

In terms of its shape, extent and mass the present factory building on the site seems a deliberate twentieth century reminder of what once stood there. The highest building of the factory, the 100 feet (30.5 metres) processing tower, standing on the same location as the Pain brothers' massive White Tower.

Garden Party

The massive edifice of Mitchelstown Castle may have overawed, or appalled, those who saw it standing in its prime and glory, but all is one with Ninevah and Tyre.[48] But the ghosts of the Anglo-Irish still linger there, wandering amidst the vats and machinery of a cheese-making factory, conjured up by the pen of Elizabeth Bowen who, in her *Bowen's Court*, writes of a memorable garden party she attended in the castle grounds on 5 August 1914, the day following Britain's declaration of war against Imperial Germany. The castle created by the Pains providing the ideal Gothic backdrop to the opening of this final scene of the Anglo-Irish, the last garden party of an epoch. The weather being made suitably windy, overcast and grey by that Great Director in the sky:

> 'Wind raced around the castle terraces, naked under the Galtees; grit blew into the ices; the band clung with some trouble to its exposed place. The tremendous news certainly made that party, which might have been rather flat. Almost everyone said they wondered if they really ought to have come, but they had - rightly; this was a time to gather. This was an assemblage of Anglo-Irish people from all over northeast Cork, from the counties of Limerick, Waterford, Tipperary. For miles around each isolated big house had disgorged its talker, this first day of the war . . . So on this day of grandeur and gravity the Ascendancy rallied, renewed itself . . .
>
> '. . . this Mitchelstown party, it was agreed, would remain in every one's memory as historic. It was, also, a more final scene than we knew. Ten years hence, it was all to seem like a dream - the castle

Engraving of Mitchelstown Castle shortly after its completion.

itself would be a few bleached stumps on the plateau. Today, the terraces are obliterated, the grass grows where the saloons were. Many of the guests, those vehement talkers, would be scattered, houseless, sonless, or themselves dead . . .The unseen descent of the sun behind the cloud sharpens the bleak light; the band, having throbbed out God Save The King, packs up its wind-torn music and goes home.'[49]

Patron and Architect

Clearly, from what we have said of Dromoland and Mitchelstown the personality of the various patrons that the Pain brothers encountered during their professional careers, and the nature of the personal relationship that developed between patron and architect, was not a negligible factor in influencing the quality of the finished architectural product. From the very first, visitors to Dromoland have always been favourably impressed by the Pain brothers' most distinguished and picturesque creation. Lady Chatterton thought it 'a splendid abode . . . and offers that phenomenon in Ireland, or indeed in any country, a magnificent place erected without ruining the possessor.'[50]

Grania O'Brien, writing of her illustrious forebears, says of Sir Edward O'Brien 'Throughout all his life, Sir Edward was conscious and careful about money and economics, sometimes to the point of fanaticism.'[51] In his wife, Lady Charlotte (1781-1856), Sir Edward had a good friend, staunch ally and worthy chatelaine who managed the estate during her husband's frequent absences as a serving Member of Parliament (until 1826) for Clare. Lady Charlotte comes over as being an extremely practical person. With two such exacting taskmasters as patrons it is little wonder that Dromoland turned out to be the most pleasing of the Pain brothers' country house work. The painstaking, patient, financially cautious approach of Sir Edward O'Brien contrasting favourably with the egotistical, money no object, I want it now! approach of the 3rd Earl of Kingston who is said to have remarked, perhaps apocryphally, to the architects. 'Build me a castle. I am no judge of architecture, but it must be larger than any other house in Ireland. No delay! It is time for me to enjoy.'[52] The difference in approach of the two patrons having no small influence on the

Picturesque view of Dromoland Castle.

final appearance of the respective houses, their personalities becoming very much part of the buildings. So, in magisterially declaring that such and such a building designed by the Pain brothers is 'good', while another is 'bad' or 'mediocre', we cannot leave the patron out of the equation in allocating fault or praise.

As well as his financial good sense it is perhaps to Sir Edward's sense of historical time that we owe Dromoland's measured development, a sense of the historical continuity of a dynasty stretching back centuries unto the Middle Ages and to Brian Bórú of Blessed Memory. An Irish family history spanning and surviving invasions, political turmoil, religious conflict and all the other vicissitudes and ups and downs of Irish history since the time of the Vikings. A fine family name that, no doubt, would stretch forth centuries. This sense of historical continuity, of historical infinity, may have influenced Sir Edward in his approach to building Dromoland Castle. If it took nigh on twenty years to build it was but a drop in the ocean of O'Brien time. When Sir Edward died in 1837 the house was still not entirely completed, for when Lady Chatterton visited Dromoland in 1838 she noted that the Castle was 'now nearly finished.'[53] There was absolutely no need to rush the building of Dromoland. "Don't worry, why rush, it will be there for ever; let's take our time and get it right" would seem to have been the approach.

Endnotes

1 Sir Edward O'Brien Correspondence with Lady Charlotte O'Brien, National Library (NCI 2972-4; 2976-7).

2 For further information concerning the building of Dromoland Castle see Richardson, Douglas Scott *Gothic Revival Architecture in Ireland*, 2 Vols., Garland Publishing Inc., New York and London, Vol. I, pp. 140-6 and Figs. 65-76.

3 Chatterton, Lady Georgina *Rambles in the South of Ireland During the Year 1838*, Two Vols., Saunder & Otley, London, 1839, Vol. II, p. 173.

4 O'Brien, Grania *These My Friends and Forebears – The O'Briens of Dromoland*, Ballinakella Press, Whitegate, Co. Clare, 1991, p. 112.

5 Correspondence of Sir Edward O'Brien 1795-1837, National Library of Ireland (NLI 2972-4.

6 O'Brien *op. cit.* p. 122.

7 Chatterton *op. cit.* pp. 173-4.

8 Scott, Walter *Ivanhoe* 1819, Chap.12.

9 *Limerick General Advertiser*, 11 February 1820.

10 Bowen, Elizabeth *Bowen's Court*, The Collins Press, Cork, 1998, p. 256.

11 *The Parliamentary Gazetteer of Ireland* 3 Vols., A. Fullarton & Co., Dublin, London and Edinburgh, 1844-46, Vol. II, p. 773.

12 Pückler-Muskau, Prince *Tour in England, Ireland and France in 1828-9 by a German Prince*, Effingham Wilson, 1832, Vol. II, pp. 21-2.

13 Robertson, N. *Crowned Harp, Memories of the Last Years of the Crown*, Dublin, 1960, p. 90.

14 Lewis, Samuel *Topographical Dictionary of Ireland*, Two Vols., London, 1837, Vol. II, p. 373.

15 Power, Bill *White Knights, Dark Earls: The Rise and Fall of an Anglo-Irish Dynasty*, The Collins Press, Cork, 2000, pp. 72-3. For a more detailed and comprehensive description of the interior and exterior of Mitchelstown, see O'Dwyer, Frederick 'A Noble Pile in the Late Tudor Style: Mitchelstown Castle', *Irish Arts Review*, 2002, p. 42; Bence-Jones, M. *A Guide to Irish Country Houses*, s.v. 'Mitchelstown', Constable, London, 1982, 2nd revised edition 1999; Hajba, Anna-Maria *Houses of Cork: Volume I, North Cork*, s.v. 'Mitchelstown Castle, Mitchelstown', Ballinakella Press, White Gate, County Clare.

16 Lewis *op. cit.* Vol. II, p. 373.

17 loc. cit.

18 Power *op. cit.* p. 84.

19 Power, Bill *Evensong: The Story of a Church of Ireland Country Parish*, Mount Cashell Books, Mitchelstown, 2004, p. 48.

20 Lewis *op. cit.* Vol. II, p. 373.

21 Lewis *op. cit.* Vol. II, p. 372-3.

22 *Parliamentary Gazetteer of Ireland* s.v. 'Mitchelstown', Vol. II, p. 774.

23 Power *Evensong*, pp. 30-1.

24 *Parliamentary Gazetteer of Ireland*, Vol. II, p. 774.

25 ibid. Vol. II, p. 736.

26 Power *Evensong*, pp. 36, 68, 70.

27 Power *White Knights, Dark Earls*, p. 84.

28 Lewis *op. cit.* p. 373.

29 Power, Bill *Mitchelstown Through Seven Centuries*, Éigse Books, Fermoy, Co. Cork, 1987, p. 51.

30 Lewis *op. cit.* s.v. 'Mitchelstown', Vol. II, p. 373.

31 Lewis's contributors were not always accurate in their architectural descriptions of churches, sometimes attributing the stock phrase 'the later English style of architecture' (i.e. Perpendicular) to the earlier Decorated style, as in the case of St. Michael and St. John Catholic church in Dublin with its Geometrical tracery windows on the central bays of its frontage. But this church is very eclectic in style, also incorporating Early English lancet windows and Tudor arch entrance. But as Lewis's Mitchelstown correspondent accurately described St. George's Anglican church as in the later English style with its Perpendicular windows it can be assumed that the same was with the case of St. Fanahan's.

32 Richardson *op. cit.* pp. 215-6.

33 Power *Evensong*, p. 49.

34 ibid. p. 77.

35 'The Will of James Pain', *Transcriptions of Wills of Limerick*, Limerick Archives and Ancestry Office, The Granary, Limerick.

36 Power *White Knights, Dark Earls*, p. 90.

37 ibid. pp. 113-6.

38 O'Dwyer *op. cit.* p. 40.

39 de Tocqueville, Alexis *Alexis de Tocqueville's Journey in Ireland July – August 1835*, Larkin, Emmet, (trans. and ed.), Wolfhound Press, Dublin, 1990. Letter dated '27 July 1835', pp. 87-8.

40 ibid. '16 July, 1835'.

41 Plowden, Francis *An Historical View of the State of Ireland*, London, 1801, Vol. IV, pp. 252-3.

42 Crookshank, Anne & the Knight of Glin *The Watercolours of Ireland; Works on Paper in Pencil, Pastel and Paint c1600-1914*, Barrie and Jenkins, London, 1994, p. 106.

43 Power *White Knights, Dark Earls*, pp. 225-7.

44 ibid. pp. 150f.

45 Hajba, Anna-Maria *Houses of Cork: Volume I, North Cork*, Ballinakella Press, White Gate, County Clare, p. 266.

46 Chatterton *op. cit.* Vol. II, p. 2.

47 O'Dwyer *op. cit.* p. 42.

48 The reference to Ninevah and Tyre comes from two lines of Rudyard Kipling's poem *Recessional* (1897),

> 'Lo, all our pomp of yesterday
> Is one with Ninevah and Tyre.'

These ancient Middle-Eastern cities, each once the centre of an empire, were overwhelmed by stronger foes.

49 Bowen *op. cit.* pp. 435-7.

50 Chatterton *op. cit.* p. 173.

51 O'Brien *op. cit.* p. 103.

52 Bowen *op. cit.* p. 256

53 Chatterton *op. cit.* p. 173.

CHAPTER EIGHT
FIRST FRUITS

James Pain is heavily identified with church architecture because *c.*1822 he was appointed as architect to the Board of First Fruits for the ecclesiastical Province of Cashel with responsibility for the erection of all new Church of Ireland churches and glebe houses in the province and the maintenance and repair of existing buildings,[1] George Richard acting as his assistant.[2] A glebe house is a parish clergyman's residence built on 'glebe land', i.e. land from which the clergyman obtained an income. Glebe land could be in one plot or divided between several parcels of land.

Typical glebe house.

It is said that John Nash exercised influence in the appointment of James to the Board of First Fruits,[3] a position that proved a steady source of income for the Pain brothers. However, it has to be said that James had earned his position on merit and not on preferment, because before his appointment he had already carried out work in association with the Board. One example is Kilnasoolagh parish church at Newmarket-on-Fergus, Co. Clare, for which he was the architect, built in 1816 and the house of worship for Sir Edward O'Brien of Dromoland. James also probably acted as the executing architect for Nash's own St. Paul's at Cahir, Co. Tipperary.

The Board of First Fruits was first established in Ireland in 1711 during the reign of Queen Anne. The term 'First Fruits' derives from a pre-Reformation obligation whereby newly promoted clergy were deducted, for their first year in office, the difference between their present and previous incomes and the

131

revenue presented to the Vatican. In England this practice continued until the Church of England broke away from the Church of Rome in the sixteenth century. During the reign of Henry VIII the monarch, as the Supreme Head of the Church in England, became the beneficiary of First Fruits. In 1704 the revenue was redirected to the poorer clergy and the Irish Board of First Fruits was established in 1711 for this purpose, the body acting under the direction of Commissioners and Trustees. Initially the value of the fund was not very high, then in 1777 legislation enacted by the Irish Parliament in Dublin paved the way for annual subventions to be paid to the Board allowing it to purchase glebe land and to finance, by the way of loans and gifts, the construction and repair of churches and glebe houses.

As the established Church in Ireland, the Church of Ireland benefited considerably from parliamentary largesse following the passage of the Act of Union (1800),[4] public monies flowing generously and copiously into the Board's coffers. The Commissioners and Trustees received about £5,000 a year from the Government for the first nine years after 1800, the grant increasing substantially to about £60,000 annually from 1810 to 1816. The grant was reduced to half that amount in the years 1817-21. From this, and other sources, between 1800 and 1823 over £1,000,000 came into the possession of the Board.[5] This was a substantial sum of money for those days, considering that a modest sized church, complete with two-storey tower and elegant spire, could be built for £1,500, as in the case of Kilnasoolagh,[6] and that the great pile of Mitchelstown Castle was erected for some £100,000.[7]

With ample funds to draw upon, church building among the Anglican community became prolific, especially so in county towns and rural areas, and during the period 1777-1829 the Board of First Fruits built, rebuilt, or enlarged a total of 697 churches. The process lasted until the Famine and in Munster alone more than 200 were erected between 1813 and 1844. Many of the Anglican churches we see today in the Irish countryside and provincial towns, whether they be in ruins, converted to secular uses such as dwellings, lovingly restored for use as heritage and arts performance centres, or still serving a religious function, date from this period of architectural renewal spanning some seventy years. In addition, a large number of glebe houses were also erected. In 1787 there were 354 such dwellings in Ireland, by 1832 there were 829.[8]

There was a parallel church-building 'frenzy' in Britain during the nineteenth century commencing in 1818. That year Parliament granted £1 million, and an additional £5000,000 in 1824, to the Church of England enabling this body to build churches in the rapidly expanding cities of the country. This was both to rectify the dire shortage of parish churches in the urban centres and to combat the growth of Nonconformist religions and sects. Between 1835 and 1875 alone almost 4,000 new or rebuilt churches were financed.[9]

Official Church Architect

For the first thirty-six years after 1777 church construction in Ireland seems to have proceeded on an ad hoc basis with no central coordination, then about 1813 the Board appointed John Bowden as retained architect to supervise the accelerating building programme at a national level. Following his death in 1822 each of the four ecclesiastical provinces appointed its own architect: William Farrell for Armagh, John Semple (assisted by his son, John Jnr.) for Dublin, Joseph Welland for Tuam, and James Pain (assisted by his brother) for Cashel,[10] *Pigot's* 1824 trade directory describing 'Pain Jas.' of Upper George's Street, Limerick as architect 'to the board of first fruits for the province of Munster'.[11] As a result of their involvement with the Board a large number of Church of Ireland structures in Munster were built, altered, restored or repaired by the architect brothers.[12]

The Archdiocese of Cashel covered the civil province of Munster (counties Limerick, Clare, Tipperary, Kerry, Cork and Waterford) with the addition of adjacent parts of counties Offaly, Kilkenny and Galway. James's geographical area of responsibility was therefore quite extensive, his jurisdiction incorporating the dioceses of Cashel and Emly, Cloyne, Cork and Ross, Killaloe and Kilfenora, Limerick and Ardfert, Waterford and Lismore. Given that the architect had to deal with a wide variety of people – builders, craftsmen, parish clergy, vestry committees, bishops and lay dignities of some wealth and prominence – diplomatic as well as architectural skills were required on his behalf. Parochial clergymen in particular sometimes being difficult to deal with as they tend to have too much time on their hands.

In 1833 the Board of First Fruits was replaced under the terms of The Church Temporalities Act by the Board of Ecclesiastical Commissioners, a body that continued on the Godly work of architectural renewal; the Commissioners retaining the services of James Pain until 1843. The Church Temporalities Act mainly concerned itself with rationalising the finances of the Church of Ireland, reducing the number of bishops and archbishops, taxing the wealthier dioceses and enabling Church tenants to purchase their holdings.

Much Admired for its Taste and Stile

Once a decision had been made by the local vestry to build a new church, or carry out major renovations on an existing one, a committee was appointed by the parish to oversee the project. Plans and drawings were sought, generally from the provincial architect, but high-spending projects might invite proposals from other architects. In January 1825, for instance, we find the committee appointed by the Parish of the Holy Trinity, Cork City meeting on Tuesday the 11th to discuss the merits or otherwise of six proposals, four from Dublin and two from Cork, a premium of £50 being awarded to George Richard Pain for submitting 'the best plan'.[13] Meeting again three weeks later the committee formally approved George Richard's proposal which was 'much admired for its taste and stile [sic]', and sought a sizeable loan of £13,500 from the Board of First Fruits. However, the scheme was not carried out due to the large expense involved, for we hear two years later that 'The parishioners of Christ Church, Cork have approved of Messrs. Pain's estimate of 2,888*l* for repairing the Old Church.'[14] Christ Church (in the Anglican parish of Holy Trinity) on Cork's South Main Street should not be confused with the Catholic Church of the Holy Trinity on Fr. Mathew Quay which was to be later built to a design by G. R. Pain.

Typically though, parish committees sought loans of £500-£900 from the Board of First Fruits or received assistance in the form of both a loan and a non-repayable gift. In some instances financial support was wholly in the form of a gift, as was the case with Bruree Church (1812) in East Co. Limerick, grant aided to the tune of £800.[15]

Serviceable houses of worship could be built with the assistance of such funding but First Fruits money was generally not sufficient in itself to cover the full cost of construction and additional funding had to be raised from local sources. For instance St. Munchin's (1827) on Limerick's King's Island was rebuilt for £1,450 of which £900 was lent by the Board, £500 raised by local subscriptions and £50 obtained by selling off the materials of the old church.[16] It was certainly helpful if a local member of the gentry or nobility, a Lord or Lady Bountiful, was on hand to make a donation to the building fund. This was often the case as the gentry generously supported the Established Church and in rural areas the Anglican house of worship was often built on or close to a demesne. Tullybrackey Church (1819)[17] near Bruff in Co. Limerick was erected conveniently outside the entrance to the Rockbarton estate of Lord Guillamore, the new church being built 1.2 kilometres northeast of the site of the previous church[18] and about 450 metres from the site of the glebe house built in 1813. With a lofty, three stage, square tower, battlemented and pinnacled, the church cost £2,500 to build of which £1,200 was in the form of grants from the Board of First Fruits and £1,300 donated by Lord Guillamore.[19] Capable of accommodating 120 persons, the church was demolished in 1959, the graveyard transferred to Limerick County Council in 1960.[20]

Some landowners were especially generous, the Waller family of Castletown, Co. Limerick not only donating £700 to the building of Kilcornan parish church (1831) near Pallaskenry, but also undertaking to repay the £800 loan. As well as paying for the entire project, the Wallers also held patronage over the parish 'living', an ecclesiastical term for a position held by a vicar or rector that has an income or property. A clergyman may have more than one such living if he was responsible for more than one parish. Although many parish livings came under the patronage of various ecclesiastical authorities - the diocesan Bishop,

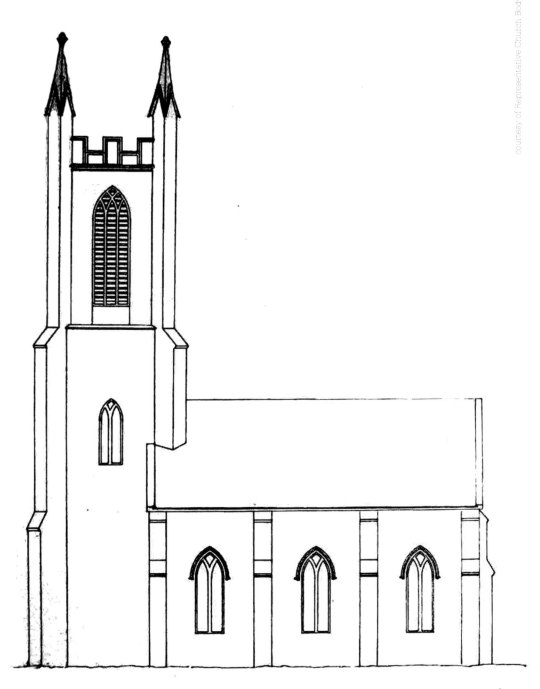

South elevation of Tullybrackey Church, Co. Limerick.

the Dean, the Vicars Choral of a cathedral, the provincial Archbishop – or, in some instances, the Crown, it was not uncommon for a prominent member of the county gentry and nobility to hold the gift of appointing local Anglican priests. The living at Newcastlewest came under the patronage of the Earl of Devon for instance; Croom was in the ownership of the Crokers of Ballynaguarde, Ballyneety, Co. Limerick; and St. John's parish in Limerick City the gift of the Earl of Limerick.[21]

This custom enabled landowners to appoint a favoured protégé, or a deserving member of their own family who had taken Holy Orders, to the position. It is therefore not surprising that among the memorial tablets in Kilcornan Church one finds mention of two offspring of the Waller family who held the rectorship: Rev. William Waller of Castletown who died in 1863, and the Rev. John Waller of Castletown who died in 1911.[22] The incumbents' no doubt less than onerous duties were not without benefits, for the 'very handsome and commodious' glebe house at Kilcornan sat on '60 acres of profitable land.'[23]

In Jane Austen's *Sense and Sensibility* Colonel Brandon, a Devonshire gentleman, offers the vacant living of Delaford parsonage to Edward Ferrars, a young clergyman. It so falls out, after much emotional turmoil, that Colonel Brandon marries Marianne Dashwood and her sister, Elinor, marries clergyman Ferrars, all four harmoniously united and bound together by ties of blood, marriage, property and religion in perfect material security.[24]

The Work of a Provincial Architect

Once a parish committee had approved a plan, and finances guaranteed, tenders were invited from builders to carry out the work, James Pain being ultimately responsible for monitoring and approving their performance:

To Builders

'Wanted, a person to undertake Building a Church in the town of Cloghjordan, according to plan and specification, to be seen at the house of Mr. R. Pyke, Churchwarden, contiguous to the site. The execution to be approved of by James Pain Esq. Provincial Architect. Ample security will be required for the fullfilling such agreement as may be entered into. Proposals to be addressed to the Rev. Edwin Palmer, or the Rev. F. Fitzwilliam Trench, Cloghjordan or to William Trench Esq. Roscrea – the committee appointed for building said Church.'
(*Limerick Chronicle*, Wednesday 31 May 1826.)

St. Kiernan's Church, Cloghjordan (Cloughjordan) in Co. Tipperary was described at the time as 'a handsome light edifice, in the later English style' i.e. Perpendicular, it was built for around £1,800 and completed in 1830. [25]

As well as constructing churches, the provision of new glebe houses for the comfort and well-being of clergymen and their families was also an important part of the work carried out by the Board of First Fruits,

To Builders and Contractors

Proposals for building a Glebe-house at Askeaton, will be received by the Rev. R. Murray, Askeaton. Plans and specifications to be seen at Mr. Payne's [sic], Limerick; or at the Rev. R. Murray's, Askeaton.

(Limerick Chronicle Saturday 29 April 1826)

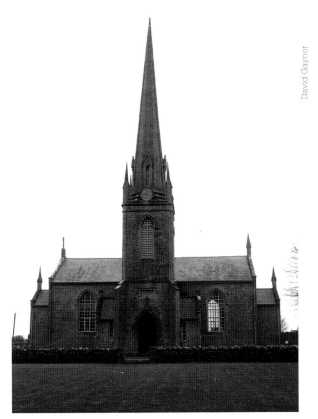

David Gaynor

137

Cloughjordan Church, Co. Tipperary.

A similar notice appeared in the same newspaper of Wednesday 30 August 1826,

Notice to Builders

Proposals will be received for building a Glebe House and Offices in the Parish of O'Brien's Bridge. Application to be made to Mr. Pain, Architect, George's Street, Limerick for Plan and Specification.

Glebe houses were invariably built to the same pattern and have distinctive features. Basically the house was a two storey 'Georgian box' having three bays on the front with a fan-lighted central door. On the ground floor, a parlour and a dining room were located on either side of a narrow hall with three bedrooms and two dressing rooms on the first floor. Two sets of chimney stacks straddle the hipped roof. Plain on the exterior, if any classical motifs were used at all they were mainly confined to decorative door and window surrounds. Costing in the region of £600-£700 they were a simple but substantial dwelling for a country person and his family and are as habitable today as when first built.

One of the tasks that James Pain undertook during his stewardship was to draw up plans and elevations of all the churches in the Archdiocese. These are presently held in the library of the Representative Church Body (RCB), Dublin in a collection of six volumes that constitute a valuable primary source. James remained with the Board of First Fruits and its successor body, the Board of Ecclesiastical Commissioners, until the early 1840s; drawings signed and dated by the architect are still extant from that period.

My Old Master

Although other architects such as G. R. Pain submitted proposals to local vestry committees, as seen in the case of Christ Church, Cork, James Pain as provincial architect would have been involved in providing plans for many of the churches built during his tenure, especially those in out of the way rural areas and small country towns. Those parishes who simply wanted a serviceable church would hardly have wanted to consult with architects up and down the country when a perfectly competent ecclesiastical architect was on hand to suggest a suitable plan to suit their needs and pockets. The execution of this work would, in most cases, be placed in the hands of a local builder or architect/builder. One such person was William Tinsley (1804-85), a Clonmel architect whose contracting company carried out some work for the Board of First Fruits and its successor body. One of Tinsley's first ecclesiastical assignments was Lisronagh Church, 'a neat edifice' completed in 1832[26] designed, according to Tinsley's biographer J. D. Forbes, 'by James Pain.'[27]

Lisronagh Church, Co. Tipperary.

A major source of information for Forbes was Tinsley's unpublished memoirs written in America (he emigrated there in 1851) which recall that in 1837, and for several years after, he was engaged by the Board to build a series of churches. Tinsley lists five built to plans provided by Pain. Three were in Tipperary, Clonbeg, Clogheen and Kilvemnon and a fourth at Kilbehenny on the border of Co. Limerick. The final church, whose name the architect could not recall, was identified only as situated 'near the borders of Co. Limerick' whose rector was Thomas Kearney 'a man with a lame foot and not much pretension to Godliness.'[28] All this was not very exciting contract work for Tinsley given the simple nature of these bell-cote churches, but in 1843 he succeeded James Pain as architect to the Waterford diocese.

In the course of the Irish phase of his career before he left for America and settled in Cincinnati, William Tinsley was involved in a number of country house commissions as well as designing churches, schools, a Protestant asylum, a convent and building a workhouse. As with other Irish architects of the period he was of necessity diverse, being schooled in Greek, Gothic and Tudor-Revival. The highlight of his career in Ireland was being employed in the early 1840s by the Earl of Glengall in remodelling Cahir town through the construction of several ranges of street houses.[29] As he worked mainly in Tipperary and Waterford his sphere of influence marched with part of that of the Pain brothers' and he appears to have greatly admired James, becoming such a close friend that he named a son, born in 1844, James Pain Tinsley.[30] The elder architect certainly exercised some influence over the younger man, but not to the extent that it was dominant. In his unpublished memoirs Tinsley writes with regret that in the 1840s, after he became architect to the Anglican diocese of Waterford, he was obliged in the course of his professional duties 'to contradict or differ with my old master (as I sometimes called Jas. Pain).' Tinsley also wrote that in the course of his early work as church architect he 'occasionally' submitted his design to James 'and had the benefit of his instruction.'[31]

Out in the Field

The duties of an ecclesiastical architect of the period could be quiet mundane. When William Tinsley was architect to the Waterford Diocese he discovered that a lot of his work involved inspecting church properties recently vacated to determine their condition and ascertain the cost of any repairs. This was to ensure that a proper accounting could be made with the outgoing clergyman and that glebe houses, as well as fences, gates etc. on glebe land, were brought back into good order for the next incumbent.[32]

140

As well as carrying out routine administrative and undertaking surveying work James, who was very much a 'hands on' architect, was also out in the field supervising work on his own projects, as in the summer of 1826: 'There is a neat and commodious church building at Emly. Mr. James Pain, who is the architect, at present superintends the work', reported the *Limerick Chronicle* of 12 August 1826. Emly, located nine miles west of Tipperary Town near the Co. Limerick border, was a diocesan seat until 1562 when Emly diocese was united with that of Cashel. Although Emly's Cathedral status was vastly diminished by the early nineteenth century, and the local Church of Ireland population falling, it was decided to demolish the old building and replace it by a new Cathedral built to the design of James Pain. Completed in 1827 for a cost of £2,521, the building, although graced with the title of 'Cathedral', really served as a parish church.[33] Despite the cost involved, Emly Cathedral was demolished in 1877.[34]

South elevation of Emly Church, Co. Tipperary.

Flush With Money

The Church of Ireland was so flush with money that it could afford to finance the erection of new churches to cater for rural parishes that had tiny Protestant populations. In 1830, for instance, James Pain designed a church at Marshalstown [35] (about 7 km. west of Mitchelstown, Co. Cork) with the aid of a £200 gift from the Earl of Kingston and £700 from the Board of First Fruits. Capable of seating 150 people, and with a standard western square tower, this expenditure was entered into to look after the spiritual needs of a total of fifteen parishioners. This contrasts with the 2,633 Catholics in the parish, the local chapel having to cater for 1,400 of them. To support the Protestant 'Establishment' in Marshalstown tithes of £330 were levied on the parish, divided equally between the vicar and a lay impropriator, a Mr. John Nason, gentleman.[36]

This situation was by no means an unusual one in rural Ireland where the Established Church was strongly supported by the local gentry and resident nobility. Another example that can be cited was Kilfane, Thomastown in Co. Kilkenny. In the autumn of 1828 Thomas Creevy MP visited Ireland and stayed at Bessborough House, Piltown, Co. Kilkenny, the home of Lord and Lady Duncannon. In early October the Duncannons, two servants and Creevy travelled twenty miles to call upon the Power family of Kilfane House. The only other prominent Protestant family in the parish, according to Creevy, was that of Chief Justice Burke. The next day Creevy attended a service at Kilfane Anglican Church. Writing of his religious experiences in a letter penned that day, he reports,

> '. . . Now I have seen a real Protestant church. When I entered it, two parsons were sitting in a row at the reading desk - one, the rector and Archdeacon of Ossory - the other his curate. We were 15 company from the house and 4 from the Chief Justice's. Duncannon and Lady Duncannon, man and maid were there, so help me God! not a soul else. The parish is a large and populous one, but without a single Protestant in it except these two families - nay, not even among their servants . . . . The living is £500 a year: the Catholic coadjutor or priest has £70 !'[37]

It is necessary at this point to clarify a number of terms such as 'vicar', 'rector' and 'impropriator'. Today the terms vicar and rector are used as synonyms but in the early nineteenth century they did have particular meanings. A rector was an Anglican parish priest who was in full possession of a fixed annual income known as a tithe. Tithes were legally binding taxes on agricultural produce levied on all producers, whether one were Catholic, Protestant or Dissenter, for the express purpose of supporting the minority Church of Ireland. These taxes were collected by a person known as a tithe-proctor who handed over a fixed sum to the parish and retained the excess amount. Whereas a rector received the full amount of this fixed allocated sum, a vicar was a priest who received only part of this annual allocation, the other portion paid to a lay person known as an impropriator. In the situation where the entire amount of the tithe went to an impropriator, the priest was known as a 'perpetual curate'.

Resistance to this unjust tax was part and parcel of popular agrarian agitation in the 1820s and '30s leading to refusal to pay tithes and intimidation of the tithe-collector and the local Anglican priest. These acts of civil disobedience leading to confrontations with the forces of law and order. The whole contentious issue was finally dealt with by legislation passed in 1838 that provided for the tithe to be subsumed into the rent paid to the landlord who then passed on the money to the appropriate beneficiary. This compromise proved acceptable because one of the outcomes of the legislation was to reduce the amount of tithe payable by agricultural producers.

Sectarian Difficulties

In the course of his duties for the Board of First Fruits James Pain would have been responsible for overseeing the rebuilding of several churches that had been burnt down during the extensive agrarian disturbances that broke out in parts of the Munster countryside during the early 1820s. Although sectarianism is commonly associated with Ulster, in the first half of the nineteenth century popular sectarianism was strong in areas of the south. A major contributing factor in rural Ireland was the payment of tithes. During the Rockite disturbances at least half a dozen Protestant churches in Kerry, Cork and Limerick were set on fire.[38] On the night of 8 February 1822 the Church of Ireland house of worship at Killeedy, four miles south of Newcastlewest, was burnt down and destroyed while that same night the church at Abbeyfeale, also in West Limerick, was attacked and badly damaged, the roof having to be taken off and repaired.[39] The glebe house at Killeedy was also burnt down - both church and glebe house were not rebuilt.[40] Another victim of the insurgents' wrath was Athlacca Church, East Limerick, similarly burnt down in 1822, but rebuilt the following year by a tax levied on the parish.[41] Elsewhere, an unsuccessful attempt was made on Bruff Church also in East Limerick. According to an account in Lewis's *Topography*, Rockites assembled 'in great numbers and made an attempt to burn the church and several private houses, but were frustrated by the active and judicious exertions of the neighbouring gentry, aided by a large body of the military stationed in the town.'[42]

Intimidation was an occupational hazard for clergymen in those times if the incumbent insisted on his pound of tithe flesh. Take the case of the Rev. Madders of Ballybrood, a parish a few miles south of Caherconlish on the road to Hospital in Co. Limerick. Not only was the church burnt down but the glebe house was also attacked, the Rev. Madders being seized, placed on his knees and several shots fired over his head. The church was rebuilt the following year in 1823.[43]

As the newly appointed provincial architect to the Board of First Fruits following the death of Board architect John Bowden in 1822, James Pain would have been busy assessing the damage to church property and arranging for repairs to be carried out and new buildings constructed to replace those damaged beyond repair. These burnings and attacks made the pages of the newspapers and were memorable enough to be recorded in memoirs and contemporary accounts, but there was probably much other low-key damage inflicted on church property, such as broken windows, that would have come to the attention of the architect, if not to the general public.

Sectarian feeling during this period manifested itself in commonplace ways as well as in overt acts of violence. In his memoirs written in 1898 the Catholic Bishop of Kansas City, John J. Hogan, recalled his childhood days in Bruff, Co. Limerick. Describing one incident that took place in 1837 he recounts how he and two or three other boys entered Tullybrackey Church when they found the door ajar and no one in the building. One of the boys, Carroll by name, seeing a large gilt King James Bible laying on the pulpit seized upon it, ripping out all its pages. This gesture, says the Bishop in retrospective justification for this act of vandalism, was an impulsive display of hatred towards the church the young Carroll had entered,

> 'It was the Church the Government of England had forced on the people against their will and had compelled the Irish people to support and maintain, although opposed to their conscience . . . Well and fully he had known that the pulpit he had entered was an intruder and plunderer in Ireland - that the gilded Bible, the glittering church, the ruddy, rotund parson, with his well-fed, well-dressed wife and children and servants around him, and who dwelt in a luxurious glebe-house with park and lawns surroundings, were not representative or expositive of the true and honest gospel of Christ. He knew too well what was in the mouths of others, that all this wealth, grandeur and show of the Church of England, as established in Ireland, was procured from the sales of church property robbed from the Irish Catholics and from tithes collected from them by distraint at the mouth of the cannon and the point of the bayonet . . .'[44]

As further justification for the incident the Irish-American prelate noted that Tullybracky Church stood outside the entrance to Rockbarton House, home to Standish O'Grady (Viscount Guillamore) who, in 1803, acted as prosecution barrister at the trial of Robert Emmet who attempted an insurrection in Dublin that year and was executed.[45] Hogan's bias is clear, but such bitter feelings were learnt at mother's knee and by family hearth.

Endnotes

1 *Pigot's* 1824 trade directory describes 'Pain Jas.' of Upper George's Street as architect ' to the board of first fruits for the province of Munster', p. 286.

2 *Dictionary of Architecture,* Architectural Publications Society s.v. 'Pain James and George Richard'.

3 loc. cit.

4 The Act of Union (1800) followed from the suppression of the 1798 Rebellion when the British Government decided to abolish the Irish Houses of Commons and Lords in Dublin and concentrate the parliamentary process at Westminster.

5 Hutchison, Sam *Towers, Spires and Pinnacles – A History of the Cathedrals and Churches of the Church of Ireland*, Wordwell, Bray, Co. Wicklow, 2003, p. 58; Richardson, Douglas Scott *Gothic Revival Architecture in Ireland*, 2 Vols., Garland Publishing Inc., New York and London, 1983, Vol. I, pp. 64-5, 193.

6 Lewis, Samuel *A Topographical Dictionary of Ireland*, 2 Vols., London, 1837, s.v. 'Kilnasoolagh'.

7 Lewis *op. cit.* Vol. II s.v. 'Mitchelstown'.

8 Somerville-Large, Peter *The Irish Country House – A Social History*, Sinclair-Stevenson, London, 1995, p. 232.

9 Hunt, Tristram *Building Jerusalem: The Rise and Fall of the Victorian City*, Weidenfeld & Nicolson, London, 2004, p. 65.

10 Craig, Maurice *The Architecture of Ireland From the Earliest Times to 1880*, B.T. Batsford Ltd., London, Eason & Son Ltd., Dublin, 1982, p. 216. The *Limerick Chronicle* for 22 March 1826 states that the Board of First Fruits 'have appointed the following Gentlemen their Architects in the four Provinces – Munster, R. [*sic*] Paine; Ulster, Wm. Farrell; Leinster, J. Semple; and Connaught, J. Welland Esqrs.' Since *Pigot's* 1824 Directory two years previously had described James Pain as architect 'to the board of first fruits for the province of Munster' the mention of an 'R. Paine' is of interest. It could be a typographical error as James Pain is mentioned as the 'Provincial Architect' in a *Limerick Chronicle* notice of 3 May 1826. On the other hand, some primary sources do sometimes refer to G. R. Pain as R. Pain(e). If so, G. R. Pain was officially functioning as a church architect for the Board of First Fruits in conjunction with his brother.

11 *Pigot's* 1824 trade directory, p. 286.

12 *Dictionary of* Architecture, Architectural Publications Society s.v. 'Pain (James and George Richard)'.

13 *Limerick Chronicle*, 15 January 1825.

14 *Limerick Chronicle*, Saturday 2 June 1827.

15 Lewis *op. cit.* s.v. 'Bruree'.

16 *Parliamentary Gazetteer of Ireland*, Vol. II, pp. 631-2.

17 Lewis *op. cit.* s.v. 'Tullybracky'.

18 Ordnance Survey, scale: 6 inches to the mile, Limerick Sheet 32, 1927.

19 Lewis *op. cit.* s.v. 'Tullybracky'.

20 Costello, James Canon 'Tullybrackey Church', *The Dawn Parish Journal for Bruff, Co. Limerick*, Issue No. 10, March 2000, p. 101.

21 Lewis *op. cit.* s.v. 'Newcastle', 'Croom', 'Limerick'; Bence-Jones, Mark *A Guide to Irish Country Houses*, revised edition, Constable, London, 1988 s.v. 'Ballynaguarde'.
22 Hewson, Adrian *Inspiring Stones- A History of the Church of Ireland Dioceses of Limerick, Ardfert, Aghadoe, Killaloe, Kilfenora, Clonfert, Kilmacduagh & Emly*, published by the Diocesan Council of Limerick, Killaloe and Ardfert in association with a FÁS Community Response Training Programme, Limerick, 1995, pp. 153-4; Lewis *op. cit.* s.v. 'Kilcornan'.
23 Lewis *op. cit.* 'Kilcornan'.
24 Austen, Jane *Sense and Sensibility* (1811).
25 Lewis *op. cit.* s.v. 'Cloghjordan'.
26 Lewis *op. cit.* s.v. 'Lisronagh'.
27 Forbes, J. D. *Victorian Architect: The Life and Work of William Tinsley*, Indiana University Press, Bloomington, 1953, p. 19.
28 Forbes *op. cit.* p. 35.
29 For Tinsley's Irish work see: Forbes *op. cit.*; Williams, Jeremy *Architecture in Ireland 1837-1921*, Irish Academic Press, Dublin, 1994; Bence-Jones, *op. cit.*
30 Forbes *op. cit.* p. 37.
31 ibid. p. 20.
32 ibid. p. 37.
33 Lewis *op. cit.* Vol. I, p. 599: 'The Cathedral, which serves also as a parish church, is a handsome structure of hewn stone, in the later English style, with a lofty spire, erected in 1827.'
34 Hewson *op. cit.* pp. 41-2.
35 Power, Bill *Evensong: The Story of a Church of Ireland Country Parish*, Mount Cashell Books, Mitchelstown, 2004, pp. 68-70.
36 *The Parliamentary Gazetteer of Ireland* s.v. 'Marshalstown', Vol. II, p. 736.
37 The *Creevy Papers: A Selection from the Correspondence & Diaries of the Late Thomas Creevy, M.P.* Edited by Maxwell, Sir Herbert, 2 Vols., John Murray, London, 1904, Vol. II. Letter dated 5 October 1828, pp. 175-6. Peggy Barry Collection.
38 Curtin, Gerald 'Religion and Social Conflict During the Protestant Crusade in West Limerick 1822-49', *The Old Limerick Journal*, Walsh, Larry ed., No. 39, Winter 2003, p. 48.
39 ibid. citing: *State of the County Papers* 1, 2350/39, 9 February 1822.
40 Lewis *op. cit.* s.v. 'Killeedy'.
41 ibid. s.v. 'Athlacca'.
42 ibid. s.v. 'Bruff'.
43 Seymour, Rev. St. John *The Diocese of Emly*, Church of Ireland Printing and Publishing Co. Ltd., Dublin, 1913, p. 264; Lewis *op. cit.* s.v. 'Ballybrood'.
44 Hogan, Right Rev. John J., Bishop of Kansas City, *Fifty Years Ago: A Memoir,* written in 1898 and published 1907 by Franklin Hudson Publishing Co., Kansas City, pp. 24-6.
45 ibid. p. 27.

CHAPTER NINE
SIMPLE GOTHIC

During their association with the Board of First Fruits and its successor body - the Board of Ecclesiastical Commissioners - the Pain brothers were involved in the design, maintenance and renovation of numerous churches throughout the Archdiocese of Cashel. To deal with each and every one of them is beyond the scope of this particular study, rather the intention is to provide a broad outline of the brothers' architectural work for the Church of Ireland.

Gothic Box Architecture

Many of the First Fruits churches erected in Ireland during the early nineteenth century were quite similar in design, typically being a fairly plain, rectangular 'Gothic box' with a square tower at the western end three stages in height, the upper stage housing a belfry with louvred openings.[1] The tower, which may or may not be topped by a spire, was battlemented and provided with pinnacles on the corners. The main doorway into the building was located in the west tower, which had an internal entrance porch on the ground floor.

Internally, the church is in many cases just simply a hall containing both the nave, where the congregation is seated, and the chancel at the East end where the high altar is located. A small first floor wooden gallery was usually placed at the western end of the nave and gained by stairs. The walls are punctuated with pointed arch windows, the East window naturally larger than the others; the window tracery modelled on styles used in English church architecture during the period 1180-1540. Built in a spare and rather austere Gothic, these churches are known as 'First Fruits Gothic', or 'Simple Gothic' to distinguish them from the more elaborate and more authentic 'Gothic Revival' church architecture that became fashionable later on during the Victorian era. The overuse of pinnacles on a church sometimes earns it the label 'Spiky Gothic'.

Great numbers of churches employing this rectangular-box pattern came off the First Fruits production line and it would be fairly accurate to describe many of these buildings as being produced according to a formula rather than being designed in the sense of the architect displaying any great originality. Having said this, the Pain brothers did bring flair and variation to the task and many of their churches have a distinctive elegance and charm, the architects receiving praise for the quality of their work. Among their most distinguished projects were the churches at Carrigaline,[2] Buttevant and Midleton,[3] all in County Cork. These, and other examples of their craft, can be counted as being in the premier league of Irish-Anglican church architecture for the period c.1815-38 when both brothers worked together as a team.

The universal employment of Gothic by the Church of Ireland was a deliberate choice, for it denoted historical continuity with pre-Reformation Christianity.

The adoption of neo-medieval architecture announced to the world that despite the split with the Roman Catholic Church in the sixteenth century Anglicans had not broken with authentic tradition. The architectural reference point for church architects was the English High Middle Ages, an epoch dominated by the pointed arch. This period of medieval church architecture has traditionally been subdivided into three main stylistic phases: Early English (c.1180-1250), Decorated (c.1250-1350) and Perpendicular (c.1350-1540). These stylistic phases are also called, respectively, First Pointed, Second Pointed and, Third Pointed. These medieval originals providing the inspiration for the window tracery, mouldings, vaulting etc. used by eighteenth and nineteenth century architects.

It was the Early English phase that first saw the use of the pointed arch, a feature introduced into Europe from the Middle East. The tall, narrow pointed windows of this period are called lancets because of their resemblance to a lance blade. It was in the Decorated period that we first see the use of tracery applied to windows. Initially very basic, window tracery became ever more sophisticated and decorative as time and skills progressed, advancing from simple forms such as Plate tracery, Y tracery and Intersecting tracery (a.k.a. 'Switch Line' tracery) to the more elaborate tracery of the late Decorated period which saw more flowing and complex styles known as Curvilinear and Flamboyant develop (see Glossary). It was in the late Decorated period that the ogee arch was first applied. Finally, the high point of medieval architecture came with the Perpendicular period characterised by large windows with flattened arches and intricate fan-lighted ceilings. Perpendicular architecture emphasised vertical elements, particularly so in window tracery with its straight verticals as well as its clearly defined horizontals.

Tullybrackey Co. Limerick

A representative example of the Gothic box at its most simplest would be Tullybrackey Church, built near Bruff in 1819 and demolished in 1959. James Pain's plan and side elevation show a rectangular hall containing both chancel and nave, the single-cell building being just three bays in length with 'Y' tracery in the side windows. The Church's principle element was a west tower crowned with battlements and with a pinnacle placed on each of the four corners. There was no Vestry Room or Robing Room built onto the church, nor was there any provision for such facilities within the church itself according to James Pain's ground plan of the church.[4]

Given the shortness of the nave/chancel and the height of the tower to the tip of its pinnacles, Tullybrackey was higher than it was long making the tower look disproportionate to the size of the church. But it did make the tower appear quite imposing in its rural setting, Bishop John J. Hogan in his 1898 memoirs of his Bruff childhood recalling an 'elegant church, with its massive

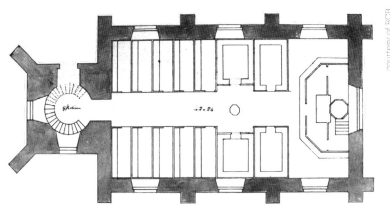

Plan of Tullybrackey Church, Co. Limerick.

tower.[5] A slight variation on this utterly simple layout is St. Munchin's (1827) on King's Island, Limerick, the vestry minutes of 27 April of that year recording the decision to proceed with a design by James Pain.[6] Similar in layout to Tullybrackey it differed in a number of regards. Firstly it is four bays in length and has therefore a better sense of proportion than Tullybrackey, and secondly the original window tracery in St. Munchin's was Perpendicular. Measuring more than 50 feet (15 metres) in height, St. Munchin's tower is supported by diagonal staged buttresses on the western corners. The tower is crowned with

St. Munchin's Church, King's Island, Limerick.

eight pinnacles, the four largest are placed on the corners of the tower and are crocketed on the spire. Four smaller-sized, uncrocketed, intermediate pinnacles are placed on the parapets. Built in a churchyard terrace overlooking the Shannon, and with the tower facing towards the river, St. Munchin's presents quite a striking sight when viewed from the opposite bank, the tower with its eight pinnacles dominating the surrounding buildings.

Normally the main entrance to a church is located in the west tower, but this is not the case with St. Munchin's. On 27 April 1827 the Vestry Committee requested that James Pain alter his design so as to move the doorway to a porch built onto a side elevation.[7] This was to avoid the inconvenience and discomfort of having the prevailing westerly winds whipping through an opening on the exposed west end. A more sheltered entrance was thereby provided in a porch built onto the northern side elevation. Constructed of local squared limestone, the Church measures approximately 72 feet (22 metres) in length and 30 feet (9 metres) in width. The doors and windows have hooded arches or drip mouldings. The Perpendicular East window was replaced during the 1880s with one decorated with Flamboyant tracery to commemorate a Major Vandeleur.[8] St. Munchin's is virtually identical to Rathkeale Holy Trinity (erected 1831)[9] in County Limerick although there are several minor differences, including the fact that the Rathkeale church retained its entrance in the west tower and there is a Vestry Room built onto the chancel end of the church on its southerly facing side elevation. The tower is, if not an identical twin, then almost the same as St. Munchin's with identical spikes and pinnacles on top of the tower, the same staged diagonal buttresses, the same pair of louvred lancets on each face of the belfry stage and a blank lancet on the second stage. Rathkeale also has Perpendicular windows and retains its original East window.

150

By convention, the chancel of a church was built to face East, but this layout was not always adhered to. In the case of St. Paul's in Cahir, Co. Tipperary, for instance, the 'East' chancel faces west and the 'west' tower looks toward the east. The 'west' tower of Kilcornan Church near Pallaskenry in County Limerick actually faces south. For the purposes of this study the chancel will always be referred to as the East end, regardless of actual orientation. This will avoid any unnecessary confusion. (When visiting a church a magnetic compass is always a useful thing to have in one's possession).

Some Gothic-box churches had a very short gabled extension added onto the East end in which the High Altar and chancel were placed. In height, these extensions reached between two-thirds to four-fifths the height of the main East gable and were about two-thirds the width of the main body of the church. An example of this layout is Killoscully Church (1829), three miles from Newport in Co. Tipperary.[10]

Variations on a Theme

While the Simple Gothic style is distinctive, it would not be correct to think that all churches were identical. There were a number of variations on the theme of a Gothic box, James Pain being able to produce an appropriate design 'model' and 'marque' to suit local needs, purse and vanities. One such variation consisted of the tower flanked on either side by a single-storey, cubic structure. An example of this type is Kilcornan (built in 1832)[11] where these additions have a pitched roof and two gables topped with a pinnacle. Kilcornan, also known as Castletown, is a cut above the average Simple Gothic church having a very attractive and stylistic tower edged with quoin work. Erected without buttresses, the tower features an unusually large lancet window on the second stage and has a pair of louvred lancets on each of the belfry faces. The curved hood-moulding over the window-heads is well

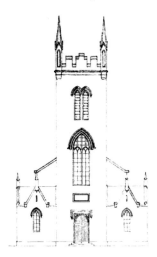

South elevation of Kilcornan Church, Co. Limerick.

executed; the west door having a label hood-mould placed over it. An extra little flourish was added with the centre merlon of the tower battlements constructed as an Irish stepped battlement. Not as stark in its finish as Simple Gothic tends to be, the masonry work and detailing at Kilcornan are excellently well done, a credit to the craftsmen working on the project and to the Waller family of Castletown who financed the entire project.[12] A number of churches with the same layout as Kilcornan had already been built in the Limerick Diocese. These included Chapel Russell Church (1822), also built near Pallaskenry, and Kilscannel Church erected near Rathkeale that same year.[13] In both these cases the single-storey 'wings' to the tower differ from Kilcornan in that they are flat roofed and embattled.[14] Projecting beyond the sides of the

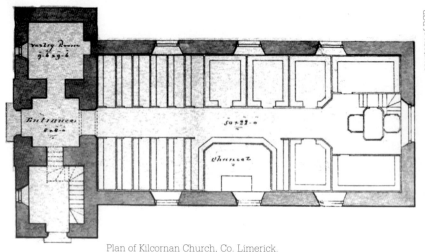

Plan of Kilcornan Church, Co. Limerick.

main body of the church, these structures usually housed a vestry room on the left-hand side of the entrance porch while the chamber on the right often contained a stair hall that led to the gallery. In the case of Kilscannel, however, an annotation by James Pain for this chamber reads 'Store, or Second Entrance.' At Kilcornan these rooms measure 9 feet 6 inches x 9 feet 6 inches (2.9 x 2.9 metres); at Kilscannel 9 feet (2.7 metres) square.[15]

A further embellishment was, of course, the placing of a spire on the top of a tower; James Pain commonly using a parapet spire on his parish churches, i.e. one arising from within the parapets of a tower. Predominately octagonal and slender, these spires give a certain elegance to churches, softening the angular lines of the supporting square tower. Spires work particularly well in partnership with modest sized towers in creating a picturesque effect, especially when the church is placed on an eminence as in the case of St. Mary's, Castletownroche (1825)[16] in north Co. Cork where a neat spire sits on a low tower. A sweet little church set on a hill overlooking the River Awbeg, St. Mary's is viewed with best effect when approaching the village along the road from Fermoy to Mallow. Bordered by trees and in harmony with its setting, St. Mary's offers a most delightful scene of idyllic rural tranquillity.

The peacefulness of this country churchyard is marred by the knowledge that one of the craftsmen working on the construction of the church tragically died there in August 1825. John Comyn, aged 27, a stonemason from Clarecastle, Co. Clare was working on the top of the steeple when he fell and was killed. Apparently his father, also a mason, was working on the site at the same time.[17] John's grave is marked by a gravestone located a few yards inside the churchyard on the left-hand side of the path leading to the church. The inscribed gravestone was erected by his brother Michael. Construction work has always traditionally been a hazardous occupation and it was even more so in the days before health and safety regulations were introduced into the

Castletownroche Church, Co. Cork showing diagonally projecting 'Vestry Room' and 'Hot Air Room'.

building trade. James Pain had personal knowledge of the dangers involved when he himself fell crashing four stories to the ground while standing on scaffolding at Lough Cutra Castle in October 1817.[18]

A reworking of the Gothic box theme is to be seen at Cloughjordan, Co. Tipperary where the pulpit was placed in front of one of the side walls of the church. The tower, surmounted by a spire, is built onto the opposite northern side elevation. On either side of the tower are single-storey additions with pitch roofs, each with an entrance door into the church (the right-hand chamber also containing stairs). On both the east and west facing gable ends of the church are gabled extensions, half the height of the main gable and

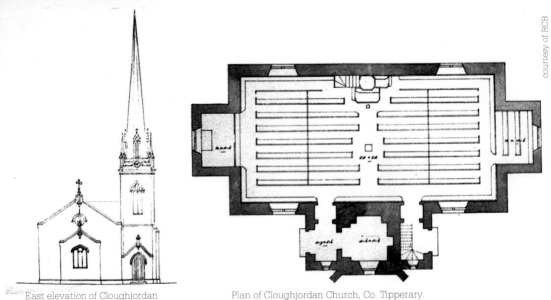

East elevation of Cloughjordan
Church, Co. Tipperary.

Plan of Cloughjordan Church, Co. Tipperary.

measuring 12 feet x 8 feet 6 inches (3.7 x 2.6 metres). That on the East end
containing the chancel and the High Altar; the other extension fitted out with
bench pews.[19]

Midleton, Co. Cork

It was in the busy, bustling town of Midleton in Co. Cork that the Pains built
one of their best regarded parish churches,[20] St. John the Baptist. It was
built in 1823 'under the immediate supervision of the Messrs. Pain'[21] with a
loan of £3,000 from the Board of First Fruits.[22] The prosperity of the town was
principally derived from a number of large breweries and distilleries giving
steady employment to many workers and craftsmen from the locality.
Within a mile of the town stood the estuary river port of Ballynacorra, the
quays and warehouses facilitating the export of agricultural products to
Britain and the import of coal, textiles and a host of other marketable goods.
Such a thriving commercial centre deserved a church of quality and the Pain
brothers duly obliged.

The Church of St. John the Baptist is a further elaboration of the Gothic box.
The most interesting feature of the composition is the three-stage tower which
is square on the first two stages turning into an octagonal upper stage, the
whole surmounted with a light, elegant octagonal spire. Large, louvred lancets
pierce the four cardinal faces of the belfry while the intermediate faces have
blank lancets. There are single-storey rooms on either side of the tower that
are flat-roofed and battlemented, but unlike Kilcornan they are rectangular in
plan, 16 x 10 feet (4.9 x 3 metres), the longest side facing west. Very much an
attention seeker, the west front of St. John the Baptist is best viewed from the
opposite side of the River Owenacurra, its eye-catching effect enhanced by an
ascending series of pinnacles. On the octagonal upper stage of the tower there

St. John the Baptist Church, Midleton, Co. Cork.

is a coronet of eight, on the corners of the square second stage there are four, while lower still a pinnacle is placed atop each corner of the nave gable.

In many churches the wooden gallery at the west end normally extended over a relatively short section of the nave. The gallery at St. Munchin's, Limerick, for instance, extended over about one third of the nave, having five rows of bench pews.[23] More prosperous and populous parishes could afford to have far grander galleries than that. At Midleton two rows of galleries, facing each other, were placed along the side walls of the nave for its full length. Each gallery was accessed by its own flight of stairs at the rear of the nave, each holding nine box pews.[24]

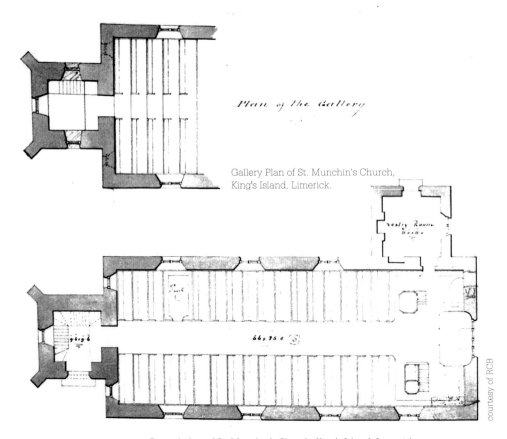

Plan of the Gallery

Gallery Plan of St. Munchin's Church, King's Island, Limerick.

Ground plan of St. Munchin's Church, King's Island, Limerick.

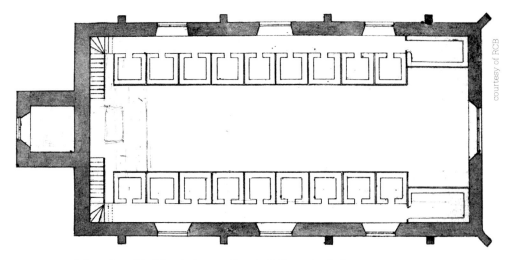

Gallery plan of St. John the Baptist Church, Midleton, Co. Cork.

Standing at the rear of the churchyard is an interesting mausoleum that is worth more than a second glance. Erected to the memory of Charles Brodrick, Archbishop of Cashel, and formerly a rector of Midleton parish, he died on 6 May 1822.[25] This large mausoleum has a Greek Revival frontage consisting of two unfluted Doric colonnettes supporting a pediment; the stonework on either side of the colonnettes is heavily rusticated. While there appears to be no architect's name inscribed on the structure the quality of the design speaks of the Pain brothers. Since the deceased gentleman was the Archbishop of Cashel and had died in 1822, about the same time that James Pain was appointed as official architect to the Archdiocese, it seems reasonable to suppose that the Church authorities would have requested the Pain brothers to provide a fitting memorial.

The Cruciform Church

More 'de-luxe' models in the Simple Gothic range featured transepts projecting north and south of the church creating a cruciform layout. There were three options available to architects: the Latin Cross, the Greek Cross and the St. Anthony's Cross (also known as the Tau Cross). The Latin Cross resembles the crucifix, with the shorter upper arm containing the chancel, and has been used as the basic form for many church plans since the Romanesque period in those areas of western and northern Europe influenced by the Roman Catholic Church and where Latin became the dominant language. The Latin Cross was hardly used by James Pain although John Nash's St. Paul's Church in Cahir, Co. Tipperary, on which the Pain brothers may have acted as the executing architects, is of this form.[26]

The Greek Cross has four arms of equal length, a church plan typically associated with Byzantine churches since the eleventh century. Byzantine

St. John's Church, Buttevant, Co. Cork

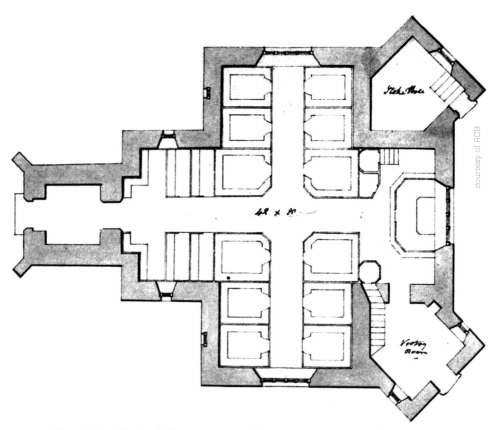

Ground plan of St. John's Church, Buttevant, Co. Cork. An example of a Greek Cross.

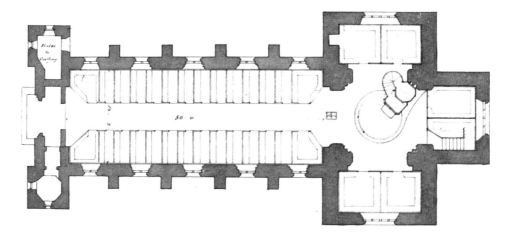

Ground plan of St. Paul's Church, Cahir, Co. Tipperary. An example of a Latin Cross.

architecture is traditional to those lands of the Eastern Roman Empire where the Orthodox Church and the Greek language became dominant. The division of the Roman Empire into eastern and western sections started at the time of the Roman Emperor Constantine (324-37), the two geographical regions gradually drifting apart until the Great Schism in the eleventh century when Christianity divided into the Orthodox and Roman Catholic Churches. The Greek Cross was also used in Italian Renaissance churches.

The Pain brothers are particularly renowned for their use of the equal-armed Greek Cross and one of the best known examples of this type is St. John's, Buttevant[27] in north County Cork on the road between Charleville and Mallow. The chancel is located in the eastern arm while the northern and southern arms formed transepts in which box pews were placed. As with other examples of the Pain brothers' Greek Cross, a tower is built onto the western arm. In the case of Buttevant it is given an octagonal spire. Jutting out diagonally from between the chancel and the transepts are two-single storey attachments that are marked on the plan drawn up by James Pain as the 'Vestry Room' and the 'Stoke Hole'.[28] This is a feature used on other of the brothers' First Fruits' work, and not solely in conjunction with a Greek Cross.

Secluded and hidden from the main road, St. John's, Buttevant does not interfere with the development of the town and is protected by the lack of development around it. Aloof and independent, it is secure in its own style, solidly grounded, compact and stocky; it looks an immovable and timeless structure planted in tradition. The church may not appeal to everyone's taste however, the blocky mass of masonry that constitutes the church and the use of dark grey limestone for the stonework may convince some that the building lacks grace and elegance. Unfortunately, when viewed from behind, where the churchyard slopes away, the East end of St. John's with its diagonal attachments spreading out wide gives the structure a rather fat-bottomed appearance. The church is in a beautiful setting, sited on an ancient sacred site and burial ground, the walled churchyard surrounded mainly by beech trees - the beech an estate tree favoured by the aristocracy and gentry for its grandeur. The building has been nurtured and cared for by a local restoration group known as The Friends of St. John's.

The Pain brothers built a number of Greek Cross churches and included among them was Mungret Church, Co. Limerick, constructed in 1822.[29] Due to the decline in Protestant numbers in the parish during the latter half of the nineteenth century the church was closed down in 1877. Unroofed in 1900 the building fell into a ruin, the stone later being used to build the parochial house at Raheen.[30] This was unfortunate and a great loss to nearby Limerick City, for the church had an interesting tower of which the upper half was octagonal with an Irish stepped battlement placed on each of the eight corners. On the cardinal faces of the belfry was a louvred lancet with blank lancets on the intermediate faces. In the south-east angle of the Greek Cross a single-storey Vestry Room, flat roofed and embattled, was placed with a length and width equal to the length of the arms of the Cross.. Unlike Buttevant, Mungret had no spire.[31]

A design with an almost identical tower to Mungret was Dromkeen Church built in 1831[32] in a parish three miles from Pallasgreen on the Limerick to Tipperary Road. In his design for Dromkeen James Pain did not include blank lancets on the intermediate faces of the belfry and he placed the Vestry Room in the north-west angle of the Cross, simply giving it a lean-to roof.

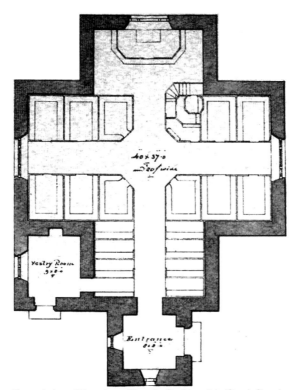

Ground plan of Dromkeen Church, Co. Limerick (Greek Cross).

Variations on the theme of a Greek Cross are Dungarvan Church (1831), which has no southern arm, and Myross Church (1827)[33] in the Diocese of Cork and Ross where the transepts are shorter than the eastern and western arms in the ratio of about 4:5.[34]

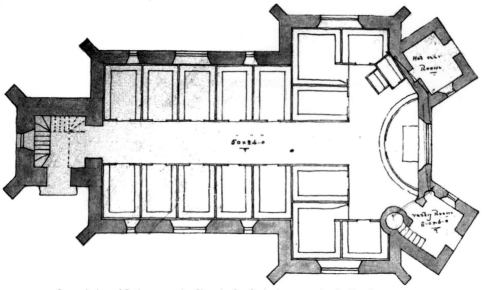

Ground plan of Catletownroche Church, Co. Cork. An example of a Tau Cross.

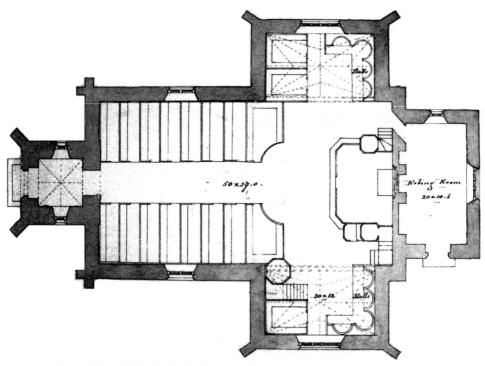

Ground plan of Emly Church, Co. Tipperary. See page 141 for side elevation.

Tau Cross

Another cruciform plan employed by the Pain brothers was the St. Anthony's Cross, or Tau Cross, which is T-shaped. This can be seen in St. Mary's at Castletownroche, Co. Cork where the transepts are placed so close to East end that there is no continuation of the northern and southern walls. The Chancel features a shallow, three-sided projection with diagonal single-storey structures attached that faced north-east and south-east respectively. One of these rooms is labelled the 'Vestry Room' on James Pain's plan of the Church while the other is called the 'Hot Air Room'.[35]

The architect's ground plan for the church at Emly, Co. Tipperary (built 1827, demolished 1877) may lead one to believe that it was a Latin Cross with its transepts and pronounced eastern arm. But this is not the case, for the eastern section houses a Robing Room that was built onto the east gable and separated by a wall from the main body of the church. Although attaining the width of the church, this room was less than half the height of the church roof. The chancel is actually centrally placed in front of the Robing Room wall at the head of the main body of the Church, which is T-shaped. This making Emly effectively a St. Anthony's Cross.[36]

A clear and unambiguous example of James Pain's affection for the St. Anthony's Cross is his proposal for Kinnitty Church in the Diocese of Killaloe.[37]

The Bell-Cote Church

The simplest of all the various formulas used by James Pain was the bell-cote church, a building consisting of a just rectangular hall with two rooms placed on either side of the entrance passage. Some of these churches lacked even pinnacles as an adornment. A distinguishing feature of this barn-like structure is a small open-arched belfry, known as a bell-cote, that straddles the west gable end and has just one single bell suspended. One of the smallest of this type of church was at Kilbehenny, Co. Limerick, the design signed James Pain, 1840. Only three bays in length, the windows were tall lancets with hood mouldings. Singe lancets on the side elevation and triple lancets on the East end were a common feature of the bell-cote church model. Utterly simple in layout, Kilbehenny was nevertheless a solid looking, robust building.[38]

An annotation in the architect's hand on one of the Kilbehenny drawings comments 'It is hoped that a porch will be built that can be used as the foundation of a future tower should funds become available. The Countess of Kingston has already given £250'.[39] Built on the borders of Co. Limerick 4 miles (6.4 km) to the north-east of Mitchelstown, the church was located near Galtee Lodge, a hunting lodge and retreat in the Galtee Mountains built for the Earls of Kingston. In 1834 the resident Protestant population of the parish amounted to twenty-two, 0.61% of the population of the parish,[40] It comes therefore of no

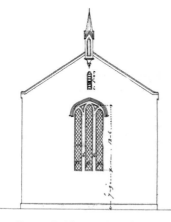

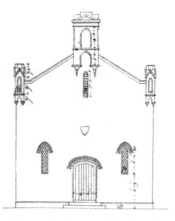

East end of Corcomohide Church,
Co. Limerick.

West end of Corcomohide Church.

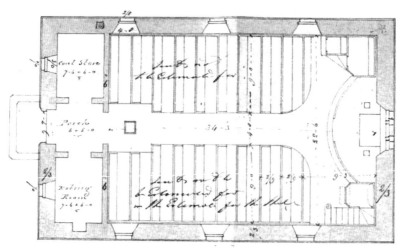

Ground plan of Corcomohide Church.

great surprise that Kilbehenny Church is no more, having been demolished in
the 1930s following the severance of the Kingston connection with the district
in the wake of the burning of Mitchelstown Castle in 1922.[41] A community hall
now occupies the site, the sole surviving remnants of the nineteenth century
churchyard are two stone gate piers and a few gravestones.

Similar to Kilbehenny was James Pain's proposed design for Corcomohide
(signed and dated July 1841), an ecclesiastical union in West Limerick that is
an amalgamation of the civil parishes of Castletown-Conyers, Dromcollogher
and Kilmeedy.[42] In this instance the architect has given the building a pinnacle
on the east gable end and provided both corners of the west elevation with just
the lower section of a pinnacle sans spire. The architect's plan shows a west

door allowing access to an internal porch with two rooms on either side. The chamber on the right is designated the 'Robing Room' while the other is a 'Coal Store', each lit by a single lancet 5 feet (1.5 metres) in height.[43] Though bell-cote churches appear to be rather small buildings when seen as architect's drawings, they were nevertheless quite large given their simplicity. The dimensions for Corcomohide are typical, being 45 feet 3 inches (13.2 metres) in length x 27 feet (8.2 metres) in width; the side walls are quite high, 21 feet 6 inches (6.6 metres), and are pieced by three lancet windows each 12 feet 6 inches (3,8 metres) tall. The top of the bell-cote is about 38 feet (11.6 metres) above ground level.[44]

Clonbeg Church

A number of very similar bell-cote designs were dashed off from the drawing boards of James Pain's Limerick office during the late 1830s and early 1840s and several of these, including Kilbehenny, were built by Clonmel architect William Tinsley. Included among Tinsley's assignments was Clonbeg Church located in the heart of the scenic Glen of Aherlow, in this instance it is a four bay, sandstone building that is mentioned in the O'Donovan Letters of 1840 as 'a neat modern little church now in the process of construction.'[45] The previous year the *Limerick Chronicle* reported that 'There is a grant of £900 by the Ecclesiastical Board to build a church at Clonbeg, Co. Tipperary and Mr. Pain has selected a site.'[46]

David Gaynor

165

Clonbeg Church, Glen of Aherlow, Co. Tipperary.

Substantial and solid despite its simple plan, the colour of the sandstone makes this isolated country church most appealing in appearance, particularly on a sunny day. Clonbeg Church is built beside the old church and all that remains of the latter is a ruined gable completely covered with ivy.[47] In the far right-hand corner of the churchyard is to be found St. Sedna's holy well, the water known for its healing properties and said to be a cure for eye aliments. When people visit the well they bring a piece of clothing from the sick person to tie onto trees behind the well. The custom is still strong, the branches festooned with items of clothing. The handsome little bell-cote straddling the west gable end is surmounted by a crucifix cross. Although the site is Church of Ireland property it has both a Catholic and Protestant burial ground. Another point of interest concerning Clonbeg Church are the stained glass windows that were inserted at a later date. Clonbeg is well worth a visit because of its setting in the natural beauty of the Glen of Aherlow and the picturesque qualities of both the church and its graveyard.

St. Sedna's holy well, Clonbeg, Co. Tipperary.

First Fruits' Alterations

As well as building new churches from the ground up, the Pain brothers' duties also involved carrying out modifications and extensions to existing buildings. We have already seen James expressing the hope that at some future date a porch and tower could be added onto Kilbehenny Church.

In 1830 the architect built a pinnacled square tower onto Kiltenanlea parish church in Clonlara, Co. Clare. It was originally erected in 1782 as a single-cell structure and when the incumbent, the Rev. Charles Massey, described the building to the Archbishop of Cashel in 1805 he had no more to say of its architectural glories other than it was 'in length 46 feet and 23 feet 6 inches wide. Wants at present some repairs to the gutters . . .' Construction of the tower was grant aided to the tune of £300 from the Board of First Fruits. Kiltenanlea was further modified in 1891 with the addition of a chancel and two small transepts, the gift of Lady Massy, providing the village with the pleasant little parish church that it is today.[48]

First Fruits' alterations could be major as well as relatively minor undertakings. Take the case of St. Carthage's Cathedral, Lismore, Co. Waterford. Founded in the medieval period, the Cathedral has undergone several changes over the centuries including major work undertaken by the Pain brothers. In 1827 the Cathedral Chapter agreed upon the following resolution,

> 'That a plan for the erection of a new tower and spire and repairs of the isle [sic] made by Messrs. Payne, to be completed for the sum of £3,500, which has been commenced under the direction of the Dean of Lismore, is unanimously and highly approved by us.'[49]

The assignment involved constructing a square tower with very tall, prominent corner pinnacles crocketed at the top. The slender octagonal parapet spire is supported by flying buttresses that leap most prettily from the pinnacles to the spire. The writer William Makepeace Thackeray, visiting Lismore in 1842, was fulsome in his praise of the Cathedral, describing the 'graceful spire of Lismore' as 'the prettiest I have seen in, or I think out of, Ireland.' He also commented that 'The church, with the handsome spire that looks so graceful among the trees, is . . . one of the neatest and prettiest edifices I have seen in Ireland.'[50] High praise indeed from such a one as Thackeray who could be quite scathing and critical of things Irish.

Because the Gothic tower and spire contrasted with the Classical style of the remainder of the Cathedral, the nave was given a fan-vaulted ceiling and the nave windows provided with pointed arches.[51] Another commission carried out for St. Carthage's Cathedral by both brothers, or by one of them, is a monument erected to the memory of Dean John Scott that took the form of an imposing Gothic interior porch to the new west tower. Porch is perhaps a far too anaemic word to describe this gateway-like structure with its buttresses, crocketed pinnacles and Tudor arch doorway. When Cork architect Henry Hill made sketches of various features of Lismore Cathedral in 1831 he remarked that the Scott memorial was 'a tasteful piece of work, J.[sic] R. Pain, Architect'.[52]

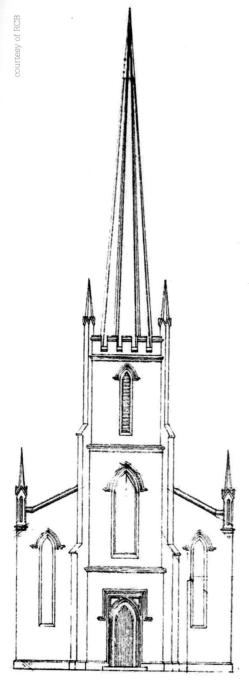

St. Michael's Church, Blackrock, Co. Cork.

George Richard Pain ▬▬▬

The younger brother's contribution to the architecture of the Church of Ireland was just as important as James's although the latter is usually referred to as the official architect to the Archdiocese of Cashel. While this may give the impression that G. R. Pain played the role of assistant to James, in practice George Richard was the equal of his brother. Interestingly, a pair of water-colour elevations of Knockavilly Church (Diocese of Cork and Ross) in the library of the Representative Church Body (RCB), are signed 'G. R. Pain. Provincial Architect. March 1836'.[53]

That James Pain was not always the sole official church architect in Munster is proved by a notice that appeared in the *Limerick Chronicle* of 7 May 1836 stating that the Ecclesiastical Commissioners were 'desirous of appointing, for the present year, one or more Architect or Architects to superintend the building and repairs of Churches in the Counties of Cork and Kerry.' Applications for the position(s) to be submitted to the Commissioners in Dublin by 14 May.

While it may be difficult to disentangle precisely what G. R. Pain's contribution was to First Fruits Gothic, given that the brothers' work in this area was generally referred to by contemporaries as by 'the Messrs. Pain', his creative input must have been quite substantial. We know what the younger brother was capable of when he worked on his own, witness the magnificent architecture he created for the Catholic Church in Cork. Indeed, some of the best Church of Ireland parish churches were built in Cork during the period when the brothers flourished as a team.

St. Michael's Church at Blackrock (1827) is certainly attention grabbing with its very tall, needle-like, 60 feet (18.3 metres) high spire that is set to pierce the heavens. Perhaps God thought that the architect was getting a bit too much above himself, for He struck both spire and tower down with lightning on 29 January 1836, but they were later restored. St. Michael's cost £2,100 to build, part of the money being raised by the sale of box pews as well as local subscriptions and the usual loan from the Board of First Fruits.[54] Another church that has been consistently picked out for praise is Carrigaline which features a tower with a large Perpendicular window on the front elevation. Opened for Divine Service in February 1824. the church looks quite superior, the press of the day commenting that Carrigaline 'built by Messrs. Payne . . . is a beautiful structure.'[55]

Endnotes

1 Stage is the correct term for a storey when discussing the structure of a tower.
2 'The new church of Carragaline [sic] County of Cork, built by Messrs. Payne [sic], was opened for Divine Service on Sunday. It is a beautiful structure.' *Limerick Chronicle*, Saturday 14 February 1824.
3 *Dictionary of Architecture*, Architectural Publication Society s.v. 'Pain, James and George Richard'.
4 Ground plan and south elevation of Tullybrackey Church by James Pain, Library of the Representative Church Body (RCB), Braemor Park, Churchtown, Dublin, Vol. 5 'Diocese of Limerick and Ardfert'. Six volumes of James Pain's plans and elevations of churches in the Archdiocese of Cashel are held in the library of the RCB.
5 Hogan, Right Rev. John J., Bishop of Kansas City *Fifty Years Ago* a memoir written in 1898 and published 1907 by Franklin Hudson Publishing Co., Kansas City, p. 24.
6 Vestry minutes of 27 April 1827 cited by Miley, Garry *History of the Church of St. Munchin*, MUBC Building Study, Limerick, 1998, copy in Limerick Civic Trust Archive; Inscribed plaque on the western tower.
7 Miley *op. cit.*
8 Miley *op. cit.*
9 Lewis, Samuel *A Topographical Dictionary of Ireland*, Two Vols., London, 1837, s.v. 'Rathkeale'.
10 Lewis *op. cit.* s.v. 'Killoscully'; Ground plan and south elevation of Killoscully Church, RCB, Vol. I, 'Diocese of Emly and Cashel'.
11 Lewis *op. cit.* s.v. 'Kilcornan'.
12 Lewis *op. cit.* 'Kilcornan'.
13 Lewis *op. cit.* s.v. 'Chapel-Russell', 'Kilscannel'.
14 Ground plans and elevations of Kilcornan, Chapel Russell and Kilscannel, RCB, Vol. 5, 'Diocese of Limerick and Ardfert'.
15 ibid.
16 Lewis *op. cit.* s.v. 'Castletownroche'.

17 Conversation with Billy Browne of Castletownroche.

18 *Limerick Gazette*, 21 October 1817.

19 Ground plan and east elevation of Cloughjordan Church, RCB, Vol. 4, 'Diocese of Killaloe and Kilfenora'.

20 *Dictionary of Architecture*, Architectural Publication Society s.v. 'Pain, James and George Richard'.

21 Lewis op. cit. s.v, 'Midleton'. The date stone on the tower of Midleton Church is inscribed '1825', presumably the date of its consecration or dedication

22 Lewis *op. cit.* s.v. 'Midleton' Vol. II. p. 369.

23 Gallery plan of St. Munchin's Church, RCB, Vol. 5 'Diocese of Limerick and Ardfert'.

24 Gallery plan of Midleton Church, RCB, Vol. II 'Diocese of Cloyne'.

25 The plaque on the mausoleum also commemorates the Archbishop's wife, the Hon. Mary Brodrick, who died in March 1799.

26 'Ground plan of Caher Church', RCB, Vol. 6 'Diocese of Waterford and Lismore'.

27 *Dictionary of Architecture*, Architectural Publication Society s.v. 'Pain, James and George Richard' credits the Pain brothers as the architects of St. John's, Buttevant.

28 Plan of St. John's, Buttevant, RCB, Vol. II, 'Diocese of Cloyne'.

29 Lewis *op. cit.* s.v. 'Mungret'.

30 O'Connor, John *Mungret: History and Antiquities*, Dalton Printers, Limerick, 1971, p. 38.

31 Ground plan and south elevation of Mungret Church, RCB, Vol. 5 'Diocese of Limerick and Ardfert'.

32 Ground floor and north elevation of Dromkeen Church, RCB, Vol. 1, 'Diocese of Emly and Cashel'; Lewis *op. cit.* s.v. 'Dromkeen'.

33 Lewis *op. cit.* s.v. 'Myross', 'Dungarvan'.

34 Ground plan of Myross Church, RCB, Vol. III, 'Diocese of Cork and Ross'.

35 Ground plan of Castletownroche Church, RCB, Vol. II 'Diocese of Cloyne'.

36 Ground plan and south elevation of Emly Church, RCB, Vol. 1, 'Diocese of Emly and Cashel'; Hewson, Adrian *Inspiring Stones: A History of the Church of Ireland Dioceses of Limerick, Ardfert, Aghadoe, Killaloe, Kilfenora, Clonfert, Kilmacduagh and Emly*, published by the Diocesan Council of Limerick, Killaloe and Ardfert in association with FÁS Community Response Training Programme, 1995, p. 42; *Limerick Chronicle* 12 August 1826; Lewis *op. cit.* Vol. I, p.599.

37 Ground plan of Kinnitty Church, RCB, Vol. 4 'Diocese of Killaloe and Kilfenora'.

38 Ground plan and elevations of Kilbehenny Church, RCB Vol. 1 'Diocese of Emly and Cashel'.

39 ibid. Although built in 1840/1 Kilbehenny Church was not dedicated until 17 October 1844 - *Index of Irish Architects* s.v. 'Pain, James', Irish Architectural Archive, Merrion Square, Dublin.

40 *The Parliamentary Gazetteer of Ireland* s.v. 'Kilbehenny'.

41 Power, Bill *Evensong: The Story of a Church of Ireland Country Parish* Mount Cashell Books, Mitchelstown, Co. Cork, 2004, p. 71.

42 Lewis *op. cit.* s.v. 'Corcomohide'. Dromcollogher is spelt 'Drumcolloher' in Lewis.

43 Ground plan and west elevation of Corcomohide, RCB, Vol. 5 'Diocese of Limerick and Ardfert'.

44 Architect's drawings of Corcomohide, RCB, Vol. 5 'Diocese of Limerick and Ardfert'.

45 Quoted in Forbes, J. D. *Victorian Architect: The Life and Work of William Tinsley*, Indiana University Press, Bloomington, 1953, p. 35.

46 *Limerick Chronicle*, 2 October 1839.

47 James Pain's south elevation of the old church at Clonbeg shows a structure that is almost cottage-like in appearance having just two rectangular windows that are slightly rounded at the top and quite domestic looking, each with nine panes of glass arranged in three rows. Although the side wall was about 39 feet (11.9 metres) long it was but 8 feet (2.4 metres) in height. Ground plan and south elevation of old Clonbeg Church, RCB, Vol. I 'Diocese of Emly and Cashel'. The building was 39 feet 2 inches (11.9 metres) long by 21 feet (6.4 metres) wide. Besides the chancel, this single cell church held just eight box pews.

48 'Parish Church and Its History', *Kiltenanlea Parish Church, Clonlara, Co. Clare, 1782-1992*, published by the Clonlara Development association, 1992.

49 Quoted in Day, J. Godfrey F., Bishop of Ossory, & Patton, Henry E., Bishop of Killaloe *The Cathedrals of the Church of Ireland*, Society for Promoting Christian Knowledge, London 1932. p. 131. Presumably the 'isle' mentioned in the resolution is a reference to the nave.

50 Thackeray, William Makepeace *The Irish Sketch Book*, London, 1843, Vol. I, pp. 93, 96.

51 Galloway, Peter *The Cathedrals of Ireland*, The Institute of Irish Studies, Queens University Belfast, 1992, p. 168.

52 Hill, H. 'Diary of an Itinerary in Ireland in 1831', *Journal of the Cork Historical and Archaeological Society* Vol. 38, No. 147, January-June, 1933, p. 31.

53 Water-colour east and south elevations of Knockavilly Church, RCB, Vol. III 'Diocese of Cork and Ross'.

54 Lewis *op. cit.* Vol. I. p. 299.

55 *Limerick Chronicle*, 14 February 1824.

CHAPTER TEN

THE GREAT GOSPEL TRUMPET

As one might expect, the name of James Pain is linked to Limerick's St. Mary's Cathedral which underwent a series of restorations, additions and alterations during the course of the nineteenth century. To compile a fully accurate list of all of the architect's work for the Cathedral may not be possible due to the patchy nature of the primary sources. However we do know that in 1826 a screen in the 'Gothic stile' was installed at the altar of St. Mary's by the Pain brothers at the expense of Bishop John Jebb (1822-33). 'The design is so chaste,' reported the *Limerick Chronicle*, 'the workmanship so correct and the whole so calculated for the venerable pile in which it is placed, as must excite general approbation.'[1]

John Paul Dowling

Gothic canopy of Bishops' Throne, St. Mary's Cathedral, Limerick.

The Bishop's Throne located in the Cathedral's Lady Chapel (formerly the Sanctuary until 1997)[2] has been attributed to James Pain.[3] Installed in 1831, the throne originally comprised a free standing chair on a dais backed by high wall panelling; overhead a Gothic canopy was attached to the wall. The dais was enclosed on its three outer sides by panelling with a doorway to allow access. Although the dais has since been removed, the wall panelling remains. Overhead still looms the substantial Gothic canopy - a dark, gloomy, wooden, crocketed affair surmounted by a weighty dome. Over the years the Cathedral clergy have not always been numbered among the greatest of admirers of this item of Pain's handiwork.

Memorial statue to Bishop Jebb, St. Mary's Cathedral, Limerick.

Near this place
are interred
the Rev. WILLIAM DEAN HOARE and
Vicar General of this Diocese
and during Twenty six Years
in discharging Clergymen in this City
A faithful preacher of the Gospel of our Lord
He never ceased to Recommend and inconceibly
Christian holiness of life
Simple and unaffected in his manners,
the law of kindness was on his lips, and
the love of God and man was in his heart
He was in the true sense of the word
a public blessing
And the following
Charitable Institutions in this City
the Lying in Hospital,
the female Orphan School,
the Widows Asylum,
the St Georges day School
and the mendicity association,
founded by his exertion,
and sustained by his watchful care,
bear testimony
to his patient continuance in well doing
born Oct st MDCCLXIII and died Oct 23rd MDCCCXXIII.
Revelations   Ch. XIV 13.

This memorial has been erected
by friends who all knew his virtues
and many of whom participated in
his labours of love

J & G.R. Pain   FitzGerald
                          Cork

Memorial tablet to Rev. William Deane Hoare, St. Mary's Cathedral, Limerick.

Following Bishop Jebb's death in 1833 a subscription fund was set up to raise money for a memorial statue and both Pain brothers made contributions. Costing over £1,100[4] the work was executed by E. H. Baily of London in 1836, the white marble statue of the Bishop consisting of a massive pedestal surmounted by a more than life-size statue of the Bishop seated in a chair, book in hand. It is presently located in the Cathedral's Jebb Chapel, formerly the Chapel of St. Nicholas and St. Catherine. A white marble plaque on the Chapel's eastern wall lists all those who subscribed to the memorial fund.[5] Bishop Jebb deserved to be commemorated by all those who knew him as he was a great benefactor to the Cathedral. Besides commissioning the Gothic screen for the altar and the Bishop's Throne, he also presented a new altar cloth and a new pulpit.[6]

Also to be seen on the eastern wall of Jebb's Chapel is a memorial tablet to the Rev. William Deane Hoare (died 1823), Vicar General of the Diocese, designed by the Pain brothers[7] and executed by Fitzgerald of Cork.[8] It may not be to modern taste, the main sculptural element being a putto (a chubby, naked male child) bewailing the demise of the exemplary Hoare by burying his tearful face in a shroud that hides his nakedness. Putti ('little boys') were a well-worn and traditional device for decorating Classical funerary monuments and tablets.

James Pain's professional association with the Cathedral also included the design in 1841 of a new entrance to the Cathedral grounds on Bridge Street opposite the old City Courthouse[9] and the insertion of a Perpendicular window, six lights in width, above the altar. There is extant in the Cathedral archives a drawing, signed by the architect and dated March 1843, of the transverse section of St. Mary's chancel showing the window in question.[10] It is no longer there, having been taken down in the late 1850s and replaced by triple lancet windows installed in 1860 by London architect William Slater.[11] James's Perpendicular was later placed in the chancel of St. Michael's Church, Pery Square when the church underwent major modifications in the 1870s. To fit into the available space the window had to be proportionately reduced in size from six to five lights in width.

James Pain is also believed to have erected a porch onto the west door of St. Mary's in 1816,[12] but this is a matter more appropriately discussed in the final chapter of this study.

Bedford Row Chapel

Besides their work for the Church of Ireland and the Catholic Church the Pain brothers were also willing to carry out commissions for other religious groupings. One known example is the New Independent Chapel, erected in 1829, by the Messrs. Pain' on Cork City's George's Street,[13] now Oliver Plunkett Street. This leads one to speculate whether or not the brothers were involved in the building in 1821 of the Primitive Methodist Preaching House on Limerick's Bedford Row. Built in the Gothic style,[14] the façade featured an attractive Perpendicular window, ogee arching over the ground floor windows and an orthodox battlemented gable roofline.[15] Given the Pain brothers' proficiency in Gothic and their local availability it is likely that the Primitive Methodists called upon their expertise to design the Chapel. When built it was set back from the pavement and protected by railings.

The background to its construction was rooted in a split in the Methodist movement caused by a dispute over their relationship with the Anglican Church. Methodism had been founded in 1739 by John Wesley (1703-91), an English Evangelist who wanted to revitalise the spiritual life of the Established

CENTRAL HALL

CENTRAL HALL

Primitive Methodist Preaching House (1821), Bedford Row, Limerick.

Church through preaching and missionary zeal, Wesley himself undertook many preaching tours of Britain and Ireland. He counselled his followers not to cut themselves off from the Established Church but urged them to take the sacraments and Holy Communion with the Anglican Congregation and to act, in effect, as a spiritual pressure group within the Church. A Methodist society was first established in Limerick in 1749,[16] that met in various venues in

Wesleyan Chapel (1812), George's (O'Connell) Street, Limerick.

Englishtown over the coming years. Finally, in 1812, a chapel was built on George Street in Newtown Pery that is still used today as a joint Methodist and Presbyterian house of worship. Known as Christ Church, it can be found at 51 O'Connell Street. But one would hardly know of its existence as the original façade has been removed and replaced with offices. Gone is the Georgian style front that featured on the ground floor rusticated stone work, round-headed windows and a large semicircular fan-light over the entrance door. Known as the Wesleyan Chapel, this building was set back from the pavement and fronted with railings. The breakfront was given emphasis by being edged with quoin work.[17] Today the Chapel is located at the rear of the offices, access to Christ Christ is through a street door and corridor.

The schism within the Methodist ranks arose due to a rising demand within the movement for the administration of the sacraments in the Methodist chapels. This was met by an equally strong, minority protest that such a move would separate the Societies from the Established Church. In 1816 the Methodist Conference gave the go-ahead for the consolidation of the Methodists into a more formal Church and the decision divided the membership, about one-third seceding and forming the Primitive Wesleyan Methodist Society to preserve their links with the Anglican Church.[18] In Limerick the newly built Chapel on George Street was retained by the majority faction, who were known as the Wesleyan Methodists,[19] while the breakaway Primitive Methodists erected their own Chapel in Bedford Row in 1821. The fact that their Chapel was in Gothic is indicative of the group's loyalty to the Established Church. This building has not served a religious purpose for some considerable time now. Most most of the façade was removed or bricked-in and the building converted into the Grand Central Cinema prior to 1924 and the building brought forward to the pavement with a normal cinema entrance. By late 1973 a shop front had been inserted into the ground floor and access to the cinema was now through a door set to one side of the shop and up two flights of stairs. The cinema closed in 2004. The removal of the Chapel's gable was not total for from street level one can still discern the battlemented roof line of the original façade. In the near future shops and offices will replace what was the hall of the Methodist Church but the surviving elements of the original Gothic façade will be retained, restored and showcased within a new façade, which will be predominately glass. This will ensure that the surviving church architecture will be featured to the best advantage. Arnold Leahy Architects are involved with this project.

John Paul Dowling

Façade of Central Cinema, Bedford Row, Limerick showing battlements of the Primitive Methodist Preaching House in background. This photo was taken in Spring 2005.

The Great Gospel Trumpet

When in early 1834 a group of Church of Ireland parishioners in St. Michael's Parish in Limerick City petitioned the Bishop that a licence be granted for Trinity Christ on Catherine Street he replied that it was his most earnest wish that:

> '. . . the Gospel Trumpet may be sounded within the walls of your beautiful chapel long after the bodies of us who are assembled shall be mouldering in our graves and our spirits shall have taken flight to the mansions of eternal rest where no jarring contention or difference of opinion shall prevail but all shall be harmony and peace.'[20]

The beautiful chapel is no more, the Gospel Trumpet now silent, the building no longer a place of worship. More recently it served as the headquarters of the Mid-Western Health Board.

Despite deconsecration, at least the building was saved and used for a beneficial and practical purpose. Other churches have not been so kindly treated over the years. Samuel Lewis noted in *Topographical Dictionary* of 1837 that Castlehyde parish church, built in 1812 two miles distant from Fermoy on the road to Mallow in County Cork, was 'much improved from a design by G. R. Pain of Cork Esq.; the interior is embellished with a richly groined ceiling and most of the windows are of stained glass.'[21] Presently (2005), Castlehyde Church is in a state of dereliction, with broken windows and damaged roof.

Which is a pity, for architecture is one of the most important primary sources we have for understanding the past and to lose even one derelict Church of Ireland church without attempting to restore or stabilise the structure is to lose a window into that past. Documents may lie, oral histories distort, but stones hold the truth of their founders, for they can often speak to the generations to come far more eloquently and convincingly than the words of men. John Ruskin, the Victorian art and social critic, once memorably remarked 'Great nations write their autobiographies in three manuscripts, the book of their deeds, the book of their words, and the book of their art. Not one of these books can be understood unless we read the two others, but of the three the only trustworthy one is the last.'

Saved From Ruin

One church that was saved from decay and ruin was St. Munchin's on King's Island, Limerick. With the decline of the Church of Ireland population in the city during the twentieth century St. Munchin's was deconsecrated in 1969 and up to 1986 it lay idle and allowed to fall into disrepair. During this period a considerable amount of vandalism and natural decay made the building derelict. It had a rather sad appearance with the doorways and the bottom half of the windows blocked up with concrete blocks. The deterioration of the building became quite advanced. The roof was beyond repair, the gutters and lead flashing had been stolen and all windows were broken with the exception of one stained glass window that had been protected from the vandals by concrete blocks and wire mesh. All electrical wiring and fittings were either stolen or broken. The surrounding graveyard was completely overgrown and the main entrance to the churchyard from Church Street bricked up.[22]

St. Munchin's was saved from a most dismal and grievous fate by the actions of Limerick Civic Trust who, in 1986, agreed to take over custody of the church from the Representative Church Body and entered into a ninety-nine year lease at a peppercorn (nominal) rent of 5 pence per year. Over the following three years Limerick Civic Trust carried out major restoration work that was sponsored by Irish Cement Ltd. to the extent of £20,000. The restoration project involved reinstating the fabric of the building by completely removing the old roof and having it replaced, providing new gutters, glazing the windows, removing the concrete blocks at the openings and providing new teak doors, as well as having the building fully rewired. The restoration also involved removing and replacing all damaged or decayed plaster and painting the entire inside of the building. The Church Street gateway was reopened and a new steel gate fitted. All this work was a direct replacement of the original and there were no alterations to the structure of any kind other than the provision of a toilet in the former vestry.[23]

In 1988 an agreement was reached with the Island Theatre Company, Limerick's only professional theatre company, to allow them under the terms of a sublease the use of the church as a theatrical workshop and headquarters. A stipulation was agreed between Limerick Civic Trust and the Representative Church Body that no commercial activity would be carried out at the venue.[24] The Company is still in residence. The building contains no church furnishings and basically the interior of the church is an open space with no partitions.

This rescue work was extremely important as St. Munchin's Church is sighted in a very critical architectural area of Limerick, located as it is beside the Villiers Alms Houses (also designed by the Pain brothers 1827) and the Bishops' Palace, once the residence of the Church of Ireland bishops of Limerick in the eighteenth century and now the headquarters of Limerick Civic Trust. This building itself had become derelict. Unroofed and gutted and almost on the verge of being demolished, the Bishops' Palace was saved by the Trust in the mid-1980s and completely renovated. In this historic part of the city is also to be found the thirteenth century King John's Castle and the ruins of the Dominican Priory built in 1227. The boundary wall of St. Munchin's graveyard, which faces towards the river Shannon, is part of the old city wall that once enclosed the medieval district of Englishtown. The work of Limerick Civic Trust in this part of the city in rescuing two buildings of architectural interest has been tremendously important in maintaining King's Island's sense of identity.

During the period 2000-2 further restorative work on the tower of St. Munchin's and the adjoining wall façade was sponsored by Limerick Civic Trust to deal with a build-up of weeds, mosses, lichen and algae on the stonework and on the pinnacles. To eradicate this growth the masonry had to be power washed and sprayed with a fungicide. The problem had arisen due to the poor condition of the pointing between the stonework that had deteriorated to such an extent as to allow weeds to take root and grow. To prevent this problem reoccurring again the old pointing had to be raked out to a minimum depth of 3/4 of an inch (1.9 cm) and the joints repointed. The work was carried out in conjunction with Limerick Corporation and Collins

Repair work on the pinnacles of St. Munchin's Church, King's Island, Limerick.

Steeplejacks & Partners Ltd. of Ardnacrusha, Co. Clare, restoration specialists who were chosen to carry out the work following a tendering process.[25]

It was also found on inspection that the uppermost stones of the pinnacles on the tower were in a loose and dangerous condition with the possibility of them eventually falling down. The top three stones of the four main corner pinnacles had to be removed, new stainless dowels inserted into each stone base and the stones re-bedded on a new mortar bed. The same system of repair was applied to the top four stones of the four intermediate pinnacles. In addition, the coping stones on the top of the battlements were also found to be in a loose condition and these had to be removed and re-bedded with stainless steel dowels. A new tower roof and replacement floor in the upper tower section were provided and a new safety staircase installed. The louvres on the belfry stage were also in poor condition and these had to be taken down to be either repaired or replicated if beyond repair.[26]

The comprehensive restorative work undertaken by Limerick Civic Trust on St. Munchin's Church indicates the detailed care and dedicated attention that needs to be lavished on heritage buildings in order to maintain them in good order for the enjoyment and use of future generations.

Endnotes

1 Limerick Chronicle, 12 September 1826.
2 In 1997 the sanctuary was deemed too far away from the congregation for modern services and was transformed into a Lady Chapel.
3 A Historic and Descriptive Sketch of St. Mary's Cathedral, G. M'Kern & Sons, Limerick, 1887, 3rd edition, p. 36; Williams, A Companion Guide to Architecture in Ireland 1837-1921, Irish Academic Press, Dublin, 1994, p. 268.
4 The New Triennial and Commercial Directory for the Years 1840, 41 and 42, printed by George M. Goggin for F. Kinder & Son, Limerick, 1840, p. 5.
5 A list of subscribers published in The Monuments of St. Mary's Cathedral Limerick, Treaty Press, Limerick, 1976, pp. 51-2, omits G. R. Pain's name from the list.
6 Lenihan, Maurice Limerick; Its History and Antiquities (1866), p. 610. Republished in facsimile in a 500 copy limited edition as History of Limerick, O'Carroll, Cian ed., The Mercier Press, Cork, 1991.
7 The initials of both brothers are inscribed on the memorial.
8 Inscription on memorial.
9 Limerick Chronicle, 10 April, 15 May, 12 August 1841.
10 Mulvin, Lynda 'St. Mary's Cathedral: Unpublished Correspondence of the Cathedral Restoration in the Nineteenth Century', Irish Architectural and Decorative Studies, The Journal of the Irish Georgian Society, Vol. IV, 2001, p. 183
11 Dowd, Rev. James History of St. Mary's Cathedral, Limerick, George

McKern & Sons, Limerick, 1899, p. 56.

12 *A Historic and Descriptive Sketch of St. Mary's Cathedral*, G. M'Kern & Sons, Limerick, 1881, p. 34.

13 Windele, J. *Historical and Descriptive Notices of the City of Cork and its Vicinity; Cougaun-Barra, Glengariff, and Killarney*, Messrs. Bolster, Cork, 1846 edition, p. 28.

14 Lenihan *op. cit.* p. 689.

15 Photograph of Bedford Row Chapel, Limerick Museum (LM 1998 0231).

16 Cooney, Dudly Levistone 'Elizabeth Bennis - Memorable Methodist'. Limerick Civic Trust Archives.

17 Photograph of original façade of George Street Wesleyan Chapel, Limerick Museum (LM 2002. 0129).

18 Cooney, Rev. Dudley Levistone *This Plain, Artless, Serious People: The Story of the Methodists of County Limerick*, 2000, p. 15.

19 Lenihan *op. cit.* p. 688.

20 Quoted in Waller, John Thomas *Trinity Church and St. Michael's Church*, McKerns Printing, Limerick, 1954.

21 Lewis *op. cit.* s.v. 'Litter, or Castlehyde' Vol. II, p. 289. The parish also went by the name Litter as well as Castlehyde.

22 St. Munchin's Church File, Limerick Civic Trust Archive.

23 ibid.

24 ibid.

25 ibid.

26 ibid.

CHAPTER ELEVEN

CORK WORK

As previously noted, George Richard Pain had moved permanently to Cork City by the early 1820s, as Pigot's 1824 Directory gives his address as 5 St. Patrick's Hill, Cork. Having one member of the family partnership with an address and office in Limerick while another was based in Cork, the two most important urban centres in Munster, gave the brothers a distinct advantage in establishing contact with potential clients and maintaining a circle of influential friends and acquaintances among 'those who mattered' in the province. Cork was to prove extremely rewarding to the brothers as a number of very prestigious commissions came their way from that part of the country, particularly to George.

Courthouse Controversy

Their most outstanding assignment in the city was the Cork City and County Courthouse[1] (1830-35) on Great George's Street, now Washington Street. Described as the Pains' Classical masterpiece[2] and the 'finest structure of the kind in the south of Ireland',[3] it boasts an immense Corinthian portico with 30 feet (9.1 metres) high columns resting on a platform gained by ascending a flight of eleven steps from street level. Projecting 20 feet (6.1 metres) from the main building, the portico has a length of 72 feet (21.95 metres). With its eight columns on its front elevation it is the only example in Ireland of a portico in Corinthian octastyle. Ten columns in all, eight on the front and one on each of the returns support the weighty pediment. The shafts are unfluted and both frieze and tympanum are left bare. There is however an impressive group of three bronze figures placed on the acroterion at the apex of the pediment representing Justice pondering profoundly between Law and Mercy. Corinthian pilasters on the front elevation of the main building complement the free-standing columns on the portico.

If the purpose of this commanding edifice in white ashlar limestone was to impress upon the mind of both felon and law-abiding citizen alike the full power and majesty of the Law then the architects certainly earned their fee. It certainly impressed the distinguished nineteenth century English historian Thomas Macaulay who commented that the Corinthian portico 'would do honour to Palladio'.[4] By way of comparison, an Ionic portico in octastyle is to be seen in Carlow Courthouse on the Dublin Road, but it is rather a plain structure when compared with the Pains' Cork work.

Controversy later arose over who actually designed the Cork City and County Courthouse, a controversy arising out of the intense rivalry that had developed between the Pains and another pair of architect brothers, Cork born Thomas and Kearns Deane. There were accusations of plagiarism, the Rev. C. B. Gibbons writing in his 1861 History of Cork that the Courthouse was 'built in 1835 by G. R. Paine after a design by Kearnes [sic] Deane'.[5] The Deanes

185

Cork City and County Courthouse.

Three bronze figures of Justice, Law and Mercy.

obviously felt very aggrieved over the whole affair, for at the Cork Exhibition of 1852 they placed on display a model of their design for the Courthouse, a model that had been submitted in 1829 as part of a competitive bid to secure the commission. Their application had been turned down and the job given to the Pains, but the Deanes clearly thought that their rivals had plagiarised their ideas[6] and that the Pains were little more than glorified contractors.

However, contemporary accounts written in the 1830s and '40s either categorically voice the opinion that the Courthouse was erected from designs by the Messrs. Pain,[7] or else attribute G. R. Pain solely as architect and contractor, the *Irish Penny Post* of 6 April 1833 reporting that 'the building is now in progress according to the design and under the inspection of G. R. Pain who has contracted for its completion at the sum of £16,000.'[8] When John Barrow viewed the Courthouse in the year of its completion in 1835 he commented that it was 'a remarkably elegant building, reflecting great credit upon Mr. Pain, the architect.'[9] Although the interior of the building was completely gutted by fire in 1891 the portico happily survived the conflagration without any damage and was retained when the Courthouses were rebuilt by Cork architect William Henry Hill (1837-1911).[10] The grandeur of the magnificent portico still impresses, even in our blasé world.

Damaging Rumours

In early June 1837 a news item surfaced in the *Cork Southern Reporter* to the effect that the Cork City and County Courthouse 'built at such an enormous cost' had been examined by architects Owens and Morrison and that 'their report is not favourable to the stability of the building.'[11] This report, republished in the *Limerick Chronicle*, drew an immediate response from

George Richard Pain who, in a letter to the Editor, forcibly challenged the potentially damaging rumours,

> 'SIR - I observe in your paper of yesterday, a short paragraph copied from the Cork Southern Reporter, alluding to the New Court Houses for this City and County. As the Architect and Contractor, in conjunction with my brother, I have to request you will give the most unqualified contradiction to the statement. The building was finished more than two years ago, and it was examined throughout last week by Mr. Owen, Mr. Leahy, and Mr. Morrison. I have not seen the report, but I have Mr. Leahy's authority (our County Engineer) to state, that not one word of the paragraph put forth by the Southern Reporter is founded in truth.'

As evidence to support his case George Richard Pain accompanied his letter with an engineer's report based on a survey of the Courthouses that had been carried out by London civil engineer Charles Vignoles in June 1836. His assessment of the structural stability of the building was also published in the same edition of the *Limerick Chronicle* along with the architect's letter. It was Vignoles's considered opinion that the Cork Courthouses were of excellent construction and that there was not the slightest apprehension concerning the solidity of the construction and the soundness of the building.

George Richard Pain concluded his letter by stating,

> 'I will now boldly assert, there is not in this City, a building of importance, so perfectly free from bulgeings, or more free from collapsion or settlement; and as to bulk - I am almost constrained to add, beauty, they all sink into nothingness. But this, perhaps, would be egotism; and although there are those who would scandalize, I wish not to praise myself,
> I am, Sir, your very obedient servant,
> G. R. PAIN.'[12]

Since the building did not fall down all in a heap in the period between the time of its construction and the fire of 1891 we can safely assume that Mr. Vignoles was correct in his assessment. However, there were long standing complaints about other aspects of the building, certain defects that were not easily resolved. In March 1837 we hear that at the Cork Grand Jury the 'new Courthouses of Cork are again' the subject of discussion concerning their comfort and ventilation, G. R. Pain arguing that 'his plans were so materially altered' as to 'affect in a great degree the proper accommodation so essential in the interior of the Courts.' [13] Six years later, despite improvements on the building carried out by Sir Thomas Deane, [14] the following account of a recent court sitting appeared in the pages of the press,

> 'The exposed condition of the Cork court-houses has been again complained of this Assizes, the rain pouring in, the Councel sitting in damp seats, and one of them applied to the Bench for leave to open his umbrella - Judge Ball's cold aggravated, his papers blown off the bench, and candles extinguished.'
>
> (*Limerick Chronicle,* Wednesday 5 April 1843.)

Sessions Houses

Although remembered for the commanding power and grandeur of their Cork City and County Courthouse the Pain brothers were also responsible for drawing up plans and specifications for a number of smaller courthouses on a far more modest scale. They submitted a 'Design for a court house and bridewell to be built in the different sessions towns in the County of Cork' (dated 6 May 1824)[15] and *c.*1826 G. R. Pain was appointed supervising architect to oversee the erection of six courthouses in County Cork - Bantry, Clonakilty, Macroom, Mallow, Midleton and Skibbereen.[16] They are all of a similar design, all, except for Clonakilty, being on the main elevation simply a single-storey, three-bay rectangle consisting of a central pedimented block flanked on either side by a recessed entrance bay. The sole feature on these recesses is a doorway over which sits a pediment resting on brackets. On the central block the fortress-like walling is only broken by a Venetian window set high up in the wall. Built for security, they were meant to intimidate in their small-town way. The Clonakilty sessions house is similar to the others except that the flanking recesses are lower in height than the wall of the central block. The building was refurbished *c.*1925 and *c.*1985 and Clonakilty Courthouse now has a hipped roof, the pediment having been removed.[17] The architects' courthouse commissions were not confined to Co. Cork, a press report for 30 May 1827 placing on record that 'The plan of a new Sessions House at Killarney by Messrs. Pain has been approved of by the Kerry Grand Jury.' A notice in the same edition of the *Limerick Chronicle* informed prospective builders that the plans and specifications could be seen at the architects' offices in both Cork and Limerick.[18] As with Clonakilty, the recesses are lower in height than the wall of the central block, but otherwise Killarney is very similar to the other courthouses in Co. Cork.[19] (For illustration see page 227).

Mysterious Rites and Rituals

In between the Corinthian magnificence of the Washington Street Courthouses and the rather modest, unadorned courthouses built for small towns such as Midleton, there was an intermediate range of county courthouses erected in Ireland during the early nineteenth century by various architects that have a rather forbidding appearance, based as they are on the Doric temples of Antiquity. This use of the stern and plain Greek Revival style with its use of imposing Doric porticos, such as at Limerick's County Courthouse, being seen as eminently suitable for projecting an image of the enduring permanence of the institutions of Law, their civilised rationality and purity of purpose. However, to the lay person, especially the uneducated and impoverished, the mysterious rites and rituals performed in these temples of justice held an awesome power. For the gowned and bewigged priests and high priests of the temple could condemn a man to death or banish him perpetually to a far and distant corner of the world. Those who performed the Legal Mysteries decided the fate of others, choosing some as sacrificial victims both for the general good of society and also to ensure that the sun remained shining on the 'better classes'; just as Aztec priests tore out the hearts of living human sacrifices to ensure that the sun did indeed rise and shine the following day.

In this sense the Greek Revival of early nineteenth century courthouse architecture does seem appropriate to the administration of justice, for it could be seen to be very cold and calculating at times, especially when dealing with instances of militant resistance to prevailing social conditions. At a special judicial commission held in Ennis Courthouse over the period of 2nd - 29th June 1831 to try cases arising from an agrarian conflict then taking place in Co. Clare between peasant secret societies and local landowners, of the 101 men found guilty six were to be hanged, others imprisoned and the majority sentenced to transportation. On Saturday 4 June 1831 following the conviction of seven men for administrating secret oaths, the prosecutor the Attorney General of Ireland, informed the judge that it was his duty to pronounce on the prisoners the required sentence,

> ". . . the sentence is, transportation for life – perpetual banishment from their native land . . . The time now draws nigh when the scene is to close on those unhappy men, and they are to be cut off for ever from their friends, their families and their country.

> "In other cases, and in other times, the criminal may be told that he has a certain time to prepare for his fate; but such is the condition to which this country is reduced, that His Majesty's Government has deemed it right that not one hour, not one instant, shall elapse between the sentence of the law and its execution . . ."[20]

Peter Gorman, an observer at the Special Commission who took shorthand notes of the proceedings, recorded that following the Attorney General's comments,

> 'Judge Jebb then proceeded, in a most impressive manner, to give judgement and sentence of transportation for life. When he concluded, these men were immediately removed to a cart, provided

for their removal to Limerick, and they were driven away amidst heart rending shrieks of an immense body of persons of their own station in life.'[21]

Suitable Premises

The Pain partnership was approached by various bodies and institutions in Cork City to devise suitable premises and among these can be counted the New Independent Chapel on George's Street (1831), a notice appearing in the 20 May 1829 edition of the *Cork Constitution* requesting that proposals from architects for the building of the Chapel according to 'plans drawn by Messrs. G. & R. Pain [*sic*]. . .' were to be submitted to the office of Mr. J. H. Manley on Grand Parade. The brothers also designed the County Club House on South Mall (1826);[22] this latter building serving as a meeting place for the county aristocracy[23] whose patronage, the Pain brothers no doubt hoped, would continue to be most liberal.

Other assignments attributable to them are the Cork Steam Packet Company building on Penrose Quay[24] and G. R. Pain's entrance gates to Lota Beg House, Glanmire[25] that feature a triumphal arch flanked by Ionic columns, two small side entrance gates and a lodge house.

They were also involved in a number of civil engineering projects including the building of two bridges. In 1820 they completed the three-arched George IV (O'Neill-Crowley) Bridge over the southern channel of the River Lee[26] and in 1830 built a three-arch bridge crossing the northern channel of the Lee, linking the Western Road with Sunday's Well. Lewis says that this structure was constructed by the Pains to a design by Richard Griffith and was called Wellington Bridge (now Thomas Davis Bridge). [27] However, this structure was referred to as Wellesley Bridge by contemporaries such as Cork historian J. Windele, who also wrote that G. R. Pain was the architect.[28] This is echoed by *The Parliamentary Gazetteer of Ireland* (1844-6) which states that 'Wellesley-bridge . . . was constructed to an elegant design by Mr. Pain.'[29]

Blackrock Castle

In contrast to their Classical masterpiece of the Cork City and County Courthouse James and George Richard were the architects of Blackrock Castle,[30] a most romantic and picturesque essay in Gothic. Majestically seated on a rocky limestone outcrop that projects into the River Lee it overlooks both the inner and outer harbour. Built near Blackrock village in 1827-9 for Cork Corporation it replaced an earlier castle on the site erected at the beginning of the seventeenth century in the form of a circular tower and held in possession by the Corporation. Here the Mayors of Cork presided over an Admiralty Court and annually celebrated their position as Admiral of the Harbour by holding a civic banquet at public expense on 1 August.[31]

Blackrock Castle, Co. Cork.

Once every three years the Mayor was required by Royal Charter to perform a ceremony known as the throwing of the Dart. A traditional and hallowed rite dating back to the time of James I (1603-25), it involved the Mayor, accompanied by his official entourage and members of the Corporation, proceeding,

> '. . . in boats from the Mayor's Slip to Blackrock Castle, and from thence to sea, where the Mayor shall throw the Dart, at the limits of his jurisdiction, for the conservancy of the river. And that an entertainment be provided for them on their return to the castle.'[32]

One such ceremony took place on 1 August 1759 when the Mayor and the 'other proper Officers of the Corporation do go in their boats to the Harbour's mouth and other parts of the channel and river, to exert their ancient rights to the government thereof . . .'[33] The purpose of the ritual was to make it publicly known that the Mayor was asserting his chartered right to hold exclusive Admiralty jurisdiction, both criminal and civil, over the River Lee from the city to the mouth of the estuary - the Dart being a symbol of his authority. The office of Admiral was not a nominal one, for it involved many duties and privileges including the imposition of fines. Other maritime cities and towns of Ireland, including Limerick, held similar ceremonies. The Mayors of Limerick being conferred with exclusive admiralty jurisdiction over the River Shannon from the city to the sea by a charter granted by King James I on 3 March 1609.[34]

Other civic events were also held at Blackrock including an annual dinner on 4th June to celebrate the birthday of George III (1760-1820) and to copiously toast the monarch's good health. These Cork banquets were occasions that, tradition has it, often became rather rowdy affairs. Indeed, it was immediately after one of these annual celebrations that the castle was accidentally burnt down in 1827 when a fire broke out in the banqueting room.[35] Such an affront to civic pride and ancient privilege by the Gods could not go unanswered and £1,000 was raised to build a replacement in Gothic, the Pain brothers completing the task in 1829. The interior layout of the new building included a magnificent ground floor banqueting room. A large wine cellar was also incorporated into the design, an architectural detail that lends credence to the story of rowdy parties enjoyed by the good burghers of Cork.

Dominating this part of the river, the principal feature of Blackrock Castle is a circular round tower, with crenellated parapet, besides which a slender turret rises above the battlements of the tower. This turret served a practical function when built, as navigation lights were attached to the top to aid shipping.[36] The large windows in the tower have label hood-moulds. With its battlemented walls adorned with turrets and bartizans Blackrock was the nearest the Pain brothers got to recreating a medieval fortress. Facing the river is a watergate, arched and castellated, from which a flight of steps leads down to a boat slip.

This essay in romantic Gothic was a jewel in the crown of Cork Corporation for many years. Much admired, it was thought by John Barrow in 1835 to be 'a structure of imposing appearance, and, . . . a clever piece of architecture.'[37] By the 1920s, however, the building had sadly fallen into disrepair, being leased in 1930 by a professor of botany at University College Cork (UCC) and privately acquired in the 1960s.[38] Purchased by Cork City Council in January 2001 the castle has taken on a new lease of life as an astronomical observatory. Following vital restoration and conservation work undertaken on Blackrock Castle the observatory was scheduled to be open to the public in September 2005 (*Irish Times*, 11 April 2005). It has two high-powered telescopes - an optical telescope placed on the castles top tower and a radio telescope located over the gallery room. A fitting location to study the works of the Grand Architect, a term James Pain would have been familiar with as a Freemason.

Although one of the Pain brothers' most romantically sited castellated creations, and a composition of great dramatic power, it must be admitted that Blackrock was not to everybody's taste. Indeed, Cork folklorist and collector of fairy legends Thomas Crofton Croker thought it a very bad day that such a thing be built at Blackrock, for in 1833 he wrote in a letter to his friend, Cork architect Thomas Deane, that the whole thing was a 'flimsy specimen of Cockney Gothic'.[39] A snide little remark that has been interpreted as a reference to the Pain brothers' London origins.[40] In making such a comment to Deane, Thomas Crofton Croker was on safe ground because of the ongoing professional rivalry in Cork between the Pain brothers and Thomas Deane, and also because the English-born architects enjoyed the patronage of the Cork county aristocracy.[41]

But bitchy begrudgery and petty jealousies aside, Blackrock Castle is nineteenth century Gothic at its best, for it did satisfy that century's need for an idealised vision of medieval social values, a pre-industrial society where 'noble acts, feates of armes of chyvalrye, prowesse, hardynesse, humanyte, love, curtoyse, and veray gentylnesse'[42] were the norm rather than the exception.

It is little wonder that this image of 'Castle Chivalrous', reflected in the still waters of the Lee on a fine summer's day, has been much admired. It had been the hope of 'Big George', 3rd Earl of Kingston, for the Pains to build an entrance lodge to Mitchelstown Castle modelled on Blackrock.[43] Dramatic especially when viewed from the river, Blackrock Castle, set on a rocky outcrop by the water's side, speaks of Arthurian legend - of the Table Round, the Holy Grail, and Excaliber:

> 'Then sir Bedwere departed and wente to the swerde and lyghtly toke hit up, and so he wente unto the watirs syde. And there he bounde the gyrdyll aboute the hyltis, and threw the swerde as farre into the

watir as he myght. And there cam an arme and an honde above the watir, and toke hit and cleyght hit, and shoke hit thryse and braundysshed, and than vanysshed with the swerde into the watir.'[44]

Ethereal Vision

As well as projects carried out in partnership with his brother, George Richard Pain also made a tremendously important contribution to Cork, his adopted city, as an independent architect in his own right. Among his achievements can be counted the Capuchin Church of the Holy Trinity on what is now Fr. Mathew Quay.[45] Commissioned in 1832[46] by Fr Mathew, the Apostle of Temperance, Holy Trinity features a marvellous Gothic portico on the west front that soars upwards, the effect created by the three tall lancet arches on the portico's front and one lancet arch on each of the returns. The dividing octagonal piers being quite narrow in comparison. This creates a very powerful impression of reaching upwards to Heaven's Gate. An impression further emphasised by the placement above the portico of a square lantern tower, with open traceried arches, which is in turn surmounted by a spire. The upward thrust of the three tiers of this celestially aspiring composition is reinforced by the tall crocketed pinnacles that adorn the structure and the octagonal piers that rise up powerfully above the roofline terminating with domed-shaped cupolas. The triple lancet arches on the front elevation of the portico have a similarity, writ large, of triple lancet window arrangements of the Early English style. However, unlike triple lancet windows, the flanking arches on Holy Trinity's portico are narrower in width than the central arch.

The brilliance of G. R. Pain's design for Holy Trinity was immediately apparent to virtually all those tasked with selecting a suitable design from among the nine architects' proposals submitted, including one from Sir Thomas Deane. In August 1832 a ballot on the various submissions was held by a body known as the Collectors (about 100 in number) and the result of the vote was quite decisive: 'Mr. Pain's Gothic plan 93; Mr. Anthony's 4; Sir Thomas Deane & Co. 1; Mr. Butler's plan 1.'[47]

Although the vision was George Richard's, Holy Trinity was not finished in his lifetime, only the portico being completed in 1837. Lewis's *Topographical Dictionary* for that year reporting that the church,

> 'built of light grey limestone is already carried up as high as the roof; when finished, it will represent a tremendous specimen... with a tower and spire, 200 feet high; the front has a portio of three lofty arches...'

Over fifty years were to elapse before the lantern tower and spire were inplemented by Dominic Coakley in 1889. Unfortunately the tower and the

Holy Trinity Church, Mathew Quay, Cork.

spire do deviate from G. R. Pain's original intention in that they were reduced in height, the architect originally entertaining the idea of a very tall spire[48] which would have added considerably to the soaring majesty of the church. As a consequence, the two upper tiers of the composition seem squat in comparison with the portico. Nevertheless, the west front of Holy Trinity stands today as an impressive testament to the younger Pain's ethereal vision.

The inspiration for his treatment of the portico may have come from the west front (c.1200-30) of Peterborough Cathedral in Cambridgeshire, England; an awe-inspiring façade featuring three massive pointed arches of identical height, but with the flanking arches wider in width than the central one. A fourteenth century porch was later placed within the thirteenth century central arch so some of the original intent of the façade did suffer a little. Although Pain's portico is, of course, very different from Peterborough's west front, the use of the pointed arch in both compositions to create a heavenwards rocket boost to the masonry is very striking.

The spiritually of Holy Trinity is further enhanced by the use of light grey/white limestone, a building material the Pain brothers used to great effect in their Cork City and County Courthouse and in G. R. Pain's St. Patrick's Church to give added grandeur and elegance to their compositions.

Another of George Richard's architectural associations with the Apostle of Temperance is the Father Mathew Memorial Tower at Glanmire, a circular battlemented Gothic tower three stages high. The entrance is in a circular stair turret that is attached to, and rises above, the tower. Funded by William O'Connor, a City merchant, it was not until 1843, five years after the architect's death, that work on the towering memorial started.[49] Prominently placed on a high ridge overlooking the estuary of the River Lee, it echoes the main tower and turret at Blackrock Castle sited on the opposite side of the river.

Fr. Mathew Memorial Tower, Glanmire, Cork.

David Gaynor

St. Patrick's Church, Lower Glanmire Road, Cork.

Distinguished Neoclassical

G. R. Pain carried out several other major assignments for the Catholic Church including his distinguished neoclassical design for St. Patrick's (1836) on the Lower Glanmire Road.[50] Funded by a wealthy Cork merchant family, the Honans,[51] St. Patrick's principal feature is a Corinthian portico in hexastyle, i.e. having six columns on the front elevation, and one on each return; the frieze and tympanum are undecorated. The columns of the deep portico are continued as Corinthian pilasters along the walls of the church giving a unified treatment to the whole structure. The composition is topped by a towering neoclassical campanile[52] (a bell tower in the Italian manner) surmounted by a sturdy stone crucifix. Located near the Railway Station on the Lower Glanmire Road, the roadway here is very wide and one has the space to stand back and fully appreciate the beauty of St. Patrick's and the outstanding quality of the architect's work.

Of interest in discussing George Richard's Cork *oeuvre* is that his Catholic churches are far more adventurous and impressive in design than the sometimes drearily repetitious, emotionless, and predictable production line work associated with early nineteenth century Church of Ireland architecture.

Having said this, the Pain brothers did bring elegance and charm to a number of their First Fruits designs.

Reconstructive Surgery

Following the burning down of the Cathedral Church of St. Mary (Roman Catholic) in 1820 and its reduction to a fire-blacked shell, G. R. Pain was chosen to remodel the Cathedral in 1828.[53] His major contribution to St. Mary's was in the remodelling of the interior, adding transepts and an apse to the East end and installing an elaborate and intricate fan-vaulted ceiling. The very striking west tower with its red sandstone dressed with white limestone is not Pain's work, having been erected in 1862-7. George Richard's interior was grievously interfered with in 1963-4 when Vatican II reconstructive surgery to the Eastern section of the Cathedral removed his apse and transepts. Despite this, the architect's fan-vaulted ceiling still lives on in the nave which survived the 1963 assault.[54] Besides working on large scale projects, George Richard is also known to have carried out relatively minor assignments for the Catholic Church. One such modest task involved roofing and slating the Chapel and house of the Church of St. Augustine on Cork's Washington Street in 1827; work costed at £350.[55] When the young Cork architect Henry Hill (1806/7-87) visited the Catholic chapel in Dungarven, Co. Waterford in 1831 he recorded in his diary for Tuesday 1 September that although the chapel was 'a large plain looking building . . . its interior is beautiful . . . An altarpiece is now in progress after the design of G. R. Pain, by whom the interior decorating has been designed.'[56]

Spa House, Mallow

As a highly accomplished architect the talents of George Richard Pain were as much in demand in the County of Cork as in the City; one example may suffice - the Spa House (1828) in Mallow, north County Cork. We commonly think of Bath in England as *the* premier spa resort in these islands, but in the eighteenth and early nineteenth century there were a number of other spa resorts in Britain and Ireland at which fashionable ladies and gentlemen took the waters. One of these was at Castleconnell in Co. Limerick and another at Mallow, Co. Cork. The geothermal spring waters at Mallow were considered a powerful restorative for those with 'debilitated constitutions', being peculiarly efficacious for those suffering from consumption (tuberculosis) and scrofula, a glandular disease associated with tuberculosis. The pleasantly warm waters, found to be about 68° Fahrenheit[57] (20°C), rise to the surface at springs in a glen on the outskirts of Mallow beside the Mitchelstown Road.

Mallow's growing popularity with the wealthier sections of society as a spa resort made the town a fashionable place to live. Known as the 'Bath of Ireland', Mallow enjoyed its boom period in the early decades of the nineteenth century with the building of many fine new residences, boarding houses and hotels; the 'season' beginning in April and lasting until the end of

Spa House, Mallow, Co. Cork.

October.[58] Such was the reputation of the town that Samuel Lewis was caused to comment in 1837, 'the spa is much frequented by persons of fashion from distant parts of the country.'[59]

One of the last developments associated with Mallow's period of fame as a spa was the construction in 1828 of the Spa House. Commissioned by Charles Jephson of Mallow Castle, it was built to counter a decline in visitor numbers. The original structure on the site, of which no description survives other than a brief reference in 1746 to a 'beautiful shell grotto and a house',[60] had obviously seen far better days, being described in 1815 as 'not unlike a pigstye.'[61] The assignment was given to George Richard Pain whose original vision was for a Greek temple, but Jephson preferred a Tudor flavour to the Spa House.[62] The resulting building is a handsome structure in Tudorish style with half-timbered gabled fronts and decorative bargeboards. It also features tall chimney stacks, a dormer window and an oriel window. Built for £1,000, the Spa House was provided with a pump house, a room for medical consultations, reading room and baths. Enclosed within the building is one of the geothermal springs.[63]

By employing the talents of the best architect in the county Charles Jephson had hoped to reverse Mallow's declining fortunes, but the writing was well and truly written on the wall, Henry Inglis reporting in 1834 that 'As a resort for invalids Mallow has greatly declined. Some years ago, during the season, it was visited by not fewer than 100 families on an average; and there are not now one-sixth part of that number . . .' He put Mallow's fall from favour down to an increase in 'steam intercourse' between Ireland and Britain allowing the affluent to resort to more fashionable spas in southern England such as Cheltenham and Clifton. Whether such places were better than Mallow or not Inglis was not prepared to say, but they had 'the superior attraction with which every distant place is invested.'[64]

By 1850 the Mallow Spa had had its day and the Spa House was closed down. It was renovated in the 1990s by Cork County Council and although not a faithful restoration, for modern materials such as uPVC windows, guttering and down pipes were used, the building is presently (2005) being usefully employed as an Energy Office to advise the general public on energy conservation and renewable energy. Sited with a pleasant little brook running close by, Mallow's Spa House is well worth a visit and during office hours the staff will show you around. Outside in the park geothermal waters can be seen gently bubbling up in a spring to be found just beyond the parking area in the front of the house, steam rising from the warm surface on cold days.

Untimely Death

As *the* leading architect in Cork it was very much regretted that George Richard Pain died in December 1838 at the age of 45 when his full potential had yet to be attained. Nevertheless, both individually and in conjunction with his brother he graced Cork with many fine buildings of which the City is justly proud. When one compares the body of work that the Pain brothers carried out in Cork City with that in Limerick the Cork architecture is on a far more grandiose scale. An indication of the greater wealth to be found in Cork, but also because, quite frankly, George Richard was the better of the two architect brothers. Indeed, in generally comparing George's personal work with that of James, the younger Pain's work is said to be more 'feminine' than that of his elder brother, a compliment to George Richard's greater artistic sensitivity and skill.

Endnotes

1 The *Dictionary of Architecture*, Architectural Publication Society s.v. 'Pain (James and George Richard)'.

2 Bence-Jones, M. 'Two Pairs of Architect Brothers', *Country Life*, 10 August 1967.

3 Windele, J. *Historical and Descriptive Notices of the City of Cork and its Vicinity*, Cork, 1846, p. 19.

4 Macaulay, Thomas *The History of England*, Chapter 12, Vol. III, 1855, reprinted in 1967 by Heron Books, London, Vol. II, p. 532.

5 Gibson, Rev. C. B. *The History of the County and City of Cork*, Cork, 1861, Vol. II, p. 324.

6 O'Dwyer, F. *The Architecture of Deane and Woodward*, Cork University Press, Cork 1997, p. 18.

7 Windele *op. cit.* p. 19; Lewis, Samuel *Topographical Dictionary of Ireland*, 2 Vols., London, 1837, Vol. I, s.v, 'Cork', p. 419; *The Parliamentary Gazetteer of Ireland* 1844-6, Vol. I, s.v. 'Cork', p. 524.

8 *Irish Penny Magazine*, 6 April 1833, pp. 105-7. Secondary sources are divided on the issue: Mark Bence-Jones in 'Two Pairs of Architect Brothers', *Country Life*, 10 August 1967 credits both Pain brothers with the design of the Cork City and County Courthouse. *The Index of Irish Architects* compiled by the Irish Architectural Archive, Merrion Square, Dublin cites George Richard Pain as the architect. While T. F. McNamara in his *Portrait of Cork*, Watermans, Cork, 1981, p. 88 states 'Considering all information available to me, I suggest Kearns Deane designed it and the Pains were the contractors.' In this matter it is perhaps a case of 'You pays your money and you takes your choice'.

9 Barrow, John *A Tour Round Ireland Through the Sea-Coast Counties, in the Autumn of 1835*, John Murray, Albemarle Street, London, 1836, p. 324.

10 Williams, Jeremy *A Companion Guide to Architecture in Ireland 1837-1921*, Irish Academic Press, 1994, p. 68. For documentation relating to the tendering process for rebuilding the Cork Courthouses see McNamara, T. F. *Portrait of Cork*, Watermans, Cork, 1981, pp. 90-102.

11 *Limerick Chronicle*, 10 June 1837.

12 *Limerick Chronicle*, 14 June 1837.

13 *Limerick Chronicle*, 18 March 1837. That same month G. R. Pain applied to the Cork County Grand Jury to reimburse him £2,400, 'a loss sustained in consequence of miscalculating the depth of the foundation of the New Courthouses.' *Limerick Chronicle*, 25 March 1837.

14 *Limerick Chronicle*, 22 March 1843. A report in the *Limerick Chronicle* of 6 August the previous year records that Sir Thomas Deane had been commissioned to improve the construction of the Cork Courthouses.

15 Copy in Irish Architectural Archive, Merrion Square, Dublin.

16 'Pain, George Richard', *Index of Irish Architects* Irish, Architectural Archive, Merrion Square, Dublin, citing NA/SPO CSORP 1826/13, 534.

17 Dunne, Mildred & Phillips, Brian *The Courthouses of Ireland – A Gazetteer of Irish Courthouses*, The Heritage Council, Kilkenny, 1999 s.v. 'Clonakilty', 'Macroom', 'Mallow', 'Midleton', 'Skibbereen'.

18 *Limerick Chronicle*, 30 May 1827.

19 Dunne *op. cit.* s.v. 'Killarney'.

20 *A Special Commission of Oyer and Terminer in the Counties of Limerick and Clare in the Months of May and June 1831*, printed by R. P. Canter, 12 Francis Street, Limerick, 1831, pp. 79-81.

21 ibid. p. 81.

22 *Dictionary of Architecture*, Architectural Publications Society s.v. 'Pain (James and George Richard).

23 O'Dwyer *op. cit.* p. 17.

24 Craig, Maurice & Glin, Knight of *Ireland Observed: A Handbook to the Buildings and Antiquities*, The Mercier Press, Cork, 1970, p. 36.

25 *Dictionary of Architecture*, Architectural Publications Society s.v. 'Pain (James and George Richard); Bence-Jones, Mark A Guide to Irish Country Houses, Constable, London, revised edition 1988, s.v. 'Lota Beg, Glanmire, Co. Cork'.

26 Rynne, Colin *The Industrial Archaeology of Cork City and its Environs*, The Stationary Office, Dublin, 1999, p. 191.

27 Lewis *op. cit.* Vol. I, s.v. 'Cork', p. 410.

28 Windele *op. cit.* p. 24.

29 *The Parliamentary Gazetteer of Ireland* 1844-6, Vol. I, s.v. 'Cork', p. 523.

30 The last line of the inscription on the plaque erected beside the entrance to Blackrock Castle reads 'James and G. R. Pain, Architects.'; *Dictionary of Architecture*, Architectural Publications Society, s.v. 'Pain (James and George Richard).

31 Croker, Thomas Crofton *Researches in the South of Ireland*, John Murray, London, 1824. Facsimile reprint, Irish University Press, 1968, pp. 211-2.

32 *Journal of the Cork Historical and Archaeological Society* Vol. II, p. 468.

33 Council Book of Cork Corporation, 30 May 1759, 'The Old Castles Around Cork Harbour', *Journal of the Cork Historical and Archaeological Society* Vol. 20, No. 104, p. 171.

34 Yeoman, Anne 'Throwing the Dart', *Remembering Limerick: Historical Essays Celebrating the 800th Anniversary of Limerick's First Charter Granted in 1197*, Lee, David, ed., Limerick Civic Trust, Limerick, 1997, pp. 327-32; Lee, David 'Fanfares of the Vanities' ibid. pp. 309-12.

35 *Journal of the Cork Historical and Archaeological Society* Vol. II, p. 468.

36 Lewis *op. cit.* Vol. I, p. 208.

37 Barrow *op. cit.* p. 327.

38 Keenan, M. 'Landmark Reflections', *The Sunday Tribune*, 2 July 2000.

39 Croker, Thomas Crofton *Recollections of Cork* (1833) unpublished MS, Trinity College Dublin.

40 O'Dwyer *op. cit.* p. 18.

41 ibid. pp. 15-18.

42 William Caxton's Preface to Sir Thomas Malory's *Le Morte Darthur* , London, 1485. See *Malory: Works*, Vinaver, Eugène ed., Oxford University Press, Oxford, 1977, p. xv.

43 Lewis *op. cit.* Vol. II, p. 373.

44 Malory, Sir Thomas 'The Most Piteous Tale of the Morte Arthur Saunz Guerdon' (Winchester Manuscript), *Malory: Works* Vinaver, Eugène ed., Oxford University Press, Oxford, 1977, pp. 715-6. A modernised version of this passage in fifteenth century English relates how ' Sir Bedevere departed, and went to the sword, and lightly took it up, and went to the water side; and there he bound the girdle about the hilts, and then he threw the sword as far into the water as he might; and there came an arm and an hand above the water and met it, and caught it, and so shook it trice and brandished, and then vanished away the hand with the sword in the water.' Sir *Thomas Malory – Le Morte D'Arthur* 2 Vols., Cowen, Janet ed., Penguin, London, 1969, Vol. II, p. 517.

45 Windele *op. cit.* p. 77.

46 The *Cork Constitution*, 8 September 1832,
'NOTICE TO ARCHITECTS
Specification and plans for the new Church of the Holy Trinity by G. R. Payne Esq., can be seen and copied by the Architects at the house of the very Rev. T. Mathew, Sullivan's Quay. Sealed estimates will be received until the 18th of the present month.'

47 *Limerick Chronicle*, 15 August 1832.

48 Williams op. cit. p. 59.

49 Howley *op. cit.* p. 54; Williams op. *cit.* pp. 75-6; 'The Mathew Tower', *Journal of the Cork Historical and Archaeological Society* Vol. 32, No. 135, January-June 1927, p. 57.

50 *The Dictionary of Architecture*, Architectural Publication Society s.v. 'Pain (James and George Richard)'.

51 Bence-Jones, M. 'Two Pairs of Architect Brothers', *Country Life*, 10 August 1967.

52 For the evolution of G. R. Pain's design for the campanile see Hill, Arthur 'St. Patrick's Church, Glanmire Road', *Journal of the Cork Historical and Archaeological Society* Vol. 14, No. 78, pp. 65-6.

53 *The Dictionary of Architecture,* Architectural Publication Society s.v. 'Pain (James and George Richard)'.

54 Galloway, Peter *The Cathedrals of Ireland*, The Institute of Irish Studies, Queens University of Belfast, 1992, pp. 63-5; Hurley, Richard *Irish Church Architecture in the Era of Vatican II*, Dominican Publications, Dublin, 2001, pp. 122-3. Vatican II (Vatican Council, Second), the twenty-first ecumenical council recognised by the Roman Catholic Church, which became the symbol of the church's openness to the modern world. The council was announced by Pope John XXIII on 25 January 1959 and held 178 meetings in the autumn

of each of four successive years. The first gathering was on 11 October 1962 and the last on 8 December 1965.

55 *Augustiniana Corcagiae 1746-1836*, 'Statement of Affairs and Inventory Presented at Visitation July 10, 1827', *Analecta Hibernia*, Vol. XII.

56 Hill, H. 'Diary of an Itinerary in Ireland in 1831', *Journal of the Cork Historical and Archaeological Society* Vol. 38, No. 147, January-June 1933, p. 32.

57 *Parliamentary Gazetteer of Ireland* s.v. 'Mallow', p. 729.

58 'History of Spa House', Energy Agency Office, Cork County Council.

59 Lewis *op. cit.* s.v. 'Mallow', Vol. II, p. 339.

60 Hajba, Anna Maria *Houses of Cork. Volume One: North Cork*, Ballinakella Press, Whitegate, Co. Clare, 2002, p. 333.

61 Townsend, Horatio *A General and Statistical Survey of the County of Cork*, Edwards and Savage, 1815.

62 Hajba *op. cit.* p. 333.

63 'History of Spa House', Energy Agency Office, Cork County Council.

64 Inglis, Henry D. *A Journey Throughout Ireland, During the Spring, Summer and Autumn of 1834*, Whittaker & Son, London, 1834, Vol. I, pp. 153-4.

CHAPTER TWELVE

POSING AS A BARON

James Pain's circle of acquaintances included Windham Henry Quin, 2nd Earl of Dunraven, and his wife Countess Caroline. The Quins of Adare are an old Irish family, not Anglo-Irish, descended from the O'Quins of Inchiquin who claimed ancestry back to a King of Munster of the 3rd century AD. Although Catholic, Valentine Quin who built an eighteenth century mansion at Adare registered himself as a Protestant in 1739. In the prevailing political climate of the time it was prudent for Catholic landowners to do so, especially when they inherited an estate.

Great Fortune came to the family when in 1810 Windham Henry Quin married Caroline Wyndham, daughter and sole heiress of Thomas Wyndham of Dunraven Castle in Glamorganshire in south Wales. Caroline was a fine catch in many ways, not only was she an intelligent, artistically gifted woman interested in architecture, there was also the small matter of her Welsh estate having coal mines. These formed the basis of Lady Caroline's wealth, such was the importance of coal in the Industrial Revolution.

Windham Henry's father, Sir Valentine Richard Quin, was obviously pleased with his son's match for when Sir Valentine was created an Earl in 1822 he took the title 1st Earl of Dunraven in honour of his daughter-in-law's Welsh property. Seven years earlier the family had hypenated their name to Wyndham-Quin.[1] The 1st Earl died in 1824, his son and Lady Caroline settling down to a comfortable life supported by money gained from the profits of coal mines as well as income from the Irish estate.

Alien Implant

In 1828 and 1829 the Pain brothers submitted proposals to the Dunravens who wished to replace their eighteenth century mansion at Adare with a residence more fitting to their self-image and station in society. James Pain had already successfully carried out a number of assignments for the 2nd Earl including the design of a family mausoleum. On 24 December 1825 Lord Dunraven had written to his wife,

> 'I have [?tried] out Mr. Pain in Limerick and he is coming here tomorrow to put into force a plan I have formed for a noble Mausoleum connected with the Church, to receive my poor father's bones.'[2]

Ten months later, on 28 October 1826, Dunraven, worried about his health and feeling a bit morbid, wrote to Caroline concerning instructions about his own burial, the letter also contained the passage,

> 'I propose next spring building the Mausoleum for my father by Mr. Pain's plan and in the spot by the Church loaned to him, and then removing my poor father's remains to it with decent privacy from Wales.'[3]

Dunraven Mausoleum, Augustinian Priory, Adare, Co. Limerick.

The site chosen was in the Augustinian Priory on the outskirts of Adare close to the bridge over the River Maigue. Founded in 1315 the Priory complex was in ruins in 1807 when its Church was given over to the Protestant community to be restored as a new house of worship, their old one being small, old and decayed. In 1814 the Refectory was re-roofed and converted into a schoolroom.⁴ The mausoleum, about 37 feet (11.3 metres) in length and about 18 feet (5.5 metres) in width, was erected on the western side of the Priory⁵ and bears the family arms and the inscription,

'This mausoleum was constructed in the year of our Lord 1826, by Windham Henry, Earl of Dunraven, for the remains of his dear father, Richard, first Earl of Dunraven, and for the family of Quin of Adare.'

To be honest, it is a rather awful, dreary, overly large, unimaginative structure that after nearly 180 years has still not been able to settle comfortably into its host body. It looks like an alien implant that the old Priory would undoubtedly vomit forth if it possibly could. This charnel house for the noble dead is not the most appealing place to lay one's bones, but there is no accounting for taste and several members of the family have been laid to rest there.

In 1831 the cloisters in the Priory were restored.[6] One assumes that James Pain supervised this work for it took place in the middle of a period when he was entrusted with a number of commissions by the Dunravens. He was also, of course, an official architect to the Board of First Fruits.

David Gaynor

Ice house, Adare Manor recently restored.

An Ice House

James Pain was certainly a welcome guest at the Dunraven household at this time, Lady Caroline's diary for 17 June 1828 recording that the architect came to visit that day to 'look for a place for an ice-house.'[7] An ice house was an outbuilding where ice was tightly stacked during the winter and used to keep game; the ice sourced from a nearby ice pond, lake or river. Ice was also used in the kitchens and cellars of great houses for keeping poultry and dairy products cool; it was also used in desserts and for the treatment of fevers. A feature in the grounds of most large country houses throughout Ireland, ice houses were built mainly in the eighteenth and nineteenth centuries until the mid-Victorian era when artificial ice production became established commercially.[8] The vaulted chamber of the Adare ice house was built of thick layers of brick over which was thrown a mound of earth giving the structure the appearance of an ancient barrow. The entrance is a short, vaulted passage that originally had an inner and outer door to help insulate the ice chamber. Recently restored, the Adare ice house can be found outside the walled garden on the side furthest away from the Manor. Behind the structure, which bears the date stone '1828', are two excavated pits that may have served as ice ponds and from where the earth to cover the ice house may have been taken. The date '1828' is similarly inscribed on the keystone over the main entrance into the walled garden and it is possible that James Pain played some role in supervising its construction.

It is at this time that the Earl and his Countess entered into serious discussions about building a new house to replace their eighteenth century mansion. Proposals were canvassed for and in September of that year William Morrison, architect, 'entertained us in the evening with a variety of plans of beautiful houses which he had superintended [?being] a celebrated Architect' records Lady Caroline's diary.[9]

Despite Morrison's best efforts it was James Pain who was most favoured and in October 1828 plans from the Limerick architect's office arrived at Adare. Consultation continued into 1829, Lady Caroline making several references to James's visits during the course of that year.[10] Although he was the contact, it was a joint approach on behalf of both brothers, an extant plan for the proposed ground floor of the new house bearing the signatures 'Jas. And G. R. Pain. May th24 '(perhaps the date referred to is 24 May 1829).[11]

The versatility of the Messrs Pain as architects is illustrated by their alternative proposals for Adare, there being extant two detailed sketches for the front elevation, one being a traditional Classical scheme with a pedimented Ionic portico, the other in the Tudor-Revival style[12] evoking the manner of a Tudor Manor House - the Tudor won. In the nineteenth century the Tudor, Elizabethan and Jacobean Manor House styles were considered the most appropriate architectural form with which to express the notion of an idealised, harmonious patriarchal landed society in which everyone knew his or her own place, but one in which tenants and retainers, for faithful duties rendered, would receive fair treatment and protection from the lord of the manor. Originating in England, Tudor-Revival was to prove popular in Ireland from 1820 up until the Famine, the Pains' Adare Manor fitting comfortably within the period of the style's vogue.

Pain brothers' alternative proposals for Adare Manor. Top drawing in Classical style.
Bottom drawing in Tudor-Revival style.

The Manor House style was an attempt to recapture the essence of an age, an English age, that was supposedly a society bound together at local level by a sense of rural community devoid of class conflict. This notion of ancient Tudor virtue is made somewhat ridiculous by Henry VIII's Dissolution of the Monasteries (1536-40) and annexation of their lands. It was one of the biggest land grabs ever staged in Britain since the Norman Conquest of 1066, the land being released onto the market by the Tudor monarch and snapped up by the nobility and wealthy interests seeking cheap land. At the time, especially in Northern England, the Dissolution of the Monasteries was seen as destroying the good feudal order of society and damaging to the poor who relied on the religious institutions for alms. It led to a widespread revolt known as the Pilgrimage of Grace (1536-7) that was eventually suppressed.

The Long Gallery

Construction on Adare Manor did not commence until 1832[13] with the erection of the kitchen wing, which has the date '1832' inscribed on the chimney gable. This functional section of the house is built in a more subdued Tudor-Revival than the rest of the Pains' work, but this is perhaps more fitting to the status of those who worked there, the full flourish of the Tudor-Revival exterior of the Manor and the Gothic flourishes of the interior being more appropriate to the living quarters of Lord and Lady Dunraven. Although the kitchen wing is linked to the northern, Long Gallery range of the house it is sited in such a way as to seem removed from the main body. This is deliberate, for whatever about the community values of Tudor-Revival it was best that the staff knew their place.

If the inspiration for Adare Manor were the halcyon days of the English Tudors, so too was its architecture chiefly inspired by English examples. The turreted Tudor entrance to the house, for example, was a copy from the entrance to the Cloister Court at Eton College, England; the Bell Tower modelled on the chapel tower at Haddon Hall, Derbyshire.[14] The Long Gallery range consisted of the Dunravens' private apartments on the ground floor and the impressive 132 feet (40.2 metres) Long Gallery on the first floor. This room is one of the marvels of Adare Manor and was even more impressive when Adare was in the ownership of the Dunravens and was used as their private living room. A mid-nineteenth century lithograph[15] depicts the Gallery in all its early Victorian-Gothic glory with its oak, medieval style hammerbeam ceiling, stained glass windows and large chivalric banners and pennants hanging from the wall.

While the shell of the house is Tudor-Revival, the interior of the Long Gallery is more Gothic influenced, the carved wooden furnishings (some authentic, others copies) ranging from a fifteenth century Gothic ogee arch doorway to a series of carved panels executed by Adare wood carvers depicting scenes from Froissart's *Chronicles*.[16] Jean Froissart (*c*.1347-*c*.1410) was a French chronicler

Long Gallery (1865), Adare Manor.

and poet who recorded the chivalric exploits of the nobles and kings of England and France from 1325 to 1400. Except for the removal of the domestic furniture and the banners, the Long Gallery today is still as it was when first built, the panels, stained glass and carved woodwork remaining.[17]

The building of Adare Manor was to proceed in two phases. During the first phase, with work proceeding on the construction of the northern section of the new house adjacent to the eighteenth century mansion, the old house was to remain standing until the Hall of the Manor had been built onto it. The old house could then be demolished with the Dunravens moving into their new living quarters in the Long Gallery range with its bedrooms, dressing rooms, bathroom etc., all located on the ground floor.[18] This paved the way for the southern section of Adare Manor to be built at a convenient time. A few of the old walls were preserved and incorporated into the new work.[19] To escape the inconvenience and nuisance of having a major construction site located next to their house the Dunravens went on an extended holiday from the autumn of 1834 until the middle of 1836 travelling on the Continent and visiting buildings of architectural interest.[20]

213

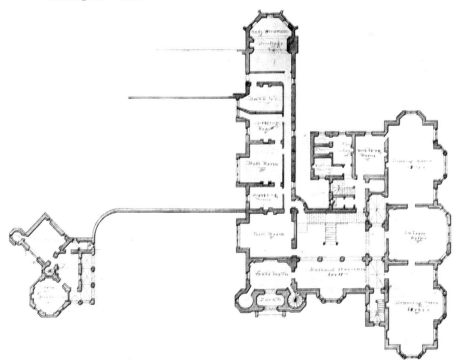

Ground plan of Adare Manor by Pain brothers.

Written Out of History

It was sometime during the latter half of the1830s following their return from the Continent that the Dunravens dispensed with the services of James Pain, even though the house was still only half complete and the old mansion still standing. In 1840, just prior to embarking on a tour of England to visit buildings there, the Earl of Dunraven wrote to the Limerick architect on 21 February,

> 'I did not cease to employ you professionally for the purpose of placing myself in any other professional hands. Building is my amusement and I am a dabbler in architecture and I have now for some years been carrying on the new work entirely from my own designs and without any assistance whatsoever.'[21]

Which would seem to indicate that James's professional relationship with the Dunravens had ceased at least two or three years previously. In the meantime George Richard Pain had died in December 1838. The high water mark of the Pain brothers involvement with Adare is indicated by a water-colour, dated September 1837, of the western front showing the Tudor entrance and the façade of the still unroofed Hall of the Manor standing beside the Dunravens' eighteenth century mansion, which is still intact and inhabited.[22] The completed Tudor-Revival work as shown in the illustration is identical with the Pains' vision for that section of the front elevation as depicted in a drawing the architects had submitted to the Dunravens in 1828-29 when the couple were still studying various proposals for the new house.[23]

After the water-colour was produced there was a pause in building [24] with a resumption at a later stage to complete the Hall and construct the southern section of the Manor containing the Library, Dining Room and Drawing Room. This work was carried out by a number of architects and designers, including Augustus Pugin and Philip C. Hardwick. The house was not entirely inhabitable until 1862 during the lifetime of the 3rd Earl,[25] but even by 1865 a number of the rooms still remained unfinished and undecorated as originally conceived by Pugin.[26] It was to be a long process and that section of the house that eventually replaced the old mansion was not designed until the early 1850s by Hardwick and it a colder, more formal Victorian design when compared to the more pleasing Tudor-Revival of the Pain brothers. Hardwick's work included the construction of the tall, square, hard edged Continental style Wyndham Tower that measures 103 feet (31.4 metres) to the top of its high pitched roof. It stands on the entrance front, rather inelegantly, in close proximity to the Pain brothers' far more pleasing Tudor gateway entrance with its slender octagonal turrets. It is on this front that one sees immediately the difference in style between the Pains' Tudor-Revival and the later Victorian work.

Front entrance to Adare Manor showing different architectural styles.

James Pain's rift with the Dunravens was not healed with the 2nd Earl's death in 1850. Imagine the hurt to his pride when it was brought to his attention that Caroline, now the Dowager Countess of Dunraven, in her *Memorials of Adare Manor*, published in 1865 and also known as the 'Green Book', had obliterated all mention of the architect brothers from her 'official' history of the house with the brazen assertion that,

> '. . . it may be remarked as an interesting fact, and one as rare as curious, that the greater portion of the building, and that the boldest in conception and most picturesque in effect, was designed by an amateur, not a single drawing having been furnished by an architect; and a still larger portion was erected without the employment of either builder or clerk of the works . . .'[27]

As well as claiming that her late husband had virtually designed Adare Manor single-handed, the Countess also claimed that the building project was carried on for twenty-one years 'solely under the superintendence' of James Conolly, a particularly talented stonemason who had been picked out from the workforce by the 'sagacious eye' of the 2nd Earl[28] and groomed for the task. In signal honour of this faithful retainer the Dunraven family erected this inscription on the eastern front of the Manor,

> 'In memory of James Conolly of Adare, mason and faithful servant of the Earl of Dunraven, and builder of this house from A.D. 1831 till his death in A.D. 1852.'[29]

Despite the Countess's admirable habit of installing memorials about the place to her faithful servants - there is a series of such memorial plaques in the cloisters of the Augustinian Abbey - nowhere on the house or in the estate is there any memorial, plaque or mention of the Pain brothers. It was as if they had never existed. Pain denied.

While it cannot be doubted that Conolly did play a major role in supervising the workforce while the architects were not on hand, and while it cannot be doubted that Lord Dunraven took an informed and active interest in the architecture of his own house, it does seem a little unfair that the Pain brothers were totally denied any credit for the work they did. No matter how highly gifted Conolly was, it seems inconceivable that Lord and Lady Dunraven should have left the building of their private apartments in Conolly's hands without any supervision from an architect when they were absent from the autumn of 1834 to the middle of 1836. Moreover, as John Cornforth points out 'it seems highly unlikely that Lord Dunraven would have left Adare for two years if he himself was the designer of all that was going on.'[30] An argument

216

that is clinched by an entry in Lady Caroline's diary for June 1836 describing Adare after her long absence; she was very much struck 'with the beauty and grandeur of the buildings and admired its style more than any I had seen. The grey stone is in my opinion so much handsomer than any other colour'.[31] Which does seem to strongly suggest that the 2nd Earl's input into the house was not quite as remarkable as she would later claim.

From the evidence it can be assumed that the Pains were involved as architects until at least June 1836 and that some time not too long after that Lord Dunraven ceased to employ them. Perhaps after being away on the Continent and absorbing new influences he gained greater self-confidence and had developed his own ideas, ideas that clashed with the Pains' desire to maintain the Tudor-Revival integrity of their design. Perhaps something had happened during their long absence on the Continent that the Dunravens disapproved of. A drastic event may have occurred that led to Lady Caroline so ruthlessly cutting the Pain brothers out of the story.

Caroline's son Edwin, the 3rd Earl, collaborated with her on the Green Book contributing historical notes to the publication. Family mythology concerning the building of the Manor continued through the generations, resurfacing again in print in 1922 when her grandson Windham Thomas, the 4th Earl of Dunraven, said in his published autobiography that his grandfather 'employed no architect, no contractor, just took the ordinary stonemason and village carpenter, trained them, and built a goodly house.'[32]

It is this version of events that entered into the folk history of Adare village and became deeply rooted. When in 1975, for instance, the Limerick branch of An Taisce published a guide to Adare village to celebrate European Architectural Year, the myth was perpetuated.[33] Several years earlier, however, in 1969, *Country Life* magazine had published a series of three articles on Adare Manor by John Cornforth dismissing as fable the story that the 2nd Earl had designed the house. Cornforth based his account on primary sources that Desmond FitzGerald, The Knight of Glin, had uncovered among the Dunraven Papers - documents and architects' plans proving conclusively that the Pain brothers were the architects of the Tudor-Revivalist portion of the building.[34]

It is not unusual for local histories to have two parallel versions of the same event, the popularly accepted story generally proving highly resistant to the findings of more academic studies since the former has become deeply embedded in the community's consciousness through song, story and constant repetition. The latter, erudite studies though they may be, tend to be little read by the general populace, especially if they cater for a specialist or an elitist market. The truth does eventually percolate down, but it drips exceedingly slow.

Unfortunately, the 2nd Earl's discarding of James Pain when Adare Manor was still only half completed and his wife's seemingly authoritative 'eyewitness' account of the doings of her husband meant that the names of James and George Richard Pain were for many years unknown and unsung in connection with one of the most architecturally rich country houses in Co. Limerick. For whatever reason, Lady Caroline felt it necessary to exorcise the name of Pain from the family home and local memory and she was very successful in this endeavour long after her own death in 1870. Whatever the reason, her treatment of the Pain brothers does seem shabby.

Noblesse Oblige

The term 'Manor' conjures up the image of a cosy rural community whereby lands were granted to tenants and everybody from labourer to lord was tied together in an understood and mutually accepted system of reciprocal duties, rights and responsibilities. As discussed earlier, in the nineteenth century the Manor House style evoked a rosy tinted view of an harmonious relationship between landlord and tenant in which the former had duties of *noblesse oblige* to perform in order to maintain social equilibrium. Privilege entails responsibility was the dictum and we see many examples in the history of Adare whereby the Dunravens, in particular Lady Caroline, cultivated the image of benign patriarchs and benevolent, bountiful chatelaines. It was her proud boast that the employment given to local labourers and craftsmen during the years of the Famine while working on Adare Manor 'proved an inestimable blessing'[35] to the community.

While it may be easy to be cynical about the Dunravens' hankering after a manorial patriarchal society, based as Lady Caroline's inherited wealth was on coal mines in Glamorgan and the fact that large scale agricultural production had for a long time been run under cash-orientated capitalist lines, there can be no doubt that Lady Caroline was sincere in her beliefs and that this attitude became an important part of the family's historical relationship with the tenantry and the village of Adare. She carried out many acts of charity and on the occasion of the coming of age of her grandson, Lord Adare, in February 1862 the Dunravens organised a series of social events that would have done the most benevolent baron proud,

> 'The first day's festivity commenced with a dinner to the tenants, to which upwards of four hundred sat down. A presentation of plate to Lord Adare from the Irish and Welsh tenantry followed, and in the evening a ball, attended by more than a thousand of the tenantry, took place. The next day there was a concert of the Adare Village Choral Society, and on the following evening a large county ball, when the great capabilities for picturesque effect of the hall and gallery were for the first time exhibited and fully brought out. The

festivities closed with a ball to the servants, and the tradesmen of the village; and thus all classes participated in the happiness of the family on this occasion.'[36]

The tradition of concern for the welfare of others by the Dunravens continued on into the twentieth century when the 4th Earl wrote an open letter to the people of Ireland calling for the provision of cheap food, in particular fish, for the populace at large,

> 'The cost of living is very high. Fish is, or could easily be made, very cheap food . . . A big business is done in all the large towns and cities in Great Britain in "fish and chips." It is quite a sufficient and dainty meal, and cheap, I do not know the exact price, but I should think a good meal could be had for sixpence. I am not aware whether there are any such shops for "fish and chips" in Ireland, but if not why should the State not try the experiment, say, in the poorer quarters of Dublin or other of our large cities.'[37]

Glenstal Castle

While the Pain brothers received some very important commissions in the course of their careers they did suffer a number of rejections. In January 1836 they were competition entrants for the new Houses of Parliament in Westminster, but their Gothic proposal was turned down, as were ninety-six other submissions, the prize going to Charles Barry (1795-1860). With far less competition they also failed to gain a lucrative commission nearer to home, Glenstal Castle built near Murroe in Co. Limerick by the wealthy Barrington family. The architectural history of Glenstal is an interesting one in the context of the development of nineteenth century Irish country house architecture for it is a prime example of an explicit statement in stone by a bourgeois family attempting to construct the image of an ancestral relationship with the land.

Glenstal Castle, now a Benedictine abbey and a boys boarding school, was begun in 1837 by Sir Matthew Barrington whose family claimed descent from Odo du Barentin, a Norman baron who came over with William of Normandy to conquer England in 1066. Perhaps this was so, but the branch of the Barringtons who settled in Limerick City at the time of the Cromwellian conquest in the mid-seventeenth century were associated with urban trades and professions over the following two hundred years, prospering through various enterprises along the way, including a clockmaking workshop, a copper foundry and a pewter ware manufacturing and dealing business. The family were also involved in mercantile activities.[38]

Pain brothers' Picturesque Gothic 1833 proposal for Glenstal Castle, Co. Limerick.

By the early nineteenth century the family had accumulated sufficient wealth to obtain a baronetcy, Joseph Barrington becoming Sir Joseph in 1831. His son Matthew had the good sense to become a lawyer and from about 1814/15 served as Crown Solicitor for Munster earning a lucrative £15,000 per annum. It was Matthew who had ambitions to own a family demesne, firstly leasing the Carbery Estate in Co. Limerick in 1818 and then purchasing it in 1831 when his father obtained his baronetcy. It was upon this property that Glenstal Castle was built as the family seat.[39]

A number of leading architects, including the Pain brothers, were approached during the course of the 1830s to submit designs and the Pain proposal, submitted in April 1833, envisaged a Picturesque castellated house in the manner of Dromoland.[40] But Matthew was anxious to proclaim his Norman ancestry and he rejected the proposal in favour of a design by William Bardwell (1795-1890)[41] that envisaged a Norman Revival castle complete with a square Norman 'keep' to be used as the main family quarters. Bardwell's grand vision called for creating the appearance of an enclosed fortress-style structure with towers and keep linked by a battlemented curtain wall of ranges enclosing a large bailey. A chapel was also to have been incorporated into the curtain walling. The design of the keep was derived from Rochester Castle in England and the impressive gateway with its two flanking round towers was modelled on that of the thirteenth century gateway at Rockingham Castle, Northamptonshire.[42] Glenstal was no means the first Norman Revival castle to be built in Ireland, that distinction going to Gosford Castle (1819-21) in Co. Armagh - the architect on that occasion was the ever versatile Thomas Hopper who also created Penrhyn Castle, Caernarvonshire, Wales in the Norman style.[43]

The Pains' flair was for Tudor-Gothic and Nashian Gothic rather than the more dour Norman Revival style that featured round-headed Romanesque doorcases and windows. Neo-Norman architectural detail was simple and austere, not only on the exterior but on the interior as well in an attempt to create the illusion of authenticity, with the use of sturdy plain columns, simple vaulting (such as rib-vaulting), and areas of the wall left unplastered revealing the masonry blocks.

William Bardwell's Norman Revival vision of Glenstal Castle.

Romanesque entrance to main living quarters in Glenstal Castle.

In the keep of Glenstal Castle there is much use of Romanesque motifs on the mouldings of the archways and doorcases. Even the fireplaces were given the full Romanesque treatment. The pride of the round tower at Glenstal is an octagonal shaped library where stone rib-vaulting springs from elaborately carved capitals, a really superb accomplishment in successfully creating a medieval ambience. If the purpose of Glenstal was to convince the Barringtons that they had baronial blood coursing through their veins then the architect and craftsmen who worked on the project certainly succeeded in their endeavours.

Matthew Barrington died in 1861 and his sons, Sir William and Sir Croker Barrington, continued construction. It was not until 1875 that Glenstal Castle was finally completed. There were a number of stops and starts during this period, with Cork architect Joshua Hargraves being appointed in 1853 to finish the work.[44] Although Glenstal was not completed in conformity with the ambitious vision of Matthew Barrington and his architect William Bardwell, sufficient was built that was still capable of cutting an impressive figure that acts as a contrast with the Pain brothers' essay in Picturesque Gothic at Dromoland Castle.

Endnotes

1 Glin, Knight of 'Adare Manor', *Adare Manor Ireland*, Catalogue of Auction at Adare Manor 9, 10 June 1982, Christie, Manson & Woods Ltd., London and Hamilton & Hamilton (Estates) Ltd., 1982. Vol. I, pp. 8-9.

2 *Dunraven Papers* D/3196/E/3/66. University of Limerick Library.

3 *Dunraven Papers* D/3196/E/3/63. University of Limerick Library.

4 Dunraven, Caroline, Countess of & Dunraven, Edwin, Earl of *Memorials of Adare Manor with Historical Notes of Adare by her son The Earl of Dunraven*, printed for private circulation, Messrs. Parker, Oxford, 1865, pp. 3-4. Lady Caroline's *Memorials of Adare* are also known as The Green Book.

5 For a scale plan of the Augustinian Priory and 1865 illustrations of the Priory's western elevation and cloisters see Dunraven, Caroline, Countess of *op. cit.* Plates 15, 16 and 17.

6 Dunraven, Caroline, Countess of *op. cit.* p. 4; a plaque in the cloisters recording the restoration bears the date '1831'.

7 Diary of Lady Caroline, Countess of Dunraven, 17 June 1828, p. 26, University of Limerick Library (D/3196/E/2/3).

8 Johnson, Máiread *Ice and Cold Storage: A Dublin History*, Dublin, 1988.

9 Diary of Lady Caroline, Sunday 21 September 1828, p. 46, University of Limerick Library (D/3196/E/2/3).

10 ibid. (D/3196/E/2/31/32).

11 *Plan; The Principal Floor. The Earl of Dunraven - Adare. Jas. And G. R. Pain. May th24*. Copy in Limerick Civic Trust Archives.

12 Drawings in the Irish Architectural Archive, Merrion Square, Dublin.

13 Caroline, Countess of Dunraven *Memorials of Adare,* p. 7.

14 Cornforth, John 'Adare Manor, Co. Limerick - I', *Country Life* Vol. CXLV, 15 May 1969, p. 1233.

15 Dunraven, Caroline, Countess of *op. cit.* Pl. 12.

16 Dunraven, Caroline, Countess of *Memorials of Adare op. cit.* p. 24.

17 For a fuller description of the Long Gallery, its furnishings and stained glass windows see: Dunraven, Caroline, Countess of *op. cit.* pp. 17-27; Cornforth *op. cit.*, pp. 1233 - 4.

18 *Plan; The Principal Floor. The Earl of Dunraven - Adare. Jas. And G. R. Pain. May th24*. Copy in Limerick Civic Trust Archives.

19 Dunraven, Caroline, Countess of *op. cit.* p. 148.

20 Glin *op. cit.* p. 9.

21 Quoted by The Knight of Glin [Desmond FitzGerald] 'Adare Manor', *Adare Manor Ireland* Vol. I. Catalogue of auction for Wednesday and Thursday 9-10 June 1982, Christie, Manson & Woods Ltd., Hamilton & Hamilton (Estates) Ltd., 1982, p. 10.

22 The water-colour was reproduced in Cornforth, John 'Adare Manor, Limerick - II', *Country Life* Vol. CXLV, 22 May 1969, Fig. 1, p. 1302.

23 Irish Architectural Archives.

24 Cornforth, John 'Adare Manor, Limerick - II' *op. cit.* p. 1303.

25 Cornforth, John 'Adare Manor, Limerick - III', *Country Life,* 29 May 1969, p. 1368.

26 Dunraven, Caroline, Countess of *op. cit.* p. 27.

27 Dunraven, Caroline, Countess of *op. cit.* pp. 147-8.

28 ibid. p. 148.

29 This contradicts by one year Lady Caroline's assertion on page 7 of her *Memorials of Adare that* construction on the house began in 1832, but perhaps preparatory work started in 1831 such as dressing stone blocks.

30 Cornforth *op. cit.* p. 1233.

31 Quoted in Cornforth 'Adare Manor, Limerick - II' *op. cit.* p. 1302.

32 Dunraven, Earl of *Past Times and Pastimes* 2 Vols., Hodder and Stoughton, London, 1922, Vol. I, p. 2. Local Studies Department, Limerick County Library.

33 *Adare,* An Taisce - Limerick, 1975, p. 22.

34 Cornforth, John 'Adare Manor, Limerick - The Seat of the Earls of Dunraven', *Country Life* Vol. CXLV, *15,* 22 & 29 May 1969.

35 Dunraven, Caroline, Countess of op. *cit.* p. 8.

36 Dunraven, Caroline, Countess of *op. cit.* p. 27*n.*

37 Dunraven, Earl of *Cheap Food for the People at Large. An Open letter from the Earl of Dunraven K.P., C.M.G., To the People of Ireland,* Eason & Son Ltd., Dublin, 1925, p. 45. Limerick City Library, Limerick Collection.

38 O'Grady, D. 'The Barrington Normans of Limerick', *The Old Limerick Journal; Barrington's Edition* No. 24, Winter, 1988.

39 Tierney, Mark 'Sir Matthew Barrington: 1788-1861', *The Old Limerick Journal; Barrington's Edition* No. 24, Winter, 1988.

40 Tierney & Cornforth 'Glenstal Castle', *Country Life,* 3 October 1974.

41 Colvin, Howard *A Biographical Dictionary of British Architects 1600-1840* s.v, 'Bardwell, William', Yale University Press, New Haven and London, 1995.

42 Tierney, M. & Cornforth, J. 'Glenstal Castle', *Country Life,* 3 October 1974.

43 Colvin *op. cit.* s.v. 'Hopper, Thomas'.

44 Tierney, Mark, O.S.B. *Glenstal Abbey: A Historical Guide,* Glenstal Abbey Publications, 2001, 4th edition, pp. 33-4.

CHAPTER THIRTEEN

ARCHITECTURAL VERSATILITY

The expertise of James Pain was called upon in a most dramatic fashion when the roof and floors of a house on Limerick's George's Street suddenly fell in with a crash at 6.30 on the morning of Friday 9 August 1834 burying a woman alive. Another woman had a miraculous escape.

The accident occurred at the house of Stephen O'Donnell, a china merchant who had contracted workmen to enlarge his ground floor shop. For that purpose they had removed the central partition wall with a view to substituting it with a bressummer which is a horizontal beam or lintel placed over an opening in an external wall, as in the case of a shop front. The foreman had supposed that sufficient precautions had been put in place to avoid any danger. At the time there were two female maids asleep in bed upstairs while the work was going on. Soon after commencing work the foreman noticed 'a settlement in the wall' and called on his men to get out quick. Scarcely had they reached the door when the dreadful crash took place, the whole of the interior of the building falling in.

Hundreds of people quickly collected on the scene and on going to the rear of the house they saw one of the maidservants, 'Mary Clanchy [*sic*]' clinging on to the sill of a window on the upper floor dressed in her chemise and night cap, and screaming loudly for help. She remained in this terrible predicament for several minutes until she was rescued, without serious injury, with a ladder. She explained that she was asleep in the same bed with her fellow servant Anne Fitzgerald, aged 23 when she heard a rumbling noise and woke Anne telling her of the danger. Mary Clanchy, aged 50, jumped out of bed and ran to the window by which she held fast until rescued. Anne Fitzgerald, however, did not follow Mary but rushed towards the stairs in the hopes of escaping. She had only reached the room door when the roof fell in and overwhelmed her in an immense mass of rubble.

224

The owners of the premises, Mr. And Mrs. Stephen O'Donnell, were initially thought to be asleep in the house but it was later found that this was not the case, Mrs. O'Donnell 'being at the sea' and her husband having slept for the last week at his father-in-law's. Within a few minutes of the collapse of the interior of the house the Mayor, John Vereker, was on the scene and immediately sent for James Pain and builders John Fogerty and Messrs. O'Farrell, father and son.

In its report of the incident the *Limerick Chronicle* stated that the advice and direction of James Pain and Fogerty was very helpful to the men who were frantically clearing away the mass of rubble in their search for Anne Fitzgerald. It was not until the early afternoon that the young woman was discovered. Mr. B. O'Farrell was the first to 'perceive her arm scarcely visible, and called to the men to cease digging, but to pull away the bricks and slates with their hands.

This was done, and the young woman was, after some difficulty taken up, but perfectly lifeless.'

It was further reported that the Mayor opened a subscription fund for the mother of the deceased and that Stephen O'Donnell's loss was serious, the house a mere shell and the destruction of property great.[1]

Courthouse Work

This terrible accident may have led to the threat of civil proceedings against the builders as disputes between builders and clients were common enough. On several occasions James Pain was called upon as an expert witness in civil actions or to act as adjudicator in disputes. One such occasion was a case taken by the owners of the flour mills at Bruree, Co. Limerick in March 1834 against contractors concerning the 'insufficientcy [sic] of the building and the machinery.' The plaintiff produced various architects and wheelwrights to substantiate his case while the defendant on the other hand called forth his expert witnesses, including the 'Messrs. Pain, Anthony, Hill and others' who spoke of the 'efficient character of the building and its suitableness for carrying on the manufacture of flour.' As one might imagine a mass of evidence was offered by the cohorts of expert witnesses of both sides and it was 'generally of very conflicting character, as to professional opinion.' The Jury took only three-quarters of an hour to return a verdict and in their wisdom they found in favour of the plaintiff who was awarded £750.[2]

As discussed previously the Pain brothers carried out work as architects on courthouses in the Munster region, their most celebrated essay in this field being the majestic Cork City and County Courthouse. But they carried out other assignments in this area, small stuff that does not usually find its way into pages of architectural histories. In 1820, for instance, the brothers were paid £118 18s 0d by the County Limerick Grand Jury to prepare and furnish a room at the County Courthouse, Merchants Quay, Limerick for the use of barristers.[3] In addition, James was paid the sum of £11 7s 6d for 'his trouble in preparing plans' for the proposed alterations to the building.[4]

Until 1863 James Pain was retained as architect by the Board of Superintendance [sic] of the County Limerick Gaol, work that involved not only maintaining the fabric of the Mulgrave Street Gaol and erecting any necessary additional buildings but also furnishing a written report on the physical state of the bridewells and courthouses in the various county towns as well. A bridewell was a small local prison where suspects could be held before being escorted to the County Gaol. Twice a year the Board of Superintendence prepared a general 'Gaol Report' for the Grand Jury which was published in the Spring and Summer Presentments. There is regular mention of James Pain having reported to the Board on the state and condition of these buildings. At the 1828 Summer Assizes, for instance, the Grand Jury was informed that the architect had found that the roof of the Courthouse at Rathkeale was in 'very bad state. The alterations and improvements in Bruff Sessions House, are nearly completed, and are found very advantageous.'[5] The following spring the situation at Rathkeale Courthouse had not been rectified as it was again found by James Pain to be 'in a very bad condition, as to the roof, and has been visited by some of the Board, and found so. Mr. Pain, being in England, prevents a regular report being furnished.'[6] The situation had not improved by the Summer Assizes of that year.[7]

As retained architect James Pain would have furnished plans and specifications for repairs, alterations and additions undertaken on buildings, as in the case of the Rathkeale Bridewell and Courthouse in June 1843 when a notice appeared in the local press advertising for builders to submit proposals, informing them that the plan and specification was to be seen in the 'Office of Mr. Pain, No. 33, George's-street, Limerick.'[8] A Mr. Fitzgerald, described as an 'architect' winning the contract.[9] One assumes that the dreadful state of the roof at Rathkeale Courthouse, as reported in 1829, had since been seen to long before the 1843 works.

Although a bridewell had been built in Glin by 1816 it soon fell into disrepair and by 1823 a report stated that it was 'holy destitute of every accommodation required by law'. It went on to say 'nothing could exceed the dirt and want of neat regular appearance' of the building.[10] At the 1824 Summer Assizes the board informed the Grand Jury that a new bridewell for Glin was 'absolutely necessary, as the old one is found to be incapable of repair.' The board also recommended building a new one at Croom.[11] At the 1827 Spring Assizes a presentment of £950 was made to build a new bridewell at Glin, and to finish the bridewells of Newcastle, Kilfinane and Croom.[12] The following spring James Pain reported to the Board that the Bridewell of Glin 'will be ready in a Week for Roof .' He also reported that the bridewells of Kilfinane and Rathkeale were completed, as was the one at Croom.[13] In its report to the Spring 1829 Assizes the Board of Superintendance remarked that 'Glin Bridewell is reported by the Knight of Glin, as finished, and ready for furniture …'[14] The Knight of Glin at the time was John Fraunceis Fitzgerald, who was known in Gaelic as the 'Knight of the Women'.[15] In 1834 the Keeper of the Glin Bridewell, Thomas Madigan, was dismissed in 1834 because he had a disagreement with the Knight. Apparently he had refused to allow the Bridewell to be used by the Knight and his mistress Mary Wright for 'improper purposes'.[16]

The architectural firm of James and George Richard Pain also carried out courthouse and bridewell work in Co. Kerry. A paragraph in the *Limerick Chronicle* of 30 May 1827 reporting that the plan of the their new Sessions House at Killarney had been approved of the Kerry Grand Jury. Also, the

Killarney Courthouse, Co. Kerry.

bridewells at Killarney, Milltown, Dingle, Tarbert, Listowel, Kenmare, Caherciveen and Castleisland 'are to be enlarged and improved according to the system recommended by the Messrs. Pain.' The same edition of the newspaper carried a notice that the new Courthouse at Tralee had been approved, but the architect in that case was William Morrison of 10 Gloucester Street, Dublin

As architect for the County Gaol James Pain was on call to carry out work on the facility, as on the occasion when the Board of Superintendence brought to the attention of the Grand Jury at the Summer 1830 Assizes 'the state of the covering of the Arcade, the greater part of which is rotten, and unsafe to walk on: they have desired Mr. Pain to report the state and expence [sic] of repairs.'[17] The arcade was the wooden walkway that ran around the second storey of the central administrative block of the prison; covered by a roof it allowed sentries to walk around the tower to keep an eye on the prison grounds below. The security was naturally an important concern for the Board and following a visit by James Pain to an English prison in the summer of 1829 he recommended the addition of loose brickwork or spiked timber to the boundary walls of the wards with a view to increase security. This work was necessary because the Lord Lieutenant of Ireland had decided to withdraw military guards from all the prisons in the country. The Board were of the opinion that additional Turnkeys (warders) need not be employed at the prison but decided to appoint four Watchmen, two of whom 'should mount every evening, and patrole [sic] within the insulating passage, until clear day light.'[18] The insulating passage being the space between the inner and outer walls of the prison. These measures, and the provision of arms for the Watchmen and Turnkeys, were considered sufficient to make the facility secure even in the absence of soldiers.

At the following Spring Assizes in 1830 it was reported that there had been an 'addition of the 3 feet 2 inches (0.92 metres) of loose brickwork, which it was found necessary to place on the top of the inside walls, and some alterations in the iron gates, to increase the security of the Prison on the removal of the Military Guards. . . . and further, an attempt at escape having been made by the Convicts under sentence of Transportation in the month of September last, by removing the flag [flagstone] placed at the back of one of the Privies - the Board found it necessary to direct all the Privies to be secured by more solid work.'[19]

Architect to the Gentry and Nobility

As well as building country mansions and churches, one of the 'bread and butter' reliables of James Pain's practice were alterations and remodelling work carried out on private houses, business premises and public buildings. Some of this work was on a very small scale such as designing cornices for the house of General Sir Richard Bourke at Thornfield, Lisnagry, Co. Limerick.[20]

In May 1833 James was in receipt of monies from Lord Viscount Guillamore's Rockbarton estate located two miles north of Bruff, Co. Limerick. According to the estate's account book the architect carried out a commission valued at £28 17s 3d for the 'New Library' of Rockbarton House and had completed work costing £10 10s in nearby Cahirguillamore House, a property on the same estate. In addition, a payment of £9 9s was made relating to the 'Church' account.[21] Presumably the church in question was Tullybrackey Church (1819, demolished 1959) sited opposite the gated entrance to Rockbarton manor and demesne.[22] These amounts are, of course, quite trivial when compared to the £100,000 plus lavished on Mitchelstown Castle by the Earl of Kingston. However, the nine guineas received by James Pain for work carried out on the

228

John Paul Dowling

Cornice detail, Thornfield, Co. Limerick.

Interior view of Thornfield.

church was more than, or the same as the annual wages received by some of the servants on the Rockbarton estate. Peg Kelly, the junior kitchen maid being in receipt of £5 a year,[23] while Thomas Keiffe, a gardener who had been appointed 'Bog Ranger', had £10 a year.[24]

Other works attributed to James Pain include the addition of a turreted porch to Castle Kevin in north Co. Cork, an 1830s castellated country house designed by an architect named Flood.[25] Some of the assignments taken on by James Pain's Limerick office were quite substantial as when major additions were made in 1835 to Loughton House, a three storey Georgian house built in 1777 near Moneygall, Co. Offaly.[26]

Curragh Chase

In 1827-8 James carried out alterations to Curragh House valued at £709 11s 3d. for Sir Aubrey Hunt (1788-1846).[27] The nature of these alterations is not known, but the work was very probably associated with a major remodelling of the eighteenth century house carried out *c.*1829 by English architect Amon Henry Wilds.[28] Wilds, a resident of Brighton, is best known for building terraces and crescents for that fashionable seaside resort.[29] According to Colvin, an 1829 edition of the *Brighton Gazette* (date not cited) noted that Wilds had just returned from Limerick where he was engaged upon 'some plans for the improvement and embellishment of that city and a house for Sir Aubrey Hunter [*sic*].'[30]

Curragh Chase House before its destruction in 1941.

230

The original house was so extensively altered by Wilds that essentially all that remains of the former Georgian structure is the front of the original building. This eighteenth century work consists of a three-sided central bow flanked on either side by two bays. The windows retain their original masonry surrounds of shouldered architraves, those on the upper storey resting on console brackets while those on the lower storey have simple entablatures and no consoles. Wilds's new, longer frontage of eleven bays faces toward the lake and is set at right angles to the earlier front, being plainer in design than the Georgian front, the windows having no surrounds. The resulting hybrid consists, therefore, of two adjoining fronts of different dates. Two storeys over a basement, Wild's composition is reminiscent of a terrace, which is not surprising given that terrace building was his main field of activity.

Sir Aubrey changed the family name from Hunt to de Vere about 1832 and renamed the estate Curragh Chase. The house was accidently burnt down in 1941 on Christmas Eve and is now a ruin. Roofless, only the walls of the house remain standing - a grey, sad ruin with windows and doors filled in with grim concrete blocks. The demesne of 777 acres is presently (2005) owned and managed by Coillte (the Irish Forestry Board) as a forest park and public amenity. Curragh Chase is mainly associated with the memory of Aubrey Thomas de Vere (1814-1902), a younger son of Sir Aubrey, who converted from the Church of Ireland to Catholicism in 1851 and developed a reputation as a minor Irish Victorian poet with patriot leanings. In the grounds of Curragh Chase can be seen the stone seat where de Vere consulted his poetic Muse, a plaque bearing the inscription *"Little Heaven" Aubrey de Vere Meditated Here*.

Locally, de Vere was not alone in converting to Catholicism, Edwin, 3rd Earl of Dunraven of Adare Manor did so as well, reconverting to the Faith of his fathers. A flavour of de Vere's patriotic verse may be had from the opening lines of his, *A Ballad of Sarsfield Or, The Bursting of the Guns A.D. 1690,*

> 'Sarsfield went out the Dutch to rout,
> And to take and break their cannon;
> To Mass went he at half-past three,
> And at four he cross'd the Shannon.'[33]

He was also responsible for *The Wail of Thomond* and *The Dirge of Kildare*, and let's not forget his *Ode to the Daffodil* (he was influenced by William Wordsworth after all), and *Ode, The Building of a Cottage,*

'Mix the mortar o'er and o'er,
Holy music singing:
Holy water o'er it pour,
Flower and tresses flinging:
Bless we now the earthen floor:
May good Angels love it!
Bless we now the new-raised door:
And that cell above it:
Holy cell, and holy shrine
For the Maid and Child divine!'[32]

As a convert Aubrey de Vere tended to wear his Catholicism on his poetic sleeve,

'Rejoice O Mary! And be glad
Thou Church triumphant here below!'[33]

Big House Work

The Pain brothers' versatility as architects was again shown in their contrasting designs for two large country houses, Clarina Castle in Co. Limerick and Convamore House in Co. Cork. Clarina Castle was built near the village of Clarina which is on the road from Limerick City to Foynes, and was constructed in the Picturesque Gothic style for Eyre Massey, 3rd Lord Clarina (1798-1872). Built in the period 1833-6 the castellated house went by various names : Clarina Castle, Elm Park Castle, or sometimes just plain Clarina House. The money for the project was provided by Lord Clarina's wife, Susan Elizabeth Barton (1810-86) who he married, when she was eighteen years old, in September 1828. Miss Barton was the daughter of wine baron Hugh Barton who was a member of an Irish-French family who had settled in France and had become extremely wealthy as wine merchants. The dowry that Susan Barton brought to her marriage to Eyre Massey was a huge one allowing Lord and Lady Clarina to employ the Pain brothers to build the castle of their dreams.[34] At one stage it was thought that the castle had been designed by C. F. Anderson who was responsible for designing a number of country houses in Ireland. However, local Limerick historian Mathew Potter has established that Clarina Castle was in fact the work of the Pain brothers. The obituary for James Pain that appeared in *The Irish Builder* on 1 January 1878 clearly states that Clarina Castle was attributable to him.

Unfortunately Clarina Castle is no more having been demolished in the early 1960s - only the outbuildings and two of the gate lodges surviving. As with Dromoland Castle, Clarina was assymetrical with a great deal of crenellation

Clarina Castle, Co. Limerick.

and adorned with both round and square towers. The central block and the tower to the right of the main entrance were three stories over a basement, the rest of the building two stories over a basement. Containing forty-nine rooms in total it had a large hall that could be used as a ballroom. Built of cut stone it cost the Masseys £50,000, worth many millions in euros today.

The Pains' work on Convamore House, Ballyhooly in north Co. Cork was, in contrast, Classically influenced. Their assignment for the Earl of Listowel, who wanted to replace the old mansion house on the site with a large building of Georgian design, involved extending considerably the size of the original house on the site. The finished work comprised an east facing two-storey, seven bay front, two of the windows on the ground floor being given pedimented tops. The adjoining north face of Convamore, also of seven bays, had a single-storey Doric portico. The south elevation of the building was given Doric plaster pilasters. Convamore, overlooking the river Blackwater, was burnt down in 1921 and is now a ruin.[35]

Before leaving the subject of the Big House mention should also be made of Strancally Castle, Co. Waterford, also in the valley of the Blackwater, built

Strancally Castle, Co. Waterford.

about 1830 for John Kiely by the Pain brothers.[36] Kiely wanted his house to be the largest and most impressive for miles around and on one occasion he visited Lough Cutra Castle (designed by John Nash, executing architect James Pain) in Co. Galway and was very much impressed by its sense of projecting an air of medieval nobility. Engaging the services of the Pain brothers, John Kiely chose a beautiful site overlooking the river but the architects said that the ground needed to be built up considerably to allow a castle to be built there. They advised Mr Kiely that it would be necessary 'to move a mountain in order to make the ground high enough' but the patron is reported to have said "If that's what it takes then that is what it will take." It is said that it took forty men two years in building up the site by over 20 feet and containing it within a castellated wall.[37] According to the *Dublin Penny Journal* of 5 July 1854 Strancally Castle was 'a modern structure built in the Gothic style from the design of Mr. G. R. Payne, of Cork.' As with other of the Pain brothers' castellated endeavours it is asymmetrical in layout but is not up to the same high standard of Dromoland Castle. Strancally, with its predominant use of square towers and turrets seems a very plain essay in Gothic.

For those estate holders anxious to establish medieval roots, whether authentic or imaginary, but who did not wish to spend vast sums of money on a new house, the job was made much easier for the architects like the Pains if one had a genuine, habitable late medieval century tower house on one's property. Then the brothers could obligingly tack on nineteenth century 'feudal' additions to the original medieval structure. At Castlegarde, Pallasgreen in Co. Limerick James and George Richard are believed to have collaborated together in about 1820 on modernising a tower house, adding a castellated wing to the structure and restoring the walls of the old castle bawn giving them battlements and a new castellated gateway.[38] The assignment was carried out for Waller O'Grady, a son of Viscount Guillamore of Rockbarton House near Bruff, Co. Limerick. In the mid-1850s James Pain carried similar work for Lord Dunboyne on his late fifteenth century medieval tower house at Knappogue Castle near Quin in Co. Clare.

Castlegarde, Pallasgreen, Co. Limerick.

In an earlier chapter the possibility that James Pain gingered up Glin House in c.1812 with Gothic battlements for John Fraunceis Fitzgerald, Knight of Glin, was discussed. It is thought that the Pain brothers carried out a more thoroughgoing make-over on Quinville House near the village of Quin in Co. Clare. Originally a fairly ordinary Georgian building it underwent a major reconstruction in 1827, being converted into a Gothic-Tudor Revivalist mansion with gable breakfronts, large oriel windows on each of the main floors and Gothicised chimney stacks.[39]

Returning to Glin Castle, the castellated entrance lodges to the estate - the Village Gate Lodge and the Western Gate Lodge - can be dated to the 1820s and 30s; the Western Gate Lodge definitely to the mid-1830s. The latter a substantial gate lodge, with square towers flanking a gateway, located on the main road to Tarbert just beyond the whitewashed Gothic Bathing Lodge that stands by the road in front of Glin Castle.[40] As with the earlier work undertaken on the Glin demesne following the inheritance of the title by John Fraunceis FitzGerald in 1812 (he died in 1854)[41] there is no documentary evidence pointing to any one particular architect. However as the pre-eminent Gothic Revivalist in the Limerick region there is a possibility, not more than that, that again the designs came off the drawing boards of James Pain's office in Limerick.[42] Evidence dating the Western Gate Lodge to 1835 is provided in an account of *Two Months at Kilkee* (1836) written by Mary John Knott. In describing the Limerick coastline as she travelled down the Shannon on 2 June 1835 by steamer from Limerick to Kilrush, Mary John Knott says of Glin,

> 'The modern castle of the present Knight is well placed on a gentle elevation; and commands a very extensive prospect up and down the river . . . a new gateway and entrance, leading up through a wood which is being made, will add to the beauty of this noble residence.[43]

236

Bank Architect

James's catalogue of commercial work included opening up 'the entrance to the New Excise office' on Limerick's Rutland Street in December 1824[44] and converting rooms in a terraced house into business offices,

THE NEW LaMERICK [*sic*] BANK

We are gratified at announcing to our readers and the public, that numerous workmen are now busily employed, under the superintendence of that eminent and respectable Architect, JAMES PAIN, Esq., in Mr. MORGAN'S house, No. 1. Rich-mond Place, preparing the Cash and other extensive Offices for THE AGRICULTURAL AND COMMERCIAL BANK OF IRE-LAND, which will be in full operation within a month, at which time the alterations in questions will have been completed.

(*Limerick Chronicle*, 17 November 1834.)

The Provincial Bank, O'Connell Street, Limerick in Classical style. Now a pub known as The Bank.

James Pain's Limerick office also drew up plans for work carried out in 1838 in Kilrush, Co. Clare converting a building into a branch bank for the Provincial Bank of Ireland. Robert Hunter, the manager of the Bank in Limerick, being responsible for examining builders' tenders. The Kilrush branch was opened in October, a sum of over £1,000 having been expended on the conversion.[45]

Robert Hunter was obviously happy with James Pain's work for he was the architect of the new Provincial Bank premises built on the corner of Mallow Street and George's Street in Limerick the following year;[46] the building still stands and is presently (2005) the home of a pub known as 'The Bank'.

Clonmel School

In April 1829 the Board of Commissioners of Education in Ireland contracted the Pain brothers to build a new Free School in Clonmel, the old school house having fallen into decay. Founded in 1685, the school was intended to provide an education for the children of local 'bakers, butchers, merchants, laundresses, semptors [seamstress], innkeepers, smiths, taverners, glovers, shoemakers, joiners, saddlers' and such like.[47] In 1824, of the sixty pupils, both boarders and day, fifty-four were members of the Church of Ireland, five were Catholics and one a Dissenter.

Proposals to build the new school had been submitted during the winter of 1825-6 by several architects, including John Welland who appears to have been the architect of first choice. But the contract with Welland and his associated contractors was not finalised due to difficulties over sureties and the contract was subsequently given to the Pains. There are a number of interesting features in their original specifications for the building, (signed and dated 'James and George Richard Pain. Limerick. 27 January 1826'), including the statement that the roof and floors were to be of 'Memel or Norway fir, no American timber to be used but in the interior finishings of the doors and shutters and skirtings.' The contract entered into by the Messrs. Pain and the Commissioners of Education on 16 April 1829 provided for an expenditure of £4000 made up as follows:

Excavating and Earth-work	... ...	£68 18 0
Mason and Bricklayers Work	... ...	£1150 0 0
Stone Cutters Work	... ...	£236 10 7
Carpenters and Joiners Work	... ...	£1509 16 1
Smiths Painter Plumber &c.	... ...	£234 14 6
Slater and Plasterer	... ...	£710 0 0
Chimney pieces Grates &c.	... ...	£89 10 0 [48]

A local architect, John Jones, was appointed to supervise construction work that was completed in the summer of 1830.[49] A large and substantial building, the new school was able to accommodate ninety pupils.[50] Due to the decline of the Protestant population in the area the school closed in 1922 and was later sold to Tipperary South Riding County Council in 1941.[51]

Villiers' Alms House, King's Island, Limerick.

Villiers' Alms House & School

The brothers were responsible for several charitable institutions in Limerick that incorporated school rooms into their design. One such being 'Madam Villiers's Alms House'[52] built in the King's Island district of Limerick as accommodation for Protestant widows. Opened in 1827, the plaque inscription on the breakfront credits the Pain brothers as the architects. Built on a site adjacent to St. Munchin's Church, construction was funded by an endowment from the will of the late Mrs. Hannah Villiers who was desirous that charity accommodation for Protestant and Presbyterian widows be provided for in the city. When built, twelve widows were catered for, each receiving £24 per annum and a room.[53]

On its front elevation, the limestone building is in the style of Tudor-Gothic Revival. Symmetrical in plan, the building has projecting wings in which schoolrooms were located, the Girls School in the northerly wing and the Boys School in the southerly.[54] These wings have gabled breakfronts. The teachers' salaries were provided for by the will of Mrs. Villiers.[55] The Alms House has lofty Tudorish chimney-stacks grouped in clusters, fourteen in all, and dormer windows. On the front elevation, over the doors and windows on the ground floor, and the three windows on the first floor, rectangular label hood-moulds are placed. The hood-mould, a characteristic feature of medieval architecture, is projecting masonry placed over an archway, door or window designed to throw rainwater clear of the opening. If rectangular in shape, as in the case of Villiers' Alms House, the hood-mould is known as a label; if curved, as over a Gothic pointed window, it is referred to as a dripstone. The use of hood-moulds was a standard device used by Gothic revivalists to give an instant look of antiquity to a building. The upper floor window of the central breakfront is flanked on either side by a slender lancet window typical of the thirteenth century while the top of the breakfront is battlemented.

T. McNamara in his *Portrait of Cork* (1981) writes that the total cost of the building came to £3,663 with the first payment to the Pains of £500 dated 10 June 1826 and a final payment of £954 10s 8d on 18 January 1827. It appears therefore that the building was completed fairly quickly.

Hannah Villiers' benevolence also provided funds for the establishment of an orphanage and school for Protestant girls that came to be built in upper Henry Street[56] in 1839. With accommodation for twenty-five to thirty orphans, the institution also catered for seventy to eighty day pupils in two schools, one for boys, the other for girls.[57] Management of the construction project came under the direction of the Rev. John Duddell who had been appointed to execute the late Mrs. Villiers's instructions.[58] Duddell had been rector of St. Munchin's when it was rebuilt in 1827; he had also overseen the Villiers' Alms House scheme.

T. McNamara in his *Portrait of Cork* states that the builders of Villiers' Orphanage and School were J. and G. R. Pain who were paid several tranches of money during the course of construction, including a sum of £600 on 27 March 1837, £1,000 on 29 July 1837 and a final payment of £788 0s 6d on 16 March 1839. McNamara cites no references however. The total expenditure came to £3,089 18s 10d.[59]

Set back from the road with a forecourt, the building is in Classical mode. Attractively designed, this two-storey, cut-limestone structure has a central block of five bays with a pedimented breakfront and a flat-roofed bow portico (single storey in height) supported by two columns. The column shafts are octagonal, the four cardinal sides about 6 inches (15.24cm) in width and the other four, intermediate faces, about 3 1/2 inches (8.89cm) in width. The pediment features an oculus window and surmounts a breakfront that is the width of the portico. Two flanking two-storey wings (not projecting) with a pedimented gable are each joined to the central block by a short section the equivalent of 1 1/2 storeys in height. Villiers School moved to Tivoli House on

Villiers School, Henry Street, Limerick.

the North Circular Road in 1953. The original premises on Henry Street was for a period, home to the Shannon Alms Hotel, and the building is presently (2005) unoccupied and advertised as having office space to let.

Numbered among the other educational institutions that appreciated the work of the Pain brothers was Trinity College, Dublin who in 1833 held a competition for a new building comprising of a hall, lecture rooms and museum to be built in Front Square. The *Limerick Chronicle* reported on 19 April 1834 that 'The design of George R. Pain Esq. For enlarging Trinity College, is preferred by the fellows, before those of near 30 other candidates.' As it turned out George Richard's design was not implemented and Trinity had to wait almost another twenty years and hold another competition before it got its Museum.[60]

241

Endnotes

1 *Limerick Chronicle*, Saturday 9 August 1834.

2 *Limerick Chronicle*, 29 March 1834.

3 *County of Limerick Grand Jury Presentments,* Summer Assizes 1820, p. 29.

4 ibid. p. 28.

5 ibid. Summer 1828, pp.17-18.

6 ibid. Spring 1829, p. 21.

7 ibid. Summer, 1829, p. 18.

8 *Limerick Chronicle*, 7 June 1843.

9 *Limerick Chronicle*, 21 June 1843.

10 Gaughan, J.A. *The Knights of Glin*, Kingdom Books, 1978, p. 114.

11 *County of Limerick Grand Jury Presentments*, Summer Assizes 1824, p. 21.

12 Donovan, Tom 'Glin Bridewell', *The Glen Corbry Chronicle*, The Glin Historical Society, 1997, p. 46.

13 *County Limerick Grand Jury Presentments*, Spring 1828, p. 26.

14 ibid. Spring, 1829, p. 21.

15 Fitzgerald, Desmond, Knight of Glin 'The Treasures of Glin Castle', *The Glen Corbry Chronicle*, The Glin Historical Society, 1997, p. 26.

16 Donovan *op. cit.* p. 47.

17 *County of Limerick Grand Jury Presentments*, Summer Assizes 1830, p. 18.

18 ibid. Summer 1829, p. 19.

19 ibid. Spring 1830, p. 21.

20 Bourke, Gerald *Out on a Limb*, Trafford Publishing, Victoria, Canada, 2003, p. 10.

21 *Account Book of Rockbarton Estate 1831-40*, p. 69, Limerick Museum (LM 2004.98).

22 Ordnance Survey, 6 inches to the mile, Limerick, Sheet 32, 1927.

23 *Account Book of Rockbarton Estate op. cit.* p. 137.

24 ibid. p. 123. Naturally, some of the staff received substantially more than these amounts and the hierarchical pecking order within servants and staff is quite evident: Patrick Dooley, groom, 14 guineas per annum; William Watson, coachman, £25; John Carroll, butler, £40.

25 Hajba, Anna-Maria *Houses of Cork Volume 1: North Cork*, Ballinakella Press, Whitegate, Co. Clare s.v. 'Castle Kevin', p.105.

26 Bence-Jones, Mark *A Guide to Irish Country Houses*, Constable, London, revised edition, 1988, s.v. 'Loughton.'

27 This information is in a notebook entitled *Timber and Turf etc* containing a list of numbered entries briefly describing the contents of various letters. Entry No. 18 reads 'Miscellaneous a/c etc. 1826. Letter [*word not legible*] James Pain's alterations to Curragh 1827-8. £709 11s 3d.', De Vere Papers, (P22 Box 3, Limerick Archives).

28 Bence-Jones *op. cit.* p. 97.

29 Colvin, Howard *A Biographical Dictionary of British Architects 1600-1840* s.v. 'Wilds, Amon Henry', Yale University Press, New Haven and London, 1995.

30 loc. cit.

31 Cronin, Patrick J. *Aubrey de Vere - The Bard of Curragh Chase: A Portrait of his Life and Poetry*, Askeaton Civic Trust, Co. Limerick, 1997, pp. 2-3, 7.

32 ibid. p. 116.

33 ibid. 'Corpus Christi', p. 187.

34 Potter, Mathew 'The Architectural Legacy of Eyre Massey, 3rd Lord Clarina (1798-1872)', *North Munster Antiquarian Journal* Vol. 42, 2002, pp. 11-20.

35 Haiba *op. cit.* s.v. 'Convamore, Ballyhooly'; Bence-Jones op. cit. s.v. 'Convamore, Ballyhooly, Co Cork'.

36 Bence-Jones *op. cit.* s.v. 'Strancally Castle, Knockanore, Co. Waterford'.

37 Billensteiner, Friedrich & Heffernan, Kieran *The History of Strancally Castle and The Valley of the Blackwater between Lismore and Yougha*, Strancally Castle Library, Knockanore, Co. Waterford, 1999, p.44.

38 Bence-Jones *op. cit.* s.v. 'Castlegarde', p. 69.

39 Weir, Hugh *Houses of Clare,* Ballinakella Press, Whitegate, Co. Clare, 1986, pp. 220-1.

40 For descriptions and illustrations of the Glin Castle gate lodges see Howley, James *The Follies and Garden Buildings of Ireland*, Yale University Press, New Haven and London, 1993, pp. 76, 92.

41 Fitzgerald *op. cit.* p. 26.

42 Conversation with Desmond FitzGerald, Knight of Glin on 12 February 2005. The Knight also suggested that Hamilton Terrace (1839), a terrace of five houses flanked on either side by two larger houses at either end built on the outskirts of Glin village and overlooking the river Shannon, may also be by James Pain.

43 Knott, Mary John *Two Months at Kilkee*, Dublin, 1836, p. 22. Reprinted facsimile published by Clasp Press, Ennis, Co. Clare, 1997.

44 *Limerick Chronicle*, 11 December 1824.

45 Limerick Chronicle, 18 August, 24 October 1838.

46 *Proceedings and Orders of the Commissioners for Improving the Parish of St. Michael* (MS), 18 January 1839.

47 Quane, Michael 'The Free School of Clonmel', *Journal of the Cork Historical and Archaeological Society* Vol. LXIX, 1964, p. 4.

48 ibid. p. 10.

49 ibid. pp. 10-11.

50 Lewis, Samuel *A Topographical Dictionary of Ireland,* Two Vols., London, 1837, Vol. I, p. 371.

51 Quane *op. cit.* P. 24.

52 *1840 Ordnance Survey*, City of Limerick, Sheet 10.

53 Lenihan *op. cit.* p. 442n.

54 *1840 Ordnance Survey*, City of Limerick, Sheet 10.

55 *Deane's Limerick Almanack, Directory and Advertiser of 1838*, p. 36; Lewis *op. cit.* Vol. II, p. 276.

56 *1840 Ordnance Survey,* City of Limerick, Sheet 18.

57 *The New Triennial and Commercial Directory for the Years 1840, 41 & 42*, printed by George M. Goggin for F. Kinder & Son, Limerick, 1840, p. 6.

58 *Deane's Limerick Almanack, Directory and Advertiser of 1838 Directory*, pp. 47-8.

59 MacNamara, T. K. *Portrait of Cork* Watermans, Cork, 1981, p. 154.

60 O'Dwyer, Frederick *Lost Dublin*, Gill & MacMillan, Dublin, 1981, p.138.

CHAPTER FOURTEEN

GEORGIAN LIMERICK

For most of his sixty-six years in Ireland James Pain lived in a Georgian terraced house on Limerick's George's Street, the main thoroughfare of the city's Georgian quarter, also known as Newtown Pery. Making Limerick his home, he seems to have settled fairly effortlessly into his new surroundings, becoming a respected figure among the professional and business classes of the city and making a distinguished contribution to its architectural development. Given that he spent two-thirds of his life working and socialising in Newtown Pery it would be of interest to have a look at the historical development of the urban context in which he lived.

A Dirty, Disagreeable Place

During the first half of the eighteenth century Limerick remained a small provincial town enclosed within restrictive medieval walls. The circuit of the city walls described an hourglass figure, Limerick being divided into two distinct quarters with Englishtown laying to the north of the Abbey River and Irishtown to the south. These two districts were linked by Baal's Bridge, a narrow structure of medieval origin having a row of houses perched on each side of the traffic way.

Englishtown, which stood upon The King's Island (an area bounded by the Shannon and the Abbey River) had traditionally been the administrative, civic and commercial centre of the city, as there were to be found the Cathedral, Bishops' Palace, Corporation offices, the Exchange, Custom House, harbour, prison, Courthouse and the principal military structure of the city, King John's Castle. Thomond Bridge, located beside the thirteenth century Castle, provided the only crossing point over the Shannon, connecting Limerick with Clare and Galway.[1]

In the mid-eighteenth century a number of suburbs composed mainly of cottages were to be found outside the walls. These extra-mural areas included Thomondgate, situated besides Thomond Bridge on the Clare side of the Shannon, and the Abbey district on King's Island. Ribbon housing ran alongside the roads leading from John's Gate in the Irishtown; these routes connecting Limerick with Cork and routes east.[2] Access into fortified Limerick was through one of seventeen city gates, twelve in Englishtown and five in Irishtown; entrances that well into the eighteenth century were closed at night for security reasons and guarded by soldiers. Limerick's reputation as a rebel city - it had thrice been subject to siege in the seventeenth century, once by Cromwellians in 1651 and twice by Williamites in 1690 and 1691 - meant that its loyalty was subject to scrutiny until the threat of a Jacobite uprising and French invasion had receded. According to Limerick historian John Ferrar, writing in 1787,

'The most severe discipline was observed in the garrison for sixty years after the siege [that of 1691]; the gates were locked every night and every Sunday . . . ; this discipline, and those walls preventing a free circulation of air, were not inviting to strangers, or men of landed property to settle here.' [3]

The streets and lanes of this cramped fortress city were positively unhealthy and a visitor to Limerick in 1752, Anglican prelate Richard Pococke,[4] described Limerick as 'a dirty, disagreeable place . . . Both the air and water are looked on as unwholesome, and the army commonly loose [sic] many of their men here.' There was little to commend the city to the traveller, its attractions were few and far between and, the prelate complained, was bereft of a decent inn.[5]

Transformation

Richard Pococke's evident dislike for Limerick was perfectly understandable, but the fortunes of the city were then on the threshold of a considerable change for the better, as from the middle of the eighteenth century the city's mercantile classes began to prosper greatly on account of Limerick's growing agricultural export trade with Britain. A prosperity that would transform Limerick from a small, grubby fortress town into a thriving port city by the first half of the nineteenth century complete with one of the most modern commercial and residential city centres in Ireland, or in Britain for that matter.

This improvement in Limerick's fortunes was directly linked to the dramatic increase in commerce between Ireland and Britain during this period. The figures speak for themselves, the value of Irish trade increasing sevenfold between 1730 and 1815, the Anglo-Irish provisions trade being particularly important. Limerick's contribution being in the form of butter, beef, bacon, pork, corn, oats, wheat and barley, as well as items such as flax, feathers and salmon, produced in the hinterlands of counties Limerick, Tipperary, Clare and parts of Kerry and exported to Bristol, London, Liverpool and Glasgow.[6]

Rising estate incomes allowed Irish landlords to build fine country homes, fashionably decorated and furnished. Economic growth also fostered the emergence of a new urban middle-class in commercial centres such as Limerick and Cork. A middle-class composed of bankers, merchants, lawyers, builders, distillers, shopkeepers and successful artisans stimulating demand for goods, services and new houses. In Limerick urban growth took the form of a Georgian new town built to the south and south-west of the old walled districts of Englishtown and Irishtown, A Georgian new town that was to be second in size only to Dublin's Georgian development.

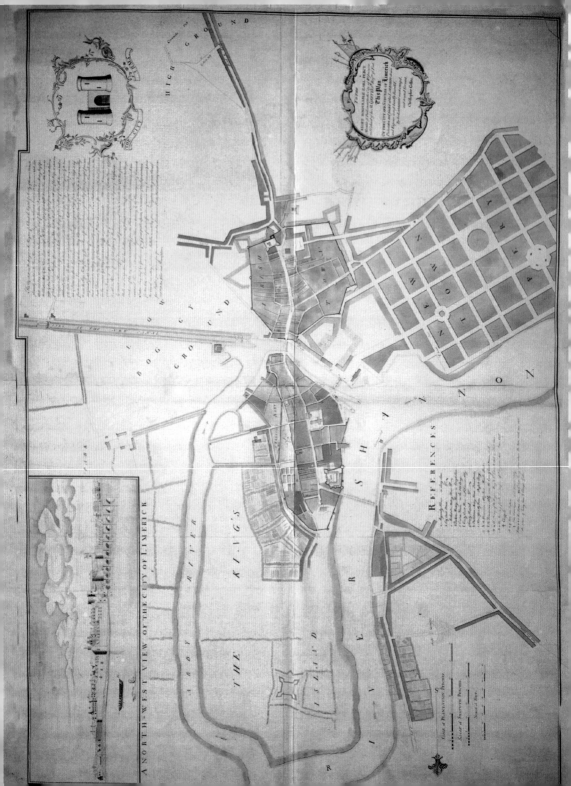

A NORTH-WEST VIEW OF THE CITY OF LIMERICK

REFERENCES

HIGH GROUND

LOW GROUND

BOGGY GROUND

THE KING'S

RIVER

ISLAND

SHANNON

R I V E R

Case of Plantation Fathom
Scale of English Perches
Scale of Feet

Georgian Limerick

In 1760 the government declared Limerick to be no longer a fortress city and within a few years the utterly useless and constricting medieval walls had been torn down, an act of symbolic and practical importance that released pent up forces of enterprise and initiative from within the business community. As local historian, newspaper proprietor and printer John Ferrar commented in 1787, it was not until these walls 'were humbled and a plan formed for raising a new city, did Limerick increase much in population, or become conspicuous for improvement.'[7] Literally a new atmosphere entered the town, with city annalist Fr. James White commenting at the end of 1760 that 'This year the city of Limerick begins to show much better than it did hitherto, and to have a wholesomer air circulating in it, and that by means of throwing down the old walls.'[8] Fifteen years later a visitor to the city, Thomas Campbell, observed that hardly a trace of the old walls and their seventeen gates remained. However, he did remark that the sanitation of the city still left much to be desired. Commenting on a local saying that the land around Limerick was so rich that people were obliged to throw their dung into the Shannon, Campbell remarked 'I wish, however, they would throw it any where out of the streets.'[9]

Campbell's comments about the sanitary habits of the people of Limerick presumably refer to the old quarters of the city, Englishtown and Irishtown, for one would hope that the citizens of the Georgian new town set higher standards. Construction on this major development began in earnest in the 1760s and continued until 1840, with merchants, speculators and developers leasing plots of land and building quays, warehouses and blocks of Georgian terraced houses. Prior to this development business and commerce had taken place in Englishtown and Irishtown, but by the end of the Georgian era with the death of George IV in 1830 all had changed utterly - the merchant houses and the successful entrepreneurs, along with the professional middle classes, had long since migrated from the old decaying quarters to their far more comfortable houses and business premises in the new town.

As a large proportion of the land on which this new quarter was constructed was owned by the Pery family the term 'Newtown Pery' was applied to the district. Built on a gridiron plan of intersecting streets meeting at right angles, the street pattern of Newtown Pery was based on a projected plan for the development of the district drawn up by architect Christopher Colles about 1769, the pattern conforming to the Classical ideal of the model city.[10] The grid had been much favoured by the Romans for their new towns, and before them the Greeks and the Etruscans. The Romans were certainly addicted to the right angle and the straight line and when they laid out a new urban settlement or a legionary fortress town in a conquered land the buildings and defensive walls were structured around a symmetrical gridiron pattern of streets intersected at fixed points. Many archaeological examples are to be found in Britain including St. Albans (known in Roman times as Verulamium) and Silchester (Calleva Atrebatum).[11] It is a street pattern that has a pronounced military character as well as being an utterly rational and practical plan for developing a new urban area. Functional, it is not everybody's vision of an ideal city, the grid being seen by some as a bit soulless.

But for those citizens of Newtown Pery who turned their back on the squalor and sordid politics of the Old Town, the well-laid out, cleansed, rationally planned streets of Georgian Limerick encapsulated the neoclassical ideals of order, regularity and restraint. What better way to design a city than in geometrically precise blocks to facilitate the leasing of speculative lots and the construction of repetitive boxes of terraced houses - Property Developing Made Easy. It made everything so much easier, from the laying down of sewers to the policing of the streets.

The Vilest Town Ever Entered

To contemporaries Newtown Pery seemed a splendid place. Exhibiting a fair and pleasing appearance, it was a modern city built in accord with best architectural practice and who better to appreciate the architecture of mercantile Limerick than a citizen of the new American Republic, the land of opportunity where the gridiron street plan became such a significant feature of many American cities. The Rev. William Stevens Balch, a preacher from Vermont, sailed into the port of Limerick on 21 May 1848 at the height of The Famine and was very favourably impressed by what he observed of Newtown Pery. In his written commentary the Rev. Balch indicated a correlation between the regularity of its predominately Georgian-style architecture and the bustling commerce of Limerick. He was impressed by the,

248

'. . . size and beautiful situation of the city, the character of its buildings, the large quantity of vessels lying along its well-built stone quays, as well as the business-like stir and bustle . . . Nor was I disappointed on entering the town. Everything I saw confirmed my first favourable impressions. The width and regularity of the streets, some of them more than a mile long, the elegance of the houses, the appearance of the well-filled stores and well dressed inhabitants . . . Everything bore the marks of wealth, prosperity and refinement, equal, if not superior, to what is common in our country. And what surprised me more, everything appeared fresh and modern. The houses, churches, stores and shops, looked as if recently erected, and with a full knowledge of all the improvements in the present system of utilitarian architecture.'[12]

Nineteenth century street scene of Newtown Pery, Limerick.

The mercantile utilitarianism of Limerick was, however, not to everyone's idea of high aesthetic taste. Ten years earlier, in 1838, travel writer Leitch Ritchie stated bluntly, 'The houses of the principle streets are like those of Belfast, nothing more than right-angled brick boxes, without any pretensions to taste.' If the terraces of Newtown Pery had no pretensions the same could not be said of the inhabitants according to Ritchie's barbed pen,

> '. . . the city contains hardly any very wealthy people; few with incomes above a thousand pounds a year, although many approaching that sum. But, though the inhabitants, therefore do not belong to the class of those who could be called wealthy people in London, there is a great deal of pretension in their way of living, and an air of fashion in their appearance, which is not surpassed in Dublin.'[13]

249

There was undoubted prosperity in the city, a welcome contrast with the depressed state Limerick had fallen into during the early part of the eighteenth century. But this golden age occurred only for the better off sections of society and those capable of grasping the opportunities presented. The least fortunate - the unskilled, the poor, the sickly - were left behind; for though Limerick experienced a rising tide of economic growth for some eighty to ninety years up to the early 1840s, despite the occasional slump, this tide did not raise all boats and the economic, social and cultural divide between those who prospered, and those who did not, widened considerably. The social landscape of the city became sharply divided between prosperity and poverty. The building of the Georgian new town, while it was certainly a major step forward for the city, also brought about a more clearly defined spatial separation of classes between those who could afford to live or earn a living in the middle-class Georgian estate of Newtown Pery and those who remained behind in the ever crumbling, festering tenements and lanes of the older quarters, particularly Englishtown.

The contrast between the two districts was quite startling, especially so to visitors,

> 'I know of no other town in which so distinct a line is drawn between the good and its bad quarters, as in Limerick,' commented Henry Inglis in 1834. 'A person arriving in Limerick by one of the best approaches . . . will probably say, "What a very handsome city this is!" while, on the other hand, a person entering the city by the old town, and taking his quarters there - a thing, indeed, not likely to happen - would infallibly set down Limerick as the very vilest he had ever entered.'[14]

Those who took the trouble to enter the poorer areas of Limerick and record their impressions were quite astonished and profoundly shocked by the depths of destitution and absolute misery to be found there, seasoned as many of these writers were to the sight and smell of poverty.[15] It was here, in the worst of the hovels, that one found emaciated adults and starving children living in rooms with no furniture and with only heaps of straw for beds. In dark, dank cellars with scarcely any light or heat, those with eyes to pry into the lower depths of society discovered appalling scenes,

> 'I found a man sitting on a little sawdust. He was naked: he had not even a shirt: a filthy and ragged mat was round him: this man was a living skeleton; the bones all but protruded through the skin: he was literally starving.'[16]

250

Poverty was endemic till well into the twentieth century.

Creating a Landscape in the Image of Man

In his *Limerick; its History and Antiquities* published in 1866 Maurice Lenihan recalled to mind the fading folk memory that the terrain on which Georgian Limerick had been built was once meadow and marshland. He recollected that in 1851 he had spoken to an elderly gentleman who 'remembered shooting snipe in Patrick Street . . . the ground in question was a marsh which the tide covered and that it was deemed unfit for building when he was a boy.'[17] It was on this virgin terrain that a new Georgian city was created, and just as Gods are created in the image of Man, so are urban landscapes.

Georgian Limerick is a bourgeois city - it was built by merchants, bankers and property speculators and prominent, at one stage, among them were the Arthur family, wealthy Catholic merchant princes who traded overseas. The Arthurs were to the forefront in developing the Arthur's Quay area of the city during the latter half of the eighteenth century, building harbour facilities, terraced houses and warehouses, and in the process leaving their name and mark on the landscape. It was Patrick Arthur, a timber merchant, who built Arthur's Quay for the berthing of his ships, a project completed in 1773. His son and business partner Francis Arthur turned his hand to property developing, financing the construction of a triangular block of thirty-seven terraced houses on the site now occupied by the Arthur's Quay shopping centre. A sketch map of the development and adjacent properties indicates that 'Mr. Arthurs house' stood at the apex of the block facing towards George's Street,[18] a site roughly approximate to the main entrances to the Arthur's Quay shopping centre.

The harbour at Arthur's Quay has since been filled in and only a handful of the original terraced houses on Patrick Street remain, but the street plan laid down by the two men in this part of the city stubbornly remains. Whether intentional or not, the plan elevation of the triangular terraced block built by Francis forms the letter 'A', for Arthur. So, in a very real sense it can be said that the Arthur family stamped their name firmly on the urban landscape. In the original street plan of the Georgian Newtown drawn up by Christopher Colles *c.*1769 the proposed layout of the Arthur's Quay housing development site was five-sided in plan;[19] an odd shape to be sure. It is possible that the Arthurs laid down a triangular plan to suit their vanity; but, then again, it was simply a case of sheer practicality rather than design in order to conform to the topography of the area. Conscious or not, the layout is nevertheless symbolic.

The important role played by the Arthur family in developing this part of Limerick is acknowledged by the fact that several city streets in the area were named after father and son in their own lifetime. Patrick Street, so named in 1780, Francis Street, and, of course, Arthur's Quay itself. Ellen Street was called after the wife of Francis Arthur while Denmark Street, where the family's

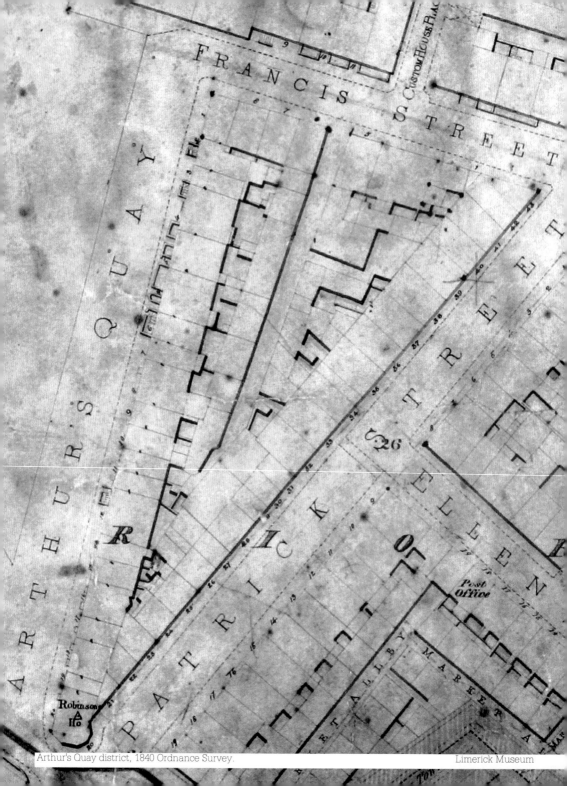

Arthur's Quay district, 1840 Ordnance Survey.

timber business was established, is said to be so-called because of their shipping links with Scandinavia.[20]

The Arthurs were not the only entrepreneurs in Georgian Limerick to be so honoured as a number of other quays constructed during the Georgian and early Victorian era were named after local merchants who privately built or conducted business from these harbour walls. Honan's Quay, built adjacent to Arthur's Quay, was erected c.1787 by Mathew Honan to facilitate his corn export trade,[21] while Spaight's Quay (now Mount Kennett) was called after merchant, timber importer and shipowner Francis Spaight,[22] to cite just two examples. Roches Street was named after the Roche brothers, bankers and merchants who assisted Edmund Sexton Pery in the building of Newtown Pery. The prosperous Barrington dynasty of businessmen and lawyers who acquired the Glenstal estate in Murroe, Co. Limerick also had a street named after them.[23]

Edmund Sexton Pery.

The most celebrated of all of Limerick's Georgian sons is Edmund Sexton Pery (1719-1806), commercially cute landowner and politician who owned most of the land on which the Georgian new town was built. Member of Parliament for Limerick and Speaker of the Irish House of Commons, he leased out his lands in lots to speculative builders, merchants, public bodies and church authorities and a new city arose beside the Shannon based on a gridiron plan of wide streets and terraced houses. Plaques to the memory of the Pery family abound on the corners of Newtown Pery in the form of street signs: Pery Square, Glentworth Street, and Mallow Street being ones that immediately spring to mind. Glentworth Street and Mallow Street were named after the Right Reverend William Cecil Pery (1721-1794), Bishop of Limerick in 1784, who was created Baron Glentworth of Mallow in 1790. Other streets named after the Pery family include Henry Street, Pery Street and Cecil Street.[24] Besides Ellen Street, two other thoroughfares in the Georgian new town were named after Limerick women. Anne Street is most probably named after Anne Rankins who was the owner of five houses in the street (c.1850) Catherine Street is said to have been named after Catherine Unthank, a member of a prominent merchant family of that name. There is no documentary evidence to support this and it seems unusual that a major street running from Hartstonge Street to William Street through the Newtown Pery development was not named after one of the Pery family.[25] A Catherine Unthank, married to John Torrance, was murdered by Rockites near Adare in June 1821,[26] but the Street had been named before her death so was not named in remembrance of her.

David Gaynor

The Seven Gates of Thebes

Whereas in the old quarters of Englishtown and Irishtown many of the street names are descriptive of the urban fabric of the walled city and were called after nearby churches - Nicholas Street, Mary Street, John Street, or just plain Church Street - or were designated according to function or description - Sheep Street, Fish Lane, Broad Street, The Parade, Merchants Quay - or location - Castle Street, Bridge Street, Exchange Street - the street names of Georgian Limerick unashamedly celebrate the spirit of individualistic capitalism and ownership of property, recalling to our memory some 200 years later the names of bankers, leaseholders, merchants and landlords. The sense of communal identity as expressed in the street names of the old city is replaced by, We name and We own this.

The place names of Newtown Pery are not politically neutral in shaping our historical consciousness, for in the process of signifying who should be remembered others are excluded. For any community to have a sense of its own unique identity it needs to know something of the origins of its place-names. Local historians, those modern day bards of Irish communities who recall the doings of our ancestors and the deeds of ancient freemen, in explaining the origins of Limerick's Georgian street names are channelled in a certain direction in which they have to discuss the evolution of the district in terms of local entrepreneurs, landowners, merchants, bankers and businessmen.

When it is written, casually, that 'Patrick Arthur built Arthur's Quay in 1773' it should bring, but hardly ever does, to mind Bertolt Brecht's poem:

> 'Who built the seven gates of Thebes?
> The books are filled with the names of kings,
> Was it kings who hauled the craggy blocks of stone?
> And Babylon, so many times destroyed,
> Who built the city up each time? In which of Lima's houses,
> That city gleaming with gold, lived those who built it?
> In the evening when the Chinese wall was finished
> Where did the masons go? Imperial Rome

Is full of arcs of triumph. Who reared them up? Over whom
Did the Caesars Triumph? Byzantium lives in song,
Were all her dwellings palaces? . . .

So many particulars
So many questions.' [27]

The point is obvious, the stonemasons, bricklayers, carpenters, plasterers and
legions of labourers who actually built Newtown Pery rarely get a mention in
the history books of the city and are certainly not commemorated in its public
plaques and monuments. The bourgeois city celebrates its bourgeois founders
and consigns to the dustbin of history the working classes. One social class is
celebrated, another ignored. The map of the city becomes an edited document
in which only selected information is provided.

As illustrated in the case of Georgian Limerick, those who exercise political
and economic power in society have the ability to name or rename the
landscape if they so wish, thereby perpetuating the memory of dominant
social groups, families and individuals and shaping the landscape of the mind
for generations to come. Place names are a powerful projector of the past into
the present as they manipulate our responses to the past, conjure up
particular historical and folk images, and in so doing condition thoughts about
the present. It was not for nothing that Leningrad was renamed St. Petersburg
when the Soviet Union collapsed. The naming of place names is a primal act
of laying claim to a territory by the use of language. But the influence of once
dominant tribes, social classes, powers, thrones and principalities wanes after
a while, allowing new forces to arise to rename the landscape in order that
they may claim and possess it for themselves. As the Canadian geographer W.
L. Morton remarked 'Nothing, no country, can be really owned except under
familiar name or satisfying phrase.' [28]

The conflict between cultures and its effect on how the Irish landscape is both
physically seen and culturally and spiritually understood was highlighted by
Daniel Corkery who, writing about Irish culture and poetry in eighteenth
century Munster, wrote,

> '. . . to recollect the place-names in certain regions was to remember
> the ancient tribes and their memorable deeds. How different it was
> with the Planters round about them. For them, all that Gaelic
> background of myth, literature and history had no existence. They
> differed from the people in race, language, religion, culture; while
> the landscape they looked upon was indeed but rocks and stones
> and trees.' [29]

Leaving behind the ancient tribes and their memorable deeds for a more recent past, we see an example of this claiming and reclaiming process taking place in Limerick itself when, due to the emergence of Irish Catholic nationalism in the nineteenth and early twentieth centuries, some of the more overtly imperial street names were consigned to the discard and replaced to make the sounds of the urban fabric more pleasing to the ears of nationalists. George Street (commonly known as George's Street in the early nineteenth century) named after King George III in 1770,[30] was renamed O'Connell Street after Daniel O'Connell who secured Catholic Emancipation and sought Repeal of the Union. Symbolically, lost territory had been regained for Ireland, the change of name signifying a change, or an aspiration for change, in the title of ownership to the land, if only in a Home Rule context.

Admiral Lord Nelson.   Charles Stewart Parnell.

Memories of past military humiliations had to go, of course, as a new political dispensation came into being. And one that was most definitely *non grata* was Cornwallis Street, named in 1799 after Lord Cornwallis who, the previous year, had been appointed Lord Lieutenant of Ireland and Commander-in-Chief of the British forces that had brutally crushed the United Irish Rebellion. Poor old Cornwallis, the same Cornwallis who had surrendered to George Washington at Yorktown during the American War of Independence, was rubbed off the map and replaced by Gerald Griffin, a mere novelist, and a Christian Brother to boot, born in Limerick in 1803.[31] Another street in the Georgian quarter with which James Pain would have been very familiar was Nelson Street, named in honour of Admiral Lord Nelson, illustrious victor of the Nile, Copenhagen and Trafalgar. It was redesignated Parnell Street [32] and an assertive imperialist statement of maritime might was replaced by the more gentler, but ultimately more potent, power of Irish constitutional nationalism.

But the nationalist sweep and purge was not entirely clean, for we still have a few Royalist hangovers in Limerick such as George's Quay named after George III and Charlotte's Quay which is probably named after his good wife, Queen Sophia Charlotte.[33] Wellesley Bridge, called after Richard, Marquis of Wellesley (a Lord Lieutenant of Ireland and brother to the Duke of Wellington) was renamed Sarsfield Bridge after General Patrick Sarsfield, Jacobite hero and dashing cavalry commander. But other streets named after former Lord Lieutenants were left unchanged. These include Mulgrave Street, Rutland Street and Bedford Row. These long forgotten and historically insignificant figures were not worth bothering about, and so they remain.

St. Michael's Parish Commissioners

Such was the political confidence of the business and middle classes in the Georgian district that by the first decade of the nineteenth century they had established their own organ of local self-government whose title was 'The Commissioners for Improving the Parish of St. Michael'. Politically independent of Limerick Corporation (also known as the 'Corrupt Corporation'), and exempt from the jurisdiction and taxes of the City Grand Jury, the St. Michael's Parish Commissioners levied rates on householders and commercial premises and looked after the policing, lighting, cleansing and maintenance of the public streets and footways, the provision of sewers and the clearing away of 'nuisances'.[34] It was a body predominately dominated by businessmen and among the twenty-one Commissioners serving in 1827 were to be found six merchants, a distiller, two businessmen involved in the drink retail trade, a member of the Roche banking family, the proprietor of a cabinetmaking business, a salt manufacturer, two members of the gentry and a Presbyterian clergyman. Other Commissioners on the Board included Lord Viscount Glentworth and Daniel Barrington, land agent to the Pery estate and member of a very wealthy family.[35]

Meeting regularly for the most part, the Board of Commissioners held vigilant watch over the public highways and pathways without encroaching on the private lives, liberties and happiness of the inhabitants. The principal functions of the Board are immediately apparent when studying the annual accounts. Those drawn up in October 1827 reveal that total expenditure on the Parish was £2938, the main items of expense being in the areas of,

Street lighting (gas)	£438	8s	0d
The Night Watch	£437	12s	2d
Repairing the streets and footways	£500	0s	0d
Sweeping the streets	£100	0s	0d
Watering the streets	£ 30	0s	0d
Annual contribution to the City Gaol	£461	10s	9d
Salary of Secretary and Treasurer	£105	0s	0d [36]

Funding for these various activities was raised by levying rates on houses and stores, these local taxes being collected twice a year and the payments recorded in Rate Books kept by the Secretary. A number of these Rate Books are extant in the Limerick Archives and although the full series has not survived they nevertheless provide very useful information about the names of ratepayers, the pace of building development in Newtown Pery and the opening up of new streets.

Up until 1840 James Pain witnessed a steady growth in Newtown Pery, a process in which he played an active role as an architect being responsible for two churches, a bank, at least one terrace[37] and probably other buildings as well. In 1814, a few years after he first came to Ireland, the number of rateable properties in St. Michael's Parish stood at 728, but by 1844, just before the Great Famine, this had increased to 1273.[38] By then Newtown Pery had reached its physical limits, the last of the terraces being erected in 1838 under James's supervision. As well as expanding southwards in the period up to 1838 with the opening of new streets such as Pery Street, Pery Square and Barrington Street, some of those streets that had already been laid down when James Pain arrived in the City saw building development continue on them as open spaces were filled in with terraced blocks and commercial premises. In Mallow Street, for example, the number of rateable properties increased from seven to forty over the period 1814-41.[39]

Fully Compliant

As a ratepayer the first mention of James Pain in the extant records is in the Rate Book covering the period September 1823 to March 1824 when a 'Mr. Pain' paid £3 17 4d on 5 April 1824 on his George's Street house; its rateable value set at £58.[40] Although in several of the earlier Rate Books the house numbers of ratepayers living in George's Street is given, in those volumes in which James Pain's name appears house numbers are not recorded. At first the architect's name is simply given as Mr. Pain in the Rate Books, but in later volumes of the series he is referred to as 'James Pain'.[41] The rateable value of houses and commercial premises, and the half-yearly tax due on them, did vary from year to year following regular reassessments of properties by persons appointed by the Board as 'valuator of houses and stores in the parish and the applotters of rates.'[42] In the period September 1828 to March 1829 the rateable value of James Pain's house was put at £54, down from £58 in 1824, on which he paid £2 14s 0d.[43]

As a fully compliant ratepayer James Pain would naturally be concerned to know if his 'tax dollars' were being wisely spent and put to good use. A valuable source of information in this regard is a set of three minute books of meetings held by the Board Commissioners over the period 1819 to 1844. This very valuable primary source details, to the last penny, the various expenses incurred by the Commissioners and records decisions taken regarding matters and issues brought to their attention.[54]

Policing

An essential function carried out by the Board was the provision of a Night Watch of watchmen to patrol the streets at night enabling citizens to sleep soundly in their beds. Such a body of men was needed to deter the criminal classes, especially on long dark nights when the streets were only dimly lit, as is evident from the following extract from the minutes,

> 'As the parish is infested in the early part of the night by villains who are watching for opportunities to rob and commit other depredations,' a meeting of the Commissioners held on 18 November 1819 resolved that 'the watchmen be put on duty at six o'clock in the evening and continue until seven o'clock the following morning - This regulation to continue until further orders - Each man is to be allowed two shillings and two pence in addition to his present wages of six shillings and six pence . . .'[45]

Night watchman.

The men were expected to work a thirteen-hour shift when their normal duties entailed patrolling the streets of Limerick for ten or eleven hours every night. They checked that doors and windows had been secured; they arrested drunks, vagrants and otherwise unruly people and brought them to the Watch House where they were either charged or placed in a cell or kept out of harm's way. In the morning prisoners became the responsibility of other authorities. The 'uniform' of the Night Watch was simply a hat and a free topcoat replaced every two years. For self-protection Night Watchmen were armed with a long pole with a metal spearhead, or, sometimes, an equally sharp hook fixed to the end. In 1819 there were thirty-two Watchmen including a Constable of the Watch, later (from 1843) known as an Inspector, by which time the

259

Watch had been reduced to twenty-two members. The night shift was long and lonely and for much of the year dark and cold. Each Watchman on the beat had two or more blocks to cover but did not spend all night walking up and down for he was given a night-box, a little collapsible box reminiscent of the bathing huts that one once saw on the beaches long ago, to sit in when things were quiet. Given the conditions of a Watchman's life it is easy to see how they might fall prey to drink.[46] One issue that frequently came before the Parish Commissioners was discipline within the force, in particular the problem of watchmen being drunk on duty; those found intoxicated being either suspended or dismissed.[47] Some men were just downright dishonest, as was the case with John Herbert who,

> 'took a gold chain and Seals from a lady at Mr. Swinburn's hotel' on the night of 3 March 1820 'as a bribe to suffer her husband who was charged with swindling, to escape through a window at which Herbert was placed as a Sentinel by Robert Murphy the City High constable with orders not to allow any person to go out that way.'

After investigating the case 'in the fullest manner' and hearing the testimony of witnesses, it was decided unanimously by the ten Commissioners present to discharge John Herbert as Constable of the Watch for conducting himself 'in the most corrupt and improper manner.'[48]

Some men, however, brought great credit to their uniform - Thomas Gorman proving himself particularly conscientious in the performance of his duties when he arrested a thief who had in his possession ' a large bag full of pigs heads.' Upon the successful prosecution of the culprit at the January 1831 Sessions the City Recorder wrote to the Board of Commissioners recommending that Gorman receive remuneration for his conduct. He was awarded £1 from the Parish funds while the thief received seven years transportation.[49]

Patrolling the streets at night had its hazards, as in the case of James Fleming who died when he fell into a basement area in Thomas Street. In recompense the Parish Fathers paid his widow, Ann Fleming, a sum of £1 2s 9d in February 1819.[50] At least one other payment was made to Ann Fleming, there being a record of £1 paid towards her relief six years later in February 1825.[51] This was the equivalent of three weeks wages for a night watchman who was paid a basic wage of 6s 6d in 1819. But not all grieving wives were treated with such kindness. When the widow of Bryan Fitzgerald sent a letter to the Board 'praying us to grant her some aid to purchase a coffin for her husband' the request was refused on the basis that her husband had been discharged from the Watch for improper conduct in getting drunk on duty and 'losing the keys of the Watch house.'[52]

The Parish Fathers were anxious not to spend the hard earned pennies of ratepayers if they could possibly avoid it so as to keep taxes down, as on the occasion when a petition from the Parish street sweepers to increase their wages from 6 shillings and 6 pence was rejected.[53] When a woman made a formal request to be reimbursed for the loss of her door knocker stolen on the night of 19 March 1839 the night watchman who patrolled her street was questioned on the matter. When it was ascertained that said door knocker was stolen before he came on duty the woman's request was turned down.[54] There was evidently a diabolical door knocker robber on the loose in the Parish at that time, as in early April that same year the Board ordered that printed notices be served on the inhabitants of the Parish notifying them to remove the knockers from their front doors at night as the night watchmen would not be held accountable for their damage or loss.[55]

Wandering Pigs

One of the responsibilities held by St. Michael's Parish Commissioners was to remove annoying public nuisances that were inconveniencing the citizenry. What constituted a public nuisance ranged from rubbish left uncollected on the streets to unemployed people lounging around outside shops. In early 1831 it was resolved 'that the Street Keeper is to look after all pigs straying in the streets and place same in the usual pound.'[56]

On 28 December 1827 John William Owens, the Parish Surveyor employed by the Commissioners, was instructed to clear away a heap of dung in Bank Place following a complaint from David Gabbett and Robert Maunsell that the offensive waste matter had been deposited 'before their windows' by persons unknown.[57] November 1821 saw the Parish Fathers dealing with a complaint from Joshua Hill that several sedan chairmen had made a stand for themselves and their sedan chairs on the flagway and gutter opposite 'his shop and concerns' at the corner of William Street 'to the great annoyance of his family and the passengers [in this context a pedestrian] by which his trade is much injured.' Finding his complaint well justified, it was resolved that Alderman Mahony be requested to use his authority as a magistrate to 'remove this nuisance from Joshua Hill's house and corner.'

Nuisances came in all shapes, sizes and persons as seen by a memorial sent to the Board in February 1833 from several householders in George's Street and Bedford Row requesting that a street lamp be placed on the corner of 'the preaching house lane' in Bedford Row. The preaching house in question was the Chapel of the Primitive Methodists, a building with a Gothic façade and plain hall that may have been designed by the Pain brothers. This lane, that once served stables at the rear of houses, still exists. The local residents' complaint was that due to the lack of a lamp 'this lane from its length and darkness at night is become a recepticle [sic] for vice and filth.' What filthiness took place there is not explained, but the Commissioners decided that sufficient depravity occurred to warrant moving a gas lamp from another part of Bedford Row and placing it so as to illuminate the mews and deter unmentionable nocturnal goings-on.[58]

James Pain himself was part-author of a complaint when he and a number of other residents living in the same row of houses on George's Street signed a letter to the Commissioners in August 1829. The nature of the complaint concerned 'their stables in the rere [sic] of their houses being completely inundated for want of some passage to carry off the water after heavy rains.' In this instance the response was positive, the Parish Surveyor being instructed to lay down a new branch sewer to 'remove the above mentioned nuisance', the expense incurred not to exceed 45 shillings.[59]

The Commissioners were very strict in drawing up a clear demarcation line as to what constituted their sphere of responsibility regarding the public highways and byways and what was the responsibility of the private citizen. At a meeting held on 8 May 1832 a letter was read from a Mr. Denis Ryan of George's Street complaining of a smell from his basement area and attributing the cause to the sewer 'being stopped'. Unfortunately for Mr. Ryan he had to sort out the problem for himself at his own expense, the Board refusing to deal with the matter as 'it is private property and cannot be complied with.' When, however, residents were to prove so bold as to encroach on the public domain it drew a very swift response from the City Fathers. They were particularly vigilant on the matter of private citizens and business interests attempting to extend their properties onto the pavement beyond the 'house line'. On one occasion Michael King was informed that he 'cannot be allowed to build pallisades [sic] round his house in Roche's Street, or make any encroachment whatever on the Street..'[60] A palisade is a fence of wooden poles or, in this case, iron railings.

When in March 1839 an application was made on behalf of the managers of the new Greek Revival style Savings Bank about to be erected in Glentworth Street that they extend the columns of the building some 4 feet beyond the range of 'the line of houses further down the street' the Board decided that the proposal could not be complied with.[61]

Lighting

Related to the security issue was the provision of street lighting at night. Up until 1824 lighting was provided in the form of oil-lit glass globes, many of them placed over the doors of houses. To light them three lamplighters were employed at 15 shillings each per week and a fourth at 10 shillings a week; each globe consuming about 4 1/2 gallons of whale oil per annum.[62] At that time whale oil was the principal means of lighting oil lamps, lubricating machinery and was used in the manufacture of soap and cosmetics.. A species known as the Baleen Whale also provided whalebone stays for ladies corsets, for which many thousands of whales were killed.[63] Whale-hunting in those days was a particularly bloody business far removed from the genteel fashionable ladies promenading up and down Limerick's George's Street on a fine summer's evening.

In May 1820 a proposal was made for improving the street lighting in Limerick by removing the globes from the walls and placing them on metal posts on the edge of footpaths. It was believed that the distance between the lights could then be doubled and still give out the same amount of light.[64] This cost-cutting measure was not carried out, but four years later the Commissioners made the decision to seek tenders from gas companies for installing gas lamps to replace the oil globes; [65] the gas lamps to be placed on posts set in the pavement. The gas was extracted from coal.

Original gaslights outside Barringtons' Hospital, Limerick. The gaslights were restored by Limerick Civic Trust.

Two proposals were received, one from Messrs. Barlow and Robinson and the other from Mr. Porter, Managing Director of the United General Gaslight Company of Kings Alms Yard, London. The former proposal was to light only some of the principal streets with gas and the rest with oil for £400 per annum for an initial contract of two years. The London company proposed to erect gaslights in all the streets and places in the parish for the sum of £420 per annum. As the terms of the contract offered by the latter were far superior to that of its competitor they gained the deal.[66] A major advantage in contracting out the supply of street lighting to a private company was that the cost was far cheaper than continuing with the Parish's own oil-lamp system, the expense to ratepayers in 1819 of lighting 470 globes being £652 1s 6d, this cost including oil, wages of lamplighters, materials and the replacement of broken globes.[67] When the new system was put in place 122 gaslights were erected on the streets of the Parish.[68]

In order to supply gas to the city a gas works had to be built nearby and the initial proposal by the United General Gaslight Company was to build their gas works on a plot of land on part of Mr. Black's ground[69] 'just without the city on the left of the Road to the barracks.'[70] This was the road known at the time as Military Walk that led from Richmond Place (The Crescent) to the New (Sarsfield) Barracks. It was in Richmond Place, the southern most part of Newtown Pery and that nearest to the proposed gas works, that some of the wealthiest residents of the city had their homes.

This plan to build a gas works in that locality drew a response from the Commissioners who advised the gas company that the siting of an industrial facility so close to a residential area inhabited by respectable citizens might cause complaint. The Secretary was instructed to write to the managers of the company seeking an assurance that no harm would befall the neighborhood and,

264

> 'to ascertain whether the smoke or smell from these or any operation therein may not incommode the inhabitants or passengers in that direction, particularly as the public walk for the respectable inhabitants of the city is [?very] contiguous to this site, and they would naturally complain of the slightest annoyance.'[71]

Although the company replied reassuring the Commissioners that the manufacture of gas was a perfectly safe procedure and free of noxious fumes, they took the hint and informed the Board in July 1824 that a decision had been made to locate its gas works at Mount Kenneth[72] near the river Shannon and well away from the residential quarters of Newtown Pery.

Endnotes

1 *Taylor and Skinner's Maps of the Roads of Ireland, Surveyed 1777*, Published 14 November 1778, pp. 99 & 200. Local Studies Department, Limerick County Library.

2 Colles, Christopher *Plan of the City and Suburbs of Limerick (c.*1769). Original in British Library, London; Copy in Limerick Museum.)

3 Ferrar, John *The History of Limerick*, 2nd Edition, A. Watson & Co., Limerick, 1787, p. 83.

4 Dr. Richard Pococke (1704-65) was Archdeacon of Dublin when he visited Limerick in 1752. He was appointed Bishop of Meath in 1756.

5 Pococke, Richard *Pocockes' Tour in Ireland in 1752*, Stokes, George T. ed., Hodges, Figgs & Co., Dublin, 1891, p. 113; *Richard Pococke's Irish Tours*, McVeagh, John ed., Irish Academic Press, Dublin, 1995, p. 96.

6 Lewis *Topographical Dictionary of Ireland*, London, 1837, Vol. II., p. 270.

7 Ferrar, John *The History of Limerick*, 2nd Edition, A. Watson & Co., Limerick, 1787, p. 83.

8 White, Fr. James *White Manuscript - The Annals of the City, County and Diocese of Limerick*, p. 171, Limerick Diocesan Library. Transcript of the English language text of the manuscript for the years 1692-1768 (pp. 74-193) in Limerick Civic Trust Archive.

9 Campbell, Thomas *A Philosophical Survey of the South of Ireland*, Thomas Campbell & William Whitestone, London, 1778, p. 230.

10 Colles, Christopher *Plan of the City and Suburbs of Limerick (c.*1769). Original in British Library, London; Copy in Limerick Museum. The name 'Newtown Pery' first appeared on Christopher Colles's map.

11 Sorrell, Alan *Roman Towns in Britain*, B.T. Batsford Ltd., London, 1976, pp. 36-43, 54-9.

12 Balch, William S. *Ireland As I Saw It*, New York, 1850. The Limerick extract republished as 'Limerick As I Saw It 1848', *The Old Limerick Journal* No. 32, p.156.

13 Leitch, Ritchie *Ireland, Picturesque and Romantic*, 1838, pp.197-8.

14 Inglis, Henry D. *A Journey Throughout Ireland During the Spring, Summer and Autumn of 1834*, Two Vols., Whittaker & Co., London, 1834, Vol. I., p. 295.

15 Barrow, John *A Tour Around Ireland*, 1835; Thackeray, W. M. *The Irish Sketch Book 1842*; Balch, William S. *Ireland As I Saw It*, New York, 1850.

16 Inglis *op. cit.* pp. 304-5.

17 Lenihan, Maurice *Limerick: Its History and Antiquities*, 1866, p. 227.

18 Sketch plan of the Arthur's Quay housing development annexed to *The Trial of Francis Arthur of the City of Limerick, Merchant, for High Treason* (MS), Local Studies Department, Limerick County Library.

19 Colles, Christopher *Plan of the City and Suburbs of Limerick c.*1769. Original in British Library, London; Copy in Limerick Museum.

20 Joyce, Gerry *Limerick Street Names*, Limerick Corporation, Limerick, 1995, pp. 15, 27-8, 29, 30, 44.

21 Lenihan *op. cit.* p. 380. The evidence that Honan's Quay was built *c.*1787 by Mathew Honan, and not by his son Martin Honan as stated in some secondary sources, is based on a number of primary sources: (1) a 1786 map ('Plan of the City of Limerick, December 1st 1786' in Ferrar, John *History of Limerick*, 1787); (2) a letter written by Mathew Honan on 1 June 1786 (Lenihan *op. cit.* 380*n1*); and (3) a 1788 Directory (Lucas, Richard *A General Directory of the Kingdom of Ireland, 1788*, 'Irish Provincial Directories – Limerick, County of Limerick' *The Irish Genealogist* Vol. 3, No12, September, 1967, pp. 529-37). Ferrar's 1786 map has no reference to Honan's Quay. Honan's 1787 letter states that he wants to acquire land on which to build and a year later Lucas's 1788 Directory carries the entry 'Honan, Mathew merchant, Honan's Quay.'

22 Joyce *op. cit.* p. 50.

23 Joyce *op. cit.* pp. 17, 47, 50.

24 Joyce *op. cit.* pp. 22, 32, 33, 37-8.

25 Joyce *op. cit.* p. 21.

26 *Limerick Chronicle*, 13 June 1821; Fitzgerald & M'Gregor 'Appendix VII', *The History, Topography and Antiquities of the County and City of Limerick*, 2 Vols., 1827, p. xl.

27 Brecht, Bertolt 'A Worker Reads History', *Bertolt Brecht, Selected Poems*, Grove Press, New York, 1959.

28 Quoted in O'Connor, Patrick J. *Living in a Coded Landscape*, Newcastle West, Co. Limerick, 1992, p. 8.

29 Corkery, Daniel *The Hidden Ireland* (1924), Gill and Macmillan, Dublin, 1967, pp. 64-5.

30 Lenihan *op. cit.* p. 370.

31 Joyce *op. cit.* p. 31; Cronin, John *Gerald Griffin 1803-1840, A Critical Biography,* Cambridge Press, 1978. Gerald Griffin (1803-40) was a dramatist, novelist and poet who entered the Christian Brothers in 1838 and taught at the North Monastery, Cork. He is best known for his novel *The Collegians* (1827) in which young Cregan, allured by wealth and beauty, permits the murder of his humble country wife. The novel is based on the infamous Colleen Bawn murder case when, in the summer of 1819, Ellen Hanley, a 15 year old from Ballingarry, Co. Limerick, was murdered on the Shannon by her husband, John Scanlan, and his servant accomplice Stephen Sullivan. Following trials in Limerick's City Courthouse, both men were convicted of the murder and executed.

32 Joyce *op. cit.* pp. 40-41, 44.

33 Joyce *op. cit.* pp. 22, 31. Joyce comments that though Charlotte's Quay is probably named after Queen Sophia Charlotte it is also possible that it was named after her granddaughter Princess Charlotte of Wales who died suddenly in 1817, the then City Council sending a message of sympathy to her husband, Prince Leopold of Saxecoburgh.

34 Lenihan *op. cit.* pp. 414-7. Established by Parliamentary legislation in

1807, the St. Michael's Parish Commissioners continued in existence until 1853.

35 List of Commissioners in 'Addenda' to Fitzgerald & M'Gregor *The History, Topography and Antiquities of Limerick* 2 Vols., 1827, Vol. II, final page (not numbered); *Pigot's Directory* 1824, pp. 282-93.

36 *Proceedings and Orders of the Commissioners for Improving the Parish of St. Michael* (MS), 5 October 1827, Limerick Archives.

37 James Pain's work in Newtown Pery includes the Dominican Church in Glentworth Street, St. Michael's Church in Pery Square, The Pery Square Tontine terrace and the Provincial Bank on the corner of George Street and Mallow Street.

38 *St. Michael's Parish Rate Book* (MS), 'March 1814 to September 1814'; '25th March 1844 to 29th September 1844', Limerick Archives.

39 ibid. 'March 1814 to September 1814'; 'September 1841 to March 1842'.

40 'George's Street' *St. Michael's Parish Rate Book (Secretary's Book) From September 1823 to March 1824* (MS), Limerick Archives.

41 For example, ibid. *March 1840 to September 1840.*

42 On 20 June 1825, for example, James Ryan, architect, of Ellen Street was appointed by the Commissioners as a 'valuator of houses and stores in the parish and the applotters of rates along with Mr. McMahon, Grocer of Patrick Street and Mr. Newell, Patrick Street. *Proceedings and Orders of the Commissioners for Improving the Parish of St. Michael*, 20 June 1825.

43 *St. Michael's Parish Rate Book September 1828 to March 1829.*

44 *Proceedings and Orders of the Commissioners for Improving the Parish of St. Michael* (MS). The three extant volumes are: Vol. I 12 April 1819 - 8 April 1833; Vol. II 9 April 1833 - 19 October 1838; Vol. III 26 October 1838 - 19 April 1844. Limerick Archives L/MP/1/1; L/MP/1/2; L/MP/1/3.

45 ibid. 18 November 1819.

46 O'Mahony, Chris 'Limerick Night Watch 1807 - 1853', *The Old Limerick Journal*, Kemmy, Jim ed. Autumn 1987 pp.9-12.

47 On 9 May 1820, for instance, Daniel Meehan and Richard Halvey were suspended from duty until 1 June for being drunk at their posts. ibid. 9 May 1820.

48 ibid. 9 March 1820.

49 ibid. 11 April 1831.

50 *St. Michael's Parish Waste Book Commencing Dec. 18th 1813 and Ending March 25th 1820* (MS), 13 February 1819. The first page of these accounts is headed 'Wastebook of the Accounts of the Commissioners for Improving the Parish of St. Michael', Limerick Archives.

51 *Proceedings and Orders of the Commissioners for Improving the Parish of St. Michael*, 17 February 1825.

52 ibid. 18 May 1832.

53 ibid. 29 June 1830.

54 ibid. 22 March 1839.

55 ibid. 5 April 1837.
56 ibid. 21 February 1831.
57 ibid. 28 December 1827.
58 ibid. 25 February 1833.
59 ibid. 28 August 1829.
60 ibid. 29 November 1819.
61 ibid. 22 March 1839.
62 ibid. 15 April 1820.
63 Ellis, Richard *Men & Whales*, Robert Hale Ltd., London, 1989, pp. 131-40, 144.
64 *Proceedings and Orders of the Commissioners for Improving the Parish of St. Michael*, 16 May 1820.
65 ibid. 5 March 1824.
66 ibid. 26 March 1824.
67 ibid. 21 October 1819.
68 ibid. 5 October 1826.
69 ibid. May 3 1824.
70 ibid. May 24 1824.
71 ibid. 3 May 1824.
72 ibid. 30 July 1824.

CHAPTER FIFTEEN

BRIDGE BUILDERS

As civil engineers the Pain brothers made a major contribution to improving the infrastructure of Limerick so as to allow the freer movement of goods and vehicles into and out of the city, their work on building Athlunkard Bridge (1830), Baal's Bridge (1831) and Thomond Bridge (1840) being their main achievements in this area. In the period leading up to the Great Famine two other bridges were constructed - Wellesley Bridge, opened 1835 and designed by Alexander Nimmo, and Mathew Bridge, contracted for in 1844 and opened 1846, architect W. H. Owens.[1] Prior to the provision of these new structures, of the four access bridges serving the city in the early decades of the nineteenth century two were very unsatisfactory, of medieval origin and in urgent need of replacement, another was a hazard to horses and pedestrians in the winter and a fourth was described as a 'mean structure'.

River Shannon with Thomond Bridge in background.

269

As the city and its trade grew in the early nineteenth century so did the need to open up new routes into the city, improve access on established routes and remove a number of traffic choke points. Before the building of Wellesley Bridge there was only one crossing over the river Shannon - Thomond Bridge - that led directly into the economically important agricultural hinterland of Clare, forcing all trade, commerce and private traffic with Clare and Galway to converge on just this one choke point. Thomond Bridge, a dilapidated structure of fourteenth century origin (not thirteenth century as some secondary sources state[2]) was narrow, dreadfully decayed and in a dire and dangerous state of disrepair. All traffic destined for Irishtown, Newtown Pery, the city markets and the quays had to pass through the congested streets of

Englishtown before passing over the Abbey River by Baal's Bridge or by the New Bridge (replaced by Mathew Bridge in 1846) located near the Customs House, now the Hunt Museum. The former was narrow, outdated and of mediaeval origin, while the latter, although built in 1762, was a humpbacked structure with steep inclines that were positively dangerous underfoot for both man and beast in frosty, icy conditions. In addition, Englishtown was getting so run-down and poverty stricken that respectable persons travelling to and from Clare and Galway would have much preferred to enter the city by an entirely different route.

Given that Limerick served quite an extensive agricultural hinterland the entire situation obviously needed to be addressed if the economic growth of the city was not to be curtailed. Limerick, as the commercial hub and port city of the Mid-West region exported the agricultural produce of counties Limerick, Clare, Tipperary and part of Kerry - beef, pork, butter, bacon, wheat, oats, barley - to Britain. The population of the city and its environs also needed to be fed and kept warm and in addition to the above items the various markets in the city demanded potatoes, milk, turf, livestock etc. as well as a plentiful supply of hay for horses. Most of this produce had to be brought to the markets and warehouses of the city by horse-drawn cars, carts and wagons, while livestock such as cattle, sheep, goats, lambs and pigs were herded along the road. When pianist Franz Liszt and his companions were travelling along the Dublin to Limerick road to play two concerts in the city in early January 1841 they heard a dreadful commotion at 6 o'clock in the morning, one hour's carriage drive from Limerick - their carriage had run over a pig on its way to market in the city. 'Poor thing - I heard a dreadful squeak' recorded vocalist John Parry in his diary for Saturday 9 January.[3]

Limerick was also importing by sea all manner of manufactured goods and raw materials that needed to be marketed and distributed - timber for the building trades, coal for the gas works, perfumes, ceramics, furnishings and all manner of general merchandise: purses, canes, gloves and garters and, lest we forget, Genuine Bears Grease for the growth of hair.[4]

To remedy the defects in the city's infrastructure a concerted programme of bridge building was undertaken from 1824 to 1846 by various public and private bodies along with the construction of new or improved approach roads. Discussions on the city's traffic problems had been taking place for many a long year before the first practical steps were taken in the 1820s. In an account of the history of Limerick ports the authors relate how since the beginning of the nineteenth century,

> '. . . the merchants of Limerick City constantly maintained that their business activities were severely handicapped by inadequate port

facilities and poor access to the City from County Clare on the north side. From 1815 onwards, the Chamber of Commerce actively pursued the case for improved land and sea access having regard to the strategic location of the City as a major trading centre.[5]

In 1814 James Pain had been commissioned to survey Thomond Bridge, drawing up a proposal for its replacement.[6] Unfortunately another twenty years were to elapse before an opportunity arose to dismantle the old stone bridge and replace it with a more modern structure. This task could not be carried out until a second bridge had been put in place over the Shannon, because the building of a new Thomond Bridge would take several years.

A revival of trade in the 1820s, following an economic slump in the post-Napoleonic War period, made the necessity of solving the city's infrastructural problems ever more urgent as traffic flows increased. The boom saw the value of agricultural products exported from Limerick almost doubling from £499,000 in 1823 to just under £1 million ten years later. This level of activity was maintained throughout the 1830s, with just over £1 million of farm produce being exported in 1838. All other indices of trade (harbour dues and customs' duties) showing increased activity on the quays of Limerick.[7]

Various ideas were mooted for bypassing the Thomond Bridge/Englishtown bottleneck, including a scheme suggested about 1820 to build a bridge from Francis Street (beside Arthur's Quay) to the House of Industry (Strand Barracks) on the North (Clancy's) Strand.[8]

David Gaynor

271

Sarsfield Bridge, Limerick previously known as Wellesley Bridge.

In 1822 John Grantham, a civil engineer appointed by the State to survey the Shannon, received representations from the Chamber of Commerce and within three months he had compiled a report that included plans, drawings and estimates for a new bridge linking Brunswick (Sarsfield) Street with what was to become the Ennis Road. Legislation was passed in June 1823 giving the authority to construct the crossing and also to establish the Limerick Bridge Commissioners, a body responsible for managing the project. Among the forty-seven Commissioners were leading representatives of the city's mercantile community and prominent members of the landed interest who would benefit from the provision of a new commercial route into the city. Alexander Nimmo, a Scottish born civil engineer living in Ireland, was appointed architect and the contractors for the scheme were Messrs. Hill and Clements. The foundation stone was laid on 25 October 1824, but it was to take eleven years to complete, not being officially opened until August 1835 at a cost of £89,061,[9] a very substantial sum. By way of comparison, the Pain brothers' great pile of Mitchelstown Castle cost just over £100,000. As Limerick historian Maurice Lenihan remarked 'A sum of £30,000 would have sufficed for an excellent suitable bridge.'[10] Named Wellesley Bridge, it later became Sarsfield Bridge.

Athlunkard Bridge

While Wellesley Bridge was designed to open up a new westerly route into Clare, there was also a need to drive a route northwards across the Shannon connecting the City with the hinterland of east and north Clare. The year 1818 saw a meeting advertised for Wednesday 22 April at Swinburn's Hotel, Limerick to which 'landed proprietors and others interested in the erection of a Bridge' across the Shannon at Corbally were invited to decide 'upon the best means to be adopted for effecting this much desired object.'[11] The outcome for the lobbyists was the setting up of the Athlunkard Bridge Commissioners in 1825 whose responsibility was not only to build Athlunkard Bridge at Corbally but also to arrange for the laying down of new access roads linking it directly with Newtown Pery.

The first phase of this major project involved driving a completely new street from the T-junction of Mary Street and Bridge Street through houses in Englishtown and lanes in the Abbey suburb to Park Bridge. Described in 1827 as a 'mean structure',[12] Park bridge was built in 1798 across the Abbey River at the bottom of what is now Athlunkard Street. The present bridge on the site, O'Dwyer Bridge, was erected in 1931.

This new, wide street, known as Athlunkard Street, bypassed Sir Harry's Mall and George's Quay and opened up a direct route into Newtown Pery via Bridge Street and the New Bridge (rebuilt 1844-6 as Mathew Bridge). The bypassing of the quays lying alongside the Abbey River was vital to avoid traffic

Athlunkard Bridge, Corbally, Limerick.

congestion and delays, especially on George's Quay. Before the construction of a new purpose-built Potato Market on Merchant's Quay in 1844, George's Quay was the location of the market for the sale of potatoes and other produce from local market gardens. Packed with pedestrians, shoppers, stalls, horses, carts, bags and baskets it had for 'so long obstructed the public thoroughfare' commented the *Limerick Chronicle* on Wednesday 6 March 1844 reporting on the opening of the 'new root market' on Merchant's Quay the previous day. It was a development much to be welcomed.

Work commenced on laying down Athlunkard Street on 26 April 1824[13] - the new road cutting through two medieval houses on Mary Street built in the manner of a fortified tower house, labourers fully demolishing one of the structures and leaving just the north gable of the other house still standing. This section of wall still survives with the interior of the house gable facing onto Athlunkard Street. This remnant marks the site of 'Bourke's House', so named because the building was listed in the Cromwellian 1654 *Civil Survey* of Limerick City as the house of 'William Bourke of Limicke [*sic*] Irish Papist'.[14]

The Pain brothers were appointed as both the architects and contractors for Athlunkard Bridge.[15] Spanning the Shannon at Corbally with five segmental arches, and costing £7,000,[16] work commenced in June 1826 and was completed by December 1830.[17] Sturdily built to withstand the full force of the Shannon when in flood, the substantial masonry of the curved cutwaters is required to cope with the worst that the river can throw at them. Given the technology of the time, and the stresses of nature that it was designed to bear, a construction period of four and a half years was reasonable.

The five segmental arches of the bridge are each 67 feet (20.4 metres) in span with a rise of 13 feet 6 inches (4.1 metres).[18] The 'rise' is the height of the arch from the 'springings' to the top, or 'crown', of the arch. A springing is the

273

lowest point of an arch where it 'springs' from a supporting abutement or pier. By way of comparison, further down the river at Thomond Bridge the rise is 10 feet (3.1 metres); while at Wellesley (Sarsfield) Bridge it is 8 feet 6 inches (2.6 metres).[19]

Because of low-lying land on either side of the river embankments had to be built to carry traffic onto the bridge. On the city side the embankment is 235 feet (71.6 metres) in length, while on the Clare side it is 111 feet (33.8 metres).[20] A neat single-storey toll-house, which still stands today, was built on the City side of the bridge and tolls were required from all crossing until 1884 when they were abolished.[21] Although taken very much for granted nowadays, Athlunkard Bridge was much admired at the time of construction by local opinion, one newspaper commenting that 'the workmanship is of the first kind',[22] while Deane's 1838 Limerick Directory remarked that the structure reflected 'much credit on the Messrs. Pain.'[23]

Toll-house, Athlunkard Bridge, Corbally.

In April 1833 the Pain brothers entered into a Bond of Agreement with the Athlunkard Bridge Commissioners to build a road across Park, as this market gardening area was known, for £2,483 linking up Athlunkard and Park bridges, the documents providing evidence that as builders and contractors the brothers were just as eager to build roads as well as great mansions for the wealthy. The contract stipulates that the work had to be completed by 1 December 1833 and that the brothers were separately and jointly bound that they, 'shall and will at his and their proper Cost and Charges and with his and their own materials in good, firm, substantial and workmanlike manner execute the works necessary for making the new Road from the end of the present new road by Patrick Doody's house at the angle of Mr. Morris's garden to within fifty feet of the bank of the Abbey River with a branch road from it to the present Causeway according to the map of the same road to the specifications, sections and plan . . .'[24]

Besides opening up another route into the agricultural hinterland, Athlunkard Bridge and its new access road provided the citizens of Limerick with a picnicking amenity on the river bank on the Clare side of the river.[25] Another advantage was that both this bridge and Wellesley Bridge opened up new sites for housing development, the *Limerick Chronicle* for 22 December 1838 reporting that,

'The number of elegant villas and handsome country houses built at the North Strand, and at Park, is no less gratifying than surprising even to the natives of Limerick. The Wellesley and Athlunkard bridges have, by facility of access, encreased [sic] the number of sites in both localities, while the delightful scenery, with commanding prospect of wood and water, render them favourite objects of general resort and recreation.'

Baal's Bridge

Another much needed improvement in the city's infrastructure took place with the demolition of old Baal's Bridge and its replacement in 1831 with a single arch bridge off the Pain brothers' drawing board.[26] Although known as Baal's Bridge in legislative Acts of the period, and is known by that name today, in the nineteenth century the structure was called 'Ball's Bridge'.[27] Dating back to the early thirteenth century when the bridge piers were first laid,[28] this antiquated four-arched bridge across the Abbey River was totally inadequate to cope with the growing traffic of an expanding commercial city. Up until 1761 Baal's Bridge supported two rows of houses on either side of an exceedingly narrow traffic way. These dwellings, erected either before or after the Williamite sieges of 1690-1,[29] were of brick, three-stories high, one room in breadth and overhanging the river at the rear.[30] The removal in 1761 of the row of houses on the eastern side of the bridge relieved some of the congestion and was 'of vast use' Limerick annalist Fr. James White remarked at the time,[31] but the entire structure was in woeful need of replacement. Upon hearing in December 1829 that this antique curiosity was to be taken down a local newspaper rejoiced,

Old Baal's Bridge, Limerick.

'We are glad to find that measures are in progress for re-building this bridge, which in its present is an abominable nuisance. The removal of the houses, now a disgrace to that entrance, and erecting a new one arch bridge across, will open a delightful view of our quays from the Dublin approach, and afford a free circulation of air to that part of the city.'[32]

The project was financed by the New Limerick Navigation Company to the tune of £600, the directors choosing a design by the Pain brothers against competition from two or three other proposals.[33] A Mr. Williams was appointed as the building contractor[34] and two months after work had commenced in November 1830[35] James Pain contracted Williams to build a temporary wooden bridge across the river[36] to relieve traffic pressue on New Bridge. Work proceeded quite swiftly, a journalist from the local press reporting in early September 1831 that construction was making rapid progress 'under the superintendence of that eminent professional gentleman Mr. Paine.' By this time the two piers of the bridge had been completed and the turning of the arch had advanced to within a few feet of the centre of the river. The 'wonderful rapidity' of the undertaking was 'highly credible' to the architect, the report concluded.[37] By late October the new bridge was already passable for horses and cars and one month later the pavements were being flagged for the convenience of pedestrians, work being completed in November.[38]

Although the local press called the Pains' design a 'handsome bridge'[39] this was perhaps just a typical case of local parochial pride puffing itself up, for it is a rather ordinary looking, functional construction. Sturdy and plain speaking, it is a competent piece of civil engineering that has stood up well to the stress and weight of modern motor traffic.

Baal's Bridge, Limerick as seen today.

John Paul Dowling

A Quaint and Curious Relic

During the course of demolition work a Freemasons' square was discovered in the foundations of old Baal's Bridge. A 'square' is an implement used by stonemasons to measure right angles and it is also a standard item of Masonic regalia, the Freemasons tracing their descent through the stonemasons' guilds of the medieval period. The relic, made of brass, bore on the reverse side the inscription, 'I will strive to live with love and care, 1507', and on the obverse, as shown below, 'Upon the level by the square'.

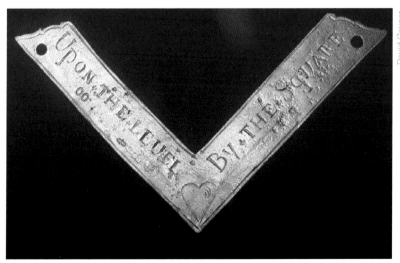

David Gaynor

277

James Pain, a Freemason, must have been quite delighted and excited when the object was discovered on the site of one of his architectural projects, for it was regarded as one of the oldest Masonic relics ever discovered in Ireland by virtue of the fact that the date '1507', or '1517', appears on the obverse. The third numeral is a bit ambiguous and has in the past been read as either '0', or '1'.[40] The relic is open to another interpretation if the inscription is read as '1517', not '1507'. When J. A. Haydn, a member of the Masonic Lodge of Research, No. 200, penned an essay on the history of Limerick's Lodge No. 13 in 1933 he wrote 'that the square bears the date 1507 (or 1517)'. This is footnoted by the comment 'Probably not a date but a reference to II. Chronicles, Chap. iii, v.v. 15 and 17. - P.C.'[41] The reference is to Verses 15 and 17, Chapter iii, of the 'Second Book of the Chronicles' in The Old Testament. These verses recording the building of the Temple of Solomon the King,[42] an important event in Masonic lore,

> 15. And he made before the house two pillars of thirty and five cubits high, and the chapiter * that was on the top of each was five cubits.
> 17.And he reared up the pillars before the temple, one on the right hand, and the other on the left; and called the name of that on the right hand Jachin, and the name of that on the left Boaz.
>> (King James Bible.)
>> *Chapiter - capital of a column.

James Pain presented the Baal's Bridge square to fellow Mason Michael Furnell. When the relic was exhibited at a dinner held by Lodge 13 on Wednesday 24 August 1842 it was described as being found by 'James Paine . . . under the foundation stone of old Baal's bridge, on which is engraved, "I will strive to liue, with loue and care and upon the leuel, by the square - 1517" [sic].'[43] However a leaflet issued by the Provincial Grand Lodge of North Munster in 2001 states that though Brother Michael Furnell believed the date to be 1517, this was 'a mistake, as the square bears the date 1507'.[44] It was naturally thought that the numerals referred to a date and this led to speculation that since the construction date of old Baal's Bridge was not certain 'the old square may have been placed under the foundation stone in 1507.'[45]

In 1872 Sophie Furnell, the widow of Frederick W. Furnell, presented the revered relic to Lodge No. 13, writing to the Worshipful Master Rev. W. F. Seymour,

> 'I send an old Masonic Square which my dear husband wished to have presented to this Lodge at his death as it is one of the oldest Masonic relics known, and I have much pleasure in giving it to those who know its value.'[46]

The prize possession of Lodge 13, the Baal's Bridge square is now safely lodged in a bank and a replica is on display in the museum of the North Munster Masonic Centre on Castle Street, King's Island, Limerick.

While the Baal's Bridge square is definitely an authentic item of Masonic regalia, precisely how it came to be lodged in the foundations of Baal's Bridge is not certain. While Michael Furnell firmly stated in 1842 in an article that the square was found under the foundation stone of old Baal's Bridge on the English town side,[47] J. A. Haydn does not commit himself so precisely, saying in his 1933 research essay that the square was 'found under its foundations.'[48]

This mystery may possibly be solved if we consider that in 1769 George Bell's house on Baal's Bridge was advertised as a meeting place for Masonic Lodge No. 36 on 'the first Wednesday of every month.'[49] The house was one of those standing in the remaining western row of dwellings, their backs facing toward the Shannon. On 4 February 1775 several of these houses collapsed following structural damage caused by a flooding high tide. A Mr. Charles Berry, a tin man by trade who dwelt on the bridge, had quite a shock that day when the floor of his house suddenly gave way and he was cast headlong into the Abbey River and swept along by the current towards the Shannon. He would surely have drowned had not a bold and manly sailor by the name of John Fitzgerald grabbed hold of him and hauled him out of the water as he passed by the slip beside the New Bridge, the site of present-day Mathew Bridge.[50] An embellishment of the story has Mr. Berry sitting at ease at the toilet when the accident happened. The *Leinster Journal* reported that following the collapse of Berry's house the inhabitants of the other dwellings on the bridge fled their 'tottering mansions which a few minutes after tumbled into ruin.'[51] The collapse resulting from the dislodgment of masonry in one of the arches by the fast flowing current.

So, it is possible that a Masonic square in George Bell's house became lodged in the foundations when the houses collapsed and was subsequently sealed up either deliberately or inadvertently when the bridge and the houses were repaired.[52] Another explanation is that the square was deliberately placed there by a member of the Freemasons during repair work. Putting a construction date of 1507 on Baal's Bridge seems to be incorrect, because there was a stone bridge on the site long before that. The available archaeological evidence points to the view that the piers of the bridge were erected in the early thirteenth century. During excavations undertaken on the Baal's Bridge area in 1999 three samples from oak timbers that revetted one of the piers of the medieval bridge were submitted for dendrochronological dating. The results suggested that the bridge piers were constructed in the early thirteenth century. [53]

The opportunity to replace the old bridge was not seized upon in 1775 because New Bridge (1762) had been recently built downstream to relieve the pressure of traffic and the 'abominable nuisance' remained in existence for another fifty-five years.

Endnotes

1 Inscription on parapet plaque.

2 Hodkinson, Brian 'Old Thomond Bridge' for publication in forthcoming edition of the *North Munster Antiquarian Journal*.

3 Parry, John Orlando 'The Diaries of John Orlando Parry', *Parry Papers*, National Library of Wales (NWL MS 17718A). For an account of Liszt's visit to Limerick see Ahern, Richard 'Liszt in Limerick', *Georgian Limerick* Vol. II, Lee, David & Gonzalez, Christine eds., Limerick Civic Trust, Limerick, 2000.

4 'Genuine Bear's Grease for the growth of Hair' was one of a number of items on sale in 1838 in the Temple of Fancy, a shop at 111 George Street, Limerick. A rhyming advertisement for the shop appeared in *Deane's Limerick Almanac Advertiser* of 1838 advertising an Aladdin's Cave of fancy goods, novelties and cosmetics, including lip-salves,

'To guard Hibernia's Daughters fair ,
From tanning sunbeam, frosty air.'

5 Donnelly, Kevin; Hoctor, Michael & Walsh, Dermot *A Rising Tide - The Story of Limerick Harbour* Limerick Harbour Commissioners, Limerick, 1994, p. 11.

6 Barry, J. G. 'Old Limerick Bridges', *Journal of the North Munster Archaeological Society* Vol. 1, 1909-11, Limerick, pp. 8-14.

7 Lenihan, Maurice *Limerick: Its History and Antiquities* (1866), republished in facsimile as *History of Limerick*, O'Carroll, Cian ed., The Mercier Press, 1991, pp. 530-3.

8 'Limerick Streets', *Limerick Leader*, 2 October 1926. Copy of article in Local Studies Department, Limerick County Library.

9 Lenihan *op. cit.* p. 471.

10 loc. cit.

11 *Limerick Gazette*, Tuesday 14 April 1818.

12 Fitzgerald, Rev. P. & M'Gregor, J. J. *The History, Topography and Antiquities of the County and City of Limerick* 2 Vols., Limerick, 1827, p. 613: 'Park Bridge is a mean structure, which crosses the Abbey River. The building of Athlunkard-bridge [*sic*] will lead to an improvement of this bridge, and all the adjacent neighbourhood.'

13 *Limerick Chronicle*, 28 April 1824. Work started at the Park Bridge end, a bridge that was called Corbally Bridge in the *Limerick Chronicle* report.

14 *The Civil Survey A.D. 1654-1656 of the County of Limerick* Vol. IV, Irish Manuscripts Commission, published by The Stationary Office, Dublin

Stationary Office, 1938, s.v. 'William Bourke of Limicke' p. 436. There is a local tradition that this remnant is part of the house belonging, in 1654, to an Alderman John Bourke, 'Irish Papist'(ibid. s.v. 'John Bourke of Limicke [*sic*] Aldr , Irish Papist.' p. 435). But research undertaken in 1988 by Claire Lane for the Limerick Museum indicates that it was Alderman John Bourke's house that was completely demolished in 1824, the surviving gable wall belonging to the adjacent house owned by William Burke. (Lane, Claire *Map of the City Based on the Civil Survey of 1654* (1988) - unpublished original in Limerick Museum archive.

15 The plaque on Athlunkard Bridge states 'THIS BRIDGE WAS DESIGNED AND BUILT BY JAMES AND GEO. RICHD. PAINE, ARCHITECTS.'

16 Lenihan *op. cit.* p. 475.

17 Inscription on bridge plaque.

18 Cox, R. C. & Gould, M. H. *Civil Engineering Heritage Ireland*, Institution of Civil Engineers and the Institution of Civil Engineers in Ireland, Thomas Telford Publications, London, 1998, p. 252.

19 ibid. pp. 247-8.

20 ibid. p. 253.

21 Dowd, Rev. James *Dowd's History of Limerick*, O'Carroll, Cian ed., The O'Brien Press, Dublin, 1990, p. 98. Originally published as *Limerick and Its Sieges* G. McKern & Sons, Limerick, 1890, p. 130

22 *The Limerick Evening Post and Clare Sentinel*, 18 December 1829.

23 *Deane's Limerick Almanack, Directory & Advertiser of 1838.*

24 *Bond for Performance of Agreement Entered into by James Pain and George Richard Pain with the Athlunkard Bridge Commissioners* (MS), April 1833, Limerick Museum (LM. 1933). The map mentioned in the document is not in the Museum archives.

25 Hannan, Kevin *Limerick – Historical Reflections*, Oireacht Publications, Castletroy, Limerick, 1996, p. 49.

26 Both plaques on Baal's Bridge record that the Pain brothers were the architects.

27 Lenihan. *op. cit.* p. 475n2.

28 During excavations undertaken on the Broad Street/George's Quay/Abbey River area of Limreck three samples from oak timbers that revetted one of the bridge piers of the mediaeval bridge were submitted for dendrochronological dating. The results suggested that the bridge piers were constructed in the early thirteenth century. *Excavations 1999: Summary Accounts of Archaeological Excavations in Ireland,* Bennett, Isabel ed., Wordwell Ltd., Bray, Co. Wicklow, 2000, s.v. '515 Broad Street/George's Quay/Abbey River'. p. 170

29 Limerick historian Maurice Lenihan writes in 1866 that the houses on Baal's Bridge were erected before the Williamite sieges (Lenihan *op. cit.* p. 476). But J.G. Barry, writing in 1909, argues that the available evidence indicates that the houses were built after 1691, see Barry, J. G. 'Old Limerick

Bridges', *Journal of the North Munster Archaeological Society*, printed by Guy & Co., Limerick, 1911, Vol. I, 1909-1910-1911, p. 10.

30 Barry *op. cit.* p. 10.

31 White, Fr. James *The White Manuscript*. Edited transcript of White Ms. in Limerick Civic Trust archive s.v. '1761', p. 171.

32 *The Limerick Evening Post and Clare Sentinel*, 18 December 1829.

33 Lenihan *op. cit.* p. 475-6.

34 *Limerick Chronicle*, 5 January 1831.

35 Inscription on bridge.

36 *Limerick Chronicle*, 5 January 1831.

37 *Limerick Chronicle*, 7 September 1831.

38 *Limerick Chronicle*, 29 October; 30 November 1831; Inscription on plaque on bridge.

39 *Limerick Chronicle*, 7 September 1831.

40 Haydn, J. A. *Ancient Union Lodge No. 13, Limerick*, essay on the Bicentenary, 1732-1932 of Ancient Union Lodge, No. 13 Limerick presented on Friday 28 April 1933, Lodge of Research, No. 200, p. 13.

41 Haydn *op. cit.* p.14.

42 Haydn *op. cit.* p. 14.

43 *Limerick Chronicle*, Wednesday 31 August 1842.

44 'The Baal's Bridge Square', Provincial Grand Lodge of North Munster, 2001.

45 Kemmy, Jim 'The Marencourt Cup', *The Old Limerick Journal - French Edition* No. 25, Summer, 1989, p. 115.

46 Haydn *op. cit.* p.13.

47 *Freemason's Quarterly Review*, 1842, p. 288. The item is dated 27 August 1842.

48 Haydn *op. cit.* p.14.

49 Ferrar, John *Limerick Trade Directory* Limerick, 1769 in *The Irish Genealogist*, October 1964, pp. 229-40. George Bell is described as a 'card-maker' in John Ferrar's 1769 Limerick Trade Directory - a 'card' being an implement much used in the textile trade for raising the nap on cloth or disentangling wool fibres prior to spinning. In 1769, seventeen tradesmen gave their address as Baal's Bridge.

50 Ferrar, John *The History of Limerick*, 2nd edition, 1787, p. 132; *Finn's Leinster Journal*, 17 February 1775.

51 *Finn's Leinster Journal*, 17 February 1775.

52 When the French Marine and Commerce attaché to Ireland visited Limerick in 1790 he recorded in his journal 'Ball's Bridge fell down some years ago. A row of houses has been rebuilt there.' De Montbret, Charles Etienne Coquebert 'A Frenchman's Impressions of Limerick', *North Munster Antiquarian Journal*, Ni Chinneide, Sighle ed., Thomond Archaeological Society, Vol. 5, (1946-9) No. 4, 1948.

53 Bennett *op. cit.* s.v. '515 Broad Street/George's Quay/Abbey River, Limerick', p. 170.

CHAPTER SIXTEEN

PERY SQUARE TONTINE

In the early years of Queen Victoria's reign a diverse range of architectural styles vied for attention in Limerick in a 'Battle of the Styles' ranging from the warm Tudor brick of Leamy's School (completed 1845)[1] on Hartstonge Street to the grey limestone of the Savings Bank's Greek Revival built on Glentworth Street in 1840. But it is in the Tontine terrace at Pery Square that we see a masterpiece of architecture that stands out as a clear victor in Limerick's stylistic conflict. The most opulent range of early nineteenth century terraced architecture to be seen in Georgian Limerick, this development of six town houses was built by the Pery Square Tontine Company and completed in 1838. It was a project with which James Pain was very closely associated, both as an investor and as the supervising architect.

A Prestigious Development

The overall design of the terrace exemplifies the Classical ideals of proportion, order and symmetry; the window arrangement in particular binding the composition together with strong horizontal and vertical lines. As such, the Pery Square Tontine contrasts with the asymmetrical lines of Picturesque Gothic. The terrace was built with the intention of encouraging a long-standing ambition to crown Newtown Pery with a prestigious residential town square. An ambition going back to 1769 when Christopher Colles drew up a draft street plan for the proposed development of Newtown Pery that included a number of squares on the map to alleviate the gridiron pattern of streets.[2]

By the 1820s, however, the only adornment to the relentless progress of the grid had been Richmond Place (The Crescent) with its double crescent of up-market terraced housing. But by the latter half of the decade the desire was to see a residential square, facing onto a park, built at a site that was to become Pery Square. An 1827 map of the city does indicate the outlines of a square on the site, but this development, marked 'New Square', was still a proposal, not an actuality. Fitzgerald and M'Gregor in their 1827 History of Limerick describing the development as a 'projected square.'[3]

One of the first indications that a name had been selected for the development appears in the 5 April 1828 minutes of St. Michael's Parish Commissioners, 'A motion for adjournment of the question of the intended Square (called Perry's [sic] Square) was called for . . .'[4] A difference of opinion had arisen at the meeting, one of the Commissioners taking a critical view of the scheme, stating that 'the intended New Square interfered with the public passage of the Parish'. However, this was not the opinion of the majority, for a resolution was passed firmly endorsing the project,

Tontine buildings, Pery Square, Limerick.

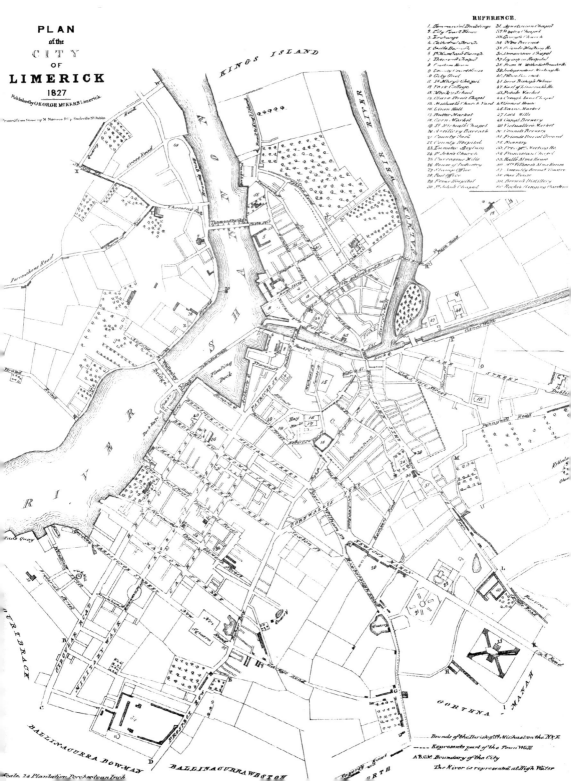

PLAN
of the
CITY
OF
LIMERICK
1827

Published by GEORGE McKERN Limerick

Printed from Stone by M. Mccune D.I.p. Sackville St. Dublin

REFERENCE.

1. Commercial Buildings
2. City Court House
3. Exchange
4. Cathedral Church
5. Castle Barrack
6. St Munchins Church
7. Thomond Chapel
8. Custom House
9. County Court House
10. City Gaol
11. St Marys Chapel
12. Park College
13. Crose Street Chapel
14. Cathedral Church Yard
15. Linen Hall
16. Butter Market
17. Corn Market
18. St Michaels Chapel
19. Artillery Barrack
20. County Gaol
21. County Hospital
22. Lunatic Asylum
23. St Johns Church
24. Currawen Wells
25. House of Industry
26. Stamp Office
27. Post Office
28. Fever Hospital
29. St Johns Chapel
31. Augustinian Chapel
32. Quaker Chapel
33. Cornwall Church
34. New Barrack
35. St Francis Abbey M.
36. Dominican Chapel
37. Lying in Hospital
38. Roman Cath Chapel
39. Independent Meeting Ho
40. Thomond Gate
41. Irish Bishops Palace
42. Earl of Limerick Ho.
43. Potatoe Market
44. Trinity Street Chapel
45. Coward House
46. Nevins Market
47. Lock Mills
48. Canal Brewery
49. Victuallers Market
50. Grounds Brewery
51. Friends Burial Ground
52. Nunnery
53. Pres. 4th Meeting Ho.
54. Primitive Chapel
55. Halls Alms House
56. McWilliams Alms House
57. Assembly Room & Theatre
58. Fire Force
59. Corrich Distillery
60. Rockes Hanging Gardens

Bounds of the Parish of St Michael on the N.Y.E.
Represents part of the Town Wall
A.B.C.D. Boundary of the City
The River is represented at High Water

Scale, 24 Plantation Perches to an Inch

'We are of the opinion that the formation of a Square and the improvement connected therewith are not only, not an encroachment, but are highly conducive to the advantage and Interest of the Parish.'[5]

Clear evidence that the city's business classes were enthusiastic about the laying down of a residential square that would be a qualitative leap in the status and standing of Limerick among the cities of Ireland.

By 1831 work had commenced in the area resulting in the provision of a landscaped park that was smaller in size than the present day Peoples' Park which incorporates the pre-Famine development. The original park was laid out in the form of an equilateral square in the centre of which stood an impressive fluted Doric column, 71 feet 6 inches (21.8 metres) high, supporting a statue to Thomas Spring Rice. A man fêted as the hero of Newtown Pery when he became MP for Limerick City in 1820 following a prolonged political tussle with the parliamentary champion of the 'Corrupt Corporation'. Erected in 1831, the inscription on the abacus at the top of the column reads 'Built by Hill Clements and Sons A.D. 1831', funding was provided by the wealthy Barrington family. The sculptor commissioned to sculpt the statue was Thomas Kirk who first came to prominence in Ireland by carving the figure of Admiral Lord Nelson for Nelson's Pillar in Dublin's Sackville (O'Connell) Street.[6] The statue of Spring Rice is not very distinguished, the most interesting feature being the Classical Roman toga in which the clothed figure is partially draped.

When completed the park was 'a formally laid out garden with paths tracing a symmetrical pattern . . . it was a relatively relaxed design with paths curving flamboyantly . . . The central area is raised, resembling a small hill, trees cluster around its limits.'[7] The amenity, enclosed within railings, was intended for the private use of local residents who paid for a gate key. On the central earthen elevation stood the Spring Rice column.

A Barrington Development

The siting of a monumental column within a landscaped park on the southern edge of the city only makes sense if it was envisaged to be the central focus of a superior residential square. The park was laid out before any houses were built facing onto it, but it would appear that by 1831 plans were far advanced to develop the area. On 31 May 1831 Joseph Barrington leased a large parcel of land from Edmond Henry Pery, Earl of Limerick[8] on part of which the six houses of Pery Square Tontine terrace were eventually to be built. The Barrington family were certainly interested in developing this part of Newtown Pery to which the wealthier citizens of the city gravitated to, the plot of land leased from the Pery Estate extending in length from Hartstonge Street to Barrington Street (yet to be built), and in width from Pery Square to the rear of the houses on The Crescent. The sketch map accompanying the lease shows the division of the property into sites intended for houses.[9] In 1833 Joseph Barrington engaged the services of James Pain to develop this prime development property.[10] The following extract from the 22 June 1831 manuscript minutes of the St. Michael's Parish Commissioners suggests that the development was to move forward fairly quickly,

> 'Resolved that our secretary do give Mr. Owens [the Parish Surveyor] instructions to pay attention to the sewer at present building by the Earl of Limerick leading from Perry's [sic] Square to the River thro' Hartstong [sic] Street so as to ascertain that said sewer is built in a workmanlike manner.'[11]

In the mid-1830s a new street, Barrington Street, had been laid down leading to Pery Square from the Crescent. According to the St. Michael's Parish Rate Book for September 1835 - March 1836, three houses had been built on Barrington Street by that time, one occupied by Sir Joseph Barrington, who had been elevated to the dignity of Baronet in September 1831,[12] and another by his son Daniel. By 1838 seven houses had appeared on the street.[13]

Work on the first of an intended series of terraced blocks on Pery Square did not commence until 1835 with the appointment of Pierse Creagh of Ennis as building contractor for the Tontine terrace. If the ambition for Pery Square had been fulfilled as envisioned, and the remaining terraces built to the same high standards as the Tontines (completed 1838), then not only would Pery Square have rivalled Dublin's Merrion and Fitzwilliam Squares, it would have been far superior. However, such was not to be the case for the Pery Square Tontine was the last of the Georgian residential terraces to be built in the city. By 1840 demand for terraced housing in Newtown Pery had been met by supply. With the coming of the Victorian era the fashion was for the wealthier business people and merchant princes of Limerick to build villas and mansions in the surrounding countryside or to live in fashionable, leafy districts such as the North Circular Road rather than in city centre terraces.

The Pery Square park was to be later considerably enlarged and converted into a public park by Limerick Corporation in 1877. Now known as Peoples' Park, the Thomas Spring Rice monument still stands, but the vast majority of the population of Limerick are totally unaware of who, exactly, that rather remote figure standing on top of the column is supposed to represent. The pigeons are much more familiar with him than the general populace. Much unappreciated, there he stands aloft, sentinel over Limerick's civic rights.

Thomas Spring Rice monument, Peoples' Park, Limerick.

A Gamble on Life

The Pery Square terrace was financed by a particular type of investment company known as a 'tontine', a term that would not be terribly familiar today. The difference between the Pery Square Tontine and a normal property company lay in the 'life and death' lottery element associated with the shares issued to investors that decided how the dividends, and ultimately the assets, of the Tontine Company were to be distributed among the shareholders.

When built the six houses in the terrace were commercially rented out and dividends paid to the shareholders. The ability of each share to earn dividends rested on the life span of a named individual nominated by the shareholder – the nominee's name, address and age appearing on the share certificate.[14] No two shares could have the same nominee. In the Pery Square scheme a total of eighty-nine numbered shares were sold to twenty-three investors and many of their chosen nominees were young relatives, or children of a friend or an acquaintance. Age was considered an important factor, for when a nominee died that particular share also 'died' in the sense that no more dividends could be collected on the share, the company's profit being distributed twice yearly among the remaining valid 'live' shares. In the event of anyone receiving or demanding a dividend following the death of a nominee the shareholder could be sued by the Company for £50 for each payment received or demanded. The schedule of nominees was finally formalised on 11 August 1840.[15]

Although shares were transferable, provided the Company Secretary was notified,[16] the name of the nominee could not be changed. For instance, Thomas Philip Vokes, Chief Magistrate for Police, owned two shares and in August 1840 he nominated Marion Madaline Spaight, aged 11, as life-nominee for Share No. 74 and George Spaight (8) for No. 75. Both were children of Francis Spaight, well-known Limerick merchant. James Pain as an investor owned five shares, Nos. 58-62.[17] When the Company was first incorporated in 1835 the shares had a purchase price of £100, however investors only had to pay an initial £5 deposit. Thereafter,

Limerick Museum

288

Pery-Square Tontine Company of the City of Limerick.

11th AUGUST, 1840.

ко. M'Kern & Sons, Limerick.

No. *51*

This is to Certify, THAT *Mathew Barrington Esquire* of *the City of Dublin* is a Proprietor of the Property and Concerns of said Company, depending on the Life of *William Button* of *Pomfret County of Galway* aged *Thirteen* years; having become entitled to a share thereof, under the Deed or Charter-Party of this date, by subscribing ONE *Eighty Ninth* Proportion of the Sum of **TEN THOUSAND SIX HUNDRED AND EIGHTY POUNDS**, Sterling, being the Capital Stock of said Company.

Henry Watson
Trustee

Geo G Wilkins
Director

Danl Barrington
Director

ENTERED,

John Mahony
Secretary.

'all future instalments shall be paid also at the rate of £5 . . . and only to be demanded as the work is proceeded with, and then only as the Committee shall deem necessary for the further progress and completion of the same.'[18]

Construction costs for the terrace, originally estimated at £9,200,[19] finally amounted to £10,680 and to cover the overrun the subscription for each of the eight-nine shares had to be increased to £120 in 1840.[20]

As the years passed the number of valid shares naturally declined as nominees died off. Under the Company's Articles of Agreement when only six of the life-nominees were left alive the holders of the remaining valid shares would each be allocated one of the six houses in the terrace.[21] It was not until 1913, seventy-five years after the terrace had been constructed, that the winners of the investment lottery were finally decided. By that time all the original shareholders had died and over the intervening years shares had passed through various hands. In 1913 the biggest beneficiary was Sophia Vanderkiste who, at the age of 77, held three of the winning shares, taking over ownership of Nos. 1, 2 and 3 Pery Square.[22]

As coincidence would have it, two of Sophia's winning shares, Nos. 58 and 60, had been originally purchased by James Pain.[23] In 1863 he transferred his shares to his niece, Sally Vereker who in turn sold them to John Vanderkiste of 6 Pery Square. John and his brother William had been attempting to buy as many shares as possible and by 1883 they had acquired twenty-three between them. When John Vanderkiste died in 1892 his shares were willed to his brother and when William, of 13 Barrington Street, in turn passed on in 1908 he left all his shares to his widow, Sophia.[24]

290

James Pain's life nominee for share No. 58 was his architect nephew James Henry Pain. Son of Henry Pain, he came to Ireland in March 1836 aged 16 to work with his uncles as an articled apprentice[25] and in 1840 was living in George Street, Limerick,[26] presumably at his uncle James's house. In 1913 James Henry Pain, then in his nineties, was living at Craigleith, Keswick Road, Putney, London.[27] He died on 12 July 1915.[28] The nominee for another winning share certificate, No. 60, was James Pain's grand niece Catherine Margaret Elphinston of Adelaide Place, Cork, aged 3, a daughter of John Elphinston and Catharine Pain (daughter of George Richard Pain). The fact that James Pain died aged 97 and that two of his relatives born in the early nineteenth century were still alive in 1913 - Catherine Elphinstone was 76 years old in 1913 - indicates a stubborn streak of healthy longevity in the family.

View of Barringtons' Hospital, George's Quay, Limerick with new office development on left.

Social Prestige

Among the original twenty-three investors in the Pery Square Tontine Company, several were leading members of Limerick society including Daniel Barrington, State Solicitor for Limerick and Land Agent for the Pery Estate,[29] who held twenty of the eighty-nine shares issued.[30] It was on family property, leased by Joseph Barrington from the Pery Estate in May 1831,[31] that the Tontine was built. Daniel's elder brother, Mathew Barrington, was also involved in the Tontine Company with six shares. Mathew served as Crown Solicitor for Munster with an annual salary of £15,000 and was later to acquire lucrative legal connections with an Irish railway company, the Great Southern Railway.[32]

Besides their leading role in the Tontine scheme and sponsorship of the Thomas Spring Rice triumphal column in the Pery Square park, the Barrington family were directly responsible for financially supporting a number of other important building projects in Limerick, including Barrington's Hospital (1829-31) built on George's Quay by the family as an infirmary for the city poor, architect Frederick Darley. Several years later Mathew was to finance the construction of the Mont de Piété (1836-7), a charitable pawn office erected adjacent to Barrington's Hospital using any profits made to support the hospital. Built in Classical style on the lines of the Temple of Vesta, the Mont de Piété had a large cupola and pillars. It ceased to function as a charitable pawn in 1845 and was eventually demolished in 1892.[33]

Mathew's long standing ambition to build a splendid and noble family home at Glenstal, near Murroe, Co. Limerick was also actively pursued at this time and in April 1833 he received a proposal from James and George Richard Pain to build Glenstal Castle in Picturesque Gothic similar to Dromoland Castle. But it was not blessed with Barrington's approval and several years later, *c.*1838, he commissioned architect William Bardwell to build Glenstal in a Neo-Norman manner.[34]

Given their social prestige, their prominent role in the Tontine Company and their experience in discussing matters of architectural style and detail with architects, it is a possibility that Daniel and Mathew Barrington may have had some say in the design of the Pery Square terrace. The fact that Daniel Barrington was the first tenant of No. 1 Pery Square and that a range of offices facing onto Barrington Street were purposely built onto his house to hold his Pery Estate records and legal papers, is circumstantial evidence to support this view.[35] Also, a distinctive feature of the side entrance portico to No. 1 is that it features Ionic columns while the side entrance portico to No. 6 and the front doors to Nos. 2-4 are framed by plainer Doric columns. Indicative of the desire by Daniel Barrington to place his stamp on his house. He did not remain in residence there beyond 1842, for by 1844 a General Lord Downes was living at No. 1 and in 1846 a General Napier was to be found there as a tenant.[36]

The fact that the Tontine terrace is far superior in architectural design to any other Georgian terrace in Limerick, indeed superior to most other Georgian terraces built in Ireland, argues for the case that an architect of quality, rather than a mere jobbing builder following pattern books by rote, was involved in the design process. As established architects, James Pain and his brother George Richard may have been invited to draw up the plans and specifications. But there is also a possibility that another architect may have been involved, for it was certainly not uncommon for non-resident architects to carry out important commissions in Limerick in the early nineteenth century. When, for instance, English architect Amon Henry Wilds came over from Britain to radically redesign Curragh House for Sir Aubrey de Vere in 1828-9 he was also involved in 'some plans for the improvement and embellishment' of Limerick City. Curragh Chase has a terraced look about it and Wilds did design a number of terraces and crescents in Brighton;[37] which is not to suggest that Wilds designed the Tontines.

The plans for the Tontine terrace were completed by the end of 1834, at the very latest, as a notice appeared in a November edition of that year's *Limerick Chronicle* informing builders and other interested parties that plans and specifications were available for inspection at Daniel Barrington's office in Mallow Street. There is no mention of plans being available in James Pain's office, which does suggest that as a major shareholder in the company Daniel was very much in control. Tenders were invited and proposals to be submitted by 20 December. A subsequent notice extended the deadline to 24 January 1835[38] and a month later the subscribers to the scheme appointed Ennis based architect Pierse Creagh as the contractor 'to build a range of houses . . . fit for the reception of tenants by next May twelve months' for a sum of £9,200.[39] By July, Creagh was seeking a subcontractor to fill in the space in front of the housing site.[40] Presumably this work involved raising up the level of the ground on which the pavement and the road was to be subsequently laid. The higher level was required to cater for the coal vaults that extended out from the basement area of each house, running under the pavement and part of the road. The deadline of May 1836 was not met, however, as the houses were not available for letting until the summer of 1838.[41]

When the company was formally incorporated in January 1835 a seven man Committee of .Management was appointed with Alderman D. F. G. Mahony acting as Treasurer and Secretary.[42] Although he did not serve on this committee, James Pain was closely involved in steering the project through to completion as the supervising architect reporting back to the shareholders, the *Limerick Chronicle*, for instance, reporting in May 1836 that,

> '. . . meetings re the Pery Square Tontine Company were held at the offices of D.F.G. Mahony & Sons and that share instalments were due to be paid.' The report then went on to say that ' a meeting was called for Tuesday 31st May 1836 when an official report is to be laid before the meeting from Mr. James Pain, architect, as to the progress of the development.'[43]

This is confirmed by a Company announcement dated 17 May 1836 which mentions that James Pain, among others, had attended a General Meeting held that day and that another General Meeting was to be held on 31 May 1836 at which 'an Official Report is to be laid before them by Mr. PAIN [sic], as to the progress of the Buildings.'[44]

Three months later, in August, James was once again reporting to a general meeting of subscribers.[45] His role as executing architect is confirmed in an announcement that appeared in the *Chronicle* of 28 April 1838 when the finishing touches to the terrace were being added,

Pery Square Tontine
> 'Proposals in writing will be received by Alderman D. F. G. MAHONY for FLAGGING in FRONT of the Houses, specifying the

rates required for best Western Flags, proper curb stones and Frames for Coal Openings, with suitable Iron Covers, finding all Materials and Workmanship. To be executed to meet the approval of James Pain, Esq.[46]

That James played a very active role professionally is therefore certain, even to the extent of looking after details such as workmanship of coal-hole covers. The square coal-hole covers for the Tontine terrace were custom-made, as they have the lettering 'PS' (for Pery Square) in the centre of the design with a shell motif in each of the four corners. Two coal-holes were set in the pavement outside each house and their purpose was to allow coal deliveries to be poured into the vaults beneath. Access to these vaults was by a door in the area in front of the basement. Today (2005), only three of the original 12 covers remain, one each outside Nos. 1, 2 and 3 Pery Square.

Armed with this knowledge, it seems reasonable to discuss the construction of the Pery Square terrace and the quality of the finished product as work that can be attributed to James Pain, even if it cannot be categorically stated that he, or his brother, were the architects.

In August 1838 Nos.1-5 had been completed and the Company placed an advertisement in the local press seeking tenants for these houses;[47] four of which had been let by October 1838.[48] The sixth house, No. 6, at the corner of Hartstonge Street was finished in 1839[49] and let to Thomas Vokes, Chief Magistrate of Police.[50]

294

David Gaynor

Coal-hole cover, Pery Square, Limerick.

Flagship Design

The Tontine may be regarded as the flagship of Newtown Pery's terraced architecture for the excellence of its design, its attractive appearance and the consistently high standard of workmanship throughout. The terrace consciously, but without ostentation, presents an image of privileged and cultured living combined with a feeling of strength, security and permanence. The two end houses of the terrace (Nos. 1 and 6), by projecting slightly forward, give a sense of country house grandeur to the front elevation, an intentional feature given that the prospect from the house is towards a park. By placing the doorways to the end houses in side pavilions, rather than on the front elevation, further emphasis is given to the 'wings'. The ashlar work on the ground and basement floors creates a sense of strength and enduring permanence. Above the ashlar, the brickwork, red/brown in colour, is well laid, the brick parapet at the top of the front, side and rear elevations hiding the double-pitched roof from view, as was standard practice for terraces of the period.

At street level iron railings, set in limestone plinths, protect the unwary passer-by from toppling over into the deep, open air, basement areas. They were indeed a danger, as witness the death in early 1825 of James Fleming, a member of the Night Watch who died when he fell into an area on Thomas Street while on duty.[51] The finials on the top of the railings are in the form of spearheads, the 'spears' ranged along the front of the building as if waiting for the hand grasp of warriors. Prior to the Victorian Age, ironwork in front of Georgian terraces was typically painted green to recall patinated bronze weapons associated with the heroic, warrior nobility of Antiquity:

> Achilles began to arm for battle . . .
> He strapped the breastplate around his chest
> Then over his shoulder Achilles slung his sword,
> The fine bronze blade with its silver studded hilt . . .
> Then lifting his rugged helmet
> He set it down on his brows, and the horsehair crest
> Shone like a star and the waving golden plumes shook . . .
> And then, at last, Achilles drew his father's spear
> From its socket stand – weighted, heavy, tough,
> No other Achaean fighter could heft that shaft,
> Only Achilles had the skill to wield it well.[52]

At intervals along the railings can be seen finials in the form of Grecian urns that are restrained in style in keeping with the architecture of the terrace. The open area in front of the basement served a functional purpose in that it permitted steam and the smell of cooking to escape from the basement kitchen without wafting up through the house. In addition, the moat-like appearance of the area kept the socially undesirable at bay.

Iron railings, Pery Square, Limerick.

This notion of the area as defensive moat is not pure fancy, for there were at least two occasions, in June 1830 and June 1840, when mobs from socially deprived Englishtown and parts of Irishtown surged into the middle class Georgian district breaking into provisions stores and bakeries and looting ships moored by the quays in sustained food rioting that required all the Sovereign's horses and all the Sovereign's men to quell the disturbances. Terrified shopkeepers closed their stores and respectable citizens bolted and shuttered their homes as the streets filled with the desperate denizens of the slums. In 1840 the high tide of the looting reached as far as a bakery in Richmond Place (The Cresent), just on the other side of the block on which Pery Square is situated. During the 1830 riots of 25 June infantrymen made bayonet charges to clear the streets. On George's Quay soldiers of the 60th Rifles opened fire hitting an innocent countryman in the knee. At the time he was bringing potatoes to the potato market and just happened to be in the wrong place at the wrong time. Until the building of a purpose-built 'root market' on Merchant's Quay in March 1844 potatoes were sold on George's Quay.[53] Another man was hit in the leg and had to have his limb amputated. In another shooting incident the military opened fire on 'a powerful mob' plundering the contents of Ballyclough Mills, several men receiving serious gunshot wounds.[54]

Unifying Features

Underneath the first floor windows of each house is placed a balcony and this line of six balconies running across the frontage of the building acts as a unifying feature linking the entire terrace together. The balconies are very simple and austere in design in comparison with the neoclassical honeysuckle balconies to be found in the nearby Georgian terrace in Barrington's Street, also constructed in the 1830s.

A building's character and aspect (its appearance) is very much defined by the arrangement of its openings - its doorways and windows. The plain and masculine approach of the Greek Revival style towards Classical decoration is very much in evidence in the layout of the door cases of Nos. 2-5 Pery Square with their stone Doric columns that stand separated from the wall. The robust Doric Order recalls the glory days of fifth century Athens when the style was used to great effect in great public buildings such as the Parthenon. The Doric columns in Pery Square are fluted on the upper two-thirds of their height, being plain and unfluted on the lower section. This partial fluting has the advantage of avoiding chipping to the stonework of the more vulnerable lower section by accidental knocks and scrapes. It also gives the columns a more solid, robust appearance; the lower unfluted section seeming to 'echo' the ashlar of the basement and ground floor of the terrace. Over the doorways of the Tontine is a fashionable segmented fanlight.

298

No. 2 Pery Square, Limerick restored by Limerick Civic Trust.

It is in the window arrangement of the terrace that the ideals of Classicism are also expressed, the fenestration making a significant contribution to the harmony, proportion and balanced elegance of the composition. The window bays are all perfectly aligned vertically from basement to top floor suggesting the monumental columns of the Ancients. The window design owes much to

Palladian precepts. The fifteenth century Renaissance architect Palladio had drawn up rules for fenestration that called for windows to be positioned one above the other and be of the same width, with the heights diminishing towards the upper floors.[55] The tallest windows being on the principle floor (usually the first floor in the terraced architecture of the period) called, in the Italian manner, the *piano nobile*, the 'noble floor'.

This window arrangement is not adhered to in most of the Georgian terraced houses in Limerick because they are generally narrower in width than the Pery Square Tontines. In order to fit two windows alongside the doorway on the ground floor the windows do not correspond to those in the upper floors, being offset. In Pery Square, happily, there is proper adherence to Palladian principals with all the windows vertically aligned. This is due the to full palatial treatment of the terrace and with the width of each house being wider than the Limerick norm.[56]

The Classical character of the exterior of the terrace was continued on into the interior of No. 2 Pery Square where the marbleised paint work on the hall and stair walls imitates the marbled walls of Greece and Rome. In terms of desirability, the Pery Square terrace had all the attributes considered important: Aspect (appearance), Prospect (view) and Locality. It was an enclave removed from the hustle and bustle of the quays and the commerce of early nineteenth century Limerick. The Tontine stands alone in Limerick for its grandeur among the generally more prosaic terraces that populate much of the rest of the city's Georgian quarter. To build the majority of such structures no art or architectural skill was required as the techniques of constructing terraces had long been established. All that the builder and his contractors needed were the easily available pattern books that laid down architectural details and dimensions so that the set pattern could be simply repeated, almost ad nauseam. It was only in the grander, more expensive terraces that a freer interpretation comes into play and an architect called upon.

Social Exclusion

The centrepiece of Pery Square, if the vision of creating a fully-fledged residential square had been realised, would have been the park. However, access to this amenity, which was enclosed by railings, was denied to the general citizenry except those who were willing to pay a yearly rent for the privilege of being a keyholder. This led the editor of *Deane's Limerick Almanack* for 1838 to complain that this was a cause of much regret because the city was 'destitute of public walks. The Wellesley Bridge is generally crowded when the weather is fine, and George Street in the evenings.'[57] It might be said that this policy of social exclusion from a park dedicated to Thomas Spring Rice, the man who 'liberated' the Newtown Pery middle classes from the parliamentary grip of the politically exclusive Corrupt

Corporation, was a bit of a contradiction. But one should not be in the least bit surprised, for what is the point of being free if one cannot deny freedom to others. However, private parks were a common feature in the layout of Georgian cities and towns.

It does appear that restrictions on entry to this park were not always strictly enforced, for we read in the diary of Ellen O'Callaghan, the socially aspiring eighteen year old daughter of a Catholic grocer and spirits dealer of 9 George Street,[58] that in the early summer of 1839 she enjoyed promenading around this garden park and being 'seen'. Although neither her family nor her friends were keyholders, Ellen's diary for 19 May records that she was walking in the park 'until near 5 – all the fashion of Limerick is to be seen there.' Six days later Ellen again passed through the gates without hindrance, finding to her delight that 'the band was playing and all the fashion of Limerick was displayed; the band plays most beautifully . . . most captivating.' But poor Miss O'Callaghan was soon to find out that she was only the grocer's daughter. On 6 June, once again intending to grace the park with her presence, she received a humiliating rebuff: 'at the gate got a very ignominious dismissal on refusing our names and not having a key.' She was rather inclined to avoid the place after that.[59]

The Restoration Project

In 1996 Limerick Civic Trust purchased one of the Pery Square Tontines, No. 2, and restored the house to its original condition over a three-year period.[60] The most successful example of architectural restoration to be found in Limerick, the project was undertaken by the Trust to create public awareness about the decline of period buildings in the city and to promote a better appreciation of the city's built heritage.

The house had been converted into flats in the 1960s, a number of the principal rooms having been subdivided by partition walls with bathrooms and kitchenettes installed. The first task of the restoration team was the removal of these twentieth century alterations revealing hidden treasures such as fireplace surrounds and the original Liscannor stone flagging on the basement kitchen floor which had been covered over with concrete. Much of the original joinery in the house was found to be in good condition and only four of the sash windows required extensive repairs.

The next phase of the project included dealing with structural problems such as dry rot and the need to strengthen the structure by inserting steel beams into the ground and first floors. This was followed by more detailed and painstaking work such as stripping away the successive layers of paint that had clogged up the plaster cornices and ceiling roses, obscuring the details.[61] Finally the house was redecorated, the paint work reproducing the colours of the period.

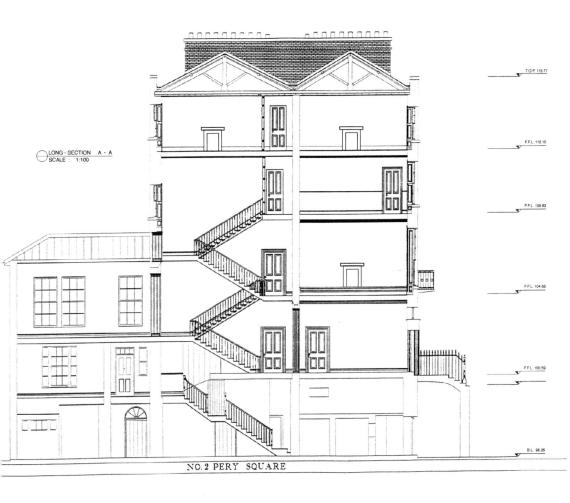

LONG · SECTION   A · A
SCALE :   1:100

T.O.P. 115.77

F.F.L. 112.10

F.F.L. 108.83

F.F.L. 104.65

F.F.L. 100.59

B.L. 96.25

NO. 2 PERY SQUARE

No. 2 Pery Square is open to the public and the remarkable nature of the workmanship by local craftsmen that went into creating the terrace, and the great attention paid to detail by supervising architect James Pain, can now be fully appreciated. It is the finest example of early nineteenth century domestic architecture in Limerick and one of the most distinguished terraces in Ireland. Of particular note in No. 2 is the distinctive mezzanine floor that divides the large and extensive basement into two floors. In terms of terraced architecture it is quite unique to Limerick, for a mezzanine is a feature not seen outside of Limerick in a house of similar size in Dublin, London or elsewhere. The mezzanine floor supports three rooms, the largest, which has a fireplace, was possibly the butler's room while the other two rooms provided sleeping accommodation for other members of staff. The kitchen, storage rooms and access doors to the area and the garden are to be found in the lower basement level.[62]

A major discovery by the restoration team was made when, under several layers of wallpaper, the original marbling paint work on the walls of the hall, stairs and landings was uncovered. On the stair and landing walls the marbling is laid out in classic block layers' pattern, the blocks being 16 x 24 inches (40.6cm x 61cm) in size. The paint scheme goes up the stairs to the top of the house, a feature which is extraordinarily rare. It is possibly the largest extent of original marbled walls to be seen in a building of this size in Ireland. In the entrance hall the size of the blocks are larger than those found on the stairs, and this, in conjunction with the archway between the entrance and staircase halls, creates the sense of a formal ante-room to the house.[63]

Socially, the most important rooms in the house are the two drawing rooms on the first floor, the *piano nobile*. In No 2 the social significance of this floor is signified by the large proportions of the rooms which are 15 feet (4.6 metres) in height, higher than elsewhere in the house, and the unusually high, 13-inch (33cm), skirting boards. Handsome white marble fireplaces with grey veining and Doric columns are to be found in both rooms, while the ceiling roses, with their alternative radiating panels of acanthus leaves and ornate fleur-de-lys, provide an interesting combination of motifs. The tall windows in these rooms reach to just a few feet above the floor providing a fine view of the park.

Another important feature of the restoration of No 2 Pery Square by Limerick Civic Trust is the Georgian town garden at the rear of the house that provides a tranquil retreat. It is the only example in Ireland of a restored urban garden of the period that is open to the public. The layout is very formal, with a rectangular lawn, straight paths and wall beds in keeping with the Classicism of the house. The reinstatement of the garden was based on both archaeological evidence and detail from the 1840 Ordnance Survey. The plants, herbs, trees and shrubs were chosen as species and varieties known to have been grown in the late eighteenth century and their positioning is correct within such a garden. The creation of the Georgian Garden was undertaken with great attention to historical accuracy by historic garden expert and designer Belinda Jupp and its primary importance is that it is integral to the house.[64]

We see in the Pery Square Tontine that terraced architecture, if approached with flair, could produce outstanding results. James Pain, and all those craftsmen and labourers who worked on the construction of the building, put in a stellar performance on this occasion.

Georgian Garden, No. 2 Pery Square, Limerick.

Endnotes

1 *Limerick Chronicle*, 22 October 1845.

2 Colles, C. *Plan of the City and Suburbs of Limerick 1769*, Limerick Museum (LM1990: 0158).

3 Fitzgerald and M'Gregor *The History, Topography and Antiquities of the County and City of Limerick* 2 Vols., Limerick, 1827, Vol. II, p. 506.

4 *Proceedings and Orders of the Commissioners for Improving the Parish of St. Michael's, Commencing April 12th 1819 and Ending April 8th 1833*, 5 April 1828, Limerick Archives. L/MP/1/1

5 loc. cit.

6 Hill, Judith *Irish Public Sculpture: A History*, Four Courts Press, Dublin, 1998, pp. 65, 78.

7 Hill, Judith *The Building of Limerick*, The Mercier Press, Cork, 1991, p. 140; Ordnance Survey, 1840, scale: 5 feet to one statute mile, City of Limerick, Sheet 19.

8 Indenture of Lease, dated 31 May 1831, of 'Part of the Lands of South Priors Land at Pery Square for lives renewal' from the Earl of Limerick to Joseph Barrington. Barrington Papers, Glenstal Abbey.

9 loc. cit.

10 *9 Barrington Street - The Heritage Angle*, A report by Limerick Chapter, Irish Georgian Society on 9 Barrington Street and an associated range of offices connected with No. 1 Pery Square, Limerick Civic Trust Archives.

11 *Proceedings and Orders of the Commissioners for Improving the Parish of St. Michael's, Commencing April 12th 1819 and Ending April 8th 1833* (MS), 22 June 1831, Limerick Archives. L/MP/1/1

12 *Limerick Chronicle*, 21 September 1831.

13 *Rate Books*, St. Michael's Parish Commissioners, Sept. 1835-March 1836, Sept. 1837 - March 1838, Limerick Archives.

14 Mathew Barrington's Share Certificate No. 49 is reproduced in Tierney, Mark 'The Barringtons and the Pery Square Tontine Company', *The Old Limerick Journal - Barrington's Edition* No. 24, Winter 1988, Kemmy, Jim ed., p. 44.

15 Articles II, III, IV, V & XXIV, *The Charter Party; or, Articles of Agreement of the Pery Square Tontine Company of the City of Limerick 11 August 1840*, printed by George M'Kern & Sons, George Street, Limerick, 1841, pp. 4-7, 18. Copy in Limerick Civic Trust Archives.

16 ibid. Article XV, pp. 12-13.

17 ibid. Schedule of Shares annexed to the Articles of Agreement.

18 *Limerick Chronicle*, 14 January 1835.

19 *Limerick Chronicle*, 25 February 1835.

20 *The Charter Party; or, Articles of Agreement of the Pery Square Tontine Company of the City of Limerick*, p. 3.

21 ibid. Article V, pp. 6-7.

22 McMahon, James *The Pery Square Tontine*, Limerick Civic Trust, Limerick, 1999.

23 Schedule of Shares annexed to *The Charter Party; or, Articles of Agreement of the Pery Square Tontine Company of the City of Limerick*.

24 *The Records of the Pery Square Tontine Company 1880-1914*, Copy in Limerick Civic Trust Archives; McMahon *op. cit.*

25 *Limerick Chronicle* 3 August 1915; A letter to *The Daily Telegraph* dated 8 September (year not known) from James Pain of Keswick Road, Putney, London recalling his boat journey from London to Cork in March 1836 and handing a letter to a Lieutenant Richard Roberts who subsequently became Captain of the *President,* a ship that floundered. Photocopy of letter is in James McMahon's 'James Pain' file, Limerick Civic Trust Archives.

26 Schedule of Shares annexed to *The Charter Party; or, Articles of Agreement of the Pery Square Tontine Company of the City of Limerick.*

27 *The Records of the Pery Square Tontine Company 1880-1914,* copy in Limerick Civic Trust Archives.

28 *Limerick Chronicle*, 3 August 1915. A son of James Henry Pain, Richard Pain, had an address at 7 Fairfax Road, Hampstead, London.

29 Daniel Barrington is described as 'the Agent for the Earl of Limerick' in the 29 March 1833 minutes of St. Michael's Parish Commissioners *Proceedings and Orders of the Commissioners for Improving the Parish of St. Michael's, Commencing April 12th 1819 and Ending April 8th 1833*, Limerick Archives Office.

30 Schedule of shares *The Charter Party* etc.

31 Indenture of Lease, dated 31 May 1831, of 'Part of the Lands of South Priors Land at Pery Square for lives renewal' from the Earl of Limerick to Joseph Barrington, Barrington Papers, Glenstal Abbey.

32 Tierney, Mark 'Mathew Barrington 1788-1861', *The Old Limerick Journal – Barrington's Edition* No. 24, Winter 1988, Kemmy, Jim ed., Limerick, 1988.

33 Tierney, Mark 'The Mont de Piété', *The Old Limerick Journal – Barrington's Edition* No. 24, Winter 1988, Kemmy, Jim ed., Limerick, 1988.

34 Tierney, Mark & Cornforth, John 'Glenstal Castle', *Country Life*, 3 October 1974; Reprinted *The Old Limerick Journal – Barrington's Edition* No. 24, Winter 1988, Kemmy, Jim ed., Limerick, 1988.

35 The St. Michael's Parish *Rate Book March 1840 – September 1840* (Limerick Archives) records that the rateable value of Daniel Barrington's 'house and office' was £100. The other five premises were rated simply as houses, No. 6 at £85 and Nos. 2-4 at £80. The six monthly rate collected from these houses was: No. 1 £5 12 6d; No. 6 £4 15s 7 1/2d; Nos. 2-4 £4 10s 0d.

36 St. Michael's Parish *Rate Book March 1842 – Sept. 1842; March 1844 – Sept. 1844; Sept. 1846 – March 1847*, Limerick Archives.

37 Colvin, H. *A Biographical Dictionary of British Architects 1600-1840* 3rd Edition, Yale University Press, New Haven & London, 1995, s.v. 'Wilds, Amon Henry'.

38 *Limerick Chronicle*, 20 November 1834, 14 January 1835.

39 *Limerick Chronicle*, 25 February 1835.

40 *Limerick Chronicle*, 29 July 1835.

41 *Limerick Chronicle*, 3 March 1838, 21 April 1838.

42 Notice dated 10 January 1835 placed in the *Limerick Chronicle* by the Pery Square Tontine Company.

43 McMahon *op. cit.*

44 *Limerick Chronicle,* 21 May 1836.

45 *Limerick Chronicle,* 10 August 1836.

46*Limerick Chronicle*, 28 April 1838.

47 Advertisement dated 15 August 1838 placed in the *Limerick Chronicle.*

48 McMahon *op. cit.*

49 ibid.

50 St. Michael's Parish Rate Book *March 1840 – September 1840*, Limerick Archives.

51 *Proceedings and Orders of the Commissioners for Improving the Parish of St. Michael's, Commencing April 12th 1819 and Ending April 8th 1833*, 17 February 1825, Limerick Archives.

52 Homer *The Iliad*, Book 19, Lines 430-60, translated by Robert Fagles, Viking Penguin, 1990.

53 *Limerick Chronicle*, Wednesday 6 March 1844 on the occasion of the opening of the new market on Merchant's Quay the previous day. Although known as the Potato Market, this new facility was described by the *Limerick Chronicle* as 'a handsome new root market' that sold the 'produce of the market gardens of the suburbs.' 1827 map of Limerick City published in Fitzgerald *op. cit.*

54 *Limerick Chronicle*, 25 June 1830; *Limerick Reporter and Tipperary Vindicator*, 2 June 1840; Lee, David 'The Food Riots of 1830 and 1840' *Made in Limerick*, Vol. I, Lee, David & Jacobs, Debbie eds., Limerick Civic Trust, Limerick, 2003.

55 Clements, Nat 'Restoration of Marble Hall and Staircase at No. 2 Pery Square'. *Georgian Limerick* Vol. II, Lee, David & Gonzalez, Christine eds., Limerick Civic Trust, Limerick, 2000.

56 Roche, Nessa 'Limerick Georgian Windows', Lee & Gonzalez op. cit.

57 *Deane's Limerick Almanack, Directory and Advertiser for 1838*, p. 57.

58 9 George Street is presently (2005) the premises of Easons book shop.

59 *Ellen O'Callaghan Diary 1838-9* (MS.), Limerick Civic Trust Archives.

60 Crowe, Catriona 'Reviving Limerick's Georgian Heritage: The Restoration Project at No. 2 Pery Square', Lee & Gonzalez *op. cit.*

61 Ó hEocha, Séamus 'Plasterwork Restoration at No. 2 Pery Square', Lee & Gonzalez *op. cit.*

62 For an informative room by room guide to No. 2 Pery Square see Leonard, Denis M. *The Georgian House & Garden: No 2 Pery Square, Tontine Buildings, Limerick*, Limerick Civic Trust, Limerick, 2003.

63 Clements, Nat 'Restoration of Marble Hall and Staircase at No. 2 Pery Square', Lee & Gonzalez, *op. cit.*

64 Jupp, Belinda 'The Georgian Garden at No. 2 Pery Square', Lee & Gonzalez *op. cit.*

CHAPTER SEVENTEEN

A NASTY, DANGEROUS AND BAD BRIDGE

The period from the mid-1820s to the mid-'40s saw an impressive burst of activity as regards bridge building in Limerick as the city successfully, if belatedly, came to grips with solving the infrastructural problems created by a sustained period of economic prosperity, population expansion and urban growth that had taken place since the mid-eighteenth century. Besides the construction of the Pain brothers' Athlunkard (1830) and Baal's (1831) bridges, other key infrastructural projects included the erection (1824-35) of Wellesley (Sarsfield) Bridge over the River Shannon improving greatly access to the agricultural hinterland of south-east Clare.

The architect was Alexander Nimmo who modelled his elegant design on the Pont Neuilly in Paris.[1] Nimmo, a civil engineer of Scottish extraction living in Ireland, is very much an unsung hero for his work in improving the road and infrastructural network of the country. His contribution was quite impressive, during his short career as an engineer (he died in 1832 aged 49) and he constructed many roads including those between Kenmare and Killarney and Glengarriff and Killarney, as well as the first road between Galway and Clifden. Nimmo was responsible for numerous piers and harbours and was also involved in the laying down of some early railway lines.[2]

Wellesley Bridge bypassed the traditional route with Clare through Thomondgate and Englishtown enabling direct access to be opened to the quays, warehouses, shops and residential quarters of Newtown Pery. A new approach road, the Ennis Road, was laid down and visitors travelling from the Clare/Galway direction could now form a favourable opinion of the city as they passed over one of the most elegant bridges in Ireland. Of five elliptical arches, each of 70 feet (21.3 metres) in span and a rise of 8 feet 6 inches (2.6 metres),[3] Wellesley is attractively built with limestone ashlar; the bridge features balustraded parapets and cutwaters whose tops are carved to resemble sea shells. As with the construction of Athlunkard Bridge, Wellesley Bridge opened up new opportunities for the wealthy to build villas and retreats in the nearby countryside removed from the bustle of the city, yet located within accessible carriage distance of the business houses and social amenities of Limerick. The leafy country suburb of the North Circular Road became a favoured location for merchants' villas and gentlemans' houses.

Old Thomond Bridge

With the opening of Wellesley Bridge in the summer of 1835 the opportunity now arose to replace Thomond Bridge, a structure of fourteenth century origin.[4] Twenty-one years had elapsed since James Pain had first surveyed the bridge in 1814 and drew up a proposal for a replacement. His report in 1816 on the condition of the old bridge drew the attention of Limerick Corporation to

Old Thomond Bridge, Limerick.

the fact that the arches were 'cracked' and the 'piers undermined'.[5] With the passing of the years the condition of Thomond Bridge had further deteriorated, it being described on one occasion as 'a nasty, dangerous and bad bridge'[6] In the winter of 1833, as a result of high and continued floods, part of the bridge had fallen in, the Corporation having to allocate £500 for repairs and to build a wooden platform across the broken arch in order to permit traffic to cross over.[7] When civil engineer W.H. Owen examined the bridge he found it to be,

> 'in a very bad state, worse than any bridge he ever saw; a portion of one of the arches had fallen down; those arches particularly were very unsafe; considered it necessary for public safety that it [Thomond Bridge] should be removed.'[8]

Following the temporary repairs undertaken in 1834 James Pain and his brother carried out an inspection of the 600 year old structure and declared in their report to the Mayor that 'it would be a complete waste of money to attempt to repair the bridge thoroughly, as it could be built anew for a very little more than it would require for a good and efficient repair.'[9] Following up this report the Common Council of the Corporation decided that a new bridge had to be built. Jacob Owen, an engineer employed by the Board of Works and father to W.H. Owen, travelled to Limerick to investigate if such a project was justified. He stated that in June 1834 he examined Thomond Bridge in conjunction with 'Mr. Pain, the Engineer, employed by the Corporation' and came to the conclusion that the structure was 'in a very ruinous and unsafe state, so that any efficient repair, would be quite impracticable . . . I do not therefore hesitate in concurring in the opinion given by Mr. Pain, that a new bridge is indispensably necessary.'[10]

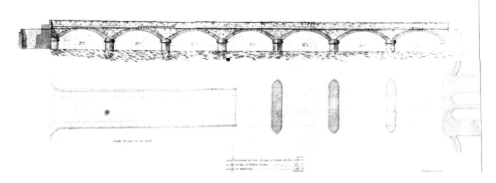

Plan and elevation (1837) of Thomond Bridge showing the old bridge in dotted lines.

The Pain brothers were given the contract for the new bridge by Limerick Corporation without any public tendering procedure taking place, articles of agreement being executed in January 1836.[11] It was estimated that the project would cost £12,139, the breakdown of costs being,

'For the Bridge	£8,709
For the Walls and Fences, and to complete the approaches	£830
For purchasing the buildings necessary to be taken down on both sides of the river and widen the streets, about	£2,500'[12]

To fund construction the Board of Works gave Limerick Corporation a loan of £9,000 at 4% interest.[13] Since the new bridge was to be double the width of the old one, increasing from 17 feet (5.2 metres) at its widest between parapets[14] to a generous and uniform width of 36 feet[15] (11 metres) the Castle Street approach had to be widened to match the bridge, the street being very narrow and only 21 feet (6.4 metres) wide.[16] At that time Castle Street was lined with two rows of houses, one of them built under the curtain wall and towers of King John's Castle - some of these houses were owned by Sir David Roche - while on the opposite side of the road a number of houses were owned by William Glover. Since some of these buildings had to be purchased and demolished to accommodate a wider street, James Pain, with over £2,000 in hand to buy land and build roads,[17] entered into negotiations with property owners during the course of 1836-7. In the event only the houses under the Castle were purchased and Sir David Roche generously compensated, leaving his rival William Glover sorely disappointed in not having sold his houses.[18]

Land and buildings were also purchased on the Thomond side of the river as a new, wide approach from the Clare direction was required. Up to that time the road took a sharp turn to the right after passing over the bridge, turning left after some 70 metres. This road, known as Thomond Gate today, meeting what is now High Road several hundred metres further on. When James Pain laid down his new road he bypassed Thomond Gate.[19]

A Catalogue of Woes

Thomond Bridge was to be a decidedly 'unlucky' bridge for James Pain as he not only encountered a series of difficulties and delays but also made several errors of judgement that did not reflect well on his professional conduct. Things went awry on the very first day of demolition work on the old bridge when, very early on the morning of 2 May 1836, the stonework of two of the arches was thrown into the water under the direction of the foreman. Apparently he had received no such instruction from the architect to do so. The problem with tumbling the masonry into the river was that the stones now had to taken out as the Pain brothers were bound under the terms of their contract to ensure that the waterways and channels between the piers were kept clear and uncongested. James now had to employ men at his own expense to remove the rubble from the river bed,[20] a labourious, time-consuming task that could only be done at certain times of the tide during the summer building season when the river was not in flood. For bridges the building season in Ireland commenced in April/May continuing until the autumn.

It could be argued that James, as the man on the spot in Limerick, should have given clear and definite instructions to the foreman as to the proper procedure for demolishing the bridge and to have had sufficient experience in the building trade not to make assumptions. Presumably the architect assumed that the foreman knew his business and therefore did not need to be informed. It was a costly assumption. There was another procedure for removing the stonework rather than simply tumbling the material into the river, a procedure known as 'centering' that allowed the stones to be removed one by one and carted off. Centering is a traditional technique used in building arches whereby a wooden frame supported by props is first built, over which the arch is laid. Demolishing a bridge by centering is the same procedure, but in reverse: first construct the wooden frame and then remove the stones.[21]

As it was, the stones of the two fallen arches had to be manually removed from the river bed, the labourers employed on this task working completely naked. This was according to an eyewitness, a William Goss, a nailer from Castle Street who recalled four years, during the course of a civil action taken against Limerick Corporation that he 'saw men naked diving for stones; they had no drawers but wore them in the summer following.' Another witness in the same case, a Mr. John Hodge, who appears to have been a lay preacher, recollected that he also saw 'naked people diving there; for a year and a half they brought up stones.' Mr. Hodge, in his account, said that he went to the foreman and said he would complain if the men did not get flannel dresses; they did so, but some of the men kept them at home.[22]

With the sudden demolition of the arches on the morning of 2 May 1836 a serious problem immediately arose for the many thousands of country people and residents of Englishtown and Thomondgate who regularly used Thomond Bridge to pursue business or pleasure in the course of their daily lives. Work on tearing down the old bridge had commenced without first putting in place a temporary wooden footbridge over the river to accommodate pedestrian traffic. This made a lot of people extremely angry, the least part of it was that anyone wanting to cross between Thomondgate and Englishtown now had to traipse all the way down to Wellesley Bridge for a journey that normally took less than a minute. The real difficulty for a lot of poor people was that Wellesley Bridge was a toll bridge, while Thomond Bridge at that time was toll free. Everything passing over Wellesley, from stage coaches to donkey carts, from flocks of lambs to foot passengers, was liable for a toll. According to a schedule of toll charges published in 1856 by the Limerick Harbour Commissioners, a single toll charge was to be levied on vehicles etc. if they were passing over the bridge and returning the same day, 'with the exception of Foot Passengers who are to pay both coming and going . . . For every Passenger passing over said Bridge, the sum of One Halfpenny, for each and every time passing.'[23] Which was all very well if one had money, but for a poor person, of which there were so many in Limerick, it naturally posed a serious problem when one considers that, at the time, labourers may have only received six pence a day in wages and there was absolutely no social security to cater for the unemployed, sick and elderly.

1840 Ordnance Survey showing new Thomond Bridge and temporary wooden bridge.

This disregard for the welfare of others in not providing a temporary crossing does display a certain arrogance on the part of Limerick Corporation and James Pain who came in for severe criticism. It was not as if the matter had not been publicly aired beforehand and the problems not foreseen, since at a meeting of the Court of D'Oyer Hundred held in the summer of 1834 this very issue was discussed. The Court of D'Oyer Hundred was a gathering of all the Freemen of the City which met on the day following one of the four quarterly meetings of the Common Council of Limerick Corporation to confirm and approve Corporate acts. Although an ancient democratic body, from the mid-eighteenth century the 'Corrupt Corporation' had allowed the Court to fall into disuse until obliged to re-establish it in 1823 under the Limerick Regulation Act.[24] According to a detailed report of the meeting carried in the *Limerick Chronicle* of 2 July 1834, following the passing of resolutions authorising the building of a new bridge,

> 'Captain Kane suggested that it would be well to erect a bridge of timber for the accommodation of the poor persons in the neighbourhood of Thomond Bridge who would be much inconvenienced by paying the toll which would be chargeable for passing the Wellesley bridge.

> 'Mr. Paine stated that he could not undertake to erect such a bridge as would be necessary for the accommodation of the vast number of persons who passed that bridge for a sum less than £500.

> 'Captain Kane - It would be a sum well applied.

> 'It was finally agreed that that the sum should be voted for the temporary bridge.

312

> 'Mr. Paine stated that he only waited the confirmation of the Court of D'Oyer Hundred before he commenced the preparation of stone for the bridge; and that he purposed commencing to take down the old stone one in the spring.'

In the event, Wellesley Bridge was not to be opened until the summer of 1835 and commencement of the Thomond Bridge project had to be deferred until May the following year. So the Messrs. Pain had almost two years to make the appropriate arrangements. The inconvenience and injustice of not providing a temporary bridge was not only felt by the poor, for at a Vestry meeting held in St. Mary's Cathedral on Monday 23 May 1836 pointed reference was made to the commitment made by the contractor that he would not disturb the old bridge until he had provided a temporary foot bridge. An angry argument then ensued and it was finally agreed by the Vestry 'to see Mr. Pain on the subject, but that gentleman being from home, the matter stands over.'[25]

Those dependent on Thomond Bridge had clearly been badly catered for. Faced with mounting criticism Limerick Corporation was obliged to provide, free of charge, three 'large ferry-boats' to carry passengers over the Shannon, the service to run from five in the morning until nine at night.[26] Not a satisfactory solution given the tidal nature of the river at that point and the strength of water flow. At the beginning of July it was finally announced that Hill & Clements had been contracted to build a temporary bridge from Brown's Quay on the Thomondgate shore to Franklin's Quay on King's Island.[27] Opened in September 1836, and known as 'Gibson's Bridge',[28] the wooden stucture was some 130 metres upstream from Thomond Bridge.[29] A period of four and a half months haved elapsed since demolition work began in May.

Arch Collapses ███████████████████████████████████████

Although the foundation stone for the new bridge was laid down in 1836 when Samuel Lewis went to print with his *Topographical Dictionary* in 1837 the old medieval structure was still 'being taken down.'[30] During the course of 1837 a number of civil engineering problems arose relating to the geology of the river bed and the fact that difficulty was encountered in building a coffer-dam, a water-tight enclosure to enable work to be carried out below the waterline on bridges, to enable inspection of the bed. The fact that the building seasons of both 1837 and 1838 were very bad due to appalling weather and river floods did not help matters.[31] These delays causing some carping criticism,

> 'Some dissatisfaction is apparent at the slow progress of Thomond Bridge, upon the rebuilding of which it is a matter of complaint that more workmen are not called in. This certainly is the season most favourable for the undertaking, and when additional hands may be had with facility.'[32]

But these are but the typical trips and problems encountered by those engaged in the building trade. Progress was being made despite the difficulties and by October 1838 all the piers of the new bridge were laid and the last archway turned.[33] A far more serious problem arose for the architect on Friday 7 June 1839 when the third arch of the new bridge fell asunder and the whole of the masonry work disappeared under the water in a few seconds. Three people who had walked over the arch just before the collapse had a very lucky escape. One man was so terrified that he 'absolutely jumped into the river'; fortunately, being a good swimmer he gained the shore. A neighbouring arch was also damaged and 'a dangerous settlement' was visible in the masonry,[34] resulting in this arch having to be dismantled.[35] Again James Pain had to stand the economic loss of removing the masonry of the fallen arch from the river-bed in addition to the extra costs he incurred in rebuilding the two arches. The circumstances surrounding the accident formed part of a civil action taken by a local resident against Limerick Corporation in July the following year.

313

Nothing daunted, James Pain soldiered on (his brother George Richard had died in December 1838), the local press optimistically reporting in July 1839 that the bridge would be passable for pedestrians in a few months time.[36] It was not until May of the following year that the new bridge was to be finally open to horses and carriages,[37] the *Limerick Chronicle* reporting on Wednesday 2 June 1840,

> 'The Limerick and Ennis Coach, yesterday for the first time, Drove over the new Thomond Bridge by Mary Street thus avoiding the toll of £50 a year by the Wellesley Bridge. The improvements apparent in the above quarter of the city, which this handsome new bridge, toll free, must greatly enhance, all gratifying to all interested in the welfare of Limerick.'

Architectural Context

Leaving aside James Pain's woes for the moment, one should consider the architectural merits of the Pain brothers' design. In styling Thomond Bridge the Pain brothers were mindful of its architectural backdrop when viewed from the Thomond shore. To the right of the bridge stands the curtain wall and towers of thirteenth century King John's Castle. To the left of the bridge a 30 metre stretch of the original town wall stands facing the river, ending at a small semicircular tower.[38] Built of limestone rubble masonary, this surviving section of Englishtown's mediaeval defences runs along Vincent Place forming the western wall of St. Munchin's terraced churchyard, the pinnacles and crenellated tower of this church rising majestically over the entire scene. To the left of St. Munchin's can be seen the Tudor-Gothic façade of the Pain brothers' Villiers' Alms House. It is in this part of Limerick that the injunction *Si monumentum requiris, circumspice!* [39] (If you seek his monument, Look About!) applies to both brothers.

314

Conscious of the need to make the new bridge harmonious with its surroundings, the outer faces of the limestone masonry blocks have been rough cut to give the structure a rusticated appearance. This contrives to produce a sense of durability, strength and venerable age, thereby integrating Thomond Bridge into its architectural backdrop. The rusticated riverside wall running along Verdant Place is a continuation of the masonry work of the bridge. It is this architectural ensemble, when viewed from Clancy Strand, that provides Limerick with its characteristic trademark image, being repeatedly used in publicity stills, film and artwork. Limerick limestone is here seen at its picturesque best, especially at low tide with the Shannon rushing and tumbling over the rugged rocks of the Curraghgower Falls.

View of Thomond Bridge, its toll-house and King John's Castle, Limerick. St. Munchin's Church stands in the background.

Associated with the bridge is the Gothick toll-house on Castle Street with its battlemented parapet, crenellated bartizans and blank arrow slits; the design and scale making it a playful, toy-box fortification rather than a serious attempt to imitate the Castle's architectural style or make it compatible with the architecture of the bridge. Although traditionally attributed to the Pain brothers' this may not be so. When they designed the new bridge for Limerick Corporation, and when it was opened in 1840, it was toll-free; so there was absolutely no need to enter into the expense of building a toll-house when the whole project was completed for a very modest and economical sum of just over £12,000. When Charles Vereker, 2nd Lord Gort and political boss of Limerick Corporation, spoke of the merits of Thomond Bridge at a meeting of the Court of D'Oyer Hundred on Tuesday 13 October 1840 he made no mention of a toll-house. As regards the scenic improvements brought about by the construction of the bridge. Vereker only mentions that with the removal of the row of houses standing immediately in front of King John's Castle the locality is improved by throwing 'open those ancient castles and towers.'[40] It was only after the abolition of Limerick Corporation in 1841 and its replacement with the Reformed Corporation that there is talk of introducing tolls. At a meeting of the new Town Council in August 1843 a committee recommended that 2 October be fixed as the date for letting the tolls and that 'the three Bridges, Wellesley, Thomondgate and Athlunkard be set up and sold in one lot.'[41] At a Town Council meeting held on 16 September 1845 it was agreed to pay James Pain £2,218 17s 6d 'for erecting a toll-house at Thomond-bridge, improving the passages and constructing slips.'[42]

Thomond Bridge consists of five segmental arches of 50 feet (15.2 metres) span and two flanking arches of 40 feet (12.2 metres). Whereas the medieval bridge measured only 17 feet (5.2 metres) between parapets at its maximum width, the new bridge had 36 feet (11 metres),[43] a substantial improvement that still serves the needs of modern traffic today. Resolute cutwaters direct the flow of the river, reducing pressure on the bridge when the Shannon is in flood as well as serving to protect the structure from floating debris.

Toll-house, Thomond Bridge, Limerick.

James Pain's Reputation Assailed

While the new bridge was a great boon and benefit to the people and trade of Limerick, not everyone was entirely happy. Certainly not William Glover, a property owner with premises on Castle Street who took a civil case in July 1840 during the Limerick Assizes against the Mayor and Limerick Corporation, seeking compensation for loss of rents arising from the Thomond Bridge works. The case was heard in the County Courthouse on Wednesday and Thursday 22 and 23 July.[44]

The plaintiff made a number of complaints, including direct criticism of the professionalism of James Pain. Glover claimed that with the closure of the bridge the trade in Castle Street had been so badly affected that two of his long-standing tenants, a blacksmith and a carpenter by trade, had moved elsewhere and the rental value of his six houses had declined. Concerning James Pain, Glover alleged that the architect/contractor was so incompetent in the performance of his duties as to delay the completion of the works, thereby causing further injury to the plaintiff's interests. There were many aspects to this case, but the main thrust of the complaint against James Pain was two-fold: (1) he wasted a considerable amount of time by demolishing the old bridge in an inappropriate manner, and (2) he was negligent during the construction of the new bridge causing an arch to collapse, thereby further delaying completion of the project.[45]

Counsel for the defendant, Limerick Corporation, argued in their rebuttal that the claim for compensation was mischievous, owing to the fact that when James Pain was buying up sites in Castle Street in 1836-7 to allow for the widening of the road William Glover had been 'exceedingly anxious' to sell his properties and premises. However, he was to be disappointed in his desire as the Corporation bought the houses on the opposite side of the road, some owned by Sir David Roche, and not Glover's. All of the plaintiff's allegations and claims therefore, including the contention that the Corporation had no legal entitlement to remove the old bridge in the first place (!), stemmed from this disappointment. The replacement of the old bridge was in the public interest, the defendant's Counsel argued, especially because it was 'exceedingly dangerous and narrow' and was 'a nasty, dangerous and bad bridge.' Glover's compensation claim was dubbed a 'fanciful case' and the jury strongly advised to refuse the plaintiff's suit for damages.[46]

One of the points raised by William Glover was that when demolition began in May 1836 James Pain allowed the masonry of two arches of the old bridge to be 'tripped' into the water rather than removed by centering. However, in his testimony to the Court, William Henshaw Owen, the superintending Engineer on the project, refuted this particular complaint against the professionalism of the Messrs. Pain. Owen stated that it was his clear recollection that on the morning of 2 May 1836 two arches were indeed thrown into the river but 'it was done by the foreman without Mr. Paine's orders.' The witness recalled 'scolding the foreman' for what he had done and that after that incident all the other arches were removed by centering. Nor was the progress of the works retarded in any way by this 'tripping', a phrase Owen stated that he had not encountered before as an engineer. If there was a delay in setting down a pier of the new bridge on the site where the two arches had been tumbled, it did not amount to a month and that was of no great consequence in a construction project of that size when twelve months had been allocated to removing the old structure. Besides, Owen stated, it was not in the architect's interests to throw any part of the bridge into the water as he would be then obliged to stand the 'great expense' of removing the stones from the river bed.[47]

The Sting for Pain

The sting for James Pain in Owen's testimony came when the engineer questioned the technique employed in the construction of the new arches, one of which had fallen into the river in June 1839 and another so unsettled that it had to be taken down. This was clearly a major setback and it took five or six months work to get the arches back to the condition they were in before the accident. According to Owen, he had on more than one occasion brought the architect's attention to the fact that the arches were being built without first erecting spandrel walls and that this an incorrect procedure and 'injudicious' when building a bridge of that size. The expert witness attributed the collapse of the arch to the fact that the spandrel walls were not filled in.[48] A spandrel is the almost triangular section of a bridge between the curves of arches, and between the curve of an arch and the ends of a bridge. A spandrel wall is built on the curve of an arch, filling in the spandrel. Presumably Owen was advising Pain that it was necessary to insert these walls as construction progressed so as to maintain the various pressures exerted on an arch in equilibrium.

318

Pain had told Owen at the time that the building of spandrel walls was not in his contract, but the clear implication in Owen's testimony is that the architect should not have continued erecting arches without making the arrangements to have spandrel walls inserted, and if the arch collapsed then it was Pain's fault for he went against the advice of a qualified civil engineer as to the correct procedure for building the arches. One can imagine the public embarrassment this evidence caused to James Pain and the possible damage to his reputation it engendered in the minds of that small circle of men in Munster and the Board of Works in Dublin whose job it was to commission and finance public works. The case certainly did not pass the notice of Pain's professional peers, for not only did W. H. Owen, Limerick architect and engineer, attend the case as an expert witness, so also did John Walker, a Co. Limerick civil engineer, and William Wallace, a well known Limerick City builder and architect, these two gentlemen supportive of the plaintiff. For those not in attendance, the entire case was reported in great detail by the local press.[49]

When the jury withdrew to consider its verdict Counsel for Limerick Corporation made several observations to the Judge, including the telling point that not only was the Corporation not responsible for the 'unskillfulness of the workmen' employed on the construction site, the Corporation were also 'not liable for the unskilful conduct of Mr. Pain.' In the event, the jury found for the plaintiff, but only awarded him £40 damages and 6d costs.[50] It appears that the jury made the award 'in consequence of the unexpected delay that occurred in throwing down the bridge' according to a Captain Kane who had spoken to some members of the jury.[51]

Spirited Defense

There was much to say in favour of James Pain's handling of the Thomond Bridge scheme. Despite the number of delays and difficulties that the contractor had encountered, the time taken to remove a sizable stone bridge and replace it with a new one was exactly four years whereas Wellesley had taken eleven. On the question of value for money, Thomond Bridge itself was built for a very modest £9,000 while Wellesley cost considerably more and was to prove a burden of debt on Limerick Harbour Commissioners for many years to come. According to Charles Vereker, 2nd Lord Gort, Wellesley cost 'to my certain knowledge £140,000'[52] although £89,061 is the figure quoted by Lenihan.[53]

Lord Gort, at a meeting of the Court of D'Oyer Hundred held on Tuesday 13 October 1840, made a very spirited defense of his friend's professional conduct and integrity. Referring to the collapse of the arch, Lord Gort described it as an accident, an Act of Providence brought about by a flood,

319

> 'But did Mr. Pain apply to the public for any remuneration on account of it? No, he never did any such thing, but he built up his bridge in a workmanlike manner creditable to himself, to the Board of Works, to the Corporation . . . without asking one farthing more than his regular contract - (Hear, hear). I say that instead of talking of his work having fallen down he should be pitied for his loss of it, and I take this opportunity of expressing my opinion that instead of finding fault with Mr. Pain for having delayed the completion of the work, he is entitled to the greatest credit for having finished it so expeditiously under the untoward circumstances in which he was placed. - (Hear, hear).[54]

At the same meeting James Pain defended his professional conduct, stating that the accident was caused by 'my pushing forward the work at an inconvenient time, but so as to convenience the public by completing it as soon as possible.' Unfortunately a flood, in conjunction with a disturbance to the river's water flow caused by two river mills, Curragour and the Golden Mills, caused the accident. The Mills should have been removed, according to Pain, 'by the Commissioners.'. To which William Glover's son, who was also present at the meeting, replied,

> 'Mr. Owen swore quite the contrary; he swore it was in consequence of your not building spandril [sic] walls as he recommended you. We have his evidence on record . . . '[55]

These critical remarks of the architect's conduct concluding the newspaper report.

James Pain appears to have been plagued by persons associated with Castle Street, as two months earlier on the night of Sunday 22 August a man had come up to the caretaker of Pain's builders' yard near Thomond Bridge and informed him that he had seen some people stealing stone flags at the other side of the bridge. The night watchman left his post and upon returning found that iron bars left in the yard had been stolen. The police were notified and early next morning Sergeant Reidy found the stolen bars in a forge in Castle Street, the alleged culprit being taken into custody.[56] James may be forgiven if he thought that the Gods of Cruel Fate had declared open season on him, for his run of bad luck with Thomond Bridge was to be further compounded when in 1842 Limerick Corporation was finally abolished - the body owing a debt of £1,855 to the architect for his work on the approaches.[57] He would now have to apply to the new Reformed Corporation for payment.

Note ██

320

When James Pain surveyed old Thomond Bridge in 1814 he proposed to rest the piers of a new bridge on top of those of the old. This was apparently the intention of the Pain brothers when they began preparations in the 1830s for building the new bridge. However, when W. H. Owen, the civil engineer on the project, inspected the site he discovered that this procedure was 'in a great measure inexpedient.' (*Limerick Chronicle* 13 July 1842). The 1837 plan and elevation for the new bridge, which was superimposed on the plan and elevation of the old structure, shows that the new piers do not conform to the position of the old ones on that half of the bridge closest to Castle Street.

Endnotes

1 Lenihan, Maurice *Limerick; Its History and Antiquities*, 1866, p. 470.

2 Somerville-Large, Peter *The Grand Irish Tour*, Hamish Hamilton, London, 1982, pp. 119-20.

3 Cox, R. C. & Gould, M.H. *Civil Engineering Heritage Ireland*, published by the Institution of Civil Engineers and the Institution of Civil Engineers in Ireland, Thomas Telford Publications, London, 1998, p. 248.

4 Hodkinson, Brian 'Old Thomond Bridge' to be published in a forthcoming edition of the *North Munster Antiquarian Journal*.

5 Barry, J.G. 'Old Limerick Bridges', *Journal of the North Munster Archaeological Society* Vol. 1, 1909-11, Limerick, p.13.

6 *Limerick Chronicle*, 2 July 1840.

7 *Limerick Chronicle*, 2 July 1834.

8*Limerick Chronicle*, 25 July 1840.

9 Limerick Chronicle, 2 July 1834.

10 A report by Jacob Owen, Civil Engineer, on the condition of Thomond Bridge, dated Dublin 16 June 1834, published in *Limerick Chronicle*, 2 July 1834.

11 *Limerick Chronicle*, 6 January 1836.The plaque on Thomond Bridge credits both James and George Richard Pain as the architects of Thomond Bridge.

12 *Limerick Chronicle*, 2 July 1834.

13 ibid.

14 Barry *op. cit.* p. 12.

15 Cox *op. cit.* p. 247.

16 *Limerick Chronicle*, 25 July 1840.

17 The figure available in January 1836 for such purposes being £2,172 0s 8d, *Limerick Chronicle*, 6 January 1836.

18 ibid.

19 The plaque on the bridge credits both George Richard and James with the architectural work.

20 *Limerick Chronicle*, 25 July 1840.

21 ibid.

22 *Limerick Chronicle*, 25 July 1840.

23 *Wellesley Bridge Toll Charges 1856*, Limerick Museum (LM1992.158). Published in *Made in Limerick* Vol. I, Lee, David & Jacobs, Debbie eds., Limerick Civic Trust, 2003, p. 104.

24 *Municipal Corporations in Ireland, Report on the County of the City of Limerick made by the Irish Corporation Commissioners following an Inquiry held in Limerick from 26th September to 11th October, 1833*, Section 70 'Court of D'Oyer Hundred'.

25 *Limerick Chronicle*, 25 May 1836.

26 *Limerick Chronicle*, 1 June 1836.

27 *Limerick Chronicle*, 2 July 1836.'

28 *Limerick Chronicle*, 14 & 17 September 1836.

29 1840 Ordnance Survey, City of Limerick, Sheet 10.
30 Lewis II, p. 268.
31 *Limerick Chronicle*, 25 July 1840.
32 *Limerick Chronicle*, 16 August 1837.
33 *Limerick Chronicle*, 13 October 1838.
34 *Limerick Chronicle*, Saturday 8 June 1839.
35 *Limerick Chronicle*, 25 July 1840.
36 ibid. 27 July 1839.
37 ibid. 20 May 1840.
38 Thomas, Avril *The Walled Towns of Ireland*, Irish Academic Press, Blackrock, Co. Dublin, 1992, p. 142.
39 Epitaph of English architect Sir Christopher Wren in St. Paul's Cathedral, London.
40 *Limerick Chronicle*, Wednesday 14 October 1840.
41 *Limerick Chronicle*, 16 August 1843.
42 *Limerick Chronicle* Wednesday 17 September 1845.
43 Cox *op. cit.* p. 247.
44 *Limerick Chronicle*, 25 July 1840.
45 ibid.
46 ibid.
47 ibid.
48 ibid.
49 ibid.
50 ibid.
51 *Limerick Chronicle*, 14 October 1840.
52 *Limerick Chronicle*, 14 October 1840.
53 Lenihan *op. cit.* p. 471.
54 *Limerick Chronicle*, 14 October 1840.
55 ibid.
56 *Limerick Chronicle*, 25 August 1840.
57 Lenihan *op. cit.* p. 498.

CHAPTER EIGHTEEN
NEW BROOMS

George Richard Pain died in Cork in 1838 on 26 December[1] aged 45 and was buried in the churchyard of St. Mary Shandon.[2] James, the man of affairs, may have found himself at a disadvantage with the death of his more artistically imaginative brother. It may be pure coincidence, but as a creative architect, and as an architect involved in large scale projects, James developed and flourished during the period 1816-38 when in association with his younger brother. A period that begun with James being awarded his first major independent commission, Limerick's County Gaol, at a time not long after George Richard makes his first appearance in Ireland, and ending with the completion in 1840 of the brothers' joint work on Thomond Bridge After that James seems to have entered a fallow period when no major works can be attributed to him for the rest of his professional career which lasted another thirty-five years until he retired in his mid-nineties. Neither James Pain's obituary, written in December 1877,[3] nor an entry compiled that same year for the *Dictionary of Architecture* when he was still alive,[4] makes any mention of any original works or major assignments carried out after the completion of Thomond Bridge. However, he was not bereft of employment for the rest of his long life as his obituary relates that he continued 'to practice his profession till within the last few years.'[5] A statement supported by various trades directories published in the latter years of his life in which he continued to advertise himself as an architect. *Bassett's Directory* for 1877-8, published in the year of his death, carrying the entry 'Payne James, architect, 17 Glentworth-street'.[6]

New Broom

The saga of woes that was Thomond Bridge may have damaged James's reputation as a civil engineer and architect, undermining his ability to successfully compete for major public works and civil engineering contracts. In the field of church architecture nothing of any great interest seems to have come off the drawing board of his Limerick office since 1838. A number of churches are attributable to James Pain after that date, but these are mostly 'production line' bell-cote churches of no great architectural merit, such as Kilbehenny Church, Co. Limerick,[7] and St. James' at Kilkee, designed 1840[8] and opened 1841.[9] The fact that no Church of Ireland churches are attributable to James after the early 1840s is explained by the fact that in 1843 the posts of the four provincial architects to the Ecclesiastical Commissioners were amalgamated under one sole architect, John Welland being appointed to the position.[10] A new broom sweeps clean, and Welland's design for the new St. John's Church (1843) in John's Square, Limerick is a refreshing change from the Simple Gothic one associates with James Pain. St. John's has door and window arches in the semicircular Norman-Romanesque style and, as opposed to the boxlike structures of Simple Gothic, it has an apse at the East end and aisles on either side of the nave with clerestorey windows featuring in the upper section of the nave wall. The belfry tower at the church's West end is offset to the right, instead of being rigidly central, as was the case with First Fruits churches. Fashionable country house architecture had also moved on from the Picturesque Gothic style with which James had been so familiar since his time with Regency architect John Nash; new, younger architects being willing to cater for Victorian tastes.

Before its demise in 1842 James had acted as architect to Limerick Corporation in matters both large and small. When builders were asked in October 1834 to submit proposals 'for putting in permanent repair the Exchange of this City' they were informed that their work would be 'subject to the Inspection of Mr. Pain.'[11] Thomond Bridge was to prove to be Limerick Corporation's last, and greatest, act in the field of public architecture and it was the Pain brothers who were given the contract without having to go through any tendering process. Charles Vereker, 2nd Lord Gort and political boss of Limerick Corporation, had always proved a great friend and staunch supporter of James, but Vereker died in 1842, the same year that the 'Corrupt Corporation' was abolished and the architect lost a source of reliable patronage. However, he still served as retained architect to the Board of Superintendence of Limerick County Gaol until 1863.

Intense Competition

By the late 1830s and early '40s James was facing far more intense competition from other architects and builders than he had ever experienced when he first came to Limerick. Sir Thomas Deane, an old rival of the Pain brothers in Cork, was being awarded assignments in Limerick including his appointment in 1839 as building contractor for the new Limerick Workhouse on Shelbourne Road[12] and the workhouse in Bruff, Co. Limerick.[13] Other local commissions were picked up by Sir Thomas Deane & Co. in direct competition with James Pain, one example being the submission in May 1837 of tenders to build quays and docks associated with Wellesley Bridge and its legislative Act. The competitors were Deane and ' Mr. Pain and Mr. Wallace of this city and Williams and Son of Dublin, but Sir Thomas Deane's proposal was £,2,000 and upwards under their's [sic]. His immediate contract is for £16,000.'[14] The commission included the construction of a quay behind the Henry Street mansion houses of Lord Limerick and the Bishop (Protestant) of Limerick.[15]

It does appear that in the matter of quays and waterways the Pains were not price competitive, their proposal in 1836 for 'Dock Works, South Quay Walls' being turned down in favour of Messrs. Henry Mullins & McMahon, Dublin.[16] Business interests in Ennis, Co. Clare had long harboured the ambition to build a lock and ship canal from Clare (now Clarecastle) to connect Ennis with the Shannon estuary. Estimates were sought and in April 1838 the *Limerick*

Chronicle briefly reported that James Pain had calculated that the project would cost £20,000 while a Mr. Grantham had forwarded a figure of £16,480. At face value James's estimate was reasonable, but the report in the *Chronicle* drew a strong rebuke in the following day's *Clare Journal,*

> 'There is a far greater difference between the estimates of Mr. Paine and Mr. Grantham, than the reader would calculate upon in this very pithy extract. Mr. Paine's estimate of £20,000 is for a "lock and small canal" to get into the deep water below the present bridge, whereas Mr. Grantham's estimate of £16,480, calculates upon continuing the improvements of the river to within fifty yards of the very centre of the town. There is a vast difference indeed between those estimates, and we expect the Chronicle will state the fact more intelligibly to its readers in the next impression.'[17]

In a competitive field other, younger, architects sought commissions. Men such as W. H. Owen who we met previously as the supervising engineer on the Thomond Bridge construction project. In 1839 he was architect of the Savings Bank [18] on Glentworth Street that took the form of a Grecian Doric temple, one of the best examples of its type in Ireland. With its four fluted, baseless columns, it is one of a number of attractive buildings erected during the 1830s and '40s in the Glentworth Street to Barrington Street district of Newtown Pery. Sir Thomas Deane & Co. were the building contractors for the Savings Bank.[19] William Henshaw Owen also designed Mathew Bridge (1846) located near the Custom House (now the Hunt Museum), replacing a structure known as the New Bridge. The plaque on Mathew Bridge credits 'W. H. Owens [sic], Architect. John Duggan, Builder'. Owen was also involved with Limerick Town Council in drawing up plans and specifications for the new Potato Market on Merchants Quay.[20]

One of the best buildings erected in Limerick in the pre-Famine period was Leamy's School (completed October 1845)[21] on Hartstonge Street. Although Leamy's, with its beautiful Tudor frontage, has traditionally been attributed to Joseph Fogerty of Henry Street, Limerick, contemporary newspaper reports clearly identify William Atkins of Cork as the architect and Fogerty as the builder.[22] William Atkins (1812-87), a former pupil of George Richard Pain and a nephew of George's second wife, Margaret Atkins,[23] had established himself as an architect in Cork and was to be responsible for, among other commissions, Our Lady's Hospital (1847-52), an asylum at Sunday's Well in that city.[24] The Tudor-Revival front elevation of Leamy's School is built in warm red brick with stone dressings and features a central embattled clock tower decorated with tall niches and a cornice enlivened with the heads of grotesque gargoyles. The building also features two oriel windows on the first floor, tall Tudor chimney stacks and a Tudor arch doorway with label hood-mould. Regrettably, only the

Leamy's School, Hartstonge Street, Limerick, in Tudor style.

front section of the building was completed in Tudor-Revival, for there were insufficient funds to carry out Atkin's design for the sides of the building as well as for the provision of canopies and statues that were originally intended to occupy the niches in the clock tower.[25] Tudor was chosen as the most appropriate architecture for the building as that style was considered to exemplify the virtues of education. Built by the Leamy Institution and Philosophical Society the school was intended to provide free education for the poor of the city regardless of religion. Although well supported by Protestant students, it had rarely more than twenty Catholics. In 1887 the Catholic bishop forbade Catholics to attend because of his opposition to the concept of non-denominational 'mixed' education.[26] Eventually Leamy's School came under the control of the Christian Brothers and was made famous in Frank McCourt's *Angela's Ashes*, an account of his Limerick childhood in the 1930s.

Gargoyles on Leamy's School.

Tribute to Departed Worth

By 1840 James Pain had reached the age of 60 and perhaps no longer felt the need to prove himself as an architect on the grand scale. As a builder, as well as an architect, there were various lucrative ways still open to him to make money, as is evident from the following notice that appeared in the *Limerick Chronicle* only four days before George Richard Pain's death,

To Builders and Capitalists.
TOWN OF KILLAOE [*sic*]
SEVERAL eligible LOTS of BUILDING GROUND
can now be had in the best part of this rapidly
improving Town, on lease for 99 years at a fair rent,
by the foot, with good accommodation in the rere.
Also, Sites for Cottages, beautifully situated, com-
manding a view of the Lake, and the Demesne of
Clarisford, and persons in business can have Lots in
the New Street, near the new Court-house, with
Stores in the rere.
Plans of the several proposed Buildings can be seen
by application to Messrs. Pain, Architects, Limerick,
and each Tenant will be bound to conform thereto,
and build within a time to be fixed on. Stephen
Moore, of Killaloe, will show the Premises and Ground Plan.
Timber, Slates, Stones, and Lime, can be had on the Spot.
And to be Let for such term as may be agreed on,
a well situated SLATE QUARRY, on Crag Hill, can
now be entered on; close to the Shannon Navigation
also, a fine site for a Flour and Meal Mill, close to
Killaloe, with a constant supply of water.
Application to be made to Charles Hunt Esq.
Manor House, Tandragee, or Messrs. Pain, Limerick
Dec.15.
(*Limerick Chronicle*, 22 December 1838)

Despite losing his position as one of the leading architects in Munster James Pain continued the family architectural practice with the help, for a period until 1842, of his nephew, James Henry Pain. The son of Henry Pain, he had moved to Ireland in 1836 at the age of 16,[27] to serve his apprenticeship with his architect uncles. In 1840 the young man is recorded as having an address at 'George-street, Limerick.'[28] James Henry Pain returned to England having served his articles marrying a Miss Glossop of Sheffield in 1845. He died aged 95 on 12 July 1915 at his house on Keswick Road, Putney, London.[29]

Another nephew of James Pain was living in his house in Limerick in 1840. This was James Richard Pain,[30] son of recently deceased George Richard Pain. James Richard was only 28 when he died at 'the house of his uncle, in George's-street, Limerick.' in February 1852.[31] A niece, Sarah (Sally), the daughter of G. R. Pain's second marriage to Miss Margaret Atkins, also settled in Limerick, marrying Henry Vereker (the son of Amos and Catherine Vereker[32]) in 1858. Sally and her husband lived at Wellington Villa, Military Road (later O'Connell Avenue), Limerick.

Until 1844 a long standing member of the Limerick office was Henry Whitestone who set up his own practice in Ennis, Co. Limerick in April of that year. In late 1845 Whitestone's plan for a new County Courthouse at Ennis was accepted by Commissioners chosen by the Grand Jury against seventeen other submissions, including those of William Atkins, William Deane and William Tinsley.[33] The courthouse was not erected until 1850.[34]

The early 1840s saw various projects handled by James Pain, including a commission from the City Grand Jury to draw up plans for a new City Courthouse on Merchants Quay.[35] In 1843 the architect generously gave, free of charge, plans for the new Adelaide School built in Bruff, Co. Limerick[36] by Rev. Godfrey Massy and which was opened on 10 July 1845.[37] Named after the Queen Dowager Adelaide (of Saxe-Meiningen), wife of William IV who died in 1837, the school was built to provide children with a Christian (Protestant) education.

James maintained his contacts with Dromoland Castle and in 1842-3 he submitted a number of drawings and plans for proposed improvements to the house to Sir Lucius O'Brien who had inherited the estate on the death of his father, Sir Edward, in 1837. Several of these sketches were signed and dated 'James Pain Jan 1843'.[38] Included among this collection is a sketch for an additional water closet in the house; a plan for the improvement of Sir Lucius's office and a proposal for the improvement of the north front by the addition of a Dining Room[39] (not carried out[40]). Also among the drawings is one dated '9 September 1842' showing elevations of a Gothic Revival chair, one of a set of seats for the Hall at Dromoland.[41] Other sketches in the collection show detailing for flues and chimney shafts.[42]

Some of these designs were executed very shortly afterwards, as in early March 1843 we hear that the Killaloe Marble Works had completed four chimney pieces for Dromoland 'in the purest white marble, and whether as regards design or workmanship, we hesitate not to pronounce fully equal to any executed in the sister kingdom.'[43] James continued to be favoured by the wealthy landed families of Limerick and Clare for house renovations, extensions and other works. In October 1844 the Earl of Clare, Mount Shannon House, Co. Limerick, erected in memory of his mother, the late Anne, Countess

Bridge Street entrance to St. Mary's Cathedral, Limerick.

of Clare 'a beautiful marble monument' in Stradbally Church, Castleconnell. The *Limerick Chronicle* commented that the 'design of this pious tribute to departed worth is by James Pain, Esq. of this city.' This sarcophagus, measuring 6 feet 6 inches (1.98 metres) in height and 5 feet long by 5 feet wide (0.6 metres^2) was described as being of, ' Italian white marble, and the . . . base of jet Galway black, resting upon carved feet. A dove, with extended wings, surmounts the coronet at the top, and the canopy is of exquisite drapery.'[44]

One of the Annoyed

In 1841 James Pain carried out an assignment for St. Mary's Cathedral, Limerick that involved opening up a new entrance to the Cathedral on Bridge Street, also known at the time as Quay Lane. To a design by James Pain[45] the cut-stone archway, completed by the end of October 1841, was described as 'a beautiful, chaste and elegant structure.'[46] Besides the gateway, which is fairly routine work for the period and not particularly attractive, and its cast iron gates the work also included erecting railings set in cut-stone plinths along Bridge Street. The newly enclosed area of the Cathedral grounds were lad out with 'grass plots and gravel walks, diversified by occasional small plantations.'[47]

Some minor controversy attended the awarding of the contract for the supply of gates and railings. Thomas Ahern, a 'Smith in General, and Ironmonmonger' of 13 Catherine Street, placed a notice in the 12 August 1841 edition of the *Limerick Chronicle* implying that he had lost the contract to Harrison Lee because of favouritism, even though Lee's quote was, according to Ahern, £17 over his rival's submission. Thomas Ahern's main complaint was,

> 'Had not I or any other Catholic Smith an equal right to the work of some of the Chapels in the town and country, that Lee got from the Clergy, that did not take his creed into account while reading over his Tender?'

Despite the new entrance there were perils posed to the pious of the Protestant persuasion in passing over from Newtown Pery to St. Mary's Cathedral in Englishtown on a Sunday were quite trying to the patience of Providence, as shown by the following letter to the Editor of the *Limerick Chronicle*,

> Sir - May I take the liberty of directing the attention of the proper authorities to the present filthy and disgraceful state of the passage leading thro' Quay-lane to the new entrance of the Cathedral. By some unaccountable mistake or oversight, the sewer of a dirty bye-lane is allowed to empty itself in the very middle of the street, which, consequently, even in very dry weather, is in a wet and foul condition. Added to this, we have a large pool of water, constantly

330

occupying the hollow of the street between the Cathedral and the New Bridge. This shameful nuisance calls loudly for a remedy, as also the insufferable annoyance occasioned by the crowded state of the New Bridge on Sundays; a number of idle fellows, regularly on that day, occupy the path-way and battlements, from which they are continually squirting tobacco juice (I will not say intentionally) on those who are obliged to take that direction to Church. A small sewer at the Cathedral side of Quay-lane would remedy the former annoyance; and I think a simple notice from our civic authorities would have the same effect with the latter, which would be a great relief to a number of your readers.

I am, Sir &c. &c.

ONE OF THE ANNOYED.

(*Limerick Chronicle*, 5 April 1843.)

The letter seems to have had some effect, for in June that year the Mayor drew the attention of the Town Council to the recent improvements that had been carried out on Quay Lane and that 'the Council would be surprised to hear that the entire work . . . had been done for the trifling cost of £10 2s 8d (hear, hear).'[48] As for the tobacco chewing, spitting Papists I know not what was done about them.

St. Michael's Church

'One of the Annoyed' was just one of the many of the annoyed Church of Ireland residents of St. Michael's Parish who had been waiting for a considerable long time for a new parish church to be opened in Newtown Pery as an alternative to St. Mary's. For almost 200 years St. Michael's Parish had had no dedicated parish church, not since 1651 when the original church, which stood outside the city walls, was demolished during the course of a siege of the city by a Cromwellian army.[49] Despite the continued growth of Newtown Pery within the boundaries of St. Michael's Parish since the mid-eighteenth century, up until 1834 the Protestant population had been served by only one small chapel, St. George's. The Methodists in Newtown Pery were better served than the Anglicans as they had two chapels, one for each of the Methodist factions, while the Catholics had three.

Since 1789 St. George's Chapel had stood on the corner of Mallow Street and George Street, a site presently occupied by a former bank building that has been converted into a public house known as 'The Bank'. Originally endowed by the Pery family as a chapel of ease,[50] St. George's was made available to accommodate the Protestant inhabitants of Newtown Pery but was capable of seating just 300. (A chapel of ease is an Anglican place of worship subordinate in status to a parish church and normally built for the convenience of remote parishioners). By the early 1830s the Protestant population in the parish numbered several thousands and the demand for better church facilities grew ever more vocal, it being claimed in an 1834 memorial presented to the Bishop that there were 'upwards of 4,000 Protestants' resident in Newtown Pery.[51] According to the Census returns for that year the number of Protestant parishioners, collectively labelled 'Churchmen', was 2,645.[52]

To relieve the pressure two churches were eventually built, one being opened on Sunday 4 May 1834 on Catherine Street. Called Trinity Church, it was also known as the Episcopal Chapel, this house of worship was funded by money personally raised by the Rev. Edward Newenham Hoare in England and Ireland.[53] Trinity went totally against the Gothic grain of the Church of Ireland by being Classically influenced, on the entrance front two sturdy Ionic columns support a plain entablature and a neat, restrained pediment. Rusticated stone work features on the ground floor of the building's central section while the rest of the façade is of dressed stone. The chapel is flanked on either side by a brick, Georgian style terraced house that is integral to the design. One of these houses was built for the Minister and the other to accommodate an Asylum for Blind Females that was attached to Trinity Church.[54] The building is quite elegant and beautiful in design and a welcome break from the relentless Simple Gothic that appeared all over the country. We must, therefore, be thankful for the independent fundraising activities of the Rev. Newenham Hoare for this building and we hope that the blind females under his care were treated with some kindness. No longer used as a church, it more recently served as the headquarters of the Mid-Western Health Board.

Trinity Church, Catherine Street, Limerick.

A Galling Situation

In 1836 the site on which St. George's stood was sold to the Provincial Bank and it was confidently expected that a new purpose-built parish church would be built fairly quickly. The Earl of Limerick gave a site, without charge, facing onto Pery Square and from the sale of St. George's he lodged £3,400 into a bank account to be used to erect the new church.[55] It would be another eight years, however, before the church was finally opened for divine worship in December 1844, the project being dogged by a series of legal and financial difficulties 'of great complexity.'[56]

In the meantime, the only Anglican church in the parish that was occasionally available was Trinity on Catherine Street, but that could only accommodate 600-700 persons and two-thirds of the sittings were reserved for those who had purchased their pews for the charitable purpose of supporting the Asylum for Blind Females.[57] St. John's Church in Irishtown was not much assistance because it was 'barely sufficient to accommodate its own congregation.'[58] There was also St. Munchin's Church near King John's Castle in Englishtown, but that part of the city had become so increasingly run-down and poverty stricken that many in Newtown Pery thought it a very disagreeable place to walk through. Indeed, in the diary of Ellen O'Callaghan, the teenage daughter of a Catholic grocer and spirits dealer living in George Street, we read that in November 1838 she 'followed Mamma's tracks through the English Town' to deliver a subscription to St. Mary's Convent, also located near the Castle. In this district the young woman saw, 'several awful houses . . . this reminded me of the road to Heaven . . . you are surprised to find so nice a place in such a neighbourhood.'[59] Some of the pressure was relieved when the Primitive Wesleyan Methodists on Bedford Row allowed their Chapel to be used for several years as a temporary church by Anglicans; but this arrangement ended immediately after Easter 1842 when the Chapel was 'required wholly for the purposes of the Wesleyan Methodist congregation.'[60] This caused a crisis for the,

PROTESTANT WIDOWS
of
Saint Michael's Parish

'It is already known to the public, that the large Congregation which has for some years past attended for Church of England worship in the Temporary Church, Bedford-Row, will, after next Sabbath, be left to seek accommodation elsewhere, till the New Church is ready for their reception.

In the interim, the Protestant Widows, who have been hitherto supported by the Sabbath collections, will be left to perish unless some provision is made for them.

It is therefore proposed by the Parishioners, that a public appeal be made, on their behalf, and accordingly on SUNDAY, April 3rd, 1842,

A Charity sermon
Will be Preached, in the Chapel, by
THE REV. JOHN ELMES,

When it is hoped that the benevolent people of the Parish will show their usual liberality in contributing to the support of these aged and helpless women, who have no resource under heaven but their bounty.

Divine Service will commence at half-past Eleven. Contributions from such as cannot attend, will be thankfully acknowledged by Henry Maunsell, Esq. and the Rev. Bryce Peacocke.

March 30.'[61]

As architect to the Ecclesiastical Commissioners James Pain was actively involved in preparing the way for the new Pery Square church, the architect being described by Daniel Barrington, Land Agent to the Earl of Limerick, as the 'superintendent of that church.'[62] A perspective drawing of the proposed new building by the Pain brothers, dated 1838[63] shows that as originally conceived it was to have a square tower surmounted by a spire supported by crocketed flying buttresses. The building was to have been far more ornate in decorative Gothic detail than that typical of most First Fruits churches, one of its attractive features being the belfry stage with its traceried openings and ogee hood-mouldings. A porch entrance was also planned to be placed on the west front. Obviously, all those involved in the planning phase thought that since Pery Square was to become *the* place to live for the elite of the city then the district needed a church of distinction.

334

The patron saint for the church was to have been St. George, not St. Michael, and in 1840 it was reported that 'a very handsome church is being built, with a tower and a spire.'[64] But the church was still incomplete in 1843, work having ceased for over a year. The building was described in April 1843 as being only 'partially erected by the proceeds of the sale of St. George's chapel.' It was 'gradually falling into decay' with the danger of 'becoming a mass of ruins.'[65] Debts were owing and a report in the *Limerick Chronicle* of 23 March 1842 stated that the new St. George's Church was 'being held over by the contractor, until certain claims are satisfied.' It appears that the total debt due on the building at that time was £1,900.[66]

A sum of £1,000 was available from the Ecclesiastical Commissioners to help finish the project, but this money could not be released because St. George's

335

Pain brothers' 1838 proposal for St. Michael's Church, Pery Square, Limerick.

had fallen into ecclesiastical limbo land. The kernal of the problem was that St. Michael's Parish was not a distinct parish in its own right, but was united with the parishes of Ardagh and Kildimo forming the Archdeanery of Limerick.[67] Technically, the Pery Square structure was neither a Chapel of Ease nor a Parish Church and since the Commissioners only had the authority to release funds to build or repair such churches they could not hand over the £1,000 required to complete the project under the terms of the Church Temporalities Act of 1833.[68] There were other complicating factors associated with this situation, such as the performance of religious duties by clergy and the allocation of revenues, but the core issue was the anomalous status of St. George's.

A frustrating situation for James Pain until the posts of the four provincial architects to the Ecclesiastical Commissioners were amalgamated into one office under John Welland in 1843. A very frustrating experience also for the over 2,000 Protestant inhabitants of St. Michael's. As a petition to the House of Lords stated in 1843, it was galling to those who lived in the parish, 'comprising within it the entire of the higher classes' of Limerick, that they could not even get married or even baptise their own children in their own church.[69]

Many agitated meetings were held by the parishioners and numerous letters of complaint and petitions were issued forth in an attempt to pressurise the highest authorities of the land, both ecclesiastical and lay, to sort out the problem The situation was finally resolved in the summer of 1843 when a Bill was passed through Parliament making the Parish of St. Michael a separate and distinct parish allowing the Pery Square church to leave limbo and be recognised as a Parish Church in its own right.[70] This enabled the £1,000 held by the Commissioners to be released. Funds were also raised by public subscription[71] allowing the church to be completed in late 1844 by building contractor William Wallace,[72] but sans spire and without the Gothic Revivalist detail of the Pain brothers' original concept. Another consequence of the legislation was that the church was now to be called St. Michael's, not St. George's as originally intended. When the church was eventually consecrated and opened for divine worship on Sunday 8 December 1844 the local press noted that a spire was still being planned for the new structure,[73] but nothing came of it. St. Michael's was capable of accommodating '1,200 people . . . of which half of the sittings were free'[74] for the use of the poor.

Despite all the time and effort spent in getting St. Michael's completed, when built it was apparently not a particularly attractive building for such a wealthy parish. This building was later described by the Rev. Robert Wyse Jackson, Rector of St. Michaels and later consecrated Church of Ireland Bishop of Limerick in 1961, in his history of St. Michael's Church as 'a plain square building, unattractive enough' with 'a plain white ceiling'[75] (and a west tower smaller in height than the present tower). In 1866 local historian Maurice

Lenihan remarked that the church 'possesses little interest' except for the east window,[76] which had originated in St. Francis Abbey, a medieval foundation outside the walls of Englishtown. At that time St. Michael's did not have the appearance it has today, having to wait until 1877 to be remodelled.[77]

Endnotes

1 *Limerick Chronicle*, 29 December 1838.

2 'Pain, George Richard', *Index of Irish Architects,* Irish Architectural Archive, Merrion Square, Dublin.

3 'The Late Mr. James Pain, Architect', *Limerick Chronicle*, 22 December 1877; *The Irish Builder*, 1 January 1878.

4 *Dictionary of Architecture*, Architectural Publication Society, Vol. VI, 'Pain (James and George Richard)' p. 6-7. The entry states in its penultimate sentence 'James retired and is living at Limerick, being now (1877) in his 98th year.'

5 'The Late Mr. James Pain, Architect', *Limerick Chronicle*, 22 December 1877; *The Irish Builder*, 1 January 1878.

6 *Bassett's Directory of the City and County and of the Principal Towns in the Counties of Tipperary and Clare 1875-6, and 1877-8*, p. 64, William Bassett, 20 George Street, Limerick.

7 Design signed James Pain, 1840, Library of the Representative Church Body (RCB), Dublin.

8 RCB Design signed and dated March 1840.

9 Hewson, Adrian *Inspiring Stones*, published by the Diocesan Council of Limerick, Killaloe and Ardfert in association with FÁS, 1995, p. 101.

10 Craig, Maurice *The Architecture of Ireland*, B. T. Batsford Ltd., London, Eason & Son, Dublin, 1982, p. 288.

11 *Limerick Chronicle*, 25 October 1834.

12 *Limerick Leader*, 28 August 1839.

13 *Limerick Chronicle*, 26 June 1839. Sir Thomas Dean was also the contractor for the Rathkeale and Newcastlewest workhouses.

14 *Limerick Chronicle*, 31 May 1837.

15 *Limerick Chronicle*, 9 September 1837.

16 *Limerick Chronicle*, 21 May 1836.

17 *The Clare Journal*, Thursday 12 April 1838.

18 In March 1839 Owen submitted to the St. Michael's Parish Commissioners, on behalf of the managers of the Savings Bank, plans and an application for permission to extend the columns of the 'new Savings Bank about to be erected some 4 feet (0.48 metres) beyond the [?range] of the line of the houses further down the street.' *Proceedings and Orders of the Commissioners for Improving St. Michael's Parish*, 22 March 1839.

19 *Limerick Chronicle*, 6 April 1839.

20 *Limerick Chronicle*, 21 June, 1843, 26 July 1843.

21 *Limerick Chronicle*, 22 October 1845.

22 *Limerick Chronicle*, 22 October 1845, 17 December 1845.

23 William Atkins became apprenticed to G. R. Pain in 1832. O'Dwyer, Frederick 'A Noble Pile in the Late Tudor Style: Mitchelstown Castle', *Irish Arts Review 2002*, p. 43n31.

24 Williams, Jeremy *Architecture in Ireland 1837-1921*, Irish Academic Press, Dublin, 1994, pp. 66-7.

25 *Limerick Chronicle*, 17 December 1845.

26 Spellissy, Sean *The History of Limerick City*, The Celtic Bookshop, Limerick, 1998, pp. 222-3.

27 Letter to the Editor of the *Daily Telegraph* dated 8 September (year not known) from 'James [Henry] Pain, Craigleith, Keswick Road, Putney.' Photocopy of the letter is in the James McMahon's 'James Pain' file, Limerick Civic Trust Archive.

28 Schedule of Shares annexed to *The Charter Party; or Articles of Agreement of the Pery Square Tontine Company of the City of Limerick*, copy in Limerick Civic Trust Archives.

29 *Limerick Chronicle*, 3 August 1915.

30 Schedule of Shares annexed to *The Charter Party; or Articles of Agreement of the Pery Square Tontine Company of the City of Limerick*, copy in Limerick Civic Trust Archives.

31 *Limerick Chronicle*, 11 February 1852.

32 *Register of St. Munchin's Parish - Baptisms* '1831 Jan. 8th, Baptised Henry, son of Amos and Catherine Vereker.'

33 *Limerick Chronicle*, 29 October 1845, 1 November 1845, 26 November 1845.

34 Williams, Jeremy *A Companion Guide to Architecture in Ireland 1837-1921*, Irish Academic Press, Dublin, 1994, p. 51.

35 *Limerick Chronicle*, 26 July 1843.

36 'The Adelaide School, Bruff', letter to the Editor from Godfrey Massy, Bruff Vicarage, dated 1 August 1843, *Limerick Chronicle*, 5 August 1843.

37 Massy, Dawson *The Faithful Shepherd: A Memoir of Godfrey Massy B. A, (Vicar of Bruff) with Sketches of his Times*, Hamilton & Co., London, 1870, pp. 421-2.

38 I wish to express my appreciation to Angela Alexander who has carried out research on James Pain's designs for furniture and furnishings for Dromoland. Angela very kindly gave me copies of James Pain's sketches she had researched in the National Library of Ireland.

39 National Library of Ireland AD 2522; 2518; 2501.

40 Richardson *Gothic Revival Architecture in Ireland* Vol. I, p. 175 n.73.

41 National Library of Ireland AD 2493.

42 NLI AD 2532. Other sketches are for the moulded jambs of doorways as well as a drawing of a section of the roof beams showing the iron trusses (NLI 2559; 2516).

43 *Limerick Chronicle*, 4 March 1843.

44 *Limerick Chronicle*, 30 October 1844.

45 *Limerick Chronicle*, 15 May 1841, 12 August 1841.

46 *Limerick Chronicle*, 27 October 1841.

47 *Limerick Chronicle*, 10 April 1841.

48 *Limerick Chronicle*, 14 June 1843.

49 Lenihan is of the reasonable opinion that since the church stood outside the walls it was demolished by the defenders before the siege in order to deny cover to the enemy. Lenihan *op. cit.* pp. 345, 427-8.

50 Lenihan *op. cit.* p. 684.

51 'Memorial to the Bishop of Limerick Presented by Residents of St. Michael's Parish 1834', Waller, John Thomas *Trinity Church and St. Michael's Church*, McKerns Printing, Limerick, 1954.

52 *Parliamentary Gazetteer of Ireland* Vol. II, p. 631.

53 Lenihan *op. cit.* p. 684.

54 Waller, John Thomas *Trinity Church and St. Michael's Church*, McKerns Printing, Limerick, 1954.

55 Letter to the Editor from Daniel Barrington, *Limerick Chronicle*, 11 September 1839.

56 Jackson, Robert Wyse *The History of St. Michael's Church, Limerick, 1844-1944*, McKerns, Limerick, 1944. Limerick Museum.

57 'St. Michael's Parish Church', *Limerick Chronicle*, 10 December 1842, 26 April 1843.

58 *Limerick Chronicle*, 10 December 1842.

59 *MS Diary of Ellen O'Callaghan*, 30 November 1838. Limerick Civic Trust Archive.

60 *Limerick Chronicle*, 23 March 1842.

61 *Limerick Chronicle*, Wednesday 30 March 1842.

62 Letter to the Editor from Daniel Barrington, *Limerick Chronicle*, 11 September 1839.

63 Drawing in the Collection of the Knight of Glin, Glin Castle, Co. Limerick. A handwritten note on the drawing reads 'Design for the Church to be built for the Parish of St. Michael, in Pery Square, Limerick – Jas. and Geo. R. Pain Architects.' Copy in Limerick Civic Trust Archives.

64 *Triennial Directory* 1840, p. 4.

65 'St. Michael's Parish Church', *Limerick Chronicle*, 26 April 1843

66 *Limerick Chronicle*, 6 April 1842.

67 'St. Michael's Church - Limerick', *Limerick Chronicle*, 12 August 1843.

68 *Limerick Chronicle*, 26 April 1843.

69 *Limerick Chronicle*, 26 April 1843.

70 For full text of the Bill see *Limerick Chronicle*, 21 June 1843; for a summary see 'St. Michael's Church - Limerick', *Limerick Chronicle*, 12 August 1843.

71 *Limerick Chronicle*,13 May 1843.

72 *Limerick Chronicle*, 10 April 1844.

73 *Limerick Chronicle*, 11 December 1844.

74 ibid.

75 Jackson *op. cit.*

76 Lenihan *op. cit.* p. 684.

77 Hewson op. cit. p. 137.

CHAPTER NINETEEN

TRIBUTE TO DEPARTED WORTH

As the main focus of this study has been the work of James Pain in Ireland prior to the Famine no further research has been carried out on the architect beyond that point, even though he was to practice for another thirty years. It was in the period *c.*1811 - 1840 that he flourished as an architect, being involved in the design and construction of very major public and private assignments with which his name, and that of his brother George Richard, are associated. One suspects that if one were to carry out an investigation into the last three decades of James Pain's professional life then one would come up with a lengthy list of minor works including house alterations,[1] office conversions, schools (he drew up plans for two new schools in Doon and Pallasgreen in Co. Limerick in 1850-1[2]) and funerary monuments. An example of the latter is to be found in Stradbally churchyard, Castleconnell, Co. Limerick where he built a plain, austere looking burial vault for General Sir Richard Bourke of Thornfield House, Lisnagry, Co. Limerick. Sir Richard, who died in 1855, had served as Governor of New South Wales in Australia during the period 1831-7.[3] There is a commemorative plaque to the General inside Stradbally Church and one assumes that James Pain, or one of his assistants, also designed this memorial as we have sufficient evidence that church plaques were a stock-in-trade of James Pain's office.

John Paul Dowling

Burial vault for General Sir Richard Bourke, Stradbally Church graveyard, Castleconnell, Co. Limerick.

Certainly, after the death of his brother and the completion of Thomond Bridge in 1840 no works of any importance have been attributed to James Pain, although one is always open to correction on these matters. It may be possible, after diligent research, to compile a list of the architect's works for the period 1845 - c.1875, but that has not been the author's brief. In its stead, one can offer a few snippets of information about his latter years highlighting a few of his professional high points, and low points. Future researchers may, if they so wish, fill in the gaps.

Famine Crisis

The skills of James Pain were called upon several times by the prison authorities during the Famine years of 1845-50 when the County Gaol on Mulgrave Street faced a crisis of chronic overcrowding. As the prison infirmary contained only twelve beds (six for males, six for females) and the ventilation was defective, the architect was called upon in 1847 to submit a plan to the Limerick County Grand Jury for building a new hospital in the southern angle of the prison.[4] In 1849 the female wing of the gaol was extended, increasing by thirty-two the number of cells. However, according to a report by the Board of Superintendence of the prison to the Grand Jury,[5] at night the new extension was occupied by male prisoners due to the overcrowded state of the facility.

That conditions in the County Gaol were particularly nightmarish at that time was indicated by the Board's remarks to the Grand Jury at the 1852 Spring Assizes recalling that the Famine years were a 'fearful period' and an 'awful crisis'.[6] Telling phrases given that Gaol Reports were typically unemotional, bureaucratic items of civic literature. At one stage, spring 1849, the numbers confined in Limerick Gaol reached 860 souls in an institution that 'legally and healthfully'[7] was supposed to accommodate, at the very most, 200.[8] The fact that at the height of the accommodation crisis in 1848-9 eight, and in many cases ten, inmates were sleeping in a small cell originally intended for just one person[9] gives some insight into the dire nature of the crisis facing both prisoners and prison authorities alike. With so many people confined in a small cell overnight, with no water closet, and with only pails for slopping out in the morning, the smell of the prison may not have been particularly pleasant. Even during the day there was no escape from the claustrophobic conditions, the Board of Superintendence reporting in the Spring of 1849 that the day-room, intended for just fifteen persons, 'has now crowded into it 302 individuals!' The inclusion by the Board of an exclamation mark in the document giving an indication of the full gravity of the situation.[10]

The reasons advanced by the prision authorities for this chronic overcrowding were two-fold: (1) the very large number of inmates held in the prison who were scheduled for transportation - in June 1849 193 men and eleven females were so classified - and, (2) the fact that the courts were sending people to jail in large numbers for committing various crimes against property. The increase in committals for minor offences was quite marked in the Famine years due to the destitution and desperation on the part of the offenders. It was the opinion of the members of the Limerick Board in June 1849 that 'a large proportion of these crimes are committed with a view of being sent to the shelter and food of a Prison.'[11] For one reason or another, these people had not been able to gain admittance to a workhouse for relief. The Board also stated that another incentive for being sent to prison was that 'prison diet was superior to pauper diet' i.e. the diet available in a workhouse.[12] As a deterrent, in September 1849 the Board of Superintendence introduced a diet into the County Gaol that was similar to that on offer in workhouses. This diet was also ordered to be the standard fare at the prisons of Rathkeale, Newcastle and Bruff.[13] The Chairman of the Board that introduced this measure was Lord Clarina of Clarina Castle, Co. Limerick, for whom James Pain had built a £50,000 castellated mansion in the 1830s and who had married the exceedingly rich daughter of a Franco-Irish wine merchant. In its report to the Grand Jury at the Spring Assizes of 1851 the Board drew attention to another change in the prison diet introduced in September 1850. Under this measure all those whose imprisonment did not exceed one month got 'in place of milk for dinner, one ounce [28.35 grams] of meal made into gruel', the Board congratulating itself that by this measure they had saved money, as 'the cost of the gruel is but one-seventh that of the milk'.[14] Gruel is a liquid food made by boiling oatmeal etc. in milk or water. Since the prison authorities were saving on milk then one assumes that prison gruel was made with water as a principle ingredient.

Knappogue Castle

With its heavy financial drain on landlords the period of the Great Famine and its aftermath was not conducive to the commencement of major building projects promoted by the gentry and aristocracy. Landlords experienced a substantial drop in rental income, were burdened by very high poor law rates and had to borrow heavily to maintain their properties and lifestyle. Many of those who put the interests of tenants before their own self-interest ended up financially ruined, their lands and properties coming onto the market under the Encumbered Estates Act (1849). This legislation simplified legal procedures involved in the sale of lands by indebted landlords. The next major phase of country house building in Ireland was not to occur until the post-Famine agricultural boom of 1854-77 when there was a substantial improvement in agricultural output and estate incomes prospered. Indeed, it was in 1856 that James, then aged 76, commenced work on major Gothic restorations and additions to Knappogue Castle, Co. Clare for Lord Dunboyne.

Knappoque Castle, Co. Clare.

Originally built by the McNamaras as a tower house in 1497, the last McNamara sold the property in 1800 to Captain John Scott of Cahircon, Co. Clare.[15] Gothic extensions to the south and east of the tower house were later added - these extensions featuring in a drawing by John Werral, a Limerick civil engineer, which appeared in the 1854 sale catalogue of the Scott estate[16] when its lands and properties came onto the market under the Encumbered Estates Act.

343

Knappogue Castle, 1854.

Designated Lot 11 in the 1854 sale, the Castle and demesne of Knappogue, with its 'highly ornamented plantations', was described as being 'beautiful' and 'splendid'. According to the agents, upwards of £8,000 had been recently expended on the castle and its attached out-offices and lands, making Knappogue a highly desirable property 'fit for the residence of a nobleman or gentleman's family.'[17] Purchased in 1855 by Theobald Butler, the 24th Lord Dunboyne, he appointed James Pain the following year to carry out major remodelling work on the Scott extensions and design an additional western wing. By comparing Werral's drawing with Knappogue Castle as it presently appears one can study Pain's contribution.

James was working for a fellow Freemason as Lord Dunboyne had served as Grand Treasurer of the Grand Lodge of Ireland between 1839 and 1842 and he affiliated to Lodge 333, Limerick, in November 1856. Dunboyne's pedigree was 'authentic' for having the right to own a medieval tower house as he was a descendant of the baronial Butler family who once held great wealth and political sway in medieval Ireland. His wife, Julia Celestina Maria, was the daughter of wealthy Surrey ship-owners and it was she who provided the wherewithal to purchase Knappogue.

On Monday 9 June 1856 the foundation stone for the new west wing was laid by Dunboyne in the presence of a 'select company of ladies and gentlemen', the inscription on the stone indicating James Payne (*sic*) as architect and Patrick Flaherty the builder. Nearby, but not too close to the proceedings as to violate social boundaries, were 'a number of the peasantry' who had assembled in the grounds adjoining the castle, 'anxious to have a view of the proceedings and testifying, by their happy looks, the sincere pleasure it afforded them.'[18] No doubt they anticipated that the solvent presence of Dunboyne at Knappogue would bring bright blessings to the local community, the previous owners, the Scotts, having had to sell out because of ruinous debts.

344

Comparing John Werral's drawing of the south-facing elevation of pre-Dunboyne Knappogue with its present appearance shows that Pain's work involved raising the left-hand, western, corner tower an extra stage creating 'a handsome clock tower, the time-piece having two faces.'[19] The clock faces have since been replaced with oculus windows. This tower flanks the main entrance to a stable yard that Pain enclosed with a medieval style curtain wall.[20] To the right of the stable yard entrance is Pain's single storey addition to the Scott extension. This addition, which projects beyond the main line of the frontage, presently holds the Castle's banqueting hall. Along the Scott frontage the Gothic Revival windows were replaced with rectangular openings to conform with those in the banqueting hall and to allow more light into the rooms. The fenestration superimposes a classical regularity on the nineteenth century neo-Gothic exterior. Despite the remodelling and additions, Pain's work has kept in sympathy with both the medieval tower house and the Scott extensions enabling the Dunboyne family to live in Victorian comfort while maintaining a comfortable historical relationship with the medieval past.

The foundation stone citing James Pain's name has disappeared from Knappogue, along with several glass bottles containing coins of the Realm, from half-farthings to sovereigns, that were placed in a large cavity chiseled out in the stone.[31] When the Dunboynes left Ireland in the 1920s the house became vacant and in the 1940s a local farmer who had acquired the property stripped the building of its roof, lead and timber and sold the material to McMahons, the Limerick timber merchants. Totally derelict until its restoration in the mid-1960s, Knappogue was totally open to the elements and the foundation stone with its treasure trove may have been taken during that period, or perhaps some time earlier. No one seems to know.[32] The Andrews family of Houston, Texas, carried out the restoration of Knappogue with assistance from Shannon Development who are the current owners of Knappogue Castle and who put on 'medieval-style' banquets for tourists..

While the sheer mass and superstructure of the tower house does tend to dominate over the nineteenth century additions, and while the proportions of the entire composition do seem to be wrong, it is easy to see why Knappogue Castle has proved consistently popular with tourists, especially Americans. It has also become an increasingly popular venue for weddings and corporate functions.

Ruthlessly Discarded

While James Pain did carry out many assignments for St. Mary's Cathedral, unfortunately for his memory some of his architectural work in St. Mary's was deemed inappropriate by later generations of architects and deans, a number of his additions and installations being removed during the latter half of the nineteenth century.

James's professional association with St. Mary's included the insertion of a Perpendicular window, six lights in width, in the East end above the altar. There is extant in the Cathedral archives a drawing, signed by the architect and dated March 1843, of a transverse section of St. Mary's Chancel showing the window in question.[23] However it is no longer there, having been taken down in the late 1850s and replaced by triple lancet windows installed in 1860.[24] The discarding of Pain's Perpendicular came about when a committee, tasked by the Cathedral authorities to recommend a fitting memorial to the late Augustus O'Brien Stafford MP decided that a stained glass window would be appropriate. At the request of the Dean the East window was selected.[25]

Transverse section (1843) of chancel of St. Mary's
Cathedral, Limerick showing James Pain's
Perpendicular window.

On the advice of William Slater, a London based architect who had been commissioned in 1857 to carry out restoration work on the Cathedral,[26] it was decided to remove the Perpendicular window 'which had not been many years in existence, and which was put up at very heavy expense by Mr. Payne, architect.'[27] The justification for the removal of this window and its replacement with the more austere Early English triple lancet arrangement was that Pains' window was 'sadly out of character with the severely plain features of the original portion of the Cathedral.'[28] At the time of its removal the window had been in place for less than twenty years. So, quite an abrupt dismissal by a new generation of architects and restorers. Slater's lancets, which face onto Nicholas Street, are still in place. Research through the comprehensive collection of papers and documents in the Limerick Archives relating to the restoration works carried out in St. Mary's during the late 1850s reveals no mention of James Pain being involved as an architect.[29]

The ruthlessness with which Pain's Perpendicular was purged may seem surprising, but it was in conformity with the ideological zeal of those associated with the Ecclesiological Society, a powerful force in the Gothic Revival movement of the Victorian era whose opinions heavily influenced Slater. (Ecclesiology is the study of churches, church history, church furnishings and decorations that considers such issues as the relationship between ritual and architecture and 'correct' restoration). Originally known as the Cambridge Camden Society (1839-46), the Ecclesiological Society set down exacting standards for the authentic restoration of medieval churches and established strict rules for the building of new churches. Their strongly held belief was that new churches should conform to thirteenth and early fourteenth century church architectural styles of the Early English and Decorated periods. Architects who did not conform were heavily criticised in the Society's journal *The Ecclesiologist*, careers being damaged as a result.

Triple lancet windows that replaced James Pain's
Perpendicular window in St. Mary's Cathedral, Limerick.

East window, St. Michael's Church, Pery Square, Limerick.

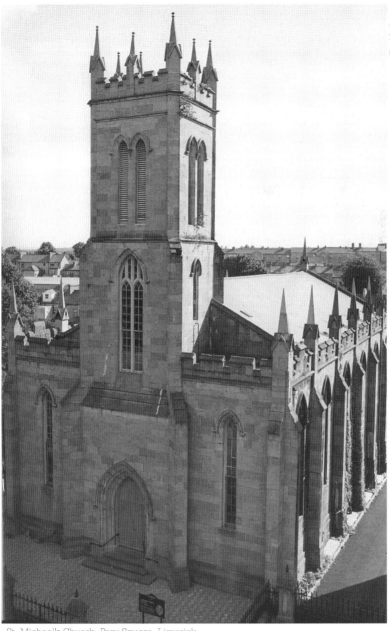

349

St. Michael's Church, Pery Square, Limerick.

Pain's offending Perpendicular was to be eventually rehabilitated, resurfacing some seventeen years later in St. Michael's (Church of Ireland), Pery Square when that church underwent extensive remodelling under the direction of architects William and Robert Fogerty in 1877, work that included heightening the tower by adding an extra stage, laying out a new forecourt and building a new chancel. The finished product being the charming church that today acts as a pleasant focal point to the view along Pery Street-Pery Square and adds considerably to the pleasing streetscape of Pery Square with its Tontine terrace and leafy park. The Rev. Wyse Jackon, the Rector of St. Michael's when he wrote his history of the church in 1944, says of the remodelling work undertaken by the Fogerty's,

> 'Perhaps the finest feature of the new work was the inclusion of the splendid window which had been in the east end of St. Mary's Cathedral until 1857. This was an 18th century copy of the perpendicular tracery in the church of St. Mary the Virgin, Oxford, cleverly modified to fit St. Michaels Church by Mr. Joseph Fogerty, C. E., the architect in charge of the alterations.'[30]

To fit into the available space the former Cathedral window had to be modified in size and proportion by reducing its width from six lights to five. However, as you enter St. Michael's Church a plaque reads,

'TO THE GLORY OF GOD

> In memory of his Reverend Father Richard Dickson for 67 years the loved and honoured rector of this parish who died April 1867 aged 90 the east window is erected by his son William R. Dickson 1871.'

The Architect Was At Fault

According to a late-nineteenth century guide book to St. Mary', James Pain built a porch onto the West door of the Cathedral in 1816. This information, the author states, was 'ascertained on the authority of a professional gentleman who had personal knowledge of the fact, that it was erected in 1816 ... by James Paine [sic]'.[31] An illustration of St. Mary's in *A Week in Killarney*, a travel account written by Mrs. Hall in 1834, shows a porch at the west end of the building.[32] Drawn from a southwestern perspective, the illustration clearly shows a rather tallish structure with pitched roof and stepped battlements along the eaves. Judging by the fenestration it may have been gloomy within, for there are only three pairs of narrow lights placed along the entire length of the porch that measured *c*.35 feet (10.7 metres) by 12 feet (3.6 metres).[33] Even then, the window openings were placed fairly high up on the wall and the natural lighting inside the structure must have been somewhat inadequate. A drawing of the interior of the porch that appeared in an 1887 Cathedral guide book seems to confirm the impression that the passageway was a bit on the gloomy side.[34]

Limerick Museum (LM 1987.0457)

Entrance porch (1816) to St. Mary's Cathedral west door. Demolished in 1892.

A photograph[35] of St. Mary's west front taken prior to the demolition of the porch in 1892 allows us to view the front of the structure, although trees obscure the side elevation. The Gothic gable had stepped Irish crenellations, a blank quatrefoil decorated the wall and a pointed arch held a doorway. Unfortunately, the porch looked like a great snout protruding from the Cathedral front obscuring one of St. Mary's architectural gems, the twelfth century Romanesque west doorway. The author of the 1881 guide to St. Mary's was not in the least bit enamoured with the appendage, for he writes that,

> '. . . the taste of the architect was at fault, as he appears to have ignored the maxim *"omne tulit punctum qui miscuit utile dulci"* [He has gained every point who has mixed the useful with the sweet], beauty not having been united with comfort, which latter, it is manifest, the structure was designed to secure.'[36]

Given such a public rebuke it comes as no surprise to learn that not long afterwards, in 1892,[37] the porch was 'swept away' by the Cathedral authorities. By so doing the Romanesque doorway was once again brought into the light of day, but the masonry of the door case had been 'terribly mangled and defaced' during the porch's construction and the necessary restoration work that had to be carried out proved to be a 'troublesome and costly operation' commented the Rev. James Dowd in 1899.[38] In his history of St. Mary's there is also mention of a 'dilapidated lodge at the northern entrance to the grounds' that was demolished in 1879 and replaced by a wall and railings.[39] A photograph of this building[40] on Bow Lane shows a lodge house built around an arched passageway that allowed carriages to pass into the Cathedral forecourt below the west front. The Bow Street gateway displays a distinct similarity with the architecture of the porch, also having

351

Romanesque west door to St. Mary's Cathedral as seen today.

Gothic gateway and lodge (1813) on Bow Lane, Limerick. Demolished in 1879.

stepped battlements and a blank quatrefoil over the archway. Evidence that this structure was built at about the same time as the western porch is supplied by Limerick historian Maurice Lenihan who, in his History of Limerick, makes mention that in December 1813 'the new Gothic gateway in Bow Lane was finished; it opens a communication for carriages to the great western door of the cathedral, which had been long since disused as a passage. Opened December 25th.'[41] Which does suggest that the porch was added to the west door at a date later than 1813. The 1840 Ordnance Survey clearly shows the layout of the forecourt complete with grassy roundabout for carriages, access to the porch being gained by a flight of steps that led up from the forecourt to the entrance door.[42] The construction of the Bow Lane gateway took place at the same time as a series of other works on St. Mary's and its approaches, including Bow Lane being 'made an inclined plane, and paved'[43] the roof of the Cathedral being extensively repaired between April and August 1815.[44] If it is correct that the porch 'was erected in 1816 ... by James Paine',[45] as the 1881 Cathedral guide informs us, then it is reasonable to suppose that all these works were carried out by the architect during the early years of his life in Limerick.

That James continued to practice as an architect until a ripe old age is illustrated by his continuing association with Limerick County Gaol, as retained architect, until 1863 when he was aged 84. Reporting to the County Grand Jury at the 1862 Summer Assizes, the Board of Superintendence wrote on 25 July that although they had 'under consideration certain plans' for improvements to the facility to meet requirements set down by a recent report compiled by the Inspectors General of Prisons, they had been hindered in presenting these to the Grand Jury due to 'the indisposition of the Architect, Mr. Pain.' But the Board entertained the hope that they would be able to present a supplementary report to the Grand Jury before the close of the Assizes in order to progress the matter.[46]

Four days later, on 29 July 1862, the Board of Superintendence gave 'instructions to their architect, Mr. Pain, for the preparation of other and preferable plans, based on the suggestions of the Governor, Mr. Eagar. Those plans they now submit to the Grand Jury, and recommend their approval and adoption.'[47] Several months before, on 31 May 1862 , Francis Eagar had been appointed as the new Governor of Limerick County Gaol following the death of the former incumbent, Henry Woodburn.[48] These plans and estimates were forwarded for the approval of the Inspectors of Prisons, one of whom, a Mr. Connellan 'pointed out that there were not a few points in which the existing building fails to comply with the requirements of the law that remained unnoticed in the proposed alterations.'[49] Following this, the Board advertised for plans from architects to carry out the necessary works to make Limerick Prison comply with the requirements of the Law. After two days' examination of the submitted plans the Board, with the assistance of the new Governor Mr. Eagar, selected those of Mr. 'Atkins' - presumably Williams Atkins (1812-87), a former pupil of the Pains'. At the Spring Assizes of 1865 it was reported that these works for the alteration of the prison were nearly completed and that 'Mr. Atkins deserves credit for his work.'[50] It would appear, therefore, that 1863 saw the ending of James Pain's long professional association with Limerick County Prison.

Death of James Pain

James survived his younger brother George Richard by almost forty years until, at the age of 98, he died at his house at 17 Upper Glentworth Street on Thursday 13 December 1877[51] from apoplexy[52] and was laid to rest in the Vereker vault at St. Mary's Cathedral[53] four days later on Monday 17 December at a funeral service conducted by the Dean and Canon Gregg.[54] James's body was found by Henry Vereker, husband of James's niece, Sarah (Sally).[55] It has generally been assumed that he never married, but this could not have been the case, for both his death and church burial certificates record his marital status as 'widower'.[56] Also, a notice in the *Limerick Chronicle* dated 12 April 1834 reports the death on, '7th inst. In Ludgate St., London, Harriet Henman, the beloved wife of James Pain of this city.'[57]

Judging by his Will, drawn up in 1863 (See Appendix IV), and the fact that he continued to work until very late in life, it can be assumed that James lived in reasonable financial comfort towards the end of his life. According to the Will, he held £5,662 of Bank of England 3% stock on which he drew dividends. At the time his housekeeper, Mrs. Moloney, received a salary of £10 per annum while his other female domestic, Anne Donnelly, was paid £7 a year.[58] Twelve years later, in January 1875, James added a codicil to the Will rearranging bequests of his bank stock to various relatives, but there had been no change in the value of the stock he held in 1863.

Among the items of interest mentioned in the Will is a model of Mitchelstown Castle that James bequeathed to his niece, Sally Vereker. Sally was also to receive the, 'small marble Bust of her late father G. R. Pain,' and, in addition, was to inherit a portrait of James Pain painted by Joseph Patrick Haverty[59] and 'my bust by Henry Vereker and the marble on which it stood in the hall.'[60] The location of these items is not presently known.

We know much about the architecture of James Pain, but little of his personality. An insight, perhaps, is offered in the obituary that appeared in *The Irish Builder* shortly after his death:

> 'He enjoyed a deservedly high reputation for his upright and honourable course of conduct, both among his employers and professional brethren, and, it may be added, was highly respected by the working men of the local building trades as a just and impartial judge of the questions which so often arise between them and their employers.'[61]

Summary

Architecture is an integral part of society expressive of its political, economic and social values and structures and the subject cannot be compartmentalised into a box labelled ' Culture and Aesthetic Taste'. Looking at the architectural practice of James Pain it is difficult not to draw the conclusion that the bulk of his work served the interests of the Anglo-Irish Establishment in attempting to preserve the status quo, whether it be building prisons and court houses to contain social unrest, peppering the landscape with the churches of a minority religion on the defensive, or building battlemented houses that sought to convince the world of the permanence of a landed social order. The only way to approach this issue is by applying the adage 'By their Works shall Ye know them.' But that is yesterday, and today is today. The architecture left behind by James Pain, both independently and in association with his brother, is a legacy that forms part of the rich and diverse cultural and architectural history of this country and as such deserves to be protected, studied and appreciated.

Water-colour of Adare Manor (1837) believed to be by Caroline, Countess of Dunraven. Painting shows the completed Tudor-Revival section standing adjacent to the eighteenth century mansion.

Endnotes

1 According to *Index of Irish Architects*, Irish Architectural Archive, Merrion Square, Dublin, s. v. 'James Pain', he worked on additions to Mount Rivers in Co. Tipperary in 1850. Mark Bence-Jones in *A Guide to Irish Country Houses* Constable, London, revised edition 1988, p. 294 suggests that *c.* 1850 James Pain may have carried out alterations to Cratloe Woods House, Cratloe, Co. Clare.

2 *The Builder*, 19 April 1851, 24 April 1852.

3 Bourke, Gerald *Out on a Limb*, Trafford Publishing, Victoria, Canada, 2003; King, Hazel 'Sir Richard Bourke: His Life and Work', *The Old Limerick Journal*, Australian edition, Kemmy, Jim ed., No. 23, Spring 1988; ibid. Reece, Bob 'Sir Richard Bourke: Irish and Colonial Liberal'.

4 *Limerick County Grand Jury Presentments*, 'County Limerick Gaol Report', Summer Assizes, 1847, p. 180.

5 ibid. 'County Limerick Gaol Report', Spring Assizes, 1849.

6 ibid. Spring Assizes, 1852, pp. 184, 185.

7 ibid. 'County Limerick Gaol Report', Spring Assizes, 1849.

8 ibid. Spring Assizes, 1852, p. 184.

9 ibid. 'County Limerick Gaol Report', Spring Assizes, 1849.

10 ibid. 'County Limerick Gaol Report', Spring Assizes, 1849.

11 ibid. 'County Limerick Gaol Report', Summer Assizes, 1849.

12 ibid. 'County Limerick Gaol Report', Spring 1850.

13 ibid. 'County Limerick Gaol Report', Spring 1850.

14 ibid. 'County Limerick Gaol Report', Spring Assizes, 1851.

15 O'Carroll, Cian *Knappogue - The Story of an Irish Castle*, Shannon Heritage, Shannon, Co. Clare, 2002, p. 21. Cian was previously chief executive of Shannon Heritage and project manager of the restoration of Knappogue Castle during the mid-1960s. He was also project manager during the restoration of Dunguaire Castle at Kinvara, Co. Galway.

16 *J. B. Scott's Property in County Clare, 1854*. The illustration of 'Knopoge [*sic*] Castle' is facing page 14. Local Studies Department, Limerick County Library

17 ibid. Lot 11 pp.14-5

18 *Clare Freeman*, 14 June 1856.

19 *Clare Journal and Ennis Advertiser*, 1872 quoted in O'Carroll *op. cit.* p. 42-3.

20 Williams, J. *A Companion Guide to Architecture in Ireland 1837-1921*, Irish Academic Press, Dublin, 1994, p. 54.

21 *Clare Freeman*, 14 June 1856.

22 Conversation with Cian O'Carroll, 16 March 2004.

23 Mulvin, Lynda 'St. Mary's Cathedral: Unpublished Correspondence of the Cathedral Restoration in the Nineteenth Century', *Irish Architectural and decorative Studies,* The Journal of the Irish Georgian Society, Vol. IV, 2001, p. 183.

24 Dowd, Rev. James *History of St. Mary's Cathedral, Limerick*,George

McKern & Sons, Limerick, 1899, p. 56.

25 O'Brien, Robert *Report on the Works Effected at St. Mary's Cathedral, Limerick, With a Statement of Accounts*, printed by Guy and Company, 114, George Street, Limerick, 1861. Limerick Archives (St. Mary's Cathedral Restoration P7). Maurice Lenihan's account of the restoration of St. Mary's Cathedral for that period in his *Limerick; its History and Antiquities* (pp. 601-3) is based on Robert O'Brien's Report.

26 ibid. p. 56.

27 Lenihan *op. cit.* p. 601.

28 Dowd *op. cit.* p. 39; O'Brian *op. cit.*

29 Limerick Archives (St. Mary's Cathedral Restoration P7). Since the collection of documents, papers and records held by the Limerick Archive is presently (2005) undergoing re-classification it is advised to consult the Archivist as to the correct Reference No. for the material relating to St. Mary's restoration.

30 Jackson, Robert Wyse *The History of St. Michael's Church, Limerick. 1844-1944*, McKerns, Limerick, 1944, p. 14, Limerick Museum; Hewson, Adrian *Inspiring Stones*, published by the Diocesan Council of Limerick, Killaloe and Ardfert in association with FÁS, 1995, p. 137.

31 *A Historic and Descriptive Sketch of St. Mary's Cathedral*, G. M'Kern & Sons, Limerick, 1881, p. 34.

32 Hall, Mrs. *A Week in Killarney* 1834.

33 Ordnance Survey 1840, City of Limerick, Sheet No. 15

34 *A Historic and Descriptive Sketch of St. Mary's Cathedral*, M'Kern & Sons, Limerick, 1887, 3rd edition, p. 5.

35 Limerick Museum (LM 1987.0457).

36 *A Historic and Descriptive Sketch of St. Mary's Cathedral*, G. M'Kern & Sons, Limerick, 1881, p. 34.

37 Hewson, R. F. 'St. Mary's Cathedral', *North Munster Antiquarian Journal*, Thomond Archaeological Society Vol. IV, No. 2.

38 Dowd *op. cit.* pp. 44, 47.

39 ibid. p. 42.

40 Limerick Museum (LM 0000.5293).

41 Lenihan *op. cit.* p. 431.

42 Ordnance Survey 1840, Sheet No. 15

43 ibid. 432.

44 ibid. p. 436.

45 *A Historic and Descriptive Sketch of St. Mary's Cathedral*, G. M'Kern & Sons, Limerick, 1881, p. 34.

46 'County of Limerick Gaol Report', 25 July 1862. List of Presentments Made by the Grand Jury of the County of Limerick, Summer Assizes, 1862. p. 137.

47 *County Limerick Grand Jury Presentments*, Spring Assizes, 1863, p. 155.

48 ibid. Summer Assizes, 1862, p.137.

49 ibid. Spring Assizes, 1863, p.154.
50 ibid. Spring Assizes, 1865, p. 150.
51 *Limerick Chronicle,* 15 December 1877.
52 *Civil Death Record* and *Burial Death Record,* James McMahon 'James Pain' file, Limerick Civic Trust Archives.
53 *A Historic and Descriptive Sketch of St. Mary's Cathedral,* printed by G. M'Kern & Sons, Limerick, 1881, 1st edition, p. 20.
54 Entry No. 620, *The Register of Burials in the United Parishes of SS Mary and Nicholas in the County of the City of Limerick.*
55 Conversation with James McMahon who carried out research on the family history of James Pain in the Genealogy Office of the Mid-West Regional Archives for his publication *The Pery Square Tontine* (1999). At the time of writing this valuable research facility has been closed down for several years and the database records are not accessible.
56 *Civil Death Record* and *Burial Death Record*, James McMahon 'James Pain' file, Limerick Civic Trust Archives.
57 *Limerick Chronicle,*12 April 1834.
58 MS of The Will of James Pain (11 January 1863) & Codicil (23 January 1875) *Limerick District Registry Will Books* Record Office of Ireland. The original document was destroyed in the explosion and fire at the Four Courts, Dublin in 1922 but there is a copy on *Transcriptions of Wills of Limerick* microfilm, Limerick Genealogy Office, The Granary, Limerick. The Limerick Genealogy Office is presently closed, but the Will is published in full as 'The Will of James Pain' in *Georgian Limerick* Vol. II, David Lee, David & Gonzalez , Christine eds., Limerick Civic Trust, Limerick, 2000, pp. 255-8.
59 Patrick Haverty was a portrait artist who worked for a period in Limerick
60 ibid.
61 'The Late Mr. James Pain, Architect', *The Irish Builder*, 1 January 1878. The obituary was signed W. F., probably William Fogerty, a Limerick architect. The obituary also appeared in the *Limerick Chronicle*, 22 December 1877.

GLOSSARY OF ARCHITECTURAL TERMS

Acanthus - Decoration based on the leaf of the acanthus plant.

Acroterion, acroterium (pl. acroteria) - Stone plinth at apex of a Classical pediment often supporting a statue or other ornament.

Antae - The short projection of side walls on the front elevation.

Apse - Semicircular east end of the chancel, typically Romanesque.

Architrave - The lowest of the three main parts of a Classical entablature. Also, the surround of a door or window.

Ashlar - Masonry blocks smoothly finished, with fine joints and laid down in regular courses.

Baluster - Upright support in a balustrade, it may be square, circular or turned.

Balustrade - Series of balusters between plinths, pedestals and cornices forming a type of parapet used on bridges, tops of walls or as a decorative parapet front to a terrace.

Barge-board - Timber board, often ornamented, placed along the slope of an eaved roof, hiding and protecting the ends of the roof timbers.

Bartizan - A small turret projecting and corbelled out from the angle at the top of a wall or tower.

Bay - The main vertical division of a building usually incorporating a window or arch.

Blank (blind) arch/arcade/window - Decorative feature on a wall or panel with the outlines of a window, arch or arcade but with no opening.

Breakfront - A slight projection in the centre of a facade, rising through its full height.

Buttress - Masonry or brickwork projecting from a wall to give added strength.

Capital - The head or crowning feature of a column or pier below the entablature; usually carved or moulded.

Castellated - A building decorated with battlements and turrets to give it the appearance of a castle, common in late eighteenth century and early nineteenth century Gothic.

Chancel - That part of a church, normally the East end, reserved for the clergy and containing the main altar.

Chinoiserie - Style of European architecture and artefacts imitating Chinese art which first appeared in the seventeenth century and became very popular in the eighteenth century especially in England, Germany, France and Italy and lingered on into the nineteenth century.

Clerestory - The upper storey of a church nave pierced by windows.

Console - Carved bracket, usually in the form of a scroll, carrying a window surround or entablature.

Corbel - A block of stone projecting from a wall supporting the beam of a roof or other member such as a bartizan or machicolation.

Corinthian Order - The third Order of Classical architecture featuring acanthus decoration on column capitals.

Cornice - In Classical architecture, the top, projecting section of an entablature. Also, any projecting ornamental moulding along the top of a building or wall finishing or crowning it.

Crenellation - Battlement.

Crocket - Projecting knob-shaped, carved foliage used to decorate pinnacles, spires and similar features characteristic in thirteenth and fourteenth century Gothic or Gothic-Revival architecture.

Cruciform - Church plan in the shape of a cross.

Curtain Wall - The outer defensive wall of a castle linking the towers.

Cutwater - The sharply pointed bottom section of a bridge pier designed to part the water and reduce the pressure on the bridge when the river is in flood.

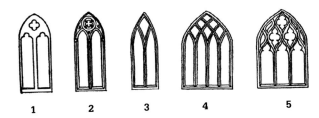

1   **2**   **3**   **4**   **5**

Decorated - English Gothic architecture of the period c.1250-1350 characterised by complex window tracery, naturalistic carvings and, in its later phase, ogee arches. The sequence of development in Decorated tracery was: 1. Plate, 2. Geometrical, 3. Y-tracery, 4. Intersecting (Switch-line), 5. Reticulated.

Dentil - A small rectangular block arranged in a series underneath a Classical cornice in tooth-like ornamentation.

Dissenters - Members of Non-conformist religious groups who refused to follow the Church of England after the Reformation, such as Presbyterians and Quakers.

Drip Mouldings - Hood mouldings over a window or doorway designed to throw off rain water.

Doric - The first, and simplest, Order in Classical architecture with no decorative feature on the capitals of columns other than horizontal bands.

Dormer - An attic window projecting from the slope of a roof.

Early English - English Gothic architecture of the period c.1190-1250 characterised by the early use of the pointed arch and lancet windows with no tracery.

Eaved roof - A roof the eaves of which overhang the walls of a house.

Elevation - the external faces of a building. Also a drawing to show any one face (or elevation) of a building.

Entablature - The upper, horizontal, part of a Classical Order consisting of three main parts; the architrave immediately above the supporting columns, the frieze in the centre, and the cornice at the top.

Engaged column - Columns attached to, or partly sunk in, the wall of a building.

Esplanade - 1. An open and level stretch of pavement or grass used as a public promenade, especially along the shore of a lake, river or sea. 2. In military architecture, the open ground separating the citadel of a fortress from the town.

.Fan -vault - Gothic form of vaulting of the English Perpendicular period with very elaborate rib design (for example see page 107).

Fanlight - Glazed light over a door, often semicircular or segmental, with radiating glazing bars suggesting the shape of an open fan.

Fenestration - The arrangement of windows in a façade.

Finial - The top of a spire, pinnacle etc.; may be sharp pointed or ornamental.

Fluted column - A column with its shaft carved with vertical grooves (flutes).

Frieze - 1. The middle division of a Classical entablature between the architrave and cornice, usually decorated but can be plain. 2. Decorative band running round a room immediately below the ceiling or the cornice.

Gable - The part of a wall filling the end of a pitched roof, normally triangular.

Gargoyle - A projecting spout from the eaves or tower of a church designed to throw off rain water. In medieval architecture they were often carved into a human or animal shape.

Gothic Revival - 1. An umbrella term to describe the various architectural styles of the eighteenth and nineteenth century based on medieval Gothic. 2. A Victorian architectural style attempting to accurately recreate medieval Gothic church architecture.

Gothick - Eighteenth century style vaguely based on medieval Gothic, but more connected with a taste for the exotic.

Hood-moulding - A projecting masonry moulding over the head of a window or doorway to throw off water. Associated with Gothic, Tudor, Gothic-Revival and Tudor-

Revival architecture. Can be either curved to conform with the head of a Gothic pointed opening or rectangular in shape to fit over a rectangular opening or Tudor arch.

Ionic Order - The second Order of Classical architecture featuring volutes (carved scrolls) on the capitals of columns.

Irish battlements - Stepped battlements characteristic of Irish architecture from the fifteenth century on.

Jacobean - Style of architecture from the reign of James I, King of England (1603-25).

Keep - The main strong point and living quarters of a castle, typically associated with Norman architecture.

Label - Rectangular moulding, with label stops, over a window or doorway.

Label stops - Decorative feature as a termination of a label or hood-mould.

Lancet window - A tall, narrow window with a pointed head and no tracery; associated with Early English architecture.

Lantern tower - Tower with window openings not filled in with glass.

Lintel - A horizontal beam or stone bridging an opening.

Louvre - One of a series of overlapping boards or slips of glass to admit air and exclude rain, often found in the belfry of a church tower.

Machicolations - 1. A corbelled gallery, either of timber or stone, built at the top of a medieval castle wall or tower supported by brackets or corbels with openings in the floor through which to drop boiling oil and/or stones on enemies at the base of the wall. A masonry feature frequently used in nineteenth century castellated houses.

Metope - Usually a plain slab between the triglyphs in a Doric frieze on the entablature.

Mezzanine - A 'half' storey between two floors of a building.

Mullion - A vertical division of a window.

Nave - The main body of a church where the congregation is seated.

Niche - A vertical recess in a wall, usually arched and containing a statue, urn or other decorative object.

Obelisk - A tapering, usually four-sided, stone pillar set up as a monument or landmark.

Oculus - A small round window.

Ogee arch - Pointed, reversed S-shaped arch with a head comprised of a compound curve of two parts, one convex and the other concave.

Order - In Classical architecture, the three classes of columns and their associated architectural features: Doric, Ionic, Corinthian.

Parapet - A low wall, sometimes battlemented, placed to protect any spot where there is a sudden drop, for example at the top of a tower, curtain wall or the edge of a bridge.

Pediment - The triangular gable of a Classical temple or portico placed over the entablature.

Perpendicular - Dominant style of English Gothic architecture c.1350-1540 characterised by large windows with panel tracery and flattened arches.

Perpendicular window - A large tracery window typical of the Perpendicular period with vertical mullions.

Piano Nobile - The storey in which the principal reception rooms of a house are situated when it is raised on a high basement, as in Palladian architecture, or at first floor level.

Pier - 1. A solid, vertical, masonry support, as distinct from a column. 2. A bridge support.

Pilaster - A shallow pier, of rectangular shape, projecting only slightly from the main body of a building.

Pinnacle - A small sharp spire used as a decoration on a tower, above a buttress or on a roof gable.

Portal - Entrance doorway or gateway of monumental character, especially if emphasised by a stately architectural treatment notably in Romanesque and Gothic architecture.

Porte-cochere - Doorway to a house or court, often very grand and large enough to permit wheeled vehicles to enter.

Portico - A projecting porch supported by columns.

Quoins - The slightly projecting dressed stones at the corners of a building, usually laid so as to have faces that are alternatively large and small, and serving as an architectural feature to give emphasis.

Rib-vaulting - Stylistically simple method of cross vaulting an arched ceiling in which thin ribs of vaulting masonry spring from capitals. (See page 13 for example).

Rubble masonry - Irregularly shaped stones fitted together in a random fashion.

Rustication - Masonry where the individual blocks are emphasied by deeply recessed joints. The face of the stonework often given a roughened surface. A treatment that is generally confirmed to the basement and lower part of a building.

Sanctuary - Part of the chancel round the altar, distinct from the choir.

Screen - In Gothic or Tudor architecture a partition of wood, often elaborately carved.

Shaft - The trunk of a column between the base and capital.

Shouldered architrave - A door or window surround with projections at the upper and sometimes also the lower corners; characteristic of eighteenth century houses.

Spandrels - The triangular spaces on either side of an arch.

Stepped battlements - Characteristic of Irish architecture from the fifteenth century on.

Switch-line tracery - Also known as Intersecting tracery. *See Decorated.*

Tetrastyle - A portico with four frontal columns.

Tower-house - Compact fortified house of several storeys, common in Ireland where many were built from the fifteenth to the seventeenth century.

Tracery - The ornamental stone ribs in the upper part of windows in Decorated and Perpendicular architecture.

Transcept - The short arms, usually north and south facing, of a cross-shaped church.

Triglyph - One of the upright blocks occurring in a series in a Doric frieze, on an entablature, separated by metopes. Each face of a triglyph has two vertical V-shaped grooves cut in it, called glyphs, and half grooves, called half-glyphs at the edges of the block, hence three glyphs in all.

Tympanum - The triangular space within the mouldings of a pediment; often ornamented, but not always.

Vault - Arched stone roof.

Venetian window - A window with three openings, that in the centre being round-headed and wider than those on either side.

Y-tracery - A mullion that branches into two, forming a Y shape; *c.*1300. *See Decorated.*

363

WORKS ATTRIBUTABLE TO JAMES PAIN

Not all the churches that James Pain was responsible for during his term of office (1822-43) as provincial architect to the Board of First Fruits, and its successor body the Ecclesiastical Commissioners, are listed in the appendices. Researchers should consult James Pain's church plans, elevations and drawings held by the Library of the Church Representative Body, Braemar Road, Churchtown, Dublin, and other primary sources. Since both brothers worked closely together on Church of Ireland commissions for the sake of convenience all the churches for the period 1822-38 have been listed under Appendix II 'Works Attributable to the Pain Brothers'.

Lough Cutra Castle, Co. Galway - John Nash design, James Pain executing architect, c.1811-17.

Rockingham House, Co. Roscommon - Nash design, James Pain may have supervised the work, c.1811.

City Gaol, Limerick - Nash design, James Pain executing architect, 1812-3.

Glin Castle, Co. Limerick - James Pain believed to have given late eighteenth century Glin House cosmetic Gothic 'makeover' c.1812 or after.

Glin Castle, Co. Limerick - other works James Pain may have carried out on demesne include design of stables, hermitage and Regency style lodge house, as well as supervising landscaping of ground in front of Castle, c.1812 or after.

Shanbally Castle, Co. Tipperary - Nash design, James Pain may have been executing architect, 1812-19.

Mount Shannon House, Co. Limerick - associated with additions, c.1813.

Dromoland House, Co. Clare - submits proposal for new house, 1813.

St. Mary's Cathedral (Church of Ireland), Limerick - Gothic gateway on Bow Lane, possibly by James Pain, 1813.

Thomond Bridge, Limerick - surveys the bridge which was first built in the fourteenth century, 1814.

County Gaol, Englishtown, Limerick - James Pain surveys state and condition of prison, 1814.

St. Mary's Cathedral, Limerick (C of I) - roof extensively repaired, possibly by James Pain, 1815.

The Exchange, Limerick - sundry repairs, 1815.

Cornmarket, Limerick - slating of market and other minor works, 1815.
Kilnasoolagh Church (C of I), Newmarket-on-Fergus, Co. Clare, 1816.

Kilfergus (Glin) Church (C of I), Co. Limerick, 1816.

St. Saviour's Church (Roman Catholic), Glentworth Street, Limerick, 1816.

St. Mary's Cathedral, Limerick (C of I) - porch added onto west door, 1816.

St. Paul's (C of I), Cahir, Co. Tipperary - Nash design, James Pain possibly executing architect, 1816-17.

Erasmus Smith School, Cahir, Co. Tipperary - Nash design, James Pain may have been executing architect, 1817.

Drumcliff Church (C of I) Ennis, Co. Clare - renovation work after lightning strike, 1817.

County Limerick Gaol, Mulgrave Street, Limerick, 1817-21.

Limerick County Gaol, Limerick - building of mill house and Cubitts treadmill commenced 1822.

Athlacca Church (C of I), Co. Limerick - burnt down by Rockites 1822, rebuilt 1823.

Ballybrood Church (C of I) - burnt down by Rockites in 1822, rebuilt 1823.

Excise Office, Rutland Street, Limerick - inserts new entrance, 1824.

Coolyhenane House, Co. Limerick - plans drawn up for, 1824.

Adare Manor, Co. Limerick - family mausoleum for the Earls of Dunraven constructed in Augustinian Priory, 1826.

Tullamore Prison, Co. Offaly - design inspired by James Pain's Limerick County Gaol, 1826-30.

Portlaoise (Maryborough) Prison, Co.Laois - design similar to Tullamore Prison, completed 1830.

Curragh (Curragh Chase) House, Co. Limerick - alterations, 1827-8.

Askeaton, Co. Limerick, glebe house, 1826.

O'Brien's Bridge, Co. Clare, glebe house, 1826.

365

Cloughjordan Church (C of I), Co. Tipperary, 1827.

Co. Limerick bridewells at Glin, Newcastlewest, Kilfinane and Croom - new structures c.1827-9.

Adare Manor, Co. Limerick - ice house in grounds of Adare House, 1828.

Adare Manor, Co. Limerick - James Pain may have supervised the erection of the walled garden, 1828.

Limerick County Gaol, Limerick - addition of loose brickwork to top of interior wall to improve security, 1829.

Limerick County Gaol, Limerick - repairs to arcade, 1830.

St. Mary's Cathedral, Limerick, Bishop's Throne, 1831.

Augustinian Priory, Adare, Co. Limerick - James Pain may have supervised restoration of cloisters, 1831.

Endowed School, Ennis, Co. Clare - repairs to school house and offices, 1832.

Barrington housing development, Limerick - Sir Joseph Barrington engages James Pain to plan housing development on property lying between Hartstonge Street and Barrington Street, 1833.

Rockbarton House, Co. Limerick - alterations for a new library, 1833.

Cahirguillamore House, Co. Limerick - alterations, 1833.

No. 1 Richmond Place (The Crescent), Limerick - conversion of rooms for the Agricultural and Commercial Bank of Ireland, 1834.

The Exchange, Limerick - supervises repairs, 1834.

Killaliathan Church (C of I), Co. Limerick, 1834.

Loughton House, Co. Offaly - major additions, 1835.

Limerick County Gaol, Limerick - plans submitted for building Female Prison, 1835.

Pery Square Tontine, Limerick - supervising architect,1836-8.

Kilrush, Co. Clare - converting a building into a branch bank for the Provincial Bank of Ireland, 1838.

St. Michael's Church (C of I), Limerick - 1838-43 supervises work as provincial ecclesiastical architect. Construction was halted and building left partially completed for several years until 1843; consecrated December 1844.

Provincial Bank, George (O'Connell) Street, Limerick - architect for new bank on the site of demolished St. George's Church, 1839-40.

Castle Kevin, Co. Cork - addition of turreted porch, 1830s.

Kilkee Church (C of I), Co. Clare 1840.

Killenaule Church (C of I), Co. Tipperary 1840

Kilbehenny Church (C of I), Co. Limerick, 1840.

Clonbeg Church (C of I), Glen of Aherlow, Co. Tipperary, 1840.

Clogheen Church (C of I), Co. Tipperary, c.1840.

Kilvemnon Church (C òf I), Co. Tipperary, 1840.

St. Mary's Cathedral, Limerick - gateway entrance on Bridge Street, associated walls and railings and landscaping of newly enclosed Cathedral grounds, 1841.

Pallasgreen Church (C of I), Co. Limerick, 1841.

Limerick County Gaol, Limerick - alteration, enlargement and repair of one of the radial wings, 1841.

George's Quay, Limerick - repairs to quay and work on Baal's Bridge, 1841.

Corcomohide Church (C of I), Co. Limerick - design signed and dated July 1841.

Dromoland Castle, Co. Clare, submits drawings and plans for improvements, 1842-3.

St. Mary's Cathedral, Limerick - Perpendicular window in Chancel, c.1843.

Rathkeale Bridewell and Courthouse, Co. Limerick - alterations, 1843.

City Courthouse, Limerick, draws up plans for, 1843.

Adelaide School, Bruff, Co. Limerick, 1843.

Stradbally Church (C of I), Castleconnell, Co. Clare, sarcophagus for Anne, Countess of Clare, 1844.

Toll-house, Thomond Bridge, Limerick - Gothic design has traditionally been attributed to the Pain brothers, but this may not be the case as the bridge was toll-free until the early 1840s. In September 1845 Limerick Town Council authorised payment to James Pain for erecting a toll-house at Thomond Bridge, c.1845.

Limerick County Gaol, Limerick - submits plans for building of hospital in prison grounds, 1847.

Limerick County Gaol, Limerick - extension to female prison, 1849-50.

Limerick County Gaol, Limerick - the 'Hospital Shed' made permanent to could accommodate 100 patients, 1850.

Mount Rivers House, Co. Tipperary - additions, 1850.

Cratloe Woods House, Co. Clare - possibly carried out additions, c.1850.

Doon School, Co. Limerick, 1851.

Pallasgreen School, Co. Limerick, 1852.

Stradbally Church (C of I), Castleconnell, Co. Limerick - burial vault for General Sir Richard Bourke, 1855.

Knappogue Castle, Quin, Co. Clare - Gothic extensions, 1856.

Limerick County Gaol, Limerick - submits plans for major renovations which are rejected by the Inspectors of Prisons, 1862.

WORKS ATTRIBUTABLE TO THE PAIN BROTHERS

Cork House of Correction, 1818-22.

The Exchange, Limerick - repairs, 1819.

Dromoland Castle, Co. Clare, 1819-37.

Castleguard, Co. Limerick - Pain brothers believed to have modernised the late medieval tower house and added castellated wing, c.1820.

George IV Bridge, Cork, 1820.

Limerick County Courthouse, Merchants Quay, Limerick - alterations, 1820.

Primitive Methodist Preaching House, Bedford Row, Limerick - possibly by Pain brothers, 1821.

Mungret Church (C of I), Co. Limerick, 1822.

Carrigaline Church of St. Mary (C of I), 1823.

Midleton Church (C of I), Co. Cork, 1823.

Cathedral of St. Mary (C of I), Limerick, memorial tablet to Rev. William Deane Hoare, 1823.

Brigown Fever Hospital, Mitchelstown, Co. Cork - possibly by Pain brothers, 1823.

Mitchelstown Castle, Co. Cork, 1823-6.

Market House and Courthouse, Mitchelstown, Co. Cork, 1823.

Carrigaline Church (C of I), Co. Cork, 1824.

Castlehaven Church (C of I), Co. Cork, 1825.

Castletownroche Church (C of I), Co. Cork, 1825.

Rathkeale Holy Trinity Church (C of I), County Limerick, 1825.

Howth Castle, Dublin - unexecuted plans, 1825.

Buttevant Church of St. John (C of I), 1826.

St. Mary's Cathedral (C of I), Limerick - Gothic screen, 1826.

County Club House, Cork, 1826.

Birr Rectory, Co. Offaly, 1826.

Stradbally Church (C of I), Castleconnell, Co. Limerick - enlargement, 1826.
Villiers' Alms House, Limerick, 1826.

Athlunkard Bridge, Corbally, Limerick, 1826-30.

Co. Cork courthouses in Bantry, Clonakilty, Macroom, Mallow, Midleton and Skibbereen - Pain brothers' designs, G.R. Pain appointed supervising architect c.1826.

St. Munchin's Church (C of I), Limerick, 1827.

Leap Church (C of I), Co. Cork, 1827.

Quinville House, Co. Clare - brothers thought to have converted Georgian house into a Gothic-Tudor mansion, 1827.

Killarney Sessions House, Co. Kerry, 1827.

Co. Kerry bridewells at Killarney, Miltown, Dingle, Tarbert, Kenmare, Cahirciveen and Castleisland - enlarged and improved according to plan by Messrs. Pain, 1827.

Emly Church (C of I), Co. Tipperary, 1827.

Blackrock Church (C of I), Co. Cork, 1827.

Lismore, Cathedral of St. Carthage (C of I), Co. Waterford - erection of new tower and internal repairs; also monument to Dean John Scott, c.1827.

Kingston School, George Street, Mitchelstown, Co. Cork - possibly by Pain brothers, 1827.

Blackrock Castle, Co. Cork, 1828-9.

Adare Manor, Co. Limerick - brothers submit proposals for Tudor Revival manor house, 1828-9.

Clonmel Free School, Co. Tipperary, 1829-30.

Independent Chapel, Oliver Plunkett Street, Cork, 1829-31.

County Club House, South Mall, Cork, 1829-31.

Strancally Castle, Co. Waterford, completed c.1830.

Wellesley Bridge, Cork, 1830.

Marshalstown Church (C of I), Co. Cork, 1830.

Castlefreke, Co. Cork - proposed additions and alterations, 1830.

St. George's Church (C of I), Mitchelstown, Co. Cork, 1830.

City and County Courthouse, Washington Street, Cork, 1830-5.

Baal's Bridge (also known as Ball's Bridge), Limerick - demolition of medieval structure commencing November 1830.

Baal's Bridge, Limerick - construction of replacement, completed November 1831.

Athlunkard Bridge, Corbally, Limerick, 1831-33.

Rathkeale Church (C of I), Co. Limerick - (very similar in design to St. Munchin's Church, Limerick), 1831.

Dromkeen Church (C of I), Co. Limerick - 1831.

Adare Manor, Co. Limerick - architects during Tudor-Revival phase, 1832 to c.1836.

Castle Bernard, Co. Offaly, 1833.

Athlunkard Bridge - construction of an approach road, 1833.

Glenstal Castle, Co. Limerick - submit castellated house design, proposal rejected, 1833.

Clarina Castle (also known as Elm Park Castle), Co. Limerick, 1833-6.

Killaliathan Church (C of I), Co. Limerick, 1834.

Church of St Mary Shandon (C of I), Shanakiel Road, Cork, c.1834.

Church of St. Luke (C of I), Summerhill, Cork, 1834-6.

Thomond Bridge, Limerick - demolition of fourteenth century structure, 1836-7

Houses of Parliament, London - competition entrant, Gothic design, 1836.

Dock works and quay walls, Limerick - competitive tender lost to Mulllins & McMahon, Dublin, 1836.

Thomond Bridge, Limerick - construction of replacement, 1837-40.

Quays and docks, Limerick - competitive tender lost to Sir William Deane, 1837.

Villiers' Orphanage and School, Henry Street, Limerick - brothers were the builders and may have designed the structure, 1837-9.

St. Michael's Church (C of I), Limerick - submitted design with spire surmounting west tower, 1838.

Killaloe, Co. Clare - house plans for sites, 1838.

Carrick-on-Suir Church (C of I), Co. Tipperary, 1838.

Ennis to Clare ship canal and lock, Co. Clare - proposals to build, not implemented, 1838.

Lough Derg, Co. Clare - cottage plans for sites overlooking the lake, 1838.

Frankfield Church (C of I) Co. Cork, 1839.

Thomond Bridge, Limerick - preparation of plans for new approaches, work completed by James Pain, c.1840.

In addition:

Convamore House, Co. Cork - replacement of fortified mansion (1617) by a large house of Georgian design, precise date unknown.

Cork Steam Packet Company building, Penrose Quay, Cork, date unknown.

APPENDIX III
WORKS ATTRIBUTABLE TO GEORGE RICHARD PAIN

Church of St. Augustine (RC) Washington Street, Cork - minor works, 1827.

Cathedral of St. Mary (RC), Cathedral Road, Cork - remodelling of the interior and insertion of elaborate fan-vaulted ceiling, 1828.

Christ Church, Parish of Holy Trinity (C of I), Main Street, Cork - internal alterations, removal of tower and construction of classical portico, 1828.

Spa House, Mallow, Co. Cork, 1828.

Castle Hyde Church (C of I), Co. Cork - remodelling and additions, 1830.

Dungarvan Church (RC) Co. Waterford - interior decorating and design of altarpiece, 1831.

Holy Trinity, Fr. Mathew Quay, Cork - (not completed in George Richard Pain's lifetime), 1832.

Trinity College, Dublin - wins competition for enlarging college with a hall, lecture rooms and museum (design not implemented), 1834.

Summerhill Church (C of I), Cork, 1834.

Church of St. Patrick (RC), Lower Glanmire Road, Cork, 1836.

Father Mathew Memorial Tower, Glanmire, Cork - designed by George Richard Pain, not completed until 1843 five years after his death.

Lota Beg House, Glanmire, Cork - entrance gates, date unknown.

THE WILL OF JAMES PAIN

In the Name of God Amen I, James Pain of No. 35 George Street Limerick, being by the mercy of God Almighty in perfect health of body and mind, do hereby indite and make this my last Will and intention of disposing of the property and effects with which the Almighty has been please to bless me Viz after my debts are paid I dispose of and give to the several persons hereinafter named the several amounts of my Bank of England 3 per cent reduced annuity, my twenty five shares in the Provincial Bank of Ireland & other sums named, my plate Books and furniture &c as herein and hereby bequeathed to them, or to be disposed as hereinafter named including any cash deposited in the Provincial Bank of Ireland, and if any 3 percent Stock in the Bank of England over and above what I may have named.

I give and bequeath to my beloved Niece Sarah (or Sally) Bendy, the daughter of my late sister Sarah (or Sally) Ostler, and wife of Mr. Richard Bendy of Mensfield Cottage Mensfield Place Kentish Town London the sum of four hundred pounds of my said Stock in the Bank of England with any Interest that may be thereon due at the time of my decease. I also give one hundred pounds of my said Stock to be divided share and share alike among the children of the said Sally & Rich Bendy. Should Mrs. Bendy die before me any bequeathments to her to be equally divided share and share alike among the said children.

I give and bequeath to my beloved Niece Sally Vereker daughter of my late Brother George Richard Pain and wife of Mr. H. Vereker of Wellington Villa Military Road Limerick the sum of four hundred pounds of my said 3 percent Stock in the Bank of England. I give of the said Stock one hundred pounds to be equally divided in sums of fifty pounds each to Catherine and Henry Vereker children of the said Sally Vereker. I also give of the said Stock Two hundred pounds to be equally divided between the two youngest children of the said Sally Vereker in sums of one hundred pounds to each of them Viz Amy and Wellington Vereker.

I also give and bequeath to my nephew James Pain son of my late Brother Henry Pain the sum of Fifty pounds of my said Stock in the bank of England. Also I give and bequeath to Mrs. Elizabeth Pain of No. 2 Elgin Villas Mother of the said James Pain the sum of Fifty pounds of my said Stock in the Bank of England. I also give and bequeath the sum of one thousand pounds of my said Stock in the Bank of England to be divided equally share and share alike of two hundred and fifty pounds each to the four children of my said Nephew James Pain Viz: to Mary Elizabeth, Sarah Anne, Richard and Olivia Pain with any Interest there may be due on the said Thousand pounds at the time of my decease. Should either of these last named six persons die before me the amount so bequeathed to be equally divided among the remainder share and share alike .

I also give and bequeath to the four children of my late brother John the sum of Twelve hundred pounds of my said Stock in the Bank of England to be divided in equal shares of Three hundred pounds Stock to each with any Interest there may be due on the same at the time of my decease. Should either of these four persons die before me the sums so bequeathed to them to be equally divided among the remainder the names of the four children are Martha, Sarah, and Henry Pain and their Sister Mrs. Elizabeth Wright married to Mr. Wright of Great College Street Camden Town.

I also give and bequeath to the four children of my late Brother Benjamin Pain the sum of Twelve hundred pounds of my said stock 3 per cent in the Bank of England to be divided among them share and share alike of 300£ stock to each. The names of these four children are George F. Pain, Mary Anne Pain, Benjamin J. Pain and Louise Pain. I also give and bequeath fifty pounds of my said Stock in the Bank of England to Mrs. Mary Anne Pain of No. 7 Milford Place Valsal Road Brixton. Should either of the last five named persons die before me the sums above given to them to be equally divided among the remainder share and share alike.

I further give and bequeath to the three children of my late niece Mrs. Catherine Tottenham wife of the Rev Richard Tottenham the sum of Nine hundred pounds of my said Stock 3 per cents in the Bank of England to be equally divided among them in shares of 300£ of the said Stock to each, their names are Belinda, Edward and Charlotte Tottenham. Should either of these three die before me the sum namedfor them to be equally divided among the remainder share and share alike.

I also give to Mrs. [one word not legible] Molony for her care and attention to me Twelve pounds of my said Stock, and to Anne Donnelly or any other person who may be with me as house Maid at the time of my decease bequeath the sum of five pounds of the said Stock of 3 per cent in the Bank of England - I hereby beg of my Legatee Sally Vereker to give to these two Servants at the time of my decease the remainder (if any) of their Several wages from the time of my decease to the end of that year to Mrs. [one word not legible] at the rate of £10 per annum of the other servant at the rate of £7 per year.

My Twenty five shares in the Provincial Bank of Ireland I give and bequeath in the following manner Viz to my Nephew James Pain eight and 1/3 of the said shares, to my Niece the aforenamed Sally Bendy eight and one third of the said shares and to my Niece the aforenamed Sally Vereker eight and one third of the said shares making the number of the 25 shares. I hereby give and bequeath to my dear Niece the aforesaid Sally Vereker - the hundred pounds (or the interest thereon) settled on my late Brother G.R. Pain by his marriage Settlement with the late Catherine Benn, which £100 I bought and received from my late niece Mrs. Catherine Tottenham and have ever since received the interest of it from Messrs. David FitzGerald & Sons of George Street Limerick Agents for Mr. Keating as the representative of the said G.R. Pain.

That the Legacy and Probate Duty cost on my will &c. may be equally divided and not fall on my Legatees. I desire that the several persons receiving sums under this will shall pay share and share alike their share of these costs as may be necessary and in proportion to the sums they may so receive.

I give to my Nephew the said James Pain my Gold Watch and chain with the Seal attached thereto and four other seals on the Ring loose in my drawer to my aforenamed Niece Sally Vereker I hereby give and bequeath all my silver plate and plated articles, eyeglasses Rings &c (which plate is named in the Box) as well as those in my general use. I hereby give unto my said Niece S Vereker, all the House Linen and the Articles of ornamental or other china, the small marble bust of her late Father G.R. Pain my Portrait (painted by Heverty) my bust by H Vereker, and the marble on which it Stands in the hall all the framed Pictures in the Parlour, entrance Halls office and the drawing Room, the two beautiful carved Panels by Gibbons the three oak chairs in the hall. The model of Mitchelstown Castle and the Table on which it stands.

All the rest of my household and office furniture, Beds, Glass and earthenware to be sold and the produce thereof to be made use of in paying any debts I may owe my funeral Expenses &c. In the foredoing of the sale of my house and office furniture I include all my library Books and engravings in the large portfolio in my office Drawer, my various account Books and papers of plans &c in the several portfolios my Executors will be so good as to look over and give to my several reletives or destroy as they may think fit.

There is due and owing to me and secured to me by the Master in Chancerys returns on the Estate of the late George earl of Kingston of Mitchelstown Castle the sum of £1096..19..3 or thereabouts, if this sum can be obtained I hereby give and bequeath it in three equal shares to my Nephew herein named James Pain and my two Nieces hereinbefore named Viz Mrs. S Bendy and Mrs. H Vereker or in case of their death their share to be given and divided equally to their several children share and share alike.

For carrying out this my last Will I appoint as my Executors my Nephew James Pain and Henry Vereker the husband of my Niece Mrs. Sally Vereker and beg of their attention to the same that it may be carried out with as little expense as possible to the several parties named herein which they residing as they do one in London and one in Limerick will be enabled to do. I beg of them to employ Mr. Davis Sims of No.3 Bartholomew Lane London Stock Broker to transact the business respecting the Bank Stock Probate &c the Will so that may be necessary as he is acquainted with these things. I also hereby name Mrs. Sally Vereker my niece as Residuary Legatee to receive all and whatever may remain after this my Will is carried out by my Executors whose necessary expenses on the transaction will of course be paid hereby - James Pain No. 35 George Street Testator.
Jany. 11 - 1863

Signed sealed and declared by the said James Pain in the presence of us present at the same time we herewith subscribe our names as Witnesses - Z.M. Ledger - Zacharias J. Ledger.

CODICIL

I, James Pain thank God am in perfect health of body and mind I do hereby make this my Codicil to be attended to, and used instead of parts of my Will and Testament which is in possession of the Rev B. Jacob of St. Michaels Limerick and dated the 13 day of Dec. 1863. The death of my late niece Mrs. Wright has left in my hand the sum of three hundred pounds, which sum of Three hundred pounds I now wish to dispose of in the following manner Viz 200£ of it in gifts of fifty pounds to each of the four children of my Nephew James Pain viz to Polly Annie, Olivia and Richard Pain, making with these additional gifts added to the sums of £250 which I had given them in my will this sum that is the same I had given to their Cousins of the families of my

Brothers John and Ben and Richard Viz 300£ each. The other hundred pounds which I had intended for Mrs. Wright to be distributed among her six children in equal shares to each of them (this disposes of the 300£ I had intended for Mrs. Wright) I do not know their names. I have named in my will £900 to be disposed of among the Tottenhams I now wish that sum to be disposed in a different manner among them Viz Three hundred pounds to Belinda and Charlotte Two to their Aunt Miss C. Tottenham. (This disposes of the 900£ I had left in my will with these changes I consider all is right) As Mrs. Howards dwelling is now known my Nephew J Pain to give her of my Bank of England Stock to give her twenty five pounds if she will except of the bequeath. Mr. Davis Sims will give information respecting my Bank of England Stock as he has received for me my dividends from it and transacted any business I had therewith - James Pain -

Testator this 23 day of January 1875 -

Signed sealed and delivered by said James Pain the Testator in our presence at which we were also both present and hereunto we subscribe our names as Witnesses - H.Y. Laud No.6 Newenham St.
Maver Prov Bank of Ireland Limerick

Affidavit of due Execution Filed -

Affidavit of Rev Benj Jacob with reference to discrepancy of date of Will as referred to by codicil, also filed, and engrossed with Will.

378

OBITUARY

The Late James Pain

On the 18th ult., died at his residence in Limerick, at the age of ninety-seven, Mr. James Pain, one of the oldest, if not the oldest, architect in the United Kingdom. The deceased gentleman was born in London, of a well-known family distinguished in architectural and building affairs. He served in the office of the late John Nash, by whom he was sent to Ireland to superintend some important works, and eventually, with his brother, Mr. George Richard Pain, settled in Cork and Limerick, in which counties, as well as in the south and west of Ireland generally, the firm of James and G. R. Pain enjoyed for many years an extensive practice. Among their works may be noted Mitchels-town Castle, erected for the Earl of Kingston, a noble pile in the late Tudor style; Dromo-land Castle, for the Earl of Inchiquin; Lough Castle, for Lord Gort; Elm Park, for Lord Clarina; and many others. Adare Manor, the residence of the Earl of Dunraven,was begun by them, and afterwards passed into the hands of the second Pugin, and finally into those of Mr. P.C. Hardwick. They also designed the Cork court-house, possessing a splendid Corinthian portico, referred to by Lord Macaulay in his history, the Cork and Limerick prisons, Thomond and Athlunkard bridges over the Shannon, and several large churches, both Protestant and Roman Catholic, in the cities of Cork and Limerick. Mr. G.R. Pain died at comparatively early age, but Mr. James Pain continued to reside in Limerick, and to practise his profession till within the last few years. He enjoyed a deservedly high reputation for his upright and honourable course of conduct, both amongst his employers and professional brethren, and, it may be added was highly respected by the working men and the local building trades as a just and impartial judge of the questions which so often arise between them and their employers. Mr. Pain was a distinguished "Mason." His remains were interred in the Cathedral of Limerick on the 17th ult.

W.F.

The Builder 1 January 1878

BIBLIOGRAPHY

PRIMARY SOURCES, MANUSCRIPT

Archer, Rev. Foster *A Journal Containing a Report on the State of Prisons, County Hospitals, Charter Schools etc. as attained in a Tour thro' the Provinces of Leinster, Munster and Connaught began July 2nd 1801, by Revd. F. Archer, inspector General of the Prisons in Ireland*, Hardwick Papers, (Additional MSS 35920) British Museum.

Beaufort, Mary *Tour from Upton to Killarney and Limerick in 1810*, MS 4036, Trinity College Dublin.

Croker, Thomas Crofton *Reflections of Cork*, Trinity College, Dublin.

De Vere Papers, Limerick Archives (P 22 Box 3).

Dunraven Papers, University of Limerick Library.

Dunraven, Countess of, Lady Caroline, *Diary*, Dunraven Papers, University of Limerick Library.

Hunt, Sir Vere, *Diary*, De Vere Papers (P22, Box 1), Limerick Archives.

O'Brien, Sir Edward correspondence with Lady Charlotte O'Brien (National Library of Ireland 2972-4; 2976-7.)

O'Callaghan, Ellen, *Diary*, Limerick Civic Trust Collection.

Pain, James, 'The Will of James Pain (11 January 1863) & Codicil (23 January 1875)', *Limerick District Registry Will Books*, Record Office of Ireland. Microfilm copy, *Transcriptions of Wills of Limerick*, Limerick Genealogy Office.

Parry, John Orlando *The Diaries of John Orlando Parry*, Parry Papers, National Library of Wales (NWL MS 17718A).

White, Fr. James *White Manuscript-The Annals of the City, County and Diocese of Limerick*, Limerick Diocesan Library.

Account Book of Rockbarton Estate 1831-40, Limerick Museum (LM 2004.98).

Archives of the Grand Lodge of Freemasons, Ireland, Molesworth Street, Dublin.

Bond for Performance of Agreement Entered into by James Pain and George Richard Pain with the Athlunkard Bridge Commissioners, April 1833, Limerick Museum (LM. 1933).

Lease Indenture between Edward Henry Pery, Earl of Limerick, and Joseph Barrington 31 May 1831, Limerick Civic Trust Collection.

Limerick Common Council, Minutes of, Limerick Archives.

Proceedings and Orders of the Commissioners for Improving the Parish of St. Michael's, 3 Vols., Limerick Archives.

Rate Books, St. Michael's Parish Commissioners, Limerick Archives.

St. Michael's Parish Waste Book, 18 December 1813 - 25 March 1820, Limerick Archives.

St. Mary's Cathedral Restoration Papers, Limerick Archives (St. Mary's Restoration Papers P7).

PRIMARY SOURCES, PRINTED

Archer, Rev. Foster 'The Reverend Foster Archer's Visit to Limerick and Clare, 1801', Lynch, Patrick B. Vol. XVIII, *The North Munster Antiquarian Journal*, 1976.

Austen Jane *Northanger Abbey* (written 1798-9, published 1818).

Austen, Jane *Sense and Sensibility* (1811).

Balch, William S. *Ireland As I Saw It,* New York, 1850, republished as 'Limerick As I Saw it 1848', *The Old Limerick Journal,* No. 32.

Barrow, John *A Tour Around Ireland Through the Sea-Coast Counties, in the Autumn of 1835*, John Murray, Albemarle Street, London, 1836.

Brewer, James, *The Beauties of Ireland*, 2 Vols., Sherwood, Jones & Co., London, 1825-6.

Campbell, Thomas *A Philosophical Survey of the South of Ireland*, Thomas Campbell & William Whitestone, London, 1778.

Carberry, J.J. *Chronological and Historical Account of Some of the Principal Events Connected with the Dominican Convent Limerick*, privately published, 1866.

de Montbret', Charles 'Charles Etienne Coquebert de Montbret', *The Grand Tour of Limerick*, Kelly, Cornelius ed., Cailleach Books, Beara, Co. Cork, 2004.

Chatterton, Lady *Rambles in the South of Ireland During the Year 1838*, 2 Vols., Saunders and Otley, London, 1839.

Creasy, Edward *Fifteen Decisive Battles of the World* (1852), republished by Dorset Press, New York, 1987.

Croker, Thomas Crofton *Researches in the South of Ireland*, John Murray, London, 1824; facsimile reprint Irish University Press, 1968.

de Tocqueville, Alex *Alex de Tocqueville's Journey in Ireland July – August 1835,* Emmet Larkin trans.& ed., Wolfhound Press, Dublin, 1990.

Dowd, Rev. James *History of St. Mary's Cathedral, Limerick,* George McKern & Sons, Limerick, 1899.

Dunraven, Caroline, Countess of & Dunraven, Edwin, Earl of *Memorials of Adare Manor,* Oxford, 1865.

Elmes, James *Hints for the Improvement of Prisons,* London, 1817.

Ferrar, John, *The History of Limerick*, 2nd edition A. Watson & Co., Limerick, 1787.

Fitzgerald, Rev. P. & M'Gregor, J.J. *The History Topography and Antiquities of the County and City of Limerick* 2 Vols., Limerick, 1827.

Gibson, Rev. C.B. *The History of the County and City of Cork*, Cork, 1861.

Hall, Mrs. *A Week in Killarney,* 1834.

Hogan, Right Rev. John J., Bishop of Kansas City *Fifty Years Ago,* Franklin Hudson Publishing Co., Kansas City, 1907.

Inglis, Henry *A Journey Throughout Ireland During the Spring, Summer and Autumn of 1834,* 2 Vols., Whittaker & Co., London, 1834.

J.B. Scott's Property in Co. Clare, 1854, Local Studies Department, County Limerick Library.

Knot, Mary John, *Two Months at Kilkee,* Dublin 1836, reprinted, Clasp Press, Ennis, Co. Clare, 1997.

Leitch, Ritchie *Ireland, Picturesque and Romantic,* 1838.

Lenihan, Maurice *Limerick; Its History and Antiquities* 1866, republished in facsimile, O'Carroll, Cian ed., Mercier Press, Dublin and Cork, 1991.

Lewis, Samuel, *Topographical Dictionary of Ireland,* 2 Vols., London, 1837. Reprint Genealogical Publishing Co. Inc., Baltimore, Maryland, 1984.

Macaulay, Thomas *The History of England,* 1855.

Massy, Dawson *The Faithful Shepherd: A Memoir of Godfrey Massy B. A. (Vicar of Bruff) with Sketches of his Times,* Hamilton & Co., London, 1870.

O'Brien, Robert *Report on the Works Effected at St. Mary's Cathedral, Limerick With a Statement of Accounts,* printed by Guy and Company, 114 George Street, Limerick, 1861. Limerick Archives (St. Mary's restoration Papers P7).

'James Pain File' compiled by James McMahon, Limerick Civic Trust Collection.

Plowden, Francis *An Historical View of the State of Ireland*, London, 1801.

Pococke, Richard *Pococke's Irish Tour 1752*, Stoke, George T, ed., Hodges & Figgis, Dublin, 1892.

Pückler-Muskau, Prince, *Tour in England, Ireland and France in 1828-9 by a German Prince*, Effingham Wilson, 1832.

Scott, Walter *Ivanhoe*, 1819.

Thackeray, William Makepeace *The Irish Sketchbook 1842*, J.M. Dent & Co., London, 1903.

Townsend, Horatio *A General and Statistical Survey of the County of Cork*, Edwards and Savage, 1815.

Trotter, J. *Walks Through Ireland in 1812, 1814 and 1817*, published 1819.

Walpole, Horace *The Castle of Otranto*, 1764.

Windele, J. *Historical and Descriptive Notices of the City of Cork and its Vicinity*, Longman & Co., London, 1846.

'An Account of all the Gaols, Houses of Correction or Penitentiaries in the United Kingdom', *Crime and Punishment – Prisons 8*, British Parliamentary Papers, 1819, Irish University Press, Shannon, Ireland, 1970.

Articles of Agreement of the Perry-Square Tontine Company of the City of Limerick, George McKern & Sons, Limerick, 1841. Limerick Civic Trust Collection.

Augustiniana Corcagiae 1746-1836, 'Statement of Affairs and Inventory Presented at Visitation July 10, 1827', *Analecta Hibernia* Vol. XII.

Civil Survey A.D. 1654-1656 of the County of Limerick, Vol. IV, Irish Manuscripts Commission, The Stationary Office, Dublin Stationary Office, 1938.

*Charter Party. The,; or, Articles of Agreement of the Pery Square Tontine Company of the City of Limerick,*1840, Limerick Civic Trust Collection.

Dictionary of Architecture, s.v. 'Pain, James and George Richard', Architectural Publications Society, entry compiled in 1877.

Freemason's Quarterly Review, 1842.

Grand Jury Presentments, County of Limerick, Local Studies Department, Limerick County Library.

Gazetteer of Ireland, The, John Parker Lawson, Edinburgh, 1845.

Historic and Descriptive Sketch of St. Mary's Cathedral, A, G. M'Kern & Sons, Limerick, 1881.

Historic and Descriptive Sketch of St. Mary's Cathedral A, M'Kern & Sons, 3rd edition, Limerick, 1887.

History of the Proceedings at the Particularly Interesting Elections for a Member to Represent The City of Limerick in Parliament; Containing . . . A List of the Electors,

Their Places of Residence, and the Quality in which they Voted, printed by William Henry Tyrrell, No. 17 College Green, Dublin, 1817. Limerick City Library.

Parliamentary Gazetteer of Ireland, The, 3 Vols., A. Fullarton & Co., Dublin, London and Edinburgh, 1844-46.

North Munster Provincial Grand Lodge, Limerick. List of officers for 24 June-17 December 1844, printed by George Morgan Goggin, Provincial Grand Librarian, 34 O'Connell Street, 1844. Limerick Museum (LM 1996.1494).

Records of the Pery Square Tontine, Limerick Civic Trust Collection.

Reports from Commissioners on Municipal Corporations in Ireland, British Parliamentary Papers, 1825.

'Report of the Commissioners of the County Limerick Gaol', *Limerick Gazette,* 9 February 1816.

'Report on the County of the City of Limerick', *Reports from Commissioners on Municipal Corporations in Ireland,* British Parliamentary Papers, 1835.

Select Committee on Petitions Relating to Limerick Taxation 1822. Limerick City Library.

Share Register Shareholders of the Pery-Square Tontine Company, 1840. Limerick Civic Trust Collection.

Special Commission of Oyer and Terminer in the Counties of Limerick and Clare in the Months of May and June 1831, A, printed by R. P. Canter, 12 Francis Street, Limerick, 1831.

NEWSPAPERS

Clare Freeman.
Clare Journal and Ennis Advertiser.
Cork Constitution.
Finn's Leinster Journal.
Irish Penny Magazine.
Irish Times.
Limerick Chronicle.
Limerick Evening Post and Clare Sentinel.
Limerick Gazette.
Limerick General Advertiser.
Limerick Reporter and Tipperary Vindicator.
The Builder.
The Irish Builder.
The Sunday Tribune.

TRADE DIRECTORIES

Ferrar, John *Limerick Directory* 1769.

Lucas, Richard *A General Directory of the Kingdom of Ireland, 1788.*

Pigot & Co's City of Dublin and Hibernian Provincial Trade Directory, J, Pigot & Co., London and Manchester, 1824.

Deane's Limerick Almanack, Directory and Advertiser of 1838.

The New Triennial and Commercial Directory for the Years 1840, 41 & 42, printed by George M. Goggin for F. Kinder & Son, Limerick, 1840.

Slater's Directory, Isaac Slater, Manchester, 1846.

Slater's Directory, 1856.

Slater's, late Pigot & Co.'s. Royal National Commercial Directory of Ireland 1870 Isaac Slater, London & Manchester, 1870.

Bassett's Directory of the City and County of Limerick and of the Principal Towns in the Counties of Tipperary and Clare 1875-6, William Bassett, 20 George Street, Limerick, 1875.

Bassett's Directory of the City and County of Limerick and of the Principal Towns in the Counties of Tipperary and Clare, 1877-8, William Bassett, Limerick, 1877.

MAPS

Colles, Christopher 'Plan of the City and Suburbs of Limerick' (*c.* 1769), original in British Library, London; copy in Limerick Museum.

Ground Plan of the Deanery Yard and Adjacent Strand, 25 March 1788. Limerick Museum (LM 0000. 1906).

Map of the City of Limerick Based on the Civil Survey 1654. Unpublished, Limerick Museum.

Ordnance Survey, City of Limerick, 1840.

'Plan of the City of Limerick, December 1, 1786' in Ferrar, John *History of Limerick,* 1787.

Taylor and Skinner's Maps of the Roads of Ireland Surveyed 1777, published 14 November 1778, pp. 99 & 200. Local Studies Department, Limerick County Library.

ARCHITECTURAL DRAWINGS

Ainslie, George 'Design for a County Goal' (1820) by *Crime and Punishment – Prisons 8*, British Parliamentary Papers, Irish University Press, Shannon, Ireland, 1970.

Nash, John 'Front Elevation of Lough Cutra Castle' (1811), in Guinness, D. & Ryan W. *Irish Houses and Castles*, Thames & Hudson Ltd., London, 1971.

Pain, James, Perspective of proposed design for Dromoland, James Pain (1813), reproduced in Richardson, D. S. *Gothic Revival Architecture in Ireland*, Garland Publishing Inc., New York and London, 1983.

Pain, James 'Plan and Elevation of Thomond Bridge' (1814), in Barry, J.G., 'Old Limerick Bridges', *Journal of the North Munster Archaeological Society*, Vol. I., 1909-11, Limerick.

Pain, James, Ground plans, gallery plans and elevations of churches in the Archdiocese of Cashel, 6 Vols., Library of the Representative Church Body, Braemar Road, Churchtown, Dublin.

Pain, James 'Plan and Elevation of Thomond Bridge', (1837), Limerick Museum (LM 1991. 0005).

Pain, James, Ground Plan of Chancel of St. Mary's Cathedral, Limerick, (March 1843), St. Mary's Archives.

Pain, James, Transverse section of Chancel of St. Mary's Cathedral, Limerick, signed and dated March 1843.

Pain, James and Pain, George Richard, Elevations and plans of Dromoland Castle, reproduced in Richardson, D.S. *Gothic Revival Architecture in Ireland*, Garland Publishing Inc., New York and London, 1983.

Pain, James and Pain, George Richard 'Plan of the Principal Floor, Adare Manor' (1828), Dunraven Papers. University of Limerick Archives.

Pain, James & Pain, George Richard *Design for the Church to be built in the Parish of St. Michael in Pery Square, Limerick* (1838).

Plan of Tullamore Gaol in Shaffrey, Patrick & Shaffrey, Maura *Buildings of Irish Towns*, The O'Brien Press Ltd., Dublin, 1983.

Sketch plan of Arthur's Quay housing development, *The Trial of Francis Arthur of the City of Limerick, Merchant for High Treason* (MS). Local Studies Department, Limerick County Library.

SECONDARY SOURCES

Adams, William Howard *Nature Perfected*, Abbeville Press, New York, 1991.

Baily, Edwin R. *Kilnasoolagh Church, Newmarket on Fergus – An Appreciation* published by Edwin Bailey for Kilnasoolagh Church, Newmarket on Fergus, Co. Clare, 1992.

Bence-Jones, Mark *A Guide to Irish Country Houses*, Constable, London, 2nd revised edition, 1988.

Bennett, Isabel, ed. *Excavations 1999: Summary Accounts of Archaeological Excavations in Ireland*, Wordwell Ltd., Bray, Co. Wicklow, 2000.

Billensteiner, Friedrich & Heffernan, Kieran *The History of Strancally Castle and the Valley of the Blackwater Between Lismore and Youghal*, Strancally Castle Library, Knockanore, Co. Waterford, 1999.

Bourke, Gerard *Out on a Limb*, Trafford Publishing, Victoria, Canada, 2003.

Bowen, Elizabeth *Bowen's Court,* The Collins Press, Cork, 1998.

Brecht, Bertolt 'A Worker Reads History', *Bertolt Brecht, Select Poems,* Grove Press, New York, 1959.

Brooks, C. *The Gothic Revival*, Phaidon, London, 1999.

Browne, Margaret 'The Limestone Industry of Limerick', *Made in Limerick*, Lee, David & Jacobs, Debbie eds., Limerick Civic Trust, 2003.

Buckley, O.P.A. 'The Present Dominican Church', *Dominicans in Limerick 1227-1977,* Limerick, 1977.

Clark, K. *The Gothic Revival: An Essay in the History of Taste*, John Murray, London, 1962.

Cooney, Rev. Dudley Levistone *This Plain, Artless, Serious People: The Story of the Methodists of County Limerick*, 2000.

Corkery, Daniel *The Hidden Ireland* 1924, Gill and Macmillan, Dublin, 1967.

Cox, R. C. & Gould, M. H. *Civil Engineering Heritage Ireland*, The Institution of Civil Engineers and the Institution of Civil Engineers in Ireland, Thomas Telford Publications, London, 1998.

Craig, Maurice *The Architecture of Ireland*, B. T. Batsford Ltd., London & Eason and Son, Dublin, 1982.

Craig, Maurice & Glin, Knight of *Ireland Observed: A Handbook to the Buildings and Antiquities,* The Mercier Press, Cork, 1970.

Cronin, John *Gerald Griffin 1803-1840, A Critical Biography*, Cambridge Press, 1978.

Cronin, Patrick J. *Aubrey de Vere-The Bard of Curragh Chase: A Portrait of his Life and Poetry*, Askeaton Civic Trust, Co. Limerick, 1997.

Crookshank, A. & Knight of Glin *The Watercolours of Ireland: Works on Paper in Pencil, Pastel and Paint c.1600-1914*, Barrie and Jenkins, London, 1994.

Cruickshank, Dan *A Guide to the Georgian Buildings of Britain and Ireland*, Weidenfeld and Nicolson, The National Trust, The Irish Georgian Society, 1985.

de Breffny, B. & ffolliott R. *The Houses of Ireland*, Thames and Hudson, London, 1975.

Day, J. Godfrey F., Bishop of Ossory, & Patton, Henry E., Bishop of Killaloe *The Cathedrals of the Church of Ireland*, Society for Promoting Christian Knowledge, London, 1932.

Donnelly, Kevin, Hoctor, Michael, & Walsh, Dermot *A Rising Tide - The Story of Limerick Harbour*, Limerick Harbour Commissioners, Limerick, 1994.

Dowd, Rev. James *Limerick and Its Sieges*, McKern & Sons, Limerick, 1890, republished as *Dowd's History of Limerick*, O'Carroll, Cian ed., The O'Brien Press, Dublin, 1990.

Dunraven, Earl of *Past Times and Pastimes*, 2 Vols., Hodder and Stoughton, London, 1922.

Dunraven, Earl of *Cheap Food for the People at Large. An Open letter from the Earl of Dunraven K.P., C.M.G., To the People of Ireland*, Easons & Son Ltd., Dublin, 1925.

Ellis, Richard *Men and Whales*, Robert Hale Ltd., London, 1989.

Evans, Robin *The Fabrication of Virtue, English Prison Architecture 1750-1840*, Cambridge University Press, Cambridge, 1982.

Forbes, J.D. *Victorian Architect: The Life and Work of William Tinsley*, Indiana University Press, Bloomington, 1953.

Galloway, Peter *The Cathedrals of Ireland*, The Institute of Irish Studies, Queens University of Belfast, 1992.

Gaughan, J.A. *The Knights of Glin*, Kingdom Books, 1978.

Guinness, D. & Ryan, W. *Irish Houses and Castles*, Thames & Hudson Ltd., London, 1971.

Hajba, Anna-Maria *Houses of Cork: Volume I, North Cork*, Ballinakella Press, Whitegate, County Clare, 2002.

Hannon, Kevin *Limerick - Historical Reflections*, Oireacht Publications, Castletroy, Limerick, 1996.

Haydn, J.A. *Ancient Union Lodge No. 13*, Limerick Lodge of Research No. 200, 1932, Limerick Civic Trust Collection.

Hewson, Adrian *Inspiring Stones: A History of the Church of Ireland Dioceses of Limerick, Ardfert, Aghadoe, Killaloe, Kilfernora, Clonfert, Kilmacduagh & Emly*, Diocesan Council of Limerick, Killaloe and Ardfert, Limerick, 1995.

Hill, Judith *The Building of Limerick*, Mercier Press, Cork & Dublin, 1991.

Hill, Judith *Irish Public Sculpture: A History*, Four Courts, Dublin, 1998.

Honour, Hugh *Romanticism*, Allen Lane, London, 1979.

Howley J. *The Follies and Garden Buildings of Ireland*, Yale University Press, New Haven and London, 1993.

Hunt, Tristram *Building Jerusalem: The Rise and fall of the Victorian City*, Weidenfeld and Nicolson, London, 2004.

Hurley, Richard *Irish Church Architecture in the Era of Vatican II*, Dominican Publications, Dublin, 2001.

Jackson, Robert Wyse *The History of St. Michael's Church, Limerick, 1844-1944*, Mckerns Printers, Limerick, 1944. Limerick Museum.

Jenkins, Elizabeth *Jane Austen*, Sphere Books, 1973, originally published by Victor Gollancz Ltd., 1938.

Johnson, Máiread *Ice and Cold Storage: A Dublin History*, Dublin, 1988.

Lamplugh, G. W. 'The Geology of the County Around Limerick', *Memoirs of the Geological Survey of Ireland*, Thom & Co., Dublin, 1907.

Leonard, Denis M. *The Georgian House and Garden: No.2 Pery Square, Tontine Buildings, Limerick*, Limerick Civic Trust, Limerick, 2003.

Lee, David *The Georgian House & Garden*, Limerick Civic Trust, Limerick, 2001.

Lee, David & Gonzalez, Christine eds., *Georgian Limerick* Vol. II, Limerick Civic Trust, Limerick, 2000.

Lee, David & Jacobs, Debbie eds., *Made in Limerick* Vol. I, Limerick Civic Trust, Limerick, 2003.

Logan, Dr. John *Learning: Schooling and the Promotion of Literacy in Nineteenth Century Ireland*, draft copy in Limerick Civic Trust Collection.

Lyons, Mary Cecelia *Illustrated Incumbered Estates: Ireland, 1850-1905*, Ballinakella Press, Whitegate, County Clare, 1993.

MacDonnell, Randal *The Lost Houses of Ireland*, Weidenfeld & Nicolson, London, 2002.

McMahon, James *The Pery Square Tontine*, Limerick Civic Trust, Limerick, 1999.

McNamara, T.F *Portrait of Cork*, Cork, 1981.

Mansbridge, Michael *John Nash: A Complete Catalogue,* Phaidon, Oxford, 1991.

O'Brien, Grania *These My Friends and Forebears: The O'Briens of Dromoland*, Ballinakella Press, Whitegate, Co. Clare, 1991.

O'Brien J. & Guinness, D. *Great Irish Houses and Castles*, George Weidenfeld & Nicolson Ltd., London, 1993.

O'Carroll, Cian *Knappogue - The Story of an Irish Castle*, Shannon Heritage, Shannon, 2002.

O'Connor, John *Mungret: History and Antiquities,* Dalton Printers, Limerick, 1971.

O'Connor, Patrick J. *Living in a Coded Landscape,* Newcastle West, Co. Limerick, 1992.

O'Dwyer, Frederick *The Architecture of Deane & Woodward*, Cork University Press, Cork, 1997.

O'Dwyer, Frederick *Lost Dublin,* Gill & McMillan, Dublin, 1981.

O'Keefe. P. & Simington, T. *Irish Stone Bridges: History and Heritage*, Irish Academic Press, Dublin, 1991.

O'Reilly, S. *The Swiss Cottage*, The Office of Public Works, Criterion Press, Dublin, 1993.

Pakenham, Valerie *The Big House in Ireland*, Cassell & Co., London.

Power, Bill *Evensong: The Story of a Church of Ireland Country Parish*, Mount Cashel Books, Mitchelstown, 2004.

Power, Bill *Mitchelstown Through Seven Centuries*, Eigse Books, Fermoy, Co. Cork, 1987.

Power, Bill *White Knights, Dark Earls: The Rise and Fall of an Anglo-Irish Dynasty*, The Collins Press, Cork, 2000.

Richardson, Douglas Scott *Gothic Revival Architecture in Ireland* 2 Vols., Garland Publishing Inc., New York and London, 1983.

Robertson, N. *Crowned Harp, Memories of the Last Years of the Crown*, Dublin, 1960.

Rynne, Colin *The Industrial Archaeology of Cork City and its Environs*, The Stationary Office, Dublin, 1999.

Sorrell, Alan *Roman Towns in Britain*, B.T. Batsford Ltd., London, 1976.

Speer, Albert *Inside the Third Reich*, Book Club Accociates/Weidenfeld & Nicoson, London, 1971 edition.

Spellissy, Sean *The History of Limerick City*, The Celtic Bookshop, Limerick, 1998.

Summerson, John *The Life and Work of John Nash, Architect*, George Allen & Unwin, London, 1980.

Tierney, M. *Glenstal Abbey: A Historical Guide*, Glenstal Abbey Publications, 2001.

Waller, John Thomas *Trinity Church and St. Michael's Church*, McKerns Printing, Limerick, 1954.

Weir, Hugh *Houses of Clare*, Ballinakella Press, Co. Clare, 1986.

Williams, Jeremy *A Companion Guide to Architecture in Ireland 1837-1921*, Irish Academic Press, Dublin, 1994.

Adare, An Taisce, Limerick, 1975.

Kiltenanlea Parish Church, Clonlara, Co. Clare, 1782-1992, Clonlara Development Association, 1992.

Monuments of St. Mary's Cathedral Limerick, The, Treaty Press, Limerick, 1976

ARTICLES

Ahern, Richard 'Liszt in Limerick', *Georgian Limerick* Vol. II, Lee, David & Gonzalez, Christine eds., Limerick Civic Trust, Limerick, 2000.

Barry, J.G. 'Old Limerick Bridges', *Journal of the North Munster Archaeological Society*, Vol. I, 1909-11, Limerick.

Bence-Jones, M. 'Two Pairs of Architect Brothers', *Country Life*, 10 August 1967.

Bence-Jones, M. 'Ravages of Time and Neglect: Lost Irish Country Houses – II', *Country Life*, 30 May 1974.

Brown, Margaret 'The Limestone Industry of Limerick', *Made in Limerick* Vol. I, Lee, David & Jacobs, Debbie eds., Limerick Civic Trust, Limerick, 2003.

Clements, Nat 'Restoration of Marble Hall and Staircase at No.2 Pery Square', *Georgian Limerick* Vol. II, Lee David & Gonzalez, Christine eds., Limerick Civic Trust, Limerick, 2000.

Cornforth, J. 'Adare Manor, Limerick - The Seat of the Earls of Dunraven', *Country Life* Vol. CXLV, 15, 22, 29 May 1969.

Crowe, Catriona 'Reviving Limerick's Georgian Heritage: The Restoration Project at No.2 Pery Square', *Georgian Limerick* Vol. II, Lee David & Gonzalez, Christine eds., Limerick Civic Trust, Limerick, 2000.

Curtin, Gerald 'Religious and Social Conflict During the Protestant Crusade in West Limerick 1822-49', *The Old Limerick Journal* No. 39, Winter 2003.

Davis, Terence 'John Nash in Ireland', *Bulletin of the Irish Georgian Society* Vol. VIII, No. 2, April-June 1965.

Donovan, Tom 'Glin Bridewell', *The Glen Corbry Chronicle*, Glin Historical Society, 1997.

Feely, Pat 'Whiteboys and Ribbonmen', *The Old Limerick Journal* No. 4, September 1980.

FitzGerald, D., Knight of Glin *Adare Manor Ireland*, Christie, Mansion & Woods Ltd., London, 1982.

FitzGerald, D., Knight of Glin 'The Treasures of Glin Castle', *The Glen Corbry Chronicle*, The Glin Historical Society, 1997.

Girouard, M. 'Swiss Cottage, Cahir', *Country Life*, 22 September 1966.

Girouard, M. 'The Swiss Cottage, Cahir, Co. Tipperary', *Country Life*, 26 October 1989.

Gonzalez, Christine 'Chancer or Hero? General Humbert's Campaign in Ireland, 1798', *Georgian Limerick* Vol. II, Lee, David & Gonzalez, Christine eds., Limerick Civic Trust, Limerick, 2000.

Green, J. F. 'James and George Richard Pain', *The Green Book, 1965: The Journal of the Architectural Association of Ireland*, Dublin, 1965.

Hill, Christopher 'The Norman Yoke', *Puritanism and Revolution: Studies in Interpretation of the English Revolution of the 17th Century*, Martin Secker & Warburg, 1958.

Hill, Henry 'Diary of and Itinerary in Ireland in 1831', *Journal of the Cork Historical & Archaeological Society* Vol. 38, No. 147, January - June 1933.

Hodkinson, Brian ' Old Thomond Bridge', to be published in a forthcoming edition of the *The North Munster Antiquarian Journal*.

Jupp, Belinda 'The Georgian Garden at No. 2 Pery Square', *Georgian Limerick* Vol. II, Lee David & Gonzalez, Christine eds., Limerick Civic Trust, Limerick, 2000.

Kemmy, Jim 'Marencourt Cup', *The Old Limerick Journal, French Edition* No. 25, Summer, 1989.

Lee, David, 'The Battle of Colloony, 1798', *Georgian Limerick* Vol. II, Lee, David & Gonzalez, Christine eds., Limerick Civic Trust, Limerick, 2000.

Lee, David 'Fanfares of the Vanities', *Remembering Limerick: Historical Essays Celebrating the 800th Anniversary of Limerick's First Charter Granted in 1197*, Limerick Civic Trust, Limerick, 1997.

Luddy, Maria 'The Lives of the Poor in Cahir in 1821', *Tipperary Historical Journal 1991*.

McDermott, Matthew 'Notable Irish Architectural Families, 4: James and George Richard Pain', *Yearbook 1971*, Royal Institute of the Architects in Ireland.

Miley, Garry *History of the Church of St. Munchin*, MUBC Building Study, Limerick, 1998. Limerick Civic Trust Collection.

Mulvin, Lynda 'St Mary's Cathedral, Limerick – Unpublished Correspondence of the Cathedral Restoration in the Nineteenth Century', Irish *Architectural and Decorative Studies*, The Journal of the Irish Georgian Society, Vol. IV, 2001.

Ni Chinneide, Sighle ed. 'A Frenchman's Impressions of Limerick, Town and People in 1791', *The North Munster Antiquarian Journal*, Thomond Archaeological Society, Vol. V (1946-1949), No. 4, 1948.

O'Dwyer, Frederick 'A Noble Pile in the Late Tudor Style: Mitchelstown', *Irish Arts Review*, 2002.

Ó hEocha, Séamus 'Plasterwork Restoration at No.2 Pery Square', *Georgian Limerick* Vol. II, Lee David & Gonzalez, Christine eds., Limerick Civic Trust, Limerick, 2000

O'Grady, D. 'The Barrington Normans of Limerick', *The Old Limerick Journal, Barrington's Edition* No. 24, Kemmy, Jim, ed., Winter, 1988.

O'Mahony, Chris 'Limerick Night Watch 1807-1853', *The Old Limerick Journal*, Kemmy, Jim ed., Autumn 1987.

Potter, Matthew 'The Architectural Legacy of Eyre Massey, 3rd Lord Clarina (1798-1872)', *The North Munster Antiquarian Journal*, Thomond Archaeological Society, Vol. 42, 2000.

Quane, Michael 'The Free School of Clonmel', *Journal of the Cork Historical & Archaeological Society* Vol. LXIX, 1964.

Roche, Nessa 'Limerick Georgian Windows', *Georgian Limerick* Vol. II, Lee David & Gonzalez, Christine eds., Limerick Civic Trust, Limerick, 2000.

Rowan, A.J. 'Georgian Castles in Ireland - 1', *Bulletin of the Irish Georgian Society* Vol. VII, No. 1, January-March 1964.

Tierney, Mark 'Sir Matthew Barrington: 1788-1861', *The Old Limerick Journal, Barrington's Edition* No. 24, Kemmy, Jim ed., Winter, 1988.

Tierney, Mark 'The Barringtons and the Pery Square Tontine', *The Old Limerick Journal, Barrington's Edition* No. 24, Kemmy, Jim ed., Winter 1988.

Tierney, Mark 'The Mont de Piété', *Barrington's Edition, The Old Limerick Journal* No. 24, Kemmy, Jim ed., Winter 1988.

Tierney, M. & Cornforth, J. 'Glenstal Castle', *Country Life*, 3 October 1974.

Yeoman, Anne 'Throwing the Dart', *Remembering Limerick: Historical Essays Celebrating the 800th Anniversary of Limerick's First Charter Granted in 1197,* Lee, David ed., Limerick Civic Trust, Limerick, 1997.

'History of Spa House', Energy Agency Office, Cork County Council.

'History of Tullamore Gaol', Offaly Historical and Archaeological Society website.

'Ld. Cahir's Cottage at Kilcommon', *Cahir Heritage Newsletter* No. 37, Swiss Cottage Edition, 1 September 1989.

9 Barrington Street - The Heritage Angle, report by Limerick Chapter, Irish Georgian Society, Limerick Civic Trust Archives.

'The Old Castles Around Cork Harbour', *Journal of the Cork Historical & Archaeological Society* Vol. 20, No. 104.

'St. Patrick's Church, Glanmire Road', *Journal of the Cork Historical & Archaeological Society* Vol. 14, No. 78.

'The Mathew Tower', *Journal of the Cork Historical & Archaeological Society* Vol. 32, No. 135, January-June, 1927.

WORKS OF REFERENCE

Byrne, Joseph *Byrne's Dictionary of Irish Local History*, Mercier Press, Cork, 2004.

Colvin, Howard *A Biographical Dictionary of British Architects 1600-1840*, 3rd edition, Yale University Press, New Haven & London, 1995.

Dunne, Mildred & Phillips, Brian *The Courthouses of Ireland - A Gazetteer of Irish Courthouses,* The Heritage Council, Kilkenny, 1999.

Jestice, P.G. *Encyclopedia of Irish Spirituality*, ABC-CLIO Inc., Santa Barbara, California, 2000.

Joyce, Gerry *Limerick Street Names*, Limerick Corporation, Limerick, 1995.

Rowan, Martha 'Pain, George Richard', *Index of Irish Architects*, Irish Architectural Archive, Merrion Square, Dublin.

Rowan, Martha 'Pain, James', *Index of Irish Architects,* Irish Architectural Archive.

Cambridge Biographical Encyclopaedia, The, 2nd edition, Cambridge University Press, 1998.

Dictionary of National Biography, Oxford University Press, 1917, reprint 1937-8.

Index of Irish Architects, The Irish Architectural Archive, Merrion Square, Dublin.

Oxford Dictionary of Architecture Curl, James Stevens, ed., Oxford University Press, 1999.

Oxford Dictionary of Classical Myth and Religion, The, Price, Simon & Kearns, Emily eds., Oxford University Press, 2003.

Oxford Names Companion, The, University Press, Oxford, 2002.

Royal Academy of Arts, The: A Complete Dictionary of Contributors and Their Work From Its Foundation in 1769 to 1904, Graves, Algernon, 9 Vols., The Royal Academy, London, 1905-6, Vol. VI, p.41.

Royal Hibernian Academy's Index of Exhibitors, 1987, III.

INDEX

398

399

416